The Automobile Industry since 1945

The Automobile Industry since 1945

Lawrence J. White

Harvard University Press
Cambridge, Massachusetts
1971

© Copyright 1971 by the President and Fellows of Harvard College

All rights reserved

Library of Congress Catalog Card Number 76-148939

SBN 674-05470-9

Printed in the United States of America

To My Parents

Preface

Automobiles hold a special place in the hearts and minds of Americans. The industry itself is important, as are the products it turns out. A discussion of automobiles and the automobile industry can, in some circles, turn into a highly passionate argument with heated opinions traded on all sides. Auto enthusiasts are perhaps exceeded only by railroad buffs in the enthusiasm with which they treat their chosen interest. I have never been part of the former group. I have been fascinated by the American automobile industry because of its economic aspects, not because of any strongly held opinions about the superiority—or inferiority—of the products that Detroit produces. This book was not conceived of as a vendetta against the industry or as a whitewash but, rather, as a scholarly attempt to describe and explain the actions of this very important American industry.

This book is a revised and edited version of my Ph.D. dissertation submitted to Harvard University in March 1969. The National Science Foundation provided fellowship support during the researching and writing of the dissertation. I owe a special debt of gratitude to Richard Caves, whose many comments and suggestions were extremely valuable, in both the early and late stages of this book's preparation. John Lintner provided useful advice and ideas. F. M. Scherer, who read the manuscript after it had largely been completed, provided further worthwhile suggestions and corrections. My fellow graduate students in the Littauer coffee lounge were a valuable sounding board. My special thanks go to Sherman Robinson, Martin Spechler, Michael Hicks, and Marc Roberts. Helen Bigelow did a masterful job of tranforming scrawled drafts into a finished manuscript, and Priscilla Read assisted with the editing.

L.J.W.

Contents

1 Introduction 1

2 A Brief Automotive History of the Postwar Period 10

3 Manufacturing Technology and the Planning Process 19

4 Estimated Economies of Scale and Minimum Efficient Size 38

5 Entry into the Automobile Industry 54

6 Integration and Diversification 77

7 The Structure of Demand 92

8 Prices and Pricing Policy 105

9 Dealers and Dealer Systems 136

10 Product Behavior: A General Summary 171

11 The Small Car Story 177

12 Product Behavior: Durability, Styling, Models, and Model Proliferation 189

13 Other Aspects of Behavior 211

14 Air Pollution and Automobile Safety Issues 228

15 Performance: An Evaluation 248

16 Recommendations for Public Policy 276

Appendix: Annual Automobile Sales (Registrations) 1946–1967 289

Bibliography 307

Notes 313

Index 343

Tables

1.1   Retail Automobile Sales (Registrations), 1967   6

2.1   Percentage Sales by Company, Independents, 1952–1953   14

3.1   Amortization of Special Tools   34

3.2   Tooling Cost per Vehicle Sold Worldwide   35

3.3   Estimated Total Development Costs and Tooling Costs, Chrysler Corporation   37

4.1   Revenue Received by Railroads for Shipments of 3,000 Pounds of Assembled Car   43

4.2   Revenue Received by Railroads for 3,000 Pounds of Shipments   43

4.3   Model Year Production: Annual Averages, Standard Deviations, and the Standard Error of Estimate around a Time Trend, 1949–1967   48

5.1   Capital Requirements at 1958 Costs to Provide Facilities to Produce and Market 250,000 Automobiles Annually   57

5.2   Manufacturing Facilities at 1958 Replacement Value to Produce 250,000 Automobiles Annually   58

5.3   Estimate of Capital Required for an Entrant at a Scale of 800,000 Units a Year   61

5.4   Balance Sheet Figures, Five Independents, 1948   69

5.5   Factory Delivered Prices (Including Federal Taxes) for Specified Four-door Sedans, April 1948   69

5.6   Factory Delivered Prices (Including Federal Taxes) of Comparable Willys and Chevrolet Cars, February 1953   71

5.7   Sales and Market Shares, Middle-level Cars   73

7.1   Estimated Division of New Car Sales to Consumers and Businesses and Fleets   93

7.2   Studies of the Demand for New Cars   94–95
7.3   Age Structure of Car Population and Number of Months
        New Car Buyer Held Previous Car, 1965   97
7.4   Income Distribution of Car Owners and New Car Buyers,
        1965   99
7.5   Median Income of New Car Buyers, by Make, March 1954   101
7.6   1967 Model Year Production by Price Class   102
8.1   Retail Prices among Chicago Automobile Dealers   108
8.2   Expected Savings from Shopping Multiple Dealers   109
9.1   Estimated per Unit Distribution Cost   146
9.2   Location of Dealer Relative to Purchaser of Car, Sample
        1960–1961   146
9.3   New Car Sales per Dealership   149
9.4   Net Dealers Handling United States Makes of Cars   149
9.5   Rates of Return on Net Worth for Corporate Automobile
        Dealers and All Corporate Retailers   153
9.6   Turnover of General Motors Dealers   158
12.1   Number of Seven-, Eight-, and Nine-Year-Old Cars, as a
        Percentage of Their Original Production, Still on the Road   194
12.2   Scrapping Rates for Cars   196
12.3   Survival Rates for Chevrolets, Fords, and Plymouths   197
12.4   Number of Models Offered and Average Output for
        Model Offered   203
12.5   Tooling (Amortization) Expenses per Car, Big Three Pro-
        ducers   204
13.1   Cases in Which One or Two Companies Clearly Led in the
        Introduction of an Innovation   214
13.2   Growth in Car Dimensions   217
13.3   Advertising, Sales, and Advertising per Car   225
15.1   Annual Rates of Return: Profits before Interest after Taxes
        Divided by Total Assets   249
15.2   Annual Rates of Return: Net Profits after Taxes Divided by
        Net Worth   251
15.3   Average Hourly Wages in Manufacturing in Certain Cities,
        Early 1967 and Early 1968   254
15.4   Prices and Price Increases   261
15.5   Auto Company Sales, Profits, Assets, 1966   266
Appendix: Annual Automobile Sales (Registrations), 1946–1967   289

Figures

2.1 Annual Market Shares, 1946–1967   11

8.1 BLS New Car Price Index, Monthly, by Model Year, 1955–1967   118

8.2 BLS New Car Price Index, Annual, Calendar Year, 1947–1967   122

9.1 Individual Dealer: Monopolistic Competition and Forcing Demand Models   140

9.2 Total Market Demand, Dealers Powerful Relative to Manufacturers   143

9.3 Total Market Demand, Manufacturers Capable of Forcing Cars on Dealers   144

12.1 Demand Model of Used Car Services   191

The Automobile Industry since 1945

1

Introduction

It is difficult to overestimate the importance of the automobile industry in the American economy. The four firms currently manufacturing automobiles are the first, third, fifth, and one-hundred-thirteenth largest industrial firms in the economy.[1] These four firms employ most of the 770,780 employees listed in the "Motor Vehicles and Parts" industry (SIC 3717) in 1965.[2] The Automobile Manufacturers Association (AMA) proudly proclaims that one business in six in the United States is automotive: "dependent on manufacturing, distribution, servicing, and use of motor vehicles."[3] During the 1957–1958 recession, many people in and out of Washington were blaming the recession on the auto industry's poor designs and consequent low sales; Detroit sneezed and America caught a cold. This book will be a study of that industry and its behavior and performance in the postwar period, 1946 through 1967.

This author believes that an "industrial organization" study of the automobile industry is long overdue. The number of areas in which public policy touches on automobiles — air pollution, traffic safety, the whole thicket of urban transportation systems and planning, the ever-present antitrust considerations — is steadily increasing. An understanding of the automobile industry and how it behaves and responds to outside influences is vital if the industry's efforts are to be harnessed to public policy goals. Further, the automobile industry is a classic case of a tight oligopoly, displaying many of the textbook symptoms and problems of oligopolies. A description and

1

analysis of this industry should provide some useful insights into the economics of this type of industrial structure.

Yet, surprisingly, the last full-length economic study of the auto industry in print was written in 1938: the Federal Trade Commission's *Report on the Motor Vehicle Industry*.[4] Since then, to this author's knowledge, only Paul H. Banner's unpublished 1953 Harvard Ph.D. thesis[5] has attempted another complete study of the industry. Lengthy chapters on the industry exist in Whitney,[6] Weiss,[7] and Adams,[8] but none of these is a truly complete study, and none concentrates on the postwar period. The same is true of the Senate Antitrust Subcommittee's *Report on Administered Prices, Automobiles*.[9] Edwards' book[10] is primarily a study of the smaller automobile companies and their struggle for survival, though his later chapters contain some useful insights into the overall industry. There are a number of general histories of the auto industry, among them books by Rae,[11] Denison,[12] Donovan,[13] and Smith,[14] but none concentrate on the economic aspects of the industry. Nothing, then, of a thorough nature exists on the economics of the postwar automobile industry. This book will attempt to close this gap.

It should be made clear that the manufacture and distribution of *automobiles* will be the main area of concern in this study. Automobiles are only assembled collections of parts; therefore, one cannot avoid dealing with the areas of technological change in automotive components, relations of the auto companies with their parts suppliers, and so forth. But a thorough study of the automotive parts industry will not be found here, nor will there be much mention of truck manufacturing. Though it would be tempting to include parts and trucks in a study of the "motor vehicles and parts industry," the subject would quickly become too complex and lengthy to be adequately dealt with here.[15] Also, an analysis of the unions and collective bargaining in the auto industry is beyond the scope of this study.[16]

We shall, then, be looking at the manufacturing of automotive components (insofar as this affects the automobile companies directly), the process of assembling these components into complete automobiles, and the distribution of the final product. We shall examine the structure of the industry and the way it has changed over the past twenty years. Entry into and exit from the industry will come under our scrutiny. Retail dealer structure and manufacturer-dealer relations will be dealt with extensively. We shall look at the pricing and product behavior of the auto companies and at their response to the outside influences of technology and Congressional pressure. We shall attempt to explain much of this behavior in terms of the structure and technology of the industry, the historical baggage that any organization must carry with it, and the perceived realities of the key characters at the time. The problems of product behavior and product variety in an oligopolistic industry will be treated extensively, and a theory of "spatial" oligopolistic product behavior will be proposed. Issues such as air pollution, auto safety, and import waves and troughs will be discussed. Finally, some comments and suggestions will be made on the role of public policy in dealing with the automobile industry.

A major theme will run through this study: the high risk aspects of automobile manufacturing and distribution and the effects of risk on the structure, behavior, and performance of the industry. The automobile business is inherently one of risks, with large swings in demand by a fickle consuming public always possible. Compounding this risk is the large size of investment needed to operate a successful car manufacturing concern and the long lag that is involved between the time at which large sums are committed and the time when the final product reaches the market.[17] The stakes are high, the penalties severe, and the uncertainties great. The now famous Edsel, a car carefully designed for a market that had greatly diminished by the time it appeared, required a $250 million investment by the Ford Motor Company, of which $100 million was eventually lost. The much more successful Ford Mustang had a $40 million investment behind it. Six postwar car manufacturers have disappeared. Since risk is a pervasive influence on the industry, it will be a pervasive theme in this study.

Design of the Study

This study will use the industrial organization tools of structure, behavior, and performance to analyze the automobile industry.[18] These categories should properly include the following elements:[19]

Structure   (1) Number and size concentration of sellers, (2) degree of differentiation of products, (3) height of barriers to entry, (4) cost and technological considerations of production, (5) extent of integration and diversification by firms, (6) structure of demand for the product, (7) the size and nature of buyers, (8) the size and nature of suppliers, and (9) the state of technological change and flux in the industry.

Behavior   (1) Prices, (2) products, (3) behavior toward suppliers and buyers, and (4) actual entry and exit.

Performance   (1) Size of profits, (2) amount of product differentiation, (3) responsiveness to technological change, (4) responsiveness to changes in consumer tastes, (5) responsiveness to public concerns (for example, auto safety, air pollution).

Traditionally, the presumption has been that structure largely determines behavior, and behavior, in turn, leads to a performance that can be judged against certain standards. In fact, structure, behavior, and performance are constantly interacting with one another, so that any effort to keep them separated analytically in watertight compartments is doomed to failure. The amount of product differentiation in a market is properly a characteristic of structure, but the differentiation itself is a result of behavior; therefore product differentiation may be one of the aspects of performance to be judged. The conditions of entry are a part of structure, but the act of entry involves behavior. Many more examples are possible.

Consequently, I have not attempted to seal off this study into separate subunits labeled "structure," "behavior," and "performance." Rather, the following chapters will have these categories intermixed as is necessary for a smooth, logical presentation. To set the later chapters in a proper perspective, Chapter 2 will offer a brief history of the industry since 1945. Chapters 3 and 4 will discuss the technology of the industry and the economies of scale that are present, while Chapter 5 will focus on the conditions of entry and the historical record of the entry that has taken place. Chapter 6 will deal with vertical integration and suppliers, Chapter 7 with the structure of demand for new automobiles, and Chapter 8 with the pricing policies of the auto companies. Chapter 9 will turn to the problems of automobile dealers. Chapter 10 will discuss some general principles of product behavior in the automobile industry; Chapter 11 will describe the development of the American compact car as a case study, displaying many of the problems of the auto industry. Chapter 12 will discuss the more general topics of product durability, styling, and proliferation, followed by Chapter 13 with a discussion of other aspects of behavior. Chapter 14 will deal with the auto safety and air pollution issues. Chapter 15 will offer a general evaluation of the performance in the industry. Chapter 16 will conclude with some observations and recommendations on public policy.

A Preliminary Resume on Structure

There are currently four major producers of passenger automobiles in the United States. In common trade usage, the term "Big Three" refers to the General Motors Corporation, the Ford Motor Company, and the Chrysler Corporation. The term "Independents" refers to any other major producers.[20] The American Motors Corporation is the only surviving Independent. There are also a number of specialty or custom car producers: Checker Motors manufactures 5–6,000 cars a year, mostly for the taxicab market, but some are sold to retail customers; International Harvester manufactures four-wheel-drive specialty vehicles and models that are similar to station wagons. But these minor producers do not exert any significant influence on the automobile market; therefore little attention will be given to them. It is on the four major producers who produce over 99 percent of American passenger cars and whose financial fortunes ride mainly on their successes in the automobile market that we will focus most of our attention.

Table 1.1 presents United States passenger car retail sales for the calendar year 1967. (Actually the figures are for new car registrations taken from state motor vehicle registration records, but they are virtually identical with domestic retail sales.) Each company's sales are broken down by "make." A make is basically a brand name that usually involves a separate design and production organization within the company, separate advertising campaigns, separate dealer organizations, and a separately designed car. Since the 1950's, though, makes have encompassed a number of separately designed car "lines"; for example, "Chevrolet" includes the Corvair, Chevy II, Camaro, Chevelle, full-sized Chevrolet, and Corvette. Each separately designed car can have a number of series; for example, the full-sized Chevrolet comes in the Biscayne, Bel Air, Impala, and Caprice series. Also, each series can have a number of models: two-door sedans, two-door hardtops, four-door sedans, and others.

The retail sales figures will differ somewhat from production figures for the same years, and both figures differ still from "factory

Table 1.1   Retail Automobile Sales (Registrations), **1967**

	Registrations	*Percent*
General Motors		
Buick	566,254	6.78
Cadillac	209,656	2.50
Chevrolet	1,979,180	23.67
Oldsmobile	552,102	6.60
Pontiac	832,682	10.00
Total	4,142,874	49.55
Ford Motor Co.		
Ford	1,522,438	18.21
Lincoln	35,221	0.42
Mercury	295,636	3.54
Total	1,853,295	22.17
Chrysler Corp.		
Chrysler	206,461	2.47
Dodge	492,500	5.89
Imperial	15,881	0.19
Plymouth	627,687	7.51
Total	1,342,529	16.06
Total American Motors	234,089	2.79
Miscellaneous	8,562	0.10
Total U.S. makes	7,581,349	90.66
Total imports	780,579	9.34
Total U.S. registrations	8,361,928	100.00

SOURCE: Data collected by R. L. Polk & Co., published in *Automotive Industries 50th Annual Engineering Specifications and Statistical Issue*, March 15, 1968, p. 105.

sales," a category of figures that appears primarily in company annual reports. The three sets differ because of exports and because of changes in company inventories, dealer inventories, and cars in transit. The retail sales figures are somewhat more detailed and accessible than the other sets; accordingly, unless otherwise indicated, the sales figures referred to in this study will be these retail figures. A complete listing of annual retail sales from 1946 through 1967 is found in the appendix.

As Table 1.1 shows, General Motors is clearly the dominant seller in the market with nearly 50 percent of sales. Its Chevrolet division alone sells more than any of the other companies. Though Ford and Chrysler were in a tight race for second place shortly after World

War II, Ford has comfortably held that position since 1952. (Ford's market share was depressed somewhat in 1967 because of a strike by the United Automobile Workers in the fall; in 1966, it held 26.08 percent of the market.) American Motors' current market share of 2.79 percent is down from a peak of 6.42 percent in 1960. Contained in the imports component are Volkswagen sales of 445,000 units in 1967 (a market share of 5.44 percent), making it in fact the fourth largest seller of cars in the United States.

Beside automobiles, all of the Big Three also produce trucks; American Motors does not. All four have automotive facilities in Canada. The Big Three have extensive automobile manufacturing facilities overseas. Outside of automotive products, the Big Three produce a variety of other goods. General Motors and Ford produce home appliances.[21] General Motors produces diesel engines and locomotives; Ford produces tractors and (through its Philco subsidiary) computers; Chrysler produces air conditioning units and marine engines. All three have defense sales. Exact sales breakdowns are difficult to ascertain, but 90 percent or more of each of the Big Three's sales are due to cars, trucks, and parts. With American Motors' sale of its Kelvinator division in June 1968, it became the only company devoted solely to automobiles. If it survives, its balance sheet figures over the next few years should give economists their first clear look in twenty years at the exact costs of producing cars.

Risk

This brief discussion of the simple analytics of risk is not intended to break new theoretical ground but, rather, to provide a background for the discussion of the risk aspects of the auto industry that will appear in subsequent chapters.

By risk, we mean a condition of uncertainty about a future outcome combined with a financial stake in the outcome. If the uncertainty can be summarized by a probability distribution of the possible outcomes and financial rewards or penalties attached to those outcomes, then the variance of these financial outcomes, relative to the mean outcome, may serve as one indicator of risk. The probability and size of possible losses of a project, irrespective of the possible gains, may serve as other indicators of risk.

We normally assume that individuals and firms are risk-averse;

that is, given their choice between a project of uncertain outcome carrying an estimated mean financial reward (but with the possibility of higher or lower rewards) and a project with a certain outcome of the same mean reward, individuals and firms will choose the latter project. For individuals, this assumption is based on the prior assumption of the declining marginal utility of income.[22] For owner-controlled firms, the same assumptions would prevail.

For firms in which management confronts a diffuse body of stockholders, none of whom individually has any measure of control over management, a different justification for risk-averse behavior can be offered. If managements are interested in security of tenure, the differential rewards and penalties to managements for exceptionally high and exceptionally low profits would seem to argue for risk-averse behavior. Stockholders, lacking detailed knowledge of the firm's operations, may remain contented with what appear to be "reasonably good" profits but will be more likely to band together to oust management if poor profits or losses have aroused them. Or poor profits or losses may depress the value of the firm's stock, making it more susceptible to a takeover by an outside firm. On the other hand, exceptionally good profits beyond the reasonable level that will keep stockholders contented would not seem to offer management any extra benefits, except insofar as management has stock holdings or a bonus system.

Some of the behavioral consequences of risk averseness can be briefly spun out. Firms and individuals will presumably have a preference pattern of trade-offs between risk and returns. They should demand a higher expected mean return, that is, a risk premium, before accepting an investment project that carries higher risks than an alternative project. The higher the risks, the higher will be the risk premium.

Once involved in a risky project, firms have a number of options that can be employed singly or in combinations: (1) They can pay someone else to absorb part of the risk (for example, a firm may elect to produce only part of its requirements of a particular input and purchase the fluctuating remainder; the supplier firm, in accepting this risky proposition, presumably will impose a risk premium on the buyer). This transference of risk can take place to the mutual profit of both because of differing degrees of risk averseness among firms and individuals in the economy. (2) They can invest resources in direct efforts to reduce the level of risk (for example, to reduce uncertainty, a firm can conduct a market survey to get a better idea of expected sales). (3) They can diversify or dilute their risk by acquiring still other risky projects with different, or at least independent, probability distributions of financial outcomes. The stability of the firm's fortunes is thereby enhanced, since the probability of all of the projects showing dismal financial results is greatly reduced. Thus, paradoxically, if a firm's sales were positively tied to the movement of the business cycle (and that business cycle is unpredictable, hence the project is risky), it would be eager to find and perhaps even willing to pay a premium for a risky project that involved sales that moved contracyclically. (4) If these risks arise from clearly perceived possibilities that rivals may achieve an important breakthrough in some area, firms can join with their rivals in explicit or implicit agreements to exchange information or license patents. In so doing, each firm loses the chance of achieving a coup at the expense of its rivals but receives the assurance, in turn, that it will not be the victim of one. As we shall see, the successful auto companies have engaged in all of these practices in their efforts to reduce the risks they face.

2

A Brief Automotive History
of the Postwar Period

In 1946 there were nine active producers of passenger automobiles, with at least twice that many hovering in the wings, eager to enter the car manufacturing business. In 1968 there were only four producers remaining. In order to put the following chapters in a proper perspective, this chapter will attempt a brief description of the intervening twenty-two years that surrounded this demise in numbers.

In addition to the Big Three, the other companies producing cars in 1946 were Studebaker, Packard, Nash, Hudson, Kaiser-Frazer, and Crosley. All but Crosley produced standard, full-sized cars, with Crosley producing a small ("bantam") four-passenger car. Figure 2.1 reproduces the market shares data from the appendix for these companies in 1946 and all of the following years.

With automobile production having been completely halted for the three and one-half years of World War II, a large backlog of demand greeted the auto companies as they geared up to resume production. Even full capacity operations for three years would not have erased the backlog, and repeated strikes in the plants of suppliers in the hectic three years that followed V-J Day made full capacity operations impossible. An automotive publication listed 143 strikes in General Motors' suppliers' plants as of May 20, 1946, while Ford faced 52 supplier strikes at the same time (not counting a national coal strike).[1] A detailed listing of the Ford components affected ranged from transmission gears and cylinder heads to automobile light bulbs and ignition locks.[2] Repeatedly, the absence of

10

items as seemingly trivial as seat cushion springs brought production lines to a halt.

Consequently, only 1.8 million new cars reached consumers' hands in 1946, followed by a still inadequate 3.2 million units in 1947.[3] Despite an end to Office of Price Administration (OPA)

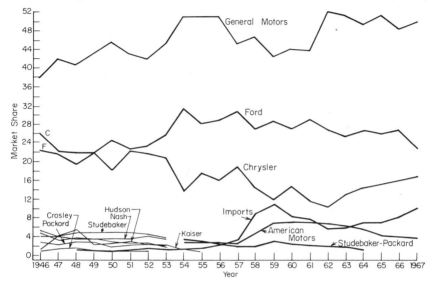

FIGURE 2.1   Annual Market Shares, 1946–1967

ceilings in November of 1946, retail list prices stayed below their market clearing levels. As late as April 1, 1948, Ford claimed that it had a backlog of 1,575,000 orders. The gray market in "new-used" cars, which had developed as soon as production had started, was still offering $700 over list price for a Chevrolet and $500 over list price for a Pontiac or Dodge in May 1948.[4]

The ability to sell every car they could produce, plus a greater willingness to "scrounge" for parts and materials and to pay premium prices for materials, carried the Independents to an expanded 18.6 percent share of the market in 1948. This was far better than the 10 percent share they occupied for the five years before the war, and it has not been equaled since. Their efforts were to pay off when the Korean War production quotas were based on the postwar average shares.

Faced with this strong demand (and an uncertain supply line

for new tooling), most auto companies refrained from any model changes, continuing to turn out what were only slightly modified prewar models. Only Kaiser-Frazer (a new entrant) and Studebaker brought out "all-new" models in 1946. Some makes brought out new models for the 1948 model year, with most holding off until the 1949 model year.

The Ford story is especially worth mentioning here. Henry Ford II took over a Ford Motor Company in 1945 that was in an advanced state of disarray. Organization, responsibility, coordination, and control had all disintegrated under the elder Henry Ford. The company was losing money, but no one knew how much; the bookkeeping system was at best rudimentary. Only later did the company discover that it had lost $50 million in the first seven months of 1946.[5] A contemporary observer described the company in the following terms:

Imagine a company with assets of $900 million, and an annual gross volume in the neighborhood of $1.5 billion, operating on a set of books that would put a country storekeeper to shame — no budget, no controls, just a how-much-comes-in, how-much-goes-out kind of calculation that would do for tax purposes. Imagine a company that boasted of a higher order of integration than any similar organization in the country, with ownership of a steel mill, glass plant, timber stands, maritime fleet, etc., and no accurate knowledge of which individual operation was paying its way, or which was padding the cost of the company's end product by open-market standards. Imagine, at the top personnel layer of a company making and selling an average of a million automobiles and trucks a year, an embittered, mutually distrustful group of executives — most of them without titles — with no clear lines of authority or responsibility anywhere delineated.[6]

One of Henry Ford II's early acts of office was to hire Ernest R. Breech away from Bendix Aviation to take over the presidency of Ford. Breech, bringing General Motors men and methods with him,[7] quickly began to pull the organization into shape. Some of the elder Ford's pet projects (the Brazilian rubber plantations that had lost $20 million between 1927 and 1945, soy bean processing factories, small-scale village industries) were sold; 8,500 unnecessary employees were pared from the payroll.[8]

But the success of the new organization really hinged on bringing out a successful postwar car. In September 1946 a crash program to bring out the car was started; in June 1948 that car, the 1949 Ford, appeared on the market. It rattled and shook, and a poorly designed fit of body and chassis allowed dust to leak into the interior (one observer claimed a count of 8,000 minor defects),[9] but the car was popular with consumers and sold well. Had it failed, the Ford organization might well have splintered into oblivion.

By early 1949 expanded production and a slackening of demand, the result of the 1948–1949 recession, had brought demand and supply back into reasonable balance at list prices, and the gray market faded out of existence.

The next jolt to the industry was the Korean War. Scare buying by long-memoried consumers in July 1950 quickly tapered off, but by the end of the year, price and production controls were imposed on the industry. Despite a war economy, consumers still managed to buy cars, with 5 million new units (the second highest figure until that time) reaching consumer hands in 1951 and a respectable 4.2 million units (fourth highest) appearing in 1952. Still, production and sales were below what the industry would have desired, since cars were selling at list prices and car dealers were making a profit on their used car resales — both forms of behavior indicating a limited supply of cars. (See Chapter 9 for a more detailed explanation of dealer behavior.)

Defense contracts served to fatten corporate treasuries, particularly among the Independents. But Crosley, never enjoying any true success with its small car (selling only 25,400 cars in its best year, 1948), was the first of the postwar Independents to fall by the wayside. General Tire & Rubber Company bought out Crosley in 1952 and promptly converted the plant to defense work. Crosley's financial losses for the fiscal year ending June 30, 1952 had been almost $2 million on sales of $5.6 million.[10]

The Korean War also had the effect of retarding planned expansion in the auto industry. Ford, particularly, was hampered in its plans to expand its V-8 engine and automatic transmission capabilities because of raw materials shortages.

The year 1953 brought a new administration to Washington, the lifting of production controls, and the end of the Korean War, in that order. Car output expanded rapidly to 3.3 million units in the second and third quarters of 1953, compared to 2.1 million units in the same period in 1952. This expanded production and the 1953 post-Korean recession brought a return to fierce selling efforts and a buyer's market. List prices were quickly forgotten, and dealer losses on used car resales mounted (due to overallowances on trade-ins for new cars, an alternative to cutting the list price).

The Independents, unprepared for the stiff competition and unwilling or unable to make sufficient price cuts quickly, found themselves in trouble. Also, a strike from April 20 through June 27 at Borg-Warner's transmission gear operations especially hurt the Independents, who relied more heavily on Borg-Warner transmissions than did the Big Three. Table 2.1 shows clearly the declining

Table 2.1   Percentage Sales by Company, Independents, 1952–1953

		1953				
	1952	1st quart.	2nd quart.	3rd quart.	4th quart.	Year
Industry sales, total	$4,158,394	$1,269,147	$1,610,878	$1,490,019	$1,368,945	$5,738,989
Independents						
Studebaker	3.80	2.45	3.29	2.83	2.56	2.81
Nash	3.43	3.26	2.80	1.99	1.56	2.40
Hudson	1.89	1.28	1.39	1.00	0.98	1.16
Kaiser-Frazer	1.72	0.90	0.71	0.52	.25	0.60
Packard	1.60	1.65	1.46	1.08	.77	1.24
Willys	0.99	1.10	0.83	0.58	.55	0.74
Misc.	.78	0.67	.56	.47	.43	.53
Total, Independents	14.21	11.31	11.04	8.47	7.10	9.48
Total, Big Three	85.79	88.69	88.96	91.53	92.90	90.52

SOURCE: *Ward's Automotive Reports*, various issues.

fortunes of the Independents during 1953. The declining market shares of the companies were joined by falling sales in absolute numbers. Falling sales were quickly reflected in falling profits and splotches of red ink. Nash lost $3.1 million before tax credits in the third quarter of 1953, and its after-tax profit in the last quarter was under $1 million. Packard's before-tax profit of $16.5 million in the first half of 1953 declined to a $4 million loss in the last half. Studebaker had a before-tax profit of $4.4 million in the first half of 1953, only $0.6 million in the last half. Hudson showed a loss of $18 million before-tax credits for the whole of 1953.[11]

Mergers appeared to be one way out of the morass. Kaiser-Frazer, which had not seen any profits since 1948, merged in April 1953 with

Willys-Overland, a profitable producer of jeeps and small trucks that had reentered the passenger car market in 1952 after a ten-year absence with a not particularly successful small car. The tax advantages of profit and loss offsetting seemed to be uppermost in the merger partners' minds. A year later, on May 1, 1954, Hudson and Nash formally merged to become the American Motors Corporation. Studebaker and Packard, after running losses of $19 million and $5.8 million, respectively, in the first half of 1954,[12] formally merged on October 1, 1954. There were now six members of the automobile industry remaining. This number was quickly cut to five, as Kaiser ceased all passenger car production of Kaisers and Willys in 1955, preferring to concentrate solely on the production of jeep vehicles.

The Chrysler Corporation had a minor debacle during this period. Its 1953 models, carried over in substance into 1954, were short and boxy compared to competitors' cars; "bigger on the inside, smaller on the outside" was the way Chrysler's president had wanted them. Though adequate for 1953, gaining 20.3 percent of the market, they proved a disaster in 1954, capturing only 12.9 percent of sales. Chrysler's before-tax profits fell from $200 million in 1953 to $21 million in 1954.[13] Hastily redesigned models for 1955 brought Chrysler's market share back to a more respectable 16.8 percent.

The year 1955 was a boom year for the auto industry, as changed styles, expanding income, and looser credit terms led to retail sales of over 7 million new cars. Despite the boom, however, the two remaining Independents continued to face hard times. American Motors sold only 137,000 units in 1955, only 1.9 percent of the market; Studebaker-Packard fared little better with 148,000 units or 2.1 percent. Red ink continued in the books of both companies.

The cars that sold particularly well that year were the larger, middle-level cars: Buick, Oldsmobile, Dodge, and others. The Ford Motor Company, feeling that it was weak in this area, began a project to develop a new middle-level car of its own. By the time the car reached the market in the fall of 1957, however, consumer preferences had changed, smaller cars were in demand, and the Edsel was a flop.

Small imported cars were suddenly reaching American shores in tidal wave proportions. From a barely perceptible 58,000 units in 1955, the tide had swollen to 207,000 units in 1957 or 3.5 percent of the United States market; in 1958 it grew to 379,000 units or 8.1 percent of the market; and in 1959 it hit a temporary peak of 610,000 units, or 10.2 percent.[14] The increased physical size and price of United States domestic makes left a wide gap on both accounts at the bottom of the scale. A recession psychology on the part of consumers looking for smaller, cheaper packages and an increased willingness and ability by Europe to export its production contributed to the tide.

American Motors, concentrating its production on its "compact"-sized Rambler, benefited from the public's preference for smaller cars and captured 4.0 percent of the market in 1958, enjoying its first profits since the merger. In 1959 sales doubled in absolute volume to 363,000 units for 6.0 percent of the market. Studebaker-Packard hastily brought out its compact Lark in November 1958 and captured 2.2 percent of the market in 1959, realizing its first profits since its merger.

Due to the change in consumer tastes, Chrysler once again fell on hard times. Its 1958 models, largely unchanged from 1957 and stressing a large, tail-finned look, fell to sales of 648,000 units and 13.9 percent of the market from 1,096,000 units and 18.3 percent the year before. A poor reputation for quality control in 1957 also contributed to this decline. Before-tax profits of $252 million in 1957 turned into a loss of $73 million before tax credits in 1958. With the same model in 1959, Chrysler's share fell to 11.3 percent of the market, but an increase in sales in absolute numbers to 683,000 units and better cost controls kept Chrysler's loss to $10 million. Newly developed models in 1960 brought sales to 921,000 units, a market share of 14.0 percent, and before-tax profits of $66 million.

After much handwringing and protestations that in building a smaller car "you take out value much faster than you can take out cost" and that "anyone who wants cheap transportation can always buy a used car," the Big Three finally brought out their own compact cars in the fall of 1959. (For a more detailed account of the small car episode, see Chapter 11.) They sold well and temporarily turned back the import tide. The compacts, originally thought of as economy cars, quickly acquired embellishments and larger versions appeared among the medium-level makes, as the companies' sales officials quickly noticed that large percentages of compact car buyers were requesting extra-cost trim outfittings, automatic transmissions, and other luxury items.

Through the early and middle 1960's, the compacts and their

middle-level counterparts gradually grew in physical size and luxury, leaving a widening gap that the imports were again ready to fill. Registrations of imported cars rose from a temporary low of 339,000 units or 4.9 percent of the market in 1962 to a peak of 781,000 units or 9.3 percent of the market in 1967. In 1968 import sales were well over 10 percent of the market; Ford, General Motors, and American Motors planned to bring out new small cars in 1969 and 1970.

For the third time, Chrysler cars lost favor with consumers. In 1961 their sales slumped to 632,000 units and a market share of 10.8 percent; the newly styled 1962 models sold only slightly better at 666,900 units and a market share of only 9.6 percent. The lack of popularity of the 1962 models is best shown by a market share of only 8.8 percent in the first six months of 1962. But better cost control was able to produce profits of $21 million and $126 million, respectively, in the two years. Chrysler's market share was 12.4 percent in 1963, and it has been climbing ever since.

Studebaker, rapidly losing momentum in the 1960's, finally left the automobile business, but in stages. In December 1963 the corporation announced a transfer of production to its Canadian plant, where a break-even point of 20,000 units a year was claimed.[15] After producing 17,614 units in 1964 and 18,542 units in 1965, Studebaker announced an end to automobile production in March 1966, leaving only the present four producers. Studebaker is now quite profitably producing a wide variety of other items.

A major style trend in the 1960's was toward "sporty" cars, best illustrated by the Ford Mustang. Introduced in the spring of 1964, the Mustang was an overnight success; in 1966, Mustang sales were 541,000 units, representing 6.0 percent of the market.[16] In 1967, when a larger number of sporty models were on the market, total sales of sporty models came to 10.8 percent of all new car sales.

Also in the 1960's, the automobile safety and air pollution issues erupted. Rumblings on both topics were heard during the 1950's, with congressional committees quietly gathering data and opinions (and opposition from the auto companies) but taking no action. California led the way in air pollution control, requiring partial smog control devices (blowby devices) on the 1961 model cars sold in the state and full control devices (exhaust devices) on the 1966 models. To ward off congressional action, the auto companies put the blowby devices on all cars, beginning with the 1963 model year.

Increasing public and congressional concern led to the Motor Vehicle Air Pollution Act of 1965,[17] which required exhaust devices on all new cars sold after January 1, 1968.

The federal government led the way on the safety issue, with Public Law 88–515[18] in 1964 requiring the General Services Administration (GSA) to set safety standards for government-purchased cars for the 1967 model year. Once the standards had been set, the companies announced their intention to put most of the safety devices on all 1966 models. But increasing publicity about auto safety and a minor scandal, revolving around the alleged unsafe characteristics of the Corvair car, led to the passage of the National Traffic and Motor Vehicle Safety Act of 1966,[19] establishing a new federal agency to set safety performance standards for all new cars sold. The first set of standards went into effect on January 1, 1968.

3

Manufacturing Technology
and the Planning Process

An automobile is composed of 15,000 parts, each one of which has to attain a high level of dimensional accuracy and must be in the right place at the right time for assembly into the finished automobile. This chapter will describe the technology involved in manufacturing a car and its components and the planning process behind the development of a car.

This description is necessary for a thorough understanding of the structure and behavior that will follow. It will allow us to see where the important economies of scale are, and at which volumes they are exhausted. This information is, of course, crucial for ascertaining the minimum size necessary for an efficient firm, which, in turn, should offer us some insight into the minimum seller concentration that could be expected in any long-run equilibrium in the industry. Further, this description will elucidate the nature of the technology involved in a key manufacturing process, the final assembly. The flexibility that has been introduced into the assembly process has had important ramifications on product behavior, particularly the proliferation of models, styles, engines, and optional accessories. Finally, the description of the planning process will bring out some of the risks involved in automobile production. Variable consumer tastes are not enough to create high risks; if products could be changed rapidly and without cost, the risks would be low. The length and nature of the lead time required between design and sale, and the costs of the design and development process, then, are crucially related to the risks of automobile production and to the structural and behavioral efforts that the auto companies have made to reduce or dilute these risks.

Much of the information in this chapter is based on visits to manufacturing operations in Detroit and interviews with executives there, supplemented by information gleaned from articles in the automotive press.

Since metal parts are about 80 percent of the weight of an assembled car[1] and provide the major cost elements and the major components with which one identifies a car (the sheet metal body, engine, bumpers, and so forth), it is on these metal manufacturing processes that we shall concentrate. They can be divided into four major categories: stamping (or pressing), casting, machining, and final assembly.

Stamping

Stamping is the process of shaping metal by the application of heavy pressure and mating dies. The familiar outer portions of a car body — the fenders, roof, hood, and door panels — as well as the unseen inner portions, are all pieces of stamped sheet metal.

Stamping operations are performed in special stamping plants, containing as many as 400 large and small presses, most of them in special sequences called press lines.[2] Each press contains a set of mating dies. Modern heavy presses are capable of ten or more strokes a minute, the smaller presses of as many as eighteen a minute.

The sheet steel enters the plant in the form of coils. The coils are cut into pieces of the proper size by blanking presses, and then the pieces begin their trip through the forming presses. A very simple piece might require only one stamping. Complex items involving deep indentations, like fenders, require multiple stampings. The appropriate dies are arranged sequentially in a number of presses. Each die makes a partial impression, and the piece is gradually shaped rather than being shaped in one fell swoop; the latter effort would probably break the metal or weaken it seriously instead of bending it.

The finished pieces are stacked and shipped off to the next stage in the manufacturing process, usually the final assembly plant. But an item like a bumper would be sent to a plating plant to be chrome-plated in an electrolytic bath before being shipped to the assembly plant.

Ten strokes a minute means that 9,600 pieces are produced in a two-shift day, or approximately 2.5 million pieces in a year. If the dies lasted that long, this would indeed be an impressive minimum efficient scale of production. But, in fact, dies do not last that long.[3] The best dies last only for "several hundred thousand pieces";[4] this author's estimate is that somewhere around 400,000 stampings is the limit for die life. Lower volume dies down to lives of 100,000 stampings are available, but the unit cost on the high volume dies is lower, and they require fewer die changes on high volume runs. Below 100,000 pieces, only very low volume dies (some of them of plastic), good for 5,000 to 10,000 pieces, are available. Despite earnest industry efforts, no intermediate volume dies between 10,000 and 100,000 have been developed. The basic problem seems to be that the smooth surface necessary for an outer-body stamping can only be obtained from a high quality steel die that will last 100,000 stampings anyway.

This 400,000 figure, then, represents the basic efficient scale of stamping. Any higher volume of production will require replacement dies for the worn-out sets.

Even with the possibility of replacement sets, rarely do dies of one type stay in a press for an entire year. Few production pieces are required in volumes of 2.5 million a year.[5] To get maximum use of the expensive presses, even when lower volumes are desired, "cycling" of the dies is practiced.[6] A set of dies will be left in a press or in a group of presses in a press line for a few days, building up an inventory of these parts. Then the first set will be pulled out and a second set put in its place, eventually to be replaced again by the first set (or by a third set). Since die sets can be changed in a few hours (and this can be accomplished over a weekend or on the third shift to avoid having the normal operators stand idle), cycling presents an efficient means of fully utilizing the presses.[7] The length of the cycle will depend on the cost and space limitations on inventorying the stampings versus the cost of changing multiple sets of dies in a press line.

Most pieces are extracted automatically from presses by mechanical hands; in all but the highest volume presses the pieces are fed in manually. The reason for this is that extracting is a comparatively low precision job, with little adjustment of the extracting machinery necessary when the dies are changed. Loading, however, requires precision placing of the piece and exact and extensive adjustment of any automatic loading device when the dies are changed. Consequently, only for high volume pieces with little or no die changing is automated loading worthwhile. This relationship is also partly self-reinforcing; automated loading permits a press to operate at higher speeds.

Thus there are some small economies to be had from very large volumes: cycling is not necessary, meaning fewer die changes, and automatic handling and faster (but more expensive) presses are possible. But these economies do not appear to be particularly significant. One middle-level car make, for example, has its right and left fender dies run on an eight-week cycle, with each set in for four weeks. This means one die change for every 70,000 fender stampings. A high volume producer who could leave his dies in continuously would have to change dies only once every 400,000 fenders. Yet, at these high volumes, the difference in cost would be at most a few cents per fender. For all practical purposes, the cost curve for stamping flattens out after a volume of 400,000 units a year has been reached.[8]

Casting

Casting is the process of pouring molten metal into a mold and allowing it to harden into a final shape. Familiar engine parts, such as the engine block itself, cylinder heads, pistons, and most crankshafts, are cast. The description that follows will be of iron casting. (Aluminum casting differs somewhat, in that different kinds of molds are used and pressure may be applied during casting.)

Casting takes place in a foundry. The molds, formed in two halves, are made of greensand, tightly compressed and shaped to form the template of the outer shape of, say, a V-8 engine block. Baked sand and resin cores (hotbox cores) or, in older plants, baked oil and sand cores, are placed in the molds to provide the hollowed-out areas (cylinders, oil lines, water jacket) around which the metal will form. The two halves are brought together, and molten metal is poured through a hole left in the top. After the molded iron has cooled, the mold is stripped away, the cores removed, and the cast part is sent to the next manufacturing stage, usually machining.

One of the newest foundries in the industry has a capacity of 110 tons of iron an hour, yielding over a thousand pieces an hour.[9] But there are a large number of parts to be cast out of iron (engine blocks, cylinder heads, oil pans, manifolds, crankshafts, and piston rods, to name a few). Also, the basic components of the casting process — a furnace and cupola for holding the hot iron, a pouring device, and the mold- and core-making machines — are fairly adaptable for casting different parts. Consequently, efficient operation over most otherwise feasible scales of production seems likely.[10] Often, casting and machining take place under the same roof, and it is the more capital-intensive machining process that will determine the overall scale of the plant.

Machining

Casting provides a piece with its general shape and dimensions. Machining is necessary to smooth the rough edges and provide the precision shaping required by the modern internal combustion engine.[11]

The machining area usually consists of a very large open room containing long rows of machine tools lined up one beside the other. On a V-8 engine line, the machine tools will be arranged in two rows facing each other, each row handling a four-cylinder half of the V. As an engine block reaches a "station" (a machine tool with a number of carbide steel machining heads) the machining heads will come into play, moving down to broach or bore or drill or hone part of the engine (for example, hone the cylinder walls). When operations are finished at this station, the block moves on to the next station, where more broaching, boring, and drilling by different machining heads will occur. The blocks are transferred from one station to another by automatic transfer machines, the whole sequence timed perfectly to allow each station adequate time to perform its operations.

At the end of the machining line, the finished engine blocks, together with the cylinder heads, crankshafts, pistons and other engine pieces that have gone through similar machining processes, are ready to be assembled into completed engines. After assembly, each engine is given a short running test. Gas, oil, and water lines are hooked up, and the engines are started and run for a minute or two. The engines are then shipped to the final assembly plant.

The speed of a machining line is determined by the length of time required for a machine to complete its job. For example, in honing the cylinder cavities, the honing head might be timed so as to take a minute to hone to the bottom of the cylinder, and the line could move no faster than 60 blocks an hour. Or one could add a second honing station and have the first set of heads hone only the top half of the cylinder for 30 seconds, the block move to the second station, and the second set of heads hone the bottom half of the cylinder. The line could thereby move at a rate of 120 blocks an hour if all of the other machines could complete their tasks in 30 seconds. Thus the speed of the line can be increased, but only by adding more machines and reducing the task of each machine. Once a volume has been attained that warrants automatic handling of the pieces, a fairly proportional relationship between speed and investment in machine tools takes hold.

What is that key volume? This author would estimate that, for a complicated piece like an engine block, that volume lies somewhere in the range of a net 65–70 pieces an hour, implying a gross rate of about 25 percent higher.[12] (Slightly higher speeds for simpler pieces seem to be warranted.) No engine plants built or expanded in the past fifteen years have planned for speeds lower than this. Officials at one machining plant that had 4 block lines (3 V-8 and 1 straight-6) producing 70 blocks an hour net (90–95 gross) from each line expressed satisfaction with their operation. Higher speeds are possible,[13] but they do not appear to be necessary for efficient production. Thus, on an annual basis, the production of 260,000 to 280,000 units per year should fully exhaust the economies of scale in this process.

Direct information about optimum scale in automatic transmission manufacturing is difficult to obtain. However, since the essential manufacturing operations are similar to those for engines, the scale economies for automatic transmissions should be approximately the same as for engines.

Assembly

It is in the assembly plant that the stamped, cast, machined, and partially assembled parts enter at one end and the finished automobile leaves at the other. The essence of the assembly process is a stream of parts, some of them partially assembled in subassembly lines, arriving at the proper time at the main assembly line and being attached to the moving "carcass" as it slowly passes by. The latter slowly grows into a completed automobile. Repetition — each worker doing essentially the same job, attaching essentially the same part as each car goes by — is the source of efficiency in the assembly process. The key elements in a successful assembly operation, as will be apparent in the description that follows, are inventorying, scheduling of the cars to be built (rarely do two identical cars follow each other down the line), and optimum utilization of the assembly labor available.

A typical assembly operation would start with the unpacking of the stamped sheet metal parts.[14] (The description that follows is for a body-on-frame type of car; a unitized type of car would be built somewhat differently,[15] but the basic processes are the same.) The sheet metal is placed on jigs and welded together to form the inner and outer portions of the body. The welds are high energy spot welds; most are done by hand and a few, such as floor pans, by machine. The higher the volume and the greater the uniformity of the pieces, the more likely is the possibility of machine welding. Solder fills and smoothes the welded edges, the metal is smoothed all around, a rust-proofing solution is applied, and the body is sent for painting. The body is dipped in a phosphate solution to allow the paint to adhere to the metal and is then given a number of sprayed-on, under- and over-layer paint coats, and baked in hot ovens between coats. After painting, the upholstery, seats, interior and exterior trim, and windows and windshields are added, and the completed body is sent up to a second floor "body bank" to be stored temporarily.

In the meantime, the frame is being built up; axles, springs, brakes, motors, and transmission are added. The various accessories and parts are retrieved either from large bins close to the workers' stations or, in the case of partially assembled items, from specially timed subassembly lines. At the proper moment, the right body drops down onto the right frame and is bolted to it; tires and wheels are added; the front fenders, grille, and bumpers are dropped into place; adjustments are made; and the car is driven to a test stand. The test stand has rollers under the rear wheels, allowing the car to be run in place. The car is run through all gears briefly and the brakes checked, all in about a minute. (The era of the road test for each car has long since passed.) The headlight aim is checked; other parts of the car are checked for proper functioning; a short waterproofing test is given; a final inspection is made; and the car is ready for shipment.[16] Cars found wanting by inspectors anywhere along the line will be pulled off the line into special repair bays and repaired before being shipped out.

In such a process, the complex operation of putting together a car has to be broken down into a large number of simple operations. Each one of the latter fully occupies a worker's time as the to-be-completed car passes by him, and each operation is capable of endless repetition. If a faster pace on an assembly line is desired, each worker would have less time to work on the car as it passed by; more workers would be necessary, with jobs broken down more finely and portions of them given to the new workers.[17]

For example, at an assembly line speed of 60 units an hour, one man's work responsibility might be the following: pick up left front wheel and place on axle, pick up five wheel nuts and hand screw them to the wheel; use five-nut torque gun to tighten wheel nuts; pick up left rear wheel and place it on the rear axle. (The next worker on the line would put on the left rear wheel nuts, and so forth.) These actions would fully (or almost fully) occupy his 60 seconds as the car went by. If a line speed of, say, 70 units per hour were desired, our worker would be relieved of placing the rear wheel on the axle. Other workers nearby would similarly be relieved of a part of their tasks, and an extra worker would be fitted into the vacant slot. Similarly, for slower speeds, more tasks can be allotted to one worker and fewer workers employed along the line.

As the previous paragraph implies, then, the speed of an assembly line is variable. A faster line requires more men; a slower line, fewer. A faster line will also require more physical space for the extra workers. It also requires more space for inventories. (If, say, an eight-hour supply of an item is desired, a faster line means a larger desired stock.) Beyond physical space, the only other limits on speed in a given plant would be paint-drying oven space — a faster line would require more oven space, since speed cannot be compensated for by just turning up the temperature — and more testing booth space at the end of the line. A faster line that is properly manned should not cause any increase in the number of repair jobs that have to be pulled off the line.

The assembly process is made yet more complex by the fact that rarely do two identical cars follow each other down the line. Cars of the same make will be of two- and four-door varieties, hardtop and regular sedans, with or without optional extras like automatic transmissions, power brakes, power steering, and radios. Further, the auto manufacturers have found it possible to mix cars of different makes along the same assembly lines. Thus, for example, in 1967 the General Motors assembly plant in Fremont, California, turned out four different "intermediate" cars: the Chevrolet Chevelle, the Pontiac Tempest, the Oldsmobile F-85, and the Buick Special.[18] Other manufacturers can turn out similar mixes.[19] The mixing of makes along one assembly line allows a better response to local market conditions, a fuller use of plant facilities, and a minimizing of expensive cross-shipment of completed cars. Thus, if Chevelle sales slacken and Tempest sales boom in California, the mix at the Fremont plant can be altered to handle this. If only Chevelles were produced, the plant would have to slow down or ship its Chevelles into another plant's area, while that plant shipped Tempests into California.

This product mix aspect introduces greater complexity into the assembly process. To make sure that the right engine, transmission, body, frame, and accessories all come together at the right time, teletype descriptions of the car and its accessories go out to as many as twelve separate points when construction of the car begins. Copies of the description will be attached to the carcass as it takes shape so that workers farther down the line know which accessories to attach. Any subassembly lines, of course, are timed so that the right parts appear at the right time.

The product mix also puts a premium on proper inventorying and scheduling. Allowing the inventory of a single item to run out can bring the entire assembly line to a halt, a very expensive proposition; yet an increasingly complex product mix could cause inventories to mushroom to uneconomic proportions. As for scheduling, a Chevrolet Impala with many extra accessories installed will require more labor effort than its simpler Biscayne sister with no accessories. A line that was geared to full effort on a Biscayne would find itself undermanned if a string of Impalas came down the line; a line geared to Impalas would be overmanned for a string of Biscaynes. Thus some intermediate planning is necessary, with proper scheduling necessary to prevent a series of identical cars from occurring on the line. A man may fall slightly behind on his task on an Impala (he can follow the Impala on foot to finish), but he gets a little bit of a breather and catches up if a Biscayne follows. The number of variables — two-door or four-door, with or without radio, deluxe trim, power steering, and so forth — can be large, and the combination problem of job definition and scheduling to ensure optimum labor utilization is correspondingly complex. The Model T days of "any color as long as it's black" and very little assembly line variation have passed into history along with the Model T.

From this description, it becomes clear that an assembly plant production manager's greatest desire is for stability: stability of product mix, and especially stability of the level of final demand and thus of the speed of the line. For it is changes in the speed of the line that create the most headaches: men have to be hired or fired; jobs have to be reallocated and the men have to learn new tasks; union grievances get filed as men complain of being overburdened on their new tasks; cars in need of repair increase in frequency while the men learn their new tasks. The settling-down time after a line speed change is about two weeks. This desire for a steady production rate will loom large in our discussion of the manufacturers' relationships with their dealers.[20]

As the previous paragraphs have indicated, there is a basic relationship between the speed of an assembly line and floor space in a plant. A faster line requires more space, both for the workers on the line and for larger inventories. (Faster replacement of inventories would increase the risk of no supplies due to a delayed shipment, and delivery carts would soon clog the aisles, requiring more aisle space; more loading dock space outside the plant would also be needed.) Also, an increasingly complex product has been requiring more space, both on the line and for inventories. An example of this latter phenomenon is the General Motors Framingham, Massachusetts, assembly plant. Built in 1948 and designed for 45 cars an hour, the same floor space now supports an optimum flow of only 30–35 cars an hour.

There is, however, an optimum rate of production for an assembly plant. All interviewed officials mentioned a plant designed for 55–65 cars an hour (that is, 180–220,000 cars a year on two-shift operations) as the optimum size plant. Faster speeds are possible; at the time of the interviews, January 1968, it was reported that the "home" Pontiac assembly plant was running at a speed of 75 cars an hour and the home Oldsmobile plant was producing 96 cars an hour. But beyond 65 cars an hour, the inventory problems, even with the greater space, begin to get troublesome. The respondents were uniform in their statements that, if they were planning a new assembly plant today, it would be in the 55–65 an hour range. The two newest assembly plants built in the industry, General Motors' 1965 Lordstown, Ohio, plant and Chrysler's 1965 Belvedere, Illinois, plant have optimum speeds of 60 cars an hour each.[21]

Interestingly, the Lordstown plant illustrates many of the points made above. The plant was originally designed for 50 cars an hour, with 1.5 million square feet of space and 4,800 employees on two shifts; in 1955 Ford opened two plants (San Jose, California, and Louisville, Kentucky) of 1.5 million square feet, which were designed for 55 cars an hour each. As optimism about future sales grew, the Lordstown plant was redesigned for a speed of 60 an hour, requiring 225,000 more square feet of floor space and 900 more employees.[22]

Though 55–65 cars an hour appears to be the optimum pace, the cost disadvantages appear to be small for lower rates, at least as far down as 30–35 an hour. Chevrolet was willing to contemplate building the Lordstown plant for 50 an hour, and General Motors has not yet found it worthwhile to close down the Framingham plant with its 30–35 an hour rate.

The Planning Process

New model cars do not appear on the scene overnight. A new model requires design, prototype building, testing, evaluation, correction, design of production machinery and tooling, and the manufacture of that machinery. The lag between drawing-board design and appearance in the car dealer showroom has run close to three years for the postwar period.

To illustrate the planning process, we can take a typical 1969 model car, which appeared in dealer showrooms in late September 1968.[23] All through 1965, preliminary sketches of this car were worked on. Sketches used to be started almost exactly three years before introduction date; recently, as the emphasis on design has increased, the preliminary sketching phase has extended to four and five years ahead. Sometime near the end of 1965, sketches were approved and the building of clay models began. The clay is covered with colored plastic and metal foil to simulate the surface of a real car.

The clay stage extended until the fall of 1966, when the clay models were approved. At this point, the basic design of the car had been set. Changes still could be, and probably were, made after this date but at a sharply increasing cost. The designs then were translated into detailed specifications, and orders for the dies for the interior and exterior sheet metal were placed. It actually takes about thirty-five weeks to cut a high quality sheet metal die; with orders piling up, thirteen months is considered a good estimate for the completion of an order. Overall, the companies have expected "an average of twenty-one to twenty-two months from the time the clay model is approved and released until dies are finished and cars come off our assembly lines." [24] Computer control of die cutting ("numerical control") is expected to cut this period to seventeen months. Also, at this point, some estimate has to be made of the expected volume so that the requisite number of duplicate die sets can be ordered.

In the meantime, work was proceeding on the interior of the car and on the engineering aspects. If a major new engine or transmission were planned that required major new manufacturing facilities, these too would have had to be planned well in advance. Otherwise the engineering people have a little more leisure in their planning. The designing and testing of most of their components took place in late 1966 and during most of 1967.

Around December of 1967, the first hand-built models of the new car were finished and tested. By March of 1968, all specifications were absolutely frozen; in June a pilot assembly line was turning out cars. These pilot-built cars were extensively tested, and "bugs" in the assembly process were hopefully eliminated at this time.[25] At the beginning of August, the regular assembly lines began full operations, and shipments to dealers began.

The process described above is the normal three-year pattern. It is possible to shorten this to about two years (that is, make a later decision on design or revise an earlier decision), but the extra cost can be steep, as overtime rates for designers, consultants, engineers, die makers, and others pile up. Given the right circumstances, however, a company will assume this burden. A case in point is the 1955 Chrysler cars, which were hurriedly redesigned as a new management realized that the original 1955 design, a continuation of the 1953 and 1954 models, would have been an invitation to disaster.

This long lag between design and delivery introduces a large element of risk into automobile manufacturing. Consumer tastes have to be predicted two to three years in advance. Millions of dollars in tooling and engineering have to be invested long before any inkling of consumer reaction to the new product has filtered in. As early as one year before delivery date, 40 percent of the new model costs have been irretrievably sunk, and the other 60 percent has been largely committed unless the project is scrapped.[26] Also, many minor — but potentially sales-losing — faults, like noise level, dust leakage, road performance, are only revealed after the basic design of the car has been accepted and the tools ordered.

The strict delivery date — the new cars have to appear within a week or so of October 1 or one's competitors will get a healthy lead and one's own cars are liable to get a reputation for mechanical difficulties[27] — places a guillotine on engineering development. A leisurely pace for solving the unexpected engineering problems of a car is not possible; and high-cost, last-minute rushes to get the quirks out of a car are not unknown. The alternatives of late introduction or consumers complaining about ill-running cars and the company incurring high repair costs because of warranty guarantees are not pleasant ones for manufacturing executives to contemplate.

Basically, then, the technology of the design process and the strict demands of an introduction date near October 1[28] introduce a basic conflict into the process of designing a car. The goal of a leisurely, less costly design and development procedure and the goal of accurately anticipating consumers' tastes in design and engineering features are fundamentally incompatible. The more leisurely the pace of development, the farther in advance of introduction day must the design be settled; the greater lead time means greater uncertainty about the state of consumer tastes on introduction day. One can short-circuit this process but only at sharply increasing costs and the attendant risk that last-minute problems might indeed be incapable of solution and there might be no time in which to find suitable alternatives.

The difficulties of car design and coordination are illustrated in the following description by a British designer involved in changing the wheel size from 15 inches to 13 inches on a Hillman Minx. The problems for an American designer would be almost identical:

1. The automatic plant that assembles the tires on the wheels may be seriously affected.
2. The supplier of the wheels has to investigate all the implications on his production line.
3. Completely new hubs have to be designed and tooled.
4. The axle ratio has to be changed.
5. The speedometer gear ratio in the gearbox has to be changed.
6. The effect of the smaller wheels on the suspension and the shock absorbers has to be investigated.
7. The braking system has to be completely revised, thus affecting the supplier of the braking equipment and his production lines.
8. The accommodation of the fatter tire in the spare wheel stowage has to be investigated, probably affecting the press tools on body work . . .
9. A whole new range of spare parts has to be gone into, with effects on literature and stocking throughout the world, and arrangements have to be made for continuing manufacture of the older-size wheels and associated components.
10. The handling of the vehicle may be influenced, particularly under braking conditions, if the offset of the wheels from the kingpin has to be changed, and the behavior of the steering gear circuit has to be investigated.
11. The question of the decorative wheel trim change has to be investigated.
12. Ground clearance may be affected and the lowest part of the vehicle, say the exhaust system, may have to be modified.
13. Finally, when any change is being made it has to be phased to an accurate deadline so that stocks of materials can be controlled, avoiding a mass of redundant material and the associated financial implications. When a vehicle is in volume production, the forward planning of production supplies always involves many thousands of parts in the "pipeline" from the raw material stage right up to the finished product.[29]

The pattern in the auto industry used to be one of major design changes, meaning a whole new car structure and body shell, every three years. "Face lift" changes of the exterior sheet metal were made in between. That the design-delivery lag and the major design change cycle were both of three years' duration was not accidental. Designers and executives liked to know how their current "all-new" model was being received before committing themselves to the next all-new model three years hence. But the three-year cycle meant that major faults (for example, the 1949–1951 Ford dust leaks and rattles) often could not be corrected for three years; if one's fundamental design were unpopular, one was still stuck with it for at least two years and usually three. The risks were obvious.

Some parts of the industry have since gone over to a two-year design change cycle. The Big Three have increased their die making capabilities, so that they are less dependent on the independent tool and die industry and less subject to the vagaries of waiting times.[30] This appears to have saved enough time (computer control of die cutting should save even more) to permit two-year cycles for some high volume lines (for example, the full-sized cars of most makes have gone over to two-year cycles, while some lower volume inter-mediates and compacts have remained with three-year cycles). Most of the preliminary design and clay work still has to be done more than two years in advance, but management is allowed a good look at the sales of the current all-new models before committing them-selves to the next all-new models of two years hence. To the extent that the designers are initially working in the dark, with no idea of how their previous all-new model has been received, risks are some-what increased. But the later final approval (closer to introduction day) and the more frequent basic style changes, meaning that one can be stuck with a bad model for only two years,[31] have served to reduce risk.

How much does the development of a new model cost? The cost elements would include the cost of the dies for the body and machining heads for the engine, special jigs and machinery for assembly, any other special machinery for new developments (for example, a fuel injection system replacing a carburetor would require a whole new set of tooling), and the design, development, engineering, and testing costs. Occasionally, a new design will require substantially changed manufacturing processes; when Chrysler changed from body-on-frame to unitized construction for the 1960 model year, the extra cost for the change was estimated at $80 million.[32]

The best figures on tooling expenses are the balance sheet amor-tization figures provided by the companies. These amortization figures effectively show the depreciation of the tools as they are used and worn out. Table 3.1 represents the relevant information on tooling expenses for the four auto companies in recent years. All four report their worldwide operations on a consolidated basis. For the Big Three, this includes American-produced cars and trucks, Cana-dian cars and trucks, and overseas car and trucks (and for Ford, domestic and overseas tractors).[33] For American Motors, only American and Canadian cars, plus some overseas sales of American

Table 3.1   Amortization of Special Tools

	Balance sheet amortization (millions)	World vehicle sales (thousands)	U.S. passenger car factory sales (thousands)
General Motors			
1962	$526.9	5,238.6	3,738.0
1963	605.4	5,974.2	4,077.7
1964	591.2	6,114.5	3,963.4
1965	744.7	7,278.1	4,941.7
1966	860.8	6,717.3	4,448.7
1967	839.6	6,271.4	4,119.7
Ford[a]			
1962	170.1	3,376.1	1,929.1
1963	188.9	3,692.3	1,959.6
1964	234.6	3,952.7	2,131.7
1965	276.4	4,595.4	2,535.0
1966	322.5	4,525.2	2,435.7
1967	331.3	3,588.6	1,720.1
Chrysler			
1962	67.2	892.3	720.7
1963	93.9	1,519.3	1,046.4
1964	95.2	1,807.5	1,231.2
1965	148.0	2,076.5	1,470.9
1966	173.2	2,134.0	1,429.1
1967	160.9	2,251.8	1,376.6
American Motors[b]			
1962	19.8	478.1	434.5
1963	19.3	511.0	454.5
1964	31.7	455.1	382.7
1965	29.4	412.7	338.2
1966	33.3	345.9	271.5
1967	38.8	291.1	232.5

SOURCE: Company annual reports and *Moody's Manual of Investments*, 1968.
  [a] Ford's world vehicle sales include sales of tractors.
  [b] For the fiscal year ending Sept. 30.

produced cars, are included. Thus the balance sheet amortization is an overstatement of the tooling expenses applicable to United States cars alone. The table shows the relation between world vehicle sales and United States car sales for each company.

Unscrambling the exact tooling costs per United States car from these totals presents an extremely difficult, if not impossible, task. The tooling costs for each type of vehicle (such as American cars,

American trucks, and European cars) should be different and should change differently over time as separate trends in styling, in added standard and optional accessories (which require additional tooling), and in the price inflation of the tooling would affect each type of vehicle differently. Also, tooling costs per vehicle should not be expected to remain constant, even in the absence of these other influences. Instead, tooling costs per vehicle for a particular model should vary somewhat erratically with the volume produced. Some tools, like carbide machining heads, wear out relatively rapidly; their costs per vehicle would remain relatively constant. But other tools, like sheet metal dies, last for relatively long periods (for example, multiples of 100,000 units), and their costs would appear in discrete lump sums. When a company has ten or more lines of cars, the variation in tooling cost per vehicle in different years could be considerable.

These difficulties rule out a simple simultaneous equation method or a least squares regression method for untwisting the tooling costs. Accordingly, we have had to fall back on the expedient of looking at the tooling costs per vehicle sold worldwide; see Table 3.2. Tooling

Table 3.2   Tooling Cost per Vehicle Sold Worldwide

Year	General Motors	Ford	Chrysler	American Motors
1962	$101	$50	$75	$ 42
1963	101	51	62	38
1964	97	59	53	68
1965	102	60	71	71
1966	127	71	81	97
1967	134	92	71	133

Data taken from Table 3.1.

costs per vehicle sold overseas and per United States truck ought to be lower than the cost per United States car, since there has been less emphasis on styling and rapid model changes in these categories (and overseas tooling costs are probably lower), while the tooling cost per Canadian car ought to be somewhat higher than per American car, since much the same model proliferation with lower volumes has meant fewer cars per set of tools.[34]

General Motors has clearly had higher tooling costs per vehicle than have its rivals. This could be due to three reasons: (1) General

Motors is more integrated than its rivals, so that it incurs tooling costs that get put on the balance sheets of its rivals' suppliers; (2) it has been overguessing its tooling requirements more than its rivals; (3) it may well be using more expensive or extensive tooling (for example, using more dies to put more wrinkles into its body designs) on comparable parts than its rivals. Some mixture of (1) and (3), but mostly (1), is probably the closest to the truth. Consistent overguessing is not likely from a corporation with the reputation of efficiency that General Motors has.

Keeping in mind that tooling costs per American car ought to be somewhat higher than the average, we can estimate that somewhere around $90–$100 per car is the minimum that auto manufacturers currently spend on tooling, with at least $50 more per car being spent by suppliers (or, in the case of General Motors, mostly in-house).[35] These figures have, of course, been smaller in the past.

Of this tooling cost, approximately $40–$50 per car is absorbed by the body dies alone. The basis for this estimate is as follows. In 1961, an Owens-Corning Fiberglas Corporation publication put the cost of high-volume steel tooling for a large four-door sedan at $10 million.[36] In 1967, a Borg-Warner engineer estimated the cost of tooling a small four-door sedan at $12 million.[37] If the additional dies required for two-door models, hardtops, and station wagons are included, a figure of $15–$20 million is reached.[38] If the dies last for approximately 400,000 stampings, a figure of $40–$50 per car is reached. The other tooling costs are absorbed by engine machining heads and tools, automatic transmission dies and heads, assembly tools and jigs, plus any tooling for in-house production of items like brakes and steering mechanisms.

On top of this tooling are the design, engineering, development, and testing costs of a new model. Table 3.3 gives the estimates, usually based on corporate announcements, that the automotive press has offered for Chrysler's overall development costs, including tooling, for each model year. It is not clear from the articles whether the costs apply just to American cars or to all North American vehicles. The latter is most likely. Since the years after 1962 include the tooling costs of Simca, Chrysler's French subsidiary, it appears that around half of the overall expenses are covered by tooling. A recent estimate for Ford's 1965 model year development and tooling expenses — $525 million, compared with $276.4 million for its worldwide tooling

Table 3.3   **Estimated Total Development Costs and Tooling Costs, Chrysler Corporation**

Year	Total development costs, including tooling, by model year (millions)	Tooling costs alone, by calendar year (millions)
1955	$250	$106.0
1956	175	118.6
1957	300	99.2
1958	150	68.6
1959	150	81.3
1960	350[a]	165.8
1961	n.a.	90.2
1962	n.a.	67.2
1963	125	93.9
1964	125	95.2
1965	300	148.0
1966	300	173.2

SOURCE: *Ward's Automotive Reports*, June 4, 1956, p. 177; *Automotive Industries* 115 (Oct. 15, 1956), p. 34; *Automotive Industries* 119 (Sept. 15, 1958), p. 33; *Automotive Industries* 121 (Oct. 1, 1959), p. 18; *Ward's Automotive Reports*, Aug. 20, 1962, p. 268; *Automotive News*, Aug. 19, 1963, p. 1; *Automotive News*, Aug. 23, 1965, p. 1; and data from Table 3.1.

[a] Of the 1960 development costs, $80 million was devoted to the changeover from body-on-frame to unitized construction.

amortization — would tend to confirm this.[39] Consequently, to the $90–$100 per car for tooling, one should add approximately an equal amount for the development expenses of bringing out a new model.

These estimates are supported by the report that Ford put $40 million into the development and tooling of the Mustang.[40] It is not unlikely that 200,000 units per year were Ford's initial hopes for the Mustang.

4

Estimated Economies of Scale and Minimum Efficient Size

After discussing the technology of the auto industry, we can now deal with the question of scale economies in the industry. What annual volume is necessary for a firm of minimum efficient size? Do risk considerations play a part here? How do the estimates derived here compare with past estimates by other sources?

The findings of Chapter 3 can be briefly summarized: in final assembly, the optimum rate is around 60 units an hour, or, on a two-shift basis, 200,000–250,000 units a year. Machining processes using automatic transfer devices run slightly higher. Casting, with a large number of different pieces to be cast, appears to be adaptable to most otherwise feasible scales of production. It is in stamping, where the best sheet metal dies have useful lives of around 400,000 stampings, that the largest volume economies are to be found.

The discussion of technology can give us some clues as to the probable shape of the cost curve for automobile manufacturing. As Bain commented, "the firms of the automobile industry seem generally uninterested in publicizing their plant and firm scale curves." [1] But, drawing on the information on the optional scale of production for the various production processes and on other information from Chapter 3 (for example, the small economies to be had from very long stamping runs, the small cost penalties incurred for suboptimal assembly voluumes until volume falls below 30–35 units an hour, and so forth), this author would estimate that the following production-cost relationship holds (in terms of relative cost):

Annual production	Relative unit cost
50,000 units	120
100,000 units	110–115
200,000 units	103–105
400,000 units	100
800,000 units and up	99+

Thus it would appear that a firm producing in the range of 400,000 cars a year would fully exhaust most of the *production* economies that exist. A larger volume would still bring slightly greater advantages: slightly cheaper handling of the sheet metal dies, fuller use of the few dies used only on two-door models or hardtops, perhaps a slightly cheaper engine assembly procedure. But the 400,000 units manufacturer ought to be able to compete effectively, especially in an oligopoly situation in which no one is ever driven to the wall for the sake of a dollar or two per car.

This would be true, however, only in a riskless world. In the real world of high risks for automobile manufacturing, a higher volume would seem to be needed for a firm to be viable in the long run, as will be argued later in this chapter. But before we turn to these risk aspects of economies of scale, there are a few other production aspects that should be discussed at this time.

Efficient Use of Tooling

Is it necessary to utilize fully the tooling in one year? What about using the sheet metal dies at a less intensive pace, say, at the rate of 200,000 units a year and extending their life over two years? If the pace of model changes had been less frequent, it has often been claimed, the Independents could have adopted this sort of practice and suffered little or no disadvantage vis-à-vis the Big Three. As it was, confronted by rapid model changes and lacking the volume to wear out their tools in one year, they faced the unappetizing choice of scrapping their still usable tools after one year, thus raising unit costs, or of extending the same design and tools for a second and third year, thus facing a competitive disadvantage on styling.[2]

This sort of claim is only partially true. What is forgotten is the payback aspect of the investment in the new model. The 400,000 unit-a-year producer invests in new tooling (and design, development, and advertising) and receives his entire returns by the end of the model year. The 200,000 unit-a-year producer makes the same investment but has to wait two model years to collect completely; the 133,000 unit-a-year producer has to wait three model years. Even if the first producer were simply to repeat the same style, the latter two would still be at a disadvantage.

A sample of this type of calculation would be as follows: Suppose a manufacturer invests in a $100 tool in January and earns $10 a month starting in October (when the new models hit the market) through the following September; the tool completely wears out after producing the model year's production. How much better off is he than the manufacturer who invests the same $100 in the tool in January and uses it less intensively, collecting $5 a month from October until September two years hence? And how do both compare with the manufacturer who collects $3.33 a month for three years?

We can compare the internal rates of return for these three alternative investments.[3] For the one-year producer, the internal rate of return is 15.4 percent; for the two-year producer, it is 11.4 percent; for the three-year producer, it is 8.7 percent.[4] The one-year producer is clearly earning an appreciably higher return than his smaller rivals.

We can further calculate by how much the one-year producer could cut his profits and still achieve the rates of return earned by his rivals. To achieve the 11.4 percent return of the two-year producer, the one-year producer could cut his monthly returns by $0.35. Since $8.33 of the $10.00 per month represents depreciation, his profit per month is $1.67. Thus the $0.35 cut would represent a 21 percent reduction in profits, which the one-year producer could endure and still earn the same return as his two-year rival. Similarly, to achieve the 8.7 percent return on the three-year producer, the one-year producer could cut his profits by $0.62 or 37 percent.

Because of the limitations of the model year cycle, the advantages of rapid use of tools do not extend appreciably beyond 400,000 units per year. If a producer with twice the volume of our one-year producer had to buy both of his tools for $100 each in January and received $20 each month over the model year, his internal rate of return would be 15.4 percent, the same as that of the one-year producer. Since all magnitudes have been doubled, the internal rate of return remains the same. If the higher volume producer could delay buying his second tool until July, his internal rate of return would be 18.6 percent. But the cut in profit he could endure and still achieve the 15.4 percent return of the smaller one-year producer would be only $0.24 or 7 percent of his monthly profit of $3.33.

In our example, of course, the one-year producer represents the manufacturer of 400,000 units a year. The actual advantage of this producer over smaller rivals would depend on the amount of specific capital invested in a model as a proportion of the total amount of general production capital (such as assembly plants, which also have to earn a return) and on the extent of the time lag between investment and receipts. An exact estimate of this advantage would require detailed accounting information that is not available. But the point still remains that the producer who can wear out his tools in one year would have an advantage over smaller rivals even if model changes did not occur, and this advantage could be significant. And, of course, in a world of model changes, the 400,000 unit-a-year producer has added advantages over his rivals.

Transportation Costs

The other production aspect that should be discussed here is the transportation cost factor. If it were cheaper to ship stacked parts and assemble them at branch plants rather than to ship finished cars, the theoretical transportation economies for larger volume would prevail over any conceivable range of output. Only if every little hamlet in the country had the capacity to consume 200,000 of a particular manufacturer's cars a year and thereby warranted an asembly plant on its outskirts would the transportation economies be exhausted.

What are the savings to be had from branch assembly plants? Obviously, the exact amount depends on the locations of the shipping and receiving plants and the particular freight rates in effect, but some estimates of the past and current savings can be made.

Until 1954, the auto manufacturers had charged "phantom freight" on car shipments to outlying areas. Though parts were shipped to branch assembly plants and the cars assembled and shipped from there, the freight charges to the consumer were based on the assembled automobile railroad freight rate from Detroit to the consumer. In 1954 and again in 1956, in response to dealer dissatisfaction, Congressional pressure, and private "bootlegging," [5] the manufacturers lowered their freight charges to outlying areas to what they claimed were roughly the real costs of shipment. To compensate for the lost revenue, they raised the wholesale prices for all cars enough so that total revenue to the companies remained constant.

This price increase offers a good estimate of the savings that were to be had from branch plants at this time.[6] The logic is as follows: Suppose that a hypothetical manufacturer produced cars only in Detroit and shipped them out to the customers who were in reality being served by the Big Three's assembly plants. Our hypothetical manufacturer would have to charge the assembled car railroad freight rate but would not profit from it. The Big Three were charging the assembled car rates but were profiting from it. When they reduced the freight charges, the subsequent price increases showed how much they were profiting from the branch plants.

General Motors' figures are clearest on this, and we shall take the Chevrolet experience as illustrative.[7] In November 1954 Chevrolet raised its list price by $20; in February 1956 the price was raised another $30, both times to cover cuts in freight charges.[8] Of the $50 list price increase, $38 actually accrued to Chevrolet; the rest was increased dealer markup. This $38 per car, then, was the added cost that a manufacturer located solely in Detroit would have incurred had he tried to duplicate Chevrolet's sales pattern (which, at the time, was roughly 1.6 million sales from nine branch assembly plants and the home plant in Flint).[9]

This $38 per car figure has surely decreased since then. Though freight rates have risen, a major technological innovation, the trilevel rack railroad car, has drastically reduced the costs of shipping assembled automobiles.[10] Exact shipping costs are hard to obtain, but a very close substitute is the revenue received by the railroads for shipments. Table 4.1 lists the relevant figures. As the costs of shipping assembled cars declined, the spread between the shipping costs of assembled cars and of stacked parts also declined; Table 4.2 shows those figures.

Table 4.2 can only be used in a general way. The assembled car rates are for shipments to all points in the state, not just to the assembly plant city, though the mileage adjustment in the table should correct for a good deal of that error. The parts rate is probably an underestimate of the total cost of sending an auto in the form of stacked parts,[11] but this bias should be present for both years. Nevertheless, the narrowing of the advantage for stacked parts is striking. If one were to take one-fourth as a rough estimate of the ratio of the 1963

Table 4.1   Revenue Received by Railroads for Shipments of 3,000 Pounds of Assembled Car (approximately one car)

Destination	Average distance (miles) of shipment in 1955	Revenue, 1955	Revenue,[a] 1963
Michigan to California	2417	$240	$128
Michigan to Texas	1384	142	79
Michigan to New Jersey	628	56	37

SOURCE: Interstate Commerce Commission, Bureau of Economics, *Carload Waybill Statistics*, 1955 and 1963.

[a] The 1963 revenues per 3,000 pound-miles have been multiplied by the 1955 distances to ensure comparability.

parts advantage to the 1955 parts advantage, the Chevrolet figure of $38 per car in 1955 would have shrunk to less than $10 by 1963.

These figures indicate, then, that though there may still be a small advantage to having branch assembly plants at very long distances from Detroit, especially on the West Coast, the advantages of branch plants any nearer to the center today are close to nonexistent. The trilevel rack railroad car has effectively reduced this former scale economy.

With parts and assembled car rates almost equal, local land and labor costs would play the dominant role in assembly plant location decisions that would otherwise be random. Also, one would want to avoid the backhauling of component parts, many of which are manu-

Table 4.2   Revenue Received by Railroads for 3,000 Pounds of Shipments

Destination	Average distance of parts shipments in 1955	Revenue, 1955			Revenue, 1963 (for the 1955 distances)		
		As-sembled car	Stacked parts[b]	Net advantage to parts	As-sembled car	Stacked parts[b]	Net advantage to parts
Michigan to California	2,395	$238[a]	$98	$140	$127[a]	$97	$30
Michigan to Texas	1,156	119[a]	59	60	66[a]	50	16
Michigan to New Jersey	647	58[a]	30	18	39[a]	34	5

[a] Assembled car costs are different from those in Table 4.2, because the mileage has been changed to the 1955 parts mileage to ensure comparability.

[b] Parts category used is "Automobile Parts, N.O.S."

factured in plants in Illinois, Indiana, and Ohio, and would want to avoid the backhauling of the assembled cars themselves. In this light, it is not surprising that the two new assembly plants built since 1960 were located outside of Detroit but in the automobile heartland: Belvedere, Illinois, and Lordstown, Ohio.[12]

One other matter on branch assembly plants needs to be disposed of. Very little local buying of components occurs, so the opportunities for in-bound transportation cost savings appear small here. Frederick G. Donner of General Motors, testifying before the Senate Committee on Interstate and Foreign Commerce at the time of the freight rate inquiry, claimed that 85–90 percent of parts, by value, at the Chevrolet plant in San Francisco came from outside the Pacific Coast area.[13]

Risk and Economics of Scale

We now turn to risk. Though a volume of 400,000 units a year might be sufficient to achieve manufacturing economies, this author is convinced that the long-run prospects for such a manufacturer would not be bright. The risks in automobile production are high. Autos have to be designed well in advance of actual confrontation with the consumer. A three-year — or even a two-year — design cycle means that a manufacturer can be stuck uncomfortably long with a badly designed car. Consumer tastes do and have changed, and what looks like a good design now could turn out to be a disaster two and one-half years later. Further, as a consumer durable item, automobiles are especially sensitive to levels of personal income (see Chapter 7). As national economic fortunes wax and wane, automobile sales expand and contract. Consumer choices among types of cars (for example, expensive or inexpensive) appear to be equally sensitive to income levels.

Examples of fluctuations among makes of cars are not difficult to find. The three nosedives of the Chrysler Corporation have already been chronicled. The fate of the Edsel is now legendary. The success of the Mustang is equally well known. The uneven fortunes of American Motors have also received wide attention.

Less well known are the rises and falls of the individual car lines, the level at which most of the tooling and development expense takes place. The Ford Falcon sold 482,000 units in 1961, its second year, and has slid downhill ever since; Falcon sales in 1967 were 110,000 units. The Chevrolet Corvair took an even steeper dive. Sales in 1965 were a respectable 209,000 units. By 1967, after Ralph Nader's claims of the dangerous qualities of earlier Corvairs,[14] sales had fallen to under 25,000 units. The Pontiac Tempest, on the other hand, grew from 110,000 sales in 1961, its first year, to a high of 363,000 sales in 1966. The full-sized Chrysler climbed from 80,000 units in 1960 to 230,000 units in 1966. Fluctuations of 80,000–100,000 units or more each year for these car lines are very common.

These fluctuations are largely unpredictable. Though one knows that the full-size Ford is going to outsell the Dodge Dart, not until the first few weeks of selling can one get a good idea of the expected sales of a car line; even then, an unexpectedly strong or weak spring selling season can alter sales of a line by as much as 50,000 units. True, if one guesses right in this sweepstakes, the rewards are large; but if one's guess is wrong, the penalties can be equally severe. The postwar history of the automobile industry (not to mention the prewar history) is littered with the hulks of six corporations[15] that guessed wrong in the passenger car business.

In this high risk environment, it is more than coincidence that the multiple-make corporations have survived and the single-make corporations have fallen by the wayside. The single-make company is betting all it has on its current model. If that design fails, it is in trouble: it has nothing to fall back on. It has to sit through a period of two or three years of poor sales—which is not only financially debilitating but can also be psychologically devastating to management morale—while finding the men and money for new designs and new facilities. In this uncertain, high risk atmosphere, banks are not particularly eager to lend money to a firm whose assets are tied up in designs that may turn out to be worthless.

In the meantime, poor sales have their effect on the company's retail dealers. The weaker ones fail, thereby reducing sales even further; the stronger ones begin to wonder if maybe they should try to get a Chevrolet franchise instead. They may stop pushing the company's cars quite so hard and instead turn their efforts to building up their service and repair businesses. The car itself may begin to acquire the reputation among consumers of being an "orphan" that will have a low trade-in value and should therefore be avoided in the first place.[16] A self-reinforcing snowball to oblivion can quickly develop.

The multiple-make manufacturer, by contrast, gambles in more than one market: if one model fails, it has the other makes to fall back on. If the swing in public taste is toward expensive cars, it has some of these; if the swing is toward cheaper cars, it also has some of these. Though the different makes of a company may in fact be constructed similarly, they are usually sold through different dealer organizations, and the public identifies them as separate entities. The company has the profits (and the psychological boost) of the successful makes to keep it going, while it applies the necessary men and money to pull the ailing make back into the black.[17] It would take simultaneous disasters in all of the company's makes — a much less likely occurrence, especially when a company produces low price and high price makes — to bring on the specter of financial ruin.[18]

Absolute size also plays a role here. The companies that failed were the smaller ones in the industry. Most had tried to diversify at one time or another by bringing out second cars, but these attempts were unsuccessful for a variety of reasons, mostly economic. They were never able to set up separate dealer organizations to market the second cars, and the price always seemed high for the quality of car they were producing. Another way of expressing this last point is that they were never able to attain a volume that would permit them to price their cars at a competitive level. (Or, they were not confident enough to price the car low enough to sell the sufficiently high volume.) Small size meant not enough volume to be able to diversify successfully.

This nexus of probability, liquidity, and technology is an important one. The basic point is that in an uncertain world of high risks and less than perfect information, the liquid resources and management morale necessary to generate a given probability of survival tend to be appreciably higher relative to sales for the single-make manufacturer than for the multiple-make manufacturer. There are definite economies of liquid and psychological capital for the multiple-make producer. But, given the technology of the industry, small producers cannot afford to have multiple makes. The small producer is at a definite disadvantage here.[19]

One way out for the small auto manufacturer might be to become part of a larger industrial complex in which auto revenues brought in no more than a third or a half of overall revenues. One might get the needed financial security in that way. But it is not clear that such a corporation would be as committed to survival in the automobile industry as would be a firm whose major revenues came from autos. A few rough years could more easily lead to the decision to "cut and run." This was the decision of the Kaiser empire in 1955. By contrast, as American Motors found itself in financial straits in the 1950's and again in the 1960's, it was the other, often profitable, divisions that were sold and the auto division that remained intact to struggle on. Thus the probability of survival of the small producer might not be appreciably increased by aligning itself with a larger nonauto empire. In terms of survival, then, the multiple-make auto producer still has an advantage.

Thus the best hope for survival in the automobile industry lies in being a multiple-make producer, the only producer who can weather the uncertainties of the industry. Again, by multiple make we mean at least two makes of cars with different brand names, at least moderately different exterior appearance, and separate dealer organizations. This last factor appears to be quite important in creating a separate identification in the consumer's mind.[20] Simply having different lines within the same make does not appear to create enough differentiation in consumers' minds. The American Motors' American, Rebel, and Ambassador cars are of different sizes and price ranges, but all have suffered recently from an "economy" image by consumers. American Motors has attempted to establish separate identities for its cars by removing the name "Rambler" from some of them and just keeping the name of the line (for example, Ambassador). But this apparently has not been successful in erasing the common image.

Though the logic of multiple-make risk spreading would indicate that the more makes a manufacturer produces the better off he is, two makes should probably be sufficient to ensure a high probability of surviving. One test of this proposition would be to look at the relationship for each firm in the industry between average model year production volumes and the standard deviation of those production volumes over time (or between average production and the standard error of estimate of a regression of production on a time trend, to allow for secular growth). Multiple makes should buffer the yearly variations of production around the mean (or around a time trend), and thus the ratio of the standard deviation (or standard error of estimate) to average production should provide an indication of the risk reduction that has occurred. A lower ratio should indicate less risk. Model year production figures were chosen for this analysis, rather than calendar year production or annual sales, because it is model year production for which the investments in design, development, and tooling are made; thus it is variations in model year production that really count in terms of risk.

Table 4.3 shows these figures for the Big Three, Nash-American

Table 4.3   Model Year Production: Annual Averages, Standard Deviations, and the Standard Error of Estimate around a Time Trend, 1949–1967

Make of car	Annual average (thousands)	Standard deviation (thousands)	Standard error of estimate (thousands)	Standard deviation divided by average	Standard error of estimate divided by average
General Motors	3,115.3	843.2	567.2	0.27	0.18
Ford Motor Co.	1,749.2	397.3	264.1	.23	.15
Chrysler Corp.	1,015.7	268.3	271.5	.26	.27
Nash—American Motors	252.5	138.2	103.9	.55	.41
Studebaker	125.7	78.3	58.5	.62	.47

SOURCE: *Ward's Automotive Yearbook*, various years.

Motors, and Studebaker. As can be seen, it is the latter two single-make firms that have the highest ratios, and there is a sizable gap between them and the Big Three. Among the Big Three, Ford, essentially a two-make firm (since Lincoln sales have been very small), has the lowest ratios in both tests. General Motors, with five makes, is highest among the Big Three for the standard-deviation/average ratio and is second for the other. Thus the important gap seems to be between the single-make firms and the multiple-make firms. At least in the postwar period, General Motors' five makes have not provided it with better buffering than Ford has received from its two makes.

Some additional arguments can be offered for the claim that two makes should be sufficient. On the production side, a firm with two makes, each being produced at an efficient level, would have a total volume of 800,000 units a year. If the two makes shared the same body shell, some additional economies on internal stampings could be achieved. They could be assembled on the same assembly lines, and the firm would gain whatever benefits there are to be had from locating one or two of its four assembly plants on the East or West Coasts. The firm would have enough volume to be able to produce efficiently three or four different engines and transmissions and thus could offer an attractive variety to the buyers of each make. A firm of this size should be sufficiently large to be able to maintain research and development facilities that would keep it abreast of advances in the industry.

On the retailing side, Bedros Peter Pashigian, studying the retail distribution of automobiles, estimated that economies in automobile distribution were significant up to sales of 600,000 units a year and continued even past 1,800,000 units a year.[21] His analysis is based on his findings that minimum retailing costs were reached when a dealer sold somewhere between 600 and 800 units a year. A dealer who sells less is at a cost disadvantage. Similar to the case of assembly plants, until sales were such that every hamlet could absorb 600–800 of a company's cars a year, there would be advantages to increasing sales volume. He does feel, though, that a company selling 600,000 units ought to be able to survive even against companies twice that size.

A number of comments can be made on Pashigian's work. First, his analysis of dealer economies is based on urban data. Land prices, the largest component of the fixed cost to be spread over sales, are appreciably lower in the small towns, where the low volume dealers would be situated. With cheap land, the minimum efficient scale of dealer may be considerably lower than 600 units a year. Second, he ignores the possibility of "dualing" dealerships — having dealers in low volume areas sell more than one make of car. The dualing could take place among one's own make or between one's makes and a rival make, thereby reducing the cost disadvantage of selling in small markets. Finally, a company might adopt the strategy of ignoring the smaller selling areas and concentrating on the larger metropolitan areas, though still on a nationwide basis. This is the strategy that Volkswagen used to great advantage.

Accordingly, a firm selling 800,000 units annually through two makes and two sets of dealers should not be at any serious disadvantage in retail distribution. Further, with proper positioning of the makes in the market, the two-make firm should be able to catch and retain the "trading-up" customer who is looking for a more expensive car than the one he owns. A firm of this size, with sales revenues close to $2 billion annually, ought to be able to afford the costs of national media advertising.

The minimum efficient size to ensure survival in the long run, then, is a firm manufacturing somewhere around 800,000 units a year split into two makes of 400,000 units each. This 800,000 units firm could gain some small economies from common internal stampings and common assembly in West Coast assembly plants (if the two makes shared the same body shell) as compared to a one-make firm of 400,000 units annual volume. But the major benefit would be from the diversification of risk.

This 800,000 units manufacturer would probably have four assembly plants, one or two casting and machining complexes, and at least one large stamping plant. An automatic transmission plant (machining and assembly) probably ought to be included. Automatic transmissions used to be bought by many manufacturers; all but American Motors now make them in-house. The advantages of integration in these areas appear to be fairly substantial (see Chapter 6). In areas like glass, upholstery, gears, electrical equipment, and brakes, the decision is a bit more marginal. A firm ought to be able to buy these from supplier firms in the industry at little or no disadvantage in cost or coordination. For a new entrant or a manufacturer short of capital, such buying decisions would be mandatory. The more seasoned firm would probably try to manufacture some of its requirements in some of these areas and contract out for the fluctuating remainder.

How do these findings compare to current company sizes and numbers? Though an 8-million-unit car market could support ten efficient, viable firms, there are only four producers in the domestic industry, of which three are clearly dominant. All of the Big Three are comfortably over the 800,000 units size and have been since the 1940's, with the exception of Chrysler's occasional styling errors. The only remaining Independent, American Motors, had a sales volume of 231,000 units in 1967, though it did reach a peak of 428,000 units in 1963. A complete explanation of this phenomenon of seller concentration that is a good deal higher than technology and risk require will be discussed in Chapter 16, after other aspects of structure and behavior have been thoroughly analyzed. But it is clear that the high barriers to entry into automobile manufacturing have been an important factor in preserving this high seller concentration. It is to the subject of entry that we will turn in Chapter 5.

Past Estimates

How does this current estimate of minimum efficient size compare with past estimates? Testifying before the Temporary National Economic Committee in 1939, Paul Hoffman, president of Studebaker, felt that a volume of 100,000 cars a year would be sufficient for him to compete successfully with the Big Three. "They, of course, have to have several sets of tools to build a million cars. One set might be good for 250,000 cars, but when you go beyond that you get into duplicate sets of toolings." [22]

The first postwar estimate was made by Joe S. Bain. On the basis of questionaires sent out to the auto firms in 1951 and 1952, he estimated that:

In general, 300,000 units per annum is a low estimate of what is needed for productive efficiency in any one line; there are probable added advantages to 600,000 units.

As regards the shape of the plant scale curve at smaller outputs, the trend of the estimates is that costs would be "moderately" higher, at 150,000 units . . . substantially higher at 60,000 units, and uneconomical at smaller scales.

The critical stage in plant economies is evidently found in the production of components and not in assembly. In assembly alone, from 60,000 to 180,000 units per annum is considered optimal, with advantages to a multi-plant decentralized development as the critical figure is passed. There are some components which are typically either integrated by the assembler or otherwise manufactured to special designs so as not to be interchangeable with those used by other firms, however, and economies of large plant in the production of these are such as to require, for best overall efficiency, a larger integrated complex than required for efficient assembly alone. The most important components of this sort under traditional automobile-industry practice (as oriented to securing distinctiveness of product) are bodies and engines, which together make up enough of the cost of an automobile to dominate the scale-economy picture.[23]

Maxcy and Silbertson, writing about the British automobile industry in the late 1950's, offered some estimates of the technological economies of the American industry. Their estimates were that the best assembly volume was in the 60,000–100,000 units range, engines were in the 500,000 range, and stampings, because of the high speed presses, were in the million or more range.[24]

In 1958, President George Romney of American Motors testified before the Senate Antitrust Subcommittee during the Kefauver investigations of "administered prices":

Our studies, based on our experience and that of our competitors, is that [sic] optimum manufacturing conditions are achieved with a production rate of 62.5 cars per hour per assembly line.

To absorb the desired machine-line and press-line rate, two final assembly lines would be required . . . This would result in production of 1,000 cars per shift.

A company that can build between 180,000 and 220,000 cars a year on a one-shift basis can make a very good profit and not take a back seat to anyone in the industry in production efficiency. On a two-shift basic, annual production of 360,000 to 440,000 cars will achieve additional small economies, but beyond that volume only theoretical and insignificant deductions in manufacturing costs are possible. It is possible to be one of the best without being the biggest.[25]

Romney later expanded on the subject of special tooling, apparently in the context of *one-shift* operations:

Now let's take tooling. There are all sorts of tooling, and when you provide tooling for high volume, you provide more expensive tooling and it costs more, and beyond these areas that I am talking about you get into duplications, and if you take the most modern tooling on a 440,000 basis or a 360,000 basis, which is that required for most highly efficient manufacturing results, then you have got double the cost for that tooling as compared to tooling for 180,000 to 220,000 units, and if you take the two sets of costs and divide them by volume per unit, it happens that the cost per unit comes out right on the button.

So all this talk about the disadvantage of lack of volume in relation to tooling costs is grossly exaggerated. What I am saying is that if you have got 180,000 to 220,000 volume a year, you can compete effectively and efficiently in the automobile industry.[26]

At first glance, these estimates range all over the board and are not very comparable to our production estimates obtained above. However, the Hoffman estimate is prewar and is included only to show the magnitude of the changes since then. Maxcy and Silbertson appear to be mostly wrong or out of date. Their assembly volume is too low; Romney's testimony at almost the same time is far more accurate. Their engine and stamping estimates are mainly from a 1952 document of the Organization for European Economic Cooperation (OEEC), *Some Aspects of the Motor Vehicle Industry in the USA*.[27] On the former, the document simply cites the highest engine rates available, without asking if any lower rates are equally efficient; on the latter, it looks at the highest press rates possible and ignores the fact that dies wear out.

This leaves the Bain and Romney estimates, which are basically in agreement with each other and with the estimates of this study. Bain's estimate of assembly efficiency is a little low for current technology, but he was probably right for the late 1940's and early 1950's on which his information was based. Romney is probably a little too emphatic in his defense of one-shift operations and too neglectful of the economies of two-shift operations. A few years later, after American Motors had had more experience working on two shifts, an executive of the company expressed the opinion that the economies of two-shift operations were "substantial" rather than "small." [28] Thus the 400,000 units production estimate of this study basically agrees with the Bain and Romney estimates of minimum efficient size.

None of the studies, however, mention risk and its relation to size.[29] Thus our estimate of 800,000 cars a year split into two makes as the minimum volume necessary for long-run survival is unique. It is the largest of any of the estimates, but it is the only one that would ensure a high chance of survival for the firm.

5

Entry into the Automobile Industry

Entry into an industry, or even the credible threat of entry, can be a beneficial influence on an industry. Entry can bring new blood, fresh ideas, new products, increased price competition, increased competition generally. Even the threat of entry can keep the current occupants on their toes and perhaps force them to keep their prices lower than otherwise to forestall entry.[1]

What are the possibilities of entry into automobile manufacturing today? What have been the conditions of entry in the past, and what has entry done for the industry?

Bain[2] has offered three general factors as determining the height of barriers to entry into an industry: (1) absolute cost advantages to established firms, (2) product differentiation advantages to established firms, and (3) significant economies of scale. All of these factors tend to raise the costs or lower the prices received by the potential entrant, thereby discouraging entry. Examples of absolute cost advantages are control of superior supplies of factors of production, control of patents, or capital market imperfections or attitudes toward risk that would impose higher interest rates upon potential entrants than upon established firms; this latter condition would become increasingly serious as the absolute size of investment rose. Effective product differentiation among established firms would force the entrant to engage in greater advertising or suffer a lower price to overcome the entrenched positions of the established firms. Significant scale economies mean that an entrant producing at efficient scale would be a noticeable part of the market; the potential entrant would have the unhappy choice

54

of entering at an efficient scale and thereby adding significantly to industry supply, depressing the price, and inviting retaliation, or of entering at a less noticeable scale but thereby suffering higher costs.

How high are the automobile industry barriers to entry? Taking the last point first, our estimated minimum efficient scale of 800,000 units per year would be between 8 and 10 percent of the current automobile market (including imports).[3] This would certainly be a noticeable intrusion. Other things being equal, if one assumes a unitary price elasticity for autos (see Chapter 7), the new entrant could cause an 8–10 percent drop in the price of autos. Since this is approximately equal to the pre-tax profit margins of Ford and Chrysler and about half the pre-tax margin of General Motors, none of the current occupants would be likely to look kindly on the entrant.[4] But antitrust fears would probably moderate any explicit retaliation and might in the end force the Big Three in particular to accommodate the new entrant by cutting back their own production. (A struggling American Motors would probably be given more leeway by the Justice Department in any sales battles with an entrant.) The newcomer, however, would have to earn his market share on his own. The selling competition would be fierce, and established auto executives, for whom maintaining and expending market shares are an important goal, could be expected to yield only grudgingly.

Product differentiation would be a difficult barrier for an entrant to hurdle. Brand names and reputations have been built up over the past forty to fifty years. Repeat buying is an important aspect of the market. Surveys show owner loyalty (repeat buying) running between 40 and 70 percent for particular makes[5] and between 60 and 80 percent for all the makes in a company (for example, Chevrolet owners "trading up" to a Buick).[6] Consumers would be wary of buying a car from a new company whose reputation for quality and service had yet to be established. Many might fear that the new firm would not survive, and they would shy away from buying a potential orphan. Introducing major innovations might not appreciably better the entrant's chances. Though there is a small minority of buyers who are willing to experiment, most American buyers tend to be conservative and stick with the tried and true. As Bain rightly points out, most buyers are technically not competent to judge the mechanical design or quality of a car.[7] A car is a "big ticket" item and is bought relatively infrequently; the opportunity for experiment by consumers is limited and the risks of experiment are great. In this environment, reputation can be crucial.[8]

Further, a new entrant would have to build up a retail dealer organization from scratch. Insofar as established dealers have built up customer loyalties based on reputations for service and fair dealing, a new entrant would have to surmount this barrier in addition to that of brand loyalty.[9] (But the scale of production envisioned for the entrant would allow adequate nationwide dealer coverage and ease the problem of "out of town" service and parts for prospective customers.)

Thus, though the 800,000 units size would be adequate for an established firm to withstand most of the risks of the auto business, a new entrant, regardless of size, would still face substantial risks in attempting to overcome the established loyalties in the automobile market.

On absolute cost advantages, the picture is mixed. There are no key patents controlling the basic manufacturing processes in the industry. Little, if any, of the technology is a secret. Supplier firms in the industry are usually willing to supply standard items like spark plugs, windshields, and carburetors at competitive prices. Monopsony buying power and the threat of in-house production can often produce this result, even in the absence of competitive structures in the auto parts industry. Even other auto manufacturers are willing to sell items to rivals at what they claim are the same prices they charge their own divisions.[10] On the other hand, an entrant might have difficulty attracting competent dealers and thereby incur higher distribution costs. The current shape of the supply curve of prospective dealers, especially for a prospective entrant,[11] is uncertain. Though every sales manager is supposed to dream of his own dealership, it is not clear that all or even most would be as competent as the current stock of dealers. In any event, the new dealer organization would have to go through a shakedown and weeding-out process, which could be costly in the interim. A commonly claimed contributing cause to the demise of the Kaiser-Frazer automobile operation was the poor quality of its dealer organization.

But it is in the capital markets that a prospective entrant would have the most difficulty. The exact value of the investment needed by an 800,000 units entrant is not available. But past and current estimates are possible. Bain in 1955 estimated that $250–$500 million would be the capital requirements for an entrant, with the latter figure required for a scale of 600,000 units a year.[12] A rough and ready expansion of Bain's estimate to 800,000 units capacity and today's real estate, construction, and machinery costs would bring the cost close to the $1 billion mark.[13]

George Romney provided the Senate Antitrust Subcommittee in 1958 with his estimate of the capital required at current prices for production of 250,000 units a year. These figures are reproduced in Tables 5.1 and 5.2. The total amount was $576,178,000, of which $374,878,000 was required for manufacturing facilities. Romney's estimate seems to be based on one-shift production and is in accord-

Table 5.1   Capital Requirements at 1958 Costs to Provide Facilities to Produce and Market 250,000 Automobiles Annually

Cash — working balance		$30,000,000
Accounts receivable		13,500,000
Inventories		56,600,000
Prepaid insurance, taxes, etc.		2,800,000
Manufacturing facilities		
Land, buildings, and building equipment	$123,712,000	
Machinery and equipment and tools and dies	251,166,000	
Total manufacturing facilities		374,878,000
Investment in Canadian assembly plant, working		
capital, etc.		7,000,000
Leasehold improvements, 21 zone sales location		3,000,000
Subtotal		487,778,000
Accounts payable	−25,000,000	
Subtotal		462,778,000
Organization expense — Underwriting discounts and		
commissions, $600,000,000 at $7\frac{1}{2}\%$		45,000,000
Institutional advertising and advertising and sales		
promotion		35,000,000
Losses		
Prior to start of production		23,000,000
First year in production		10,400,000
Total corporation requirements		576,178,000

SOURCE: Figures provided by American Motors to the Senate Subcommittee on Antitrust and Monopoly. See U.S. Senate, Committee on the Judiciary, Subcommittee on Antitrust and Monopoly, *Administered Prices — Automobiles*, Report, 85th Congress, 2nd session 1958, p. 17.

Table 5.2   Manufacturing Facilities at 1958 Replacement Value to Produce 250,000 Automobiles Annually

Land, buildings, and building equipment:			
Land and land improvements		$ 5,812,000	
Buildings:			
Press	$11,000,000		
Drop forge	1,250,000		
Foundry	3,750,000		
Powerhouse	1,600,000		
Manufacturing	62,270,000		
Service parts	8,125,000		
Office, cafeteria, etc.	5,139,000		
Total buildings (6,500,000 square feet)		93,134,000	
Building equipment:			
General factory	23,630,000		
Service parts	1,136,000		
Total building equipment		24,766,000	
Total land, buildings, and building equipment			123,712,000
Machinery and equipment and tools and dies:			
Machinery:			
Foundry department	2,800,000		
Motor department	26,560,000		
Miscellaneous machining department	6,255,000		
Transmission department	12,020,000		
Rear axle department	5,391,000		
Forge department	3,859,000		
Heat treat department	193,000		
Body department and assembly	1,243,000		
Press department	37,543,000		
Nonproductive departments, etc.	21,808,000		
Total machinery		117,672,000	
Equipment, all departments		55,621,000	
Tools and dies, all departments		77,873,000	
Total machinery and equipment			251,166,000
Total manufacturing facilities			374,878.000

Source: See Table 5.1

ance with his 180,000–220,000 units optimum size estimates in earlier testimony. The capital estimates are obviously based on American Motors' situation and experience. The current assets listed in the table are very close to American Motors' holdings at the time. As of September 30, 1958, American Motors held $34.5 million in cash, $10.0 million in accounts receivable, and $59.9 million in inventories.[14] In 1958 American Motors produced 217,332 cars.

Romney's estimate of the cost of manufacturing facilities seems too high, however, when compared to contemporary balance sheet figures. American Motors' balance sheet listed its gross (that is, adding back in depreciation reserves) property, plant, and equipment at only $107.1 million in 1958. Even though this is at historic cost, it is nowhere near Romney's estimate, and the balance sheet figures included plant and equipment for the Kelvinator division. Only in 1965, after two years of over 400,000 sales, did this category reach $362.3 million. Within this category, Romney's tool and die estimate is $77.9 million; the 1958 balance sheet listed tools and dies at $11.9 million. The highest tool and die holdings ever listed by American Motors were $56.1 million in 1966. Machinery and equipment seem to be similarly overestimated.

A better estimate for manufacturing facilities in Romney's context would probably have been around $250 million. Since this was for one-shift operations, two-shift production of 400,000 units for one make should not have required any more capital for manufacturing facilities. Two makes with a total of 800,000 units a year would require double that, or $500 million. Introducing a 30 percent inflation factor and expending and adding in Romney's cash, inventory, and other estimates would bring the overall estimate for an entrant's capital requirements toward close to $1 billion, consistent with the modified Bain estimate.

Another current estimate can be made by building up the capital cost from the costs of the individual physical requirements of an entrant. The entrant would need four assembly plants, one or two casting and machining complexes capable of 800,000 engines and parts, an automatic transmission plant, stamping facilities adequate for 800,000 cars, head offices, testing facilities, parts warehouses, inventories, cash-on-hand, special tools and dies, and an investment in the design and development of the car model.

The Chrysler Belvedere, Illinois, assembly plant, built in 1965 with a capacity of 200,000 cars a year, cost $50 million for land, plant, and equipment.[15] Four such plants would cost $200 million.

No new engine plants have been built recently. American Motors, however, in 1963 spent $42 million to add 288,000 square feet of space and equipment to its engine and axle plant.[16] Chrysler's Trenton, Michigan, engine plant, with 1,150,000 square feet of space, produced 820,000 engines in the 1964 model year.[17] A combination of the two figures yields a rough estimate of a $160 million investment necessary for machining operations. The addition of casting facilities would push this investment close to $200 million. This estimate appears reasonable in light of the past cost of engine plants. The first Ford Cleveland engine plant, built in 1951 and capable of producing over 900,000 engines a year, cost $143 million including casting facilities.[18] A plant designed for 800,000 units would have cost somewhat less; allowance for subsequent inflation would bring that cost to the $200 million range.

The only price tag ever put on an automatic transmission plant was for Chrysler's Indianapolis plant. Built in the early 1950's, the plant cost $25 million and had a capacity of 3,000 units a day.[19] An investment of $40–$50 million would probably be required for these facilities today.[20]

Ford's 1966 Woodhaven, Michigan, stamping plant cost $90 million and has a capacity of 1,500 tons of sheet metal a day.[21] A full-size, four-door sedan body weighs slightly over 1,000 pounds; a medium-size sedan would weigh somewhat less. Depending on the size of car and allowing for some waste metal, the equivalent of somewhere under 3,000 car bodies a day will emerge from this plant. With 200–225 working days a year possible, a slightly larger stamping facility would be necessary. A cost of $100–$110 million is probably justified.

So far, the manufacturing facilities have summed to $550 million. Head offices, warehouses, and testing facilities would probably add another $30–$40 million.[22]

Chapter 4 revealed that tooling costs come to a minimum of $100 per car and that testing and development expenses add another $100 per car. For 800,000 cars, this would mean another $160 million investment.

Finally, current assets — cash, marketable securities, accounts receivable, and inventories — could require another $300 million. On September 30, 1963, American Motors had $280 million in current assets, of which $47.6 million was cash, $47.8 million was marketable securities, $53.1 million in accounts receivable, and $127.4 million in inventories. American Motors produced 480,000 cars that year. The cash and securities positions were probably a little high. The following year they fell to $29.1 million and $16.0 million, respectively, as total current assets fell to $232.5 million and production fell to 493,000 units. Part of the current assets, perhaps an eighth, were attributable to Kelvinator operations; since there are economies of scale in holding current assets, a $300 million estimate for an entrant is reasonable, although perhaps a trifle on the low side.

The total, then, comes to around $1 billion. Table 5.3 summarizes

Table 5.3   Estimate of Capital Required for an Entrant at a Scale of 800,000 Units a Year (millions)

Four assembly plants	$200
Machining and casting facilities	200
Automatic transmission machining and assembly facilities	40–50
Stamping facilities	100–110
Head offices, warehouses, and testing facilities	30–40
Tooling and product development investment	160
Current assets	300
Total	$1,030–1,060

the estimates made above. The total is in basic agreement with the modified Bain and Romney estimates. Over all, then, it appears that a viable entrant would need $1 billion to set up in the automobile manufacturing business. This would not include the investments that would be required of the dealers. Figuring perhaps $100,000 per dealer and 2,000 dealers selling the entrant's cars, we get a total dealer investment of at least $200 million that would also be required.[23]

Could an entrant get $1 billion in financing under any circumstances? The *Fortune* 1968 list of the 500 largest industrial corporations shows only 73 corporations with assets of over $1 billion (and three of those are automobile companies).[24] Billion dollar corporations are not common phenomena, and forming one from scratch would be virtually impossible. Even among existing industrial giants, few, if any, would be willing to bring together the capital to enter the auto market. The high risks of entry and the dismal history of past attempts would surely scare away even the most intrepid investors. Even established Independents have never reached 8–10 percent market share size. Why should anyone believe that a newcomer could achieve this? On absolute capital cost requirements alone, one can consider entry at an efficient scale as effectively blockaded.

What are the other hypothetical possibilities? One could attempt to enter with only one make at a technically efficient scale of 400,000 units a year. Such an entrant might recognize that the long-run risks of such a scale were appreciably higher than for two makes but would hope either for exceptionally good fortune or the opportunity to expand to a second make and dealer organization, after the first make was established. Or the entry could be by an established firm in another field that was willing to absorb the risks and cover the possible losses of an automobile division. Entry at this scale would require "only" $500 million. This capital requirement would still be fearsome, and entry can be considered only slightly more likely than in the previous case.

Or one might try to enter at a scale of 200,000 units a year. In the current oligopoly structure, one might well be able to overcome the added unit costs incurred at this scale if one were able to exploit a special niche in the auto market. The absence of high volume competition in some niches makes the 200,000 units volume less of a handicap. (Many lines of established auto firms sell in the 200,000 range. Current newspaper reports claim that Pontiac is expecting its new 1969 Grand Prix model to sell 165,000 units; Pontiac does not seem at all dismayed by the extra cost burden that this volume imposes.) The entrant would have to have great confidence in the enduring nature of his niche or in his ability to forecast accurately the position of new niches. Entry at this scale would probably require $300 million and carry high long-run risks. It is only yet slightly more likely than the previous two cases.

Implicitly, however, we have been assuming that an entrant would have to build up his manufacturing operations instantly from scratch. In fact, a more likely occurrence would be a greater degree of integration into the industry by a firm that was already partially there. Perhaps most likely would be entry into United States manufacturing operations by a foreign manufacturer who was already selling his cars in the United States market. A little-noticed instance of this sort of entry almost took place in 1955. The Volkswagen organization bought an assembly plant in New Brunswick, New Jersey, from Studebaker, expecting to assemble cars partly from United States components and partly from German components.[25] The initial United States supplier estimates turned out to be too low. After they discovered that the Volkswagen components required separate tooling, the suppliers raised their prices, and Volkswagen gave up the idea and sold the plant.[26] One can only idly wonder what the effects of Volkswagen's entry into manufacturing on American soil would have been on the rest of the industry.[27]

The pattern for foreign entry into United States manufacturing might well follow the intended Volkswagen scheme. The entrant might begin by only assembling in the United States, buying some components locally, and importing the rest from the home base. As volume and confidence in United States manufacturing operations grew, more parts could be purchased and/or produced in the United States. Engine and stamping plants might be built, and the entrant would be a full-fledged American manufacturer. The beginnings of a dealer organization would already have been in existence and would need to be strengthened, rather than started from scratch. The existence of the foreign automobile home base, with its different market, would serve to absorb a great deal of the risk involved and perhaps eliminate the need for a second make and dealer organization.

Currently, only Volkswagen at 450,000 United States sales in 1967 has the volume to contemplate this kind of entry. The number two import, Opel (50,000 units), is a General Motors subsidiary. The next three imports — Datsun, Volvo, and Toyota — are each close to the 35,000 units mark. This is not, of course, large enough for an efficient assembly plant, but the act of establishing manufacturing operations in the United States might well attract customers who would otherwise not consider a foreign car.[28] Still, if Volkswagen has not made the move, we cannot expect any of the less popular imports to take the chance. Perhaps fast rising wages in Germany, plus a revaluation of the mark, might make Volkswagen more interested in entering United States manufacturing in the future.

What about American truck manufacturers? They have the technological skills and at least some of the manufacturing facilities that could be converted or expanded for auto production. They also have dealer organizations that could be expanded (though many of their dealers are currently in bad locations for selling passenger cars). However, four of the five leading truck makes are divisions of the Big Three auto manufacturers.[29] Only International Harvester, in third place with 150,000 sales in 1967 (9.9 percent of the truck market), represents an independent volume producer. (The number six and seven producers, Kaiser Jeep and White Motor, sold 43,000 and 20,000 units, respectively, in 1967.) International Harvester produces a station-wagon-like vehicle and in 1960 introduced the Scout, a four-wheel drive "personal" vehicle, and the Jeep line competes with passenger cars in some respects; but the prospects for full-scale entry are not promising. International Harvester has shown no desire to plunge any further into auto competing vehicles. In late 1969, Kaiser sold its jeep operations to American Motors. This effectively ended whatever possibility there was of Kaiser's reentering the automobile market with a new model.[30] None of the other producers has the resources or the inclinations to make the attempt.

Checker Motors is officially in the industry, with annual sales of around 5,000 units, mostly taxicabs but also some passenger cars. As other Independents have fallen, there have been recurrent rumors that Checker might try to acquire their dealer organizations and go into volume production.[31] But no action has ever been taken. Volume production would mean a vast increase in Checker's facilities, almost comparable to entry from outside. For a company that has lost money for ten of the past thirteen years, the possibility is remote.

The only other possibility is a radical change in technology that could reduce the required scale of entry or otherwise attract established firms in other industries. A significant lowering of the raw materials costs of fiber glass for automobile bodies might reduce the necessary scale of entry. Currently, fiber glass tooling is much cheaper than sheet metal tooling, but fiber glass is more costly than steel. Consequently, for high volume runs, sheet metal bodies have a clear cost advantage. Lowering the cost of fiber glass to the point where it is competitive with steel might make small scale manufacture comparatively more efficient, since a much lower tooling cost would have to be spread over production volume.

Or breakthroughs in electric car or even steam engine technology might attract firms in these fields to enter passenger car production. General Electric, Westinghouse, or Radio Corporation of America (RCA) would all have the resources, technical abilities, and framework of a retail distribution system if the required breakthroughs in electric car technology occurred. But the electric car's prospects are not bright for the future (see Chapter 14), and the current automobile producers could very likely make the breakthroughs themselves or prove to be the most attractive licensees for anyone else who did develop the technology. Interest in steam cars grew in the late 1960's, largely fed by the publicity given to William Lear's efforts toward developing a steam car. His decision in late 1969 to withdraw from the field probably signaled the end of any serious efforts to develop steam technology for automobiles.

One must conclude that the probability of entry into automobile manufacturing in the near future is rather low. The leading prospects are Volkswagen and/or an electric car manufacturer, but neither can really be considered likely entrants.

Past Entry

The barriers to entry into automobile manufacturing were not always so high, even in the postwar era. The past attempts to enter and the conditions surrounding those attempts can serve as a useful backdrop for the current situation.

The years immediately after 1945 provided a period of low barriers, probably the only such period in the thirty-five years since the development of the all-metal body in the 1930's significantly raised the economies of scale in auto manufacturing. The low barriers were a result of three factors: (1) the large backlog of consumer demand for automobiles, (2) the existence of government surplus factories and machine tools, and (3) the willingness of potential dealers to buy franchises.

First, all automobile production had ceased shortly after Pearl Harbor. Through the war years, car owners made do with their old jalopies, and potential owners waited. On V-J Day the public was holding a car stock that was smaller and three and one-half years older than it otherwise would have been. Consumers were ready to beat down the doors of dealers (and occasionally did). High levels of liquid assets, formed from wartime savings, provided the ammunition for the consumer assault. Popular accounts of war-developed advances in engines, transmissions, and light metals only whetted their appetites. Consumers were willing to buy almost anything that had four wheels (and occasionally only three) and an engine. Common estimates were that the market would absorb 20–25 million new cars in the first five years of postwar production;[32] the five years prior to the war had seen sales of only 15 million units. This pent-up demand promised high profits for successful entrants. It also reduced the economies of scale barrier to entry, since the corollary to high profits was the ability of an entrant to produce at less than efficient scale and still make reasonable profits. Further, an entrant would not have to fight so hard for sales, nor worry so much about his effect on other members of the industry.

Second, as war production ceased, the Federal Government found itself holding empty factories and idle machinery. Having very little use for them, the Truman Administration began to sell the plants and machinery, often at a fraction of their original price, or rented them with an option to buy. The famous Willow Run plant, originally costing $100 million, was rented to Kaiser-Frazer for $500,000 the first year, $850,000 the second, and $1,250,000 the third, and Kaiser-Frazer eventually bought it for $15 million.[33] Preston Tucker negotiated a lease for the large Chicago Dodge war production plant at $500,000 a year for the first two years and $2.4 million a year (or 3 percent of gross sales, whichever was higher) after that, with an option to buy the plant for $30 million and its machinery for $10 million.[34] The original cost of the plant was $75.8 million for the real estate and buildings, and there was $30 million in machinery still in the plant.[35] Other would-be entrants were able to get similar bargains. This cut by a considerable amount the capital investment that an entrant needed. (Also, if one heeded Paul Hoffman's prewar testimony, a volume of only 100,000 units was all one really needed to survive, reducing the physical plant requirements significantly from the present-day requirements cited above.)

Finally, potential dealers were willing to buy franchises. Sensing consumer eagerness for cars and seeing how well-established dealers fared during the first months of renewed sales, many businessmen saw automobile dealerships as potential gold mines. Tucker, the most successful of the "almost" entrants, netted $7,284,215 from the sale of franchises and distributorships.[36] The Playboy Motor Corporation obtained $2,093,636 from the sale of its franchises.[37] Such sales, of course, reduced the entrants' capital requirements.

In this environment, almost any engineer or designer with a design for a car could step forward and announce the imminent production of the XYZ car and receive serious attention. Paul H. Banner found that thirty-two firms had been reported attempting entry into automobile production in the late 1940's. Of these,

9 intended three-wheelers
5 intended flying cars
9 intended midget cars
2 intended light-weight cars
3 were custom builders
4 intended standard-size cars.[38]

Many of the entrants' cars contained "new" and progressive ideas. Independent four-wheel suspensions, disc brakes, torsional springing, torque converter transmissions, fuel injection, front-wheel drive, and rear air-cooled engines were among the features proposed. None of these ideas was really radical, having appeared on past American cars, trucks, or European cars at some time, but none was on production American cars at the time.

But the barriers were not as low as they looked. Few of the entrants got past the hand-built prototype stage. All but Kaiser-Frazer neglected to raise even close to enough capital. Tucker, in addition to the franchise revenue, received $15 million from the sale of stock and hoped that more capital would become available after production started, which it never did.[39] Playboy Motor Corporation originally intended a $20 million stock issue but could not float it, tried to settle for a $3.5 million issue, and eventually crumbled. Most entrants never even got to the capital-raising stage and sank without a trace.[40] Even had they been able to raise sufficient capital, most would have run into the raw materials shortages that plagued the one large entrant, Kaiser-Frazer.

The example of Kaiser-Frazer is instructive in illustrating the problems of entry.[41] During the war, Henry J. Kaiser had become interested in the possibilities of postwar car production. In 1945 he joined forces with Joseph W. Frazer, chairman of Graham-Paige, a small prewar auto producer. On July 25, 1945, the Kaiser-Frazer Corporation was formed. Shortly after, Willow Run was leased from the government.

To raise capital, stock issues were floated in 1945 and 1946, bringing in a total of $54 million. Here, perhaps, was the fatal error. Kaiser-Frazer had underestimated its capital needs and soon ran short of money. The stock issues had been oversubscribed, and Kaiser-Frazer could have raised much more. Lamented Henry Kaiser later, "It was our big mistake. We should have raised $150 million or $200 million." [42] In 1947 the company borrowed $28 million from banks;

in 1948 another stock issue was tried, but it was then too late. The public was no longer so sanguine about Kaiser-Frazer's future and would not absorb the stock.[43] As a consequence, the company was hard pressed for the remainder of its automotive life and never really recovered from this shock.

The Kaiser was originally designed with front-wheel drive and torsional springing. The Frazer was to be conventionally designed. To get rapidly into production, however, the special Kaiser features had to be scrapped, and conventional drive and springing were adopted; this resulted in Kaisers and Frazers sharing essentially the same body and frame. It is reported that the basic design was a Chrysler design, obtained when Henry Kaiser hired Chrysler engineers and stylists en masse.[44]

Shortages of raw materials, particularly iron and steel, plagued the company; it frequently bartered and shipped pig iron and steel around the country to get the particular steel that it wanted.[45] The company's steel costs were around $50 higher per car than if it had been able to get steel at list prices.[46] The company also experienced difficulty getting an adequate supply of engines from its supplier, Continental Motors, and finally had to lease and operate the engine plant itself. Kaiser-Frazer also claimed that it had supplier difficulties because the established manufacturers were given priority by suppliers.[47]

Despite these difficulties, Kaiser-Frazer managed to sell 51,000 Frazers and 56,000 Kaisers in 1947 for 3.4 percent of the market, and 58,000 Frazers and 108,000 Kaisers in 1948 for 4.8 percent of the market. In both years it was the leading Independent producer, a remarkable feat for a new entrant. But it paid a high price to get that production. Its manufacturing costs were higher than its competitors. Not only was it paying higher prices for materials but it was also inefficiently organizing production. D. K. Smith quotes United Automobile Workers (UAW) officials as saying that Kaiser-Frazer was overstaffing its production lines as late as 1949.[48] Preliminary estimates had been that the company would show a profit when sales rose above a rate of 75,000 units a year; in fact, 125,000 units a year proved to be the break-even point. Table 5.4 shows the profit squeeze that faced Kaiser-Frazer as compared to its Independent competitors. In addition, Kaiser-Frazer employed a system of wholesale distributors

Table 5.4   Balance Sheet Figures, Five Independents, 1948

Make of car	Unit sales	Sales revenues (millions)	Total assets (millions)	Pretax operating profit (millions)
Kaiser-Frazer	166,361	$341.6	$124.9	$20.3
Studebaker	143,120	383.6	129.2	33.8
Hudson	109,497	274.7	108.4	22.0
Nash	104,156	302.9	153.6	36.4
Packard	77,843	232.0	107.2	23.6

SOURCE: *Moody's Manual of Investments, 1952.*

to get its cars to its dealers, which added $50 per car to the wholesale price.

As a consequence of the above factors, its cars were overpriced; and as competition reentered the automobile market, its sales were the first to suffer. Table 5.5 shows the list prices of Kaisers and Frazers and

Table 5.5   Factory Delivered Prices (Including Federal Taxes) for Specified Four-door Sedans, April 1948

Buick 50, Super	$1,929
Oldsmobile 8, 98	1,993
Hudson Super 6, 481	2,004
Hudson Super 8, 483	2,092
Kaiser K-481	2,104
Chrysler 8, C-39	2,106
Studebaker Land Cruiser, 15A	2,144
Packard 8, 2201	2,150
Buick 70, Roadmaster	2,232
Frazer, F-485	2,294

SOURCE: *Consumer Reports* 13 (May 1948), pp. 207–208.

other similarly priced cars as of April 1948. Neither the Kaiser nor the Frazer were in the Buick-Chrysler-Packard quality and image class. Consumers Union's initial analysis of the Kaiser in May 1947 was that it was essentially a sound car but "much overpriced even in today's market." [49] A year later, Consumers Union again considered Kaisers and Frazers overpriced.[50] In fact, most Kaisers and Frazers were sold at below list price, and the company was forced to give a $200 trading allowance to its dealers. Even at $200 under list, the cars were probably still excessively priced. A *Fortune* article considered them over-priced by $500 or more.[51]

Increasing supplies of other makes cut into Kaiser and Frazer sales and demand slackened generally as the 1948–1949 recession set in. Regulation W consumer credit controls were reimposed, which hurt further. Kaiser-Frazer production rates slackened from 675 a day to 400 a day in January 1949 and kept falling. List prices were cut $200–$333 in March, but the $200 trading allowance was eliminated and the dealer discount margin was shaved by 2 percent, so that the net prices to consumers (and to Kaiser-Frazer) did not change appreciably.[52] Not too surprisingly, sales failed to respond. Kaiser sales in 1949 were 58,000 and Frazer sales were 16,000, the total being 1.5 percent of industry sales. Kaiser-Frazer had slipped to eighth place in the industry, ahead only of Crosley. The income statement showed an operating loss of $36 million.

By now the ailing car producer syndrome had set in. The inability to raise new capital in 1948 precluded the development of new models. Falling sales meant that there would be little or no profits to finance new models or even to finance cost-saving machinery. The dealer body fell from 4,700 to 2,700. Used Kaisers and Frazers were severely discounted.

Total sales rose to 112,000 in 1950, buoyed somewhat by the introduction of the compact Henry J, but the organization was not geared to make money at that volume, losing $13.3 million. (By contrast, Packard, selling only 73,000 cars that year, made an operating profit of $7 million.) Sales slipped to 104,000 in 1951 (yielding a $12.3 million loss) and kept on slipping. Government loans and defense contracts and a merger with Willys only delayed the day of reckoning. Kaiser-Frazer's fate had been sealed in 1948 when it had failed to raise additional capital. In 1955 the Kaiser Motors Corporation (the surviving corporation) ended United States passenger car production.

Had Kaiser-Frazer raised more capital in 1946, had its 1948 stock issue succeeded, had the company made greater efforts to cut its manufacturing costs, it might have survived as an auto producer. In fact, these events did not happen, and the company sank. One thing, though, can be ascertained from this experience. Entry capital requirements were well over $60 million in 1945. Henry Kaiser's lamented $150 million or $200 million was probably much closer to the mark.

Crosley Motors was another postwar entrant that actually got into production. Its largest sales year was 1948, with sales of 25,400 units. Its bantam-size car, with an 80-inch wheelbase (the current Volkswagen "beetle" has a wheelbase of 94.5 inches), was never very popular; and its price, at about two-thirds of a Chevrolet's, did not compensate enough. It died a quiet death in 1952 when the General Tire and Rubber Company bought the plant and converted it to defense production.

Willys, a prewar automobile producer and a successful wartime and postwar producer of jeeps, decided to try to reenter the passenger car market in 1952. The Willys Aero was a compact car with a 108-inch wheelbase (the 1968 Plymouth Valiant has a 108-inch wheelbase) but otherwise undistinguished. It is not clear that Americans were ready to buy compact cars at the time, but Willys' pricing eliminated any chance that they might buy the Aero. Table 5.6 gives the Willys Aero

Table 5.6   Factory Delivered Prices (Including Federal Taxes) **of Comparable Willys and Chevrolet Cars, February 1953**

Willys (108-inch wheelbase)		*Chevrolet (115-inch wheelbase)*	
Aero Lark		Special 1500	
2-door	$1,646	2-door	$1,613
4-door	1,732	4-door	1,670
Aero Falcon		Deluxe 2100	
2-door	1,796	2-door	1,707
4-door	1,861	4-door	1,761
Aero Ace		Bel Air 2400	
2-door	1,963	2-door	1,820
4-door	2,038	4-door	1,874
Aero Hardtop	2,162	DeLuxe 2100 Sport Coupe	
		(Hardtop)	1,967
		Bel Air 2400 Sport Coupe	
		(Hardtop)	2,051

SOURCE: *Automotive Industries, 35th Annual Statistical Issue* 108 (March 15, 1953), p. 125.

prices as of February 24, 1953, alongside the most comparable Chevrolet (115-inch wheelbase). The Aero was definitely overpriced. Its easier handling properties and greater gasoline economy[53] could not hope to compensate for its higher price.[54] The Aero — and similarly designed and priced cars, like the Kaiser Henry J and Hudson Jet — was a victim of cost-oriented pricing in which the basic confidence to set a low price and aim for a volume that would justify that price did not exist. Perhaps the demand elasticity for this product did not warrant it, but pricing it, model for model, above a popular car like the Chevrolet doomed the Aero from the beginning. Sales were poor for three years,[55] and Aero production was ended in 1955 when the merged Kaiser-Willys organization decided to cease United States passenger car production.

The only other new domestic make to enter the market in the 1950's was the Ford Motor Company's ill-fated Edsel. The Edsel story has been told in very readable detail elsewhere by John Brooks,[56] so that only the major features need be repeated here.

The Edsel was basically a victim of the inescapable time lag between design and delivery in the auto industry. The Edsel was planned and designed in 1955, the year of booming sales by the large middle-level cars: the Oldsmobile, Dodge, and Buick. By the time the Edsel appeared in the fall of 1957, this market had shrunk considerably (see Table 5.7).

Ford had concluded that its middle level car, the Mercury, was not adequately representing it in the middle-level market. Ford owners, when they "traded-up," were not buying Mercurys. Ford decided that it needed another car in that field, a "smart car for the younger executive or professional family on the way up." [57] The 1955 middle-level car boom underlined this need.

One might argue that the market for middle-level cars was never quite as large as Ford thought it was. The year 1955 was also the first year of the four-door hardtop style, a very popular style that only Buick and Oldsmobile had for most of the calendar year. Four-door hardtop sales more than account for the increases in Buick and Oldsmobile market shares and account for most of the rise in Pontiac's share (it introduced these models in October 1955).[58] The Chrysler Corporation's middle-level cars were following the disastrous 1954 model year, so that they would have been expected to increase their market shares anyway. That leaves only Mercury's market share increase, and it was among the smallest in the group. In 1956, when all Big Three makes had four-door hardtops, Buick, Oldsmobile, and Pontiac all settled back to market shares that were at or below their 1954 levels.

This is not to deny that the middle-level market was a solid one and one in which Ford was underrepresented. It is just that 1955, which

Table 5.7 Sales and Market Shares, Middle-level Cars

Make of car	1954 Sales	1954 Percent of market	1955 Sales	1955 Percent of market	1956 Sales	1956 Percent of market	1957 Sales	1957 Percent of market	1958 Sales	1958 Percent of market
Buick	513,497	9.28	737,879	10.29	529,371	8.89	394,553	6.60	263,981	5.67
Oldsmobile	407,150	7.35	589,515	8.22	437,896	7.35	371,596	6.21	306,566	6.59
Pontiac	358,167	6.47	530,007	7.39	358,668	6.02	319,719	5.35	229,831	4.94
Chrysler	101,741	1.84	156,458	2.18	106,853	1.79	106,436	1.78	58,573	1.26
De Soto	76,739	1.39	118,062	1.65	100,766	1.69	103,915	1.74	47,894	1.03
Dodge	154,789	2.80	284,323	3.96	220,208	3.70	257,488	4.31	135,538	2.91
Mercury	296,926	4.88	371,837	5.19	274,603	4.61	260,573	4.36	136,295	2.93
Edsel							26,681	0.44	38,601	0.83
Total market shares		34.01		38.88		34.05		30.79		26.16
Total U.S. car sales	5,535,464		7,169,908		5,955,248		5,982,342		4,654,514	

SOURCE: *Automotive News Almanac, 1961*, p. 54.

seems to have particularly swayed Ford's management, appears to have been the year of the four-door hardtop and Chrysler's resurgence rather than the year of the middle-level car per se. In any event, by 1958 the market shares and absolute sales for all middle-level cars had fallen seriously, far below the 1954 levels.

Ford invested $250 million in the Edsel: $150 million in production facilities, including conversion of Ford and Mercury plants to share facilities with the Edsel (for example, common assembly lines); $50 million on special Edsel tooling; and $50 million on initial advertising and promotion.[59] Twelve hundred dealers were signed up. Ford figured that the break-even point on the car would come at 200,000 units a year.[60]

The car, of course, failed. It sold 106,000 units in slightly over two years of production. In November 1959, as a nationwide steel strike began to dry up automobile steel supplies, Ford announced the end of the Edsel. "If we knew the reason people aren't buying the Edsel, we'd probably have done something about it," commented a company spokesman making the announcement.[61]

Ford lost approximately $100 million on the venture. Brooks estimated a loss of $350 million,[62] but this figure seems too high. His estimate is composed of the $250 million originally sunk, plus $200 million lost by the company after the Edsel appeared, less $100 million in salvageable facilities. In his figures, he includes the initial investment and then counts again as a loss the Edsel's failure to cover its fixed costs. Rather, the Edsel had to be making an out-of-pocket profit. If sales of 200,000 a year were needed to break even, the expected out-of-pocket profit must have been somewhere between $750 and $1,250 per car.[63] Even with the extra advertising expenses and dealer discounts that the company incurred, an out of pocket profit of $500 per car does not appear to be unreasonable, which would yield $50 million to be offset against the original $250 million. That, plus the $100 million in salvageable facilities, would leave a net loss of $100 million, still a healthy loss by any measure.

Many blamed the Edsel's failure on its styling; some on the name itself; others on initial sloppy production; and one Ford official blamed it on the October 4, 1957, launching of the first Soviet sputnik which had the effect of "shattering the myth of American technical preeminence and precipitating a public revulsion against Detroit's fancier baubles." [64] But more fundamentally, the market had moved out from under the Edsel.[65] Middle-level cars were in the doldrums, Ramblers and small imported cars were booming. The Edsel had emerged three years too late.

The wave of imports that began in 1956 and 1957 can also be considered a form of entry, though just at the marketing level. With their foreign manufacturing bases, they were able to bypass the high capital requirements and economies of scale barriers; by offering a product very different from that which Detroit was producing, they were able to skirt the product differentiation barrier. The largest barrier they faced was that of establishing a viable retailing system. Some, notably Volkswagen, and, to a lesser extent, Volvo and Mercedes Benz and, recently, Datsun and Toyota, were able to succeed. Others, notably Renault and Fiat, faltered. The import phenomenon will be treated more thoroughly in the discussion of "the small car story" in Chapter 11.

It is interesting to note that the record of the existing firms has been "good" with respect to behavior toward entrants (and toward struggling survivors). General Motors was willing to sell its Hydra-Matic transmission to Kaiser-Frazer and to other Independents. We have Romney's testimony that, even after the Livonia fire of 1953 that burned down the Hydra-Matic plant, General Motors was very fair in its treatment of its customer-rivals: "they (GM) went out of their way to make sure not only that they got back into production as quickly as possible, but that their other automobile company customers received preferential treatment as automatic transmissions became available." [66] Similarly, in 1951, when Kaiser-Frazer found itself with excess stamping capacity because of poor sales, General Motors arranged to buy some stampings from them. These transactions were certainly profitable for General Motors, and one would not want to imply that GM undertook them simply out of the goodness of its corporate heart. But a company determined to drive its rivals out of the market might have foregone a short-run profit and refused to sell Hydra-Matics or buy stampings. Chrysler, when it bought out the Briggs body-making operations, offered to continue producing bodies for Packard, a Briggs customer, and eventually rented a former Briggs plant to Packard. Finally, in February 1967, when American Motors lowered its prices on its American models, the Big Three refrained from lowering prices on competitive models; more rapacious rivals might have acted differently.

Antitrust fears may have been the guiding force behind all of this "good-hearted" behavior, but, for whatever reason, it has occurred. On the other hand, one might argue that there is something wrong with an industry in which firms can have the luxury of a choice as to whether or not they should be nice to their rivals.

Overall, it is hard to claim that the entry that has occurred, with the exception of the imports, has had a lasting effect on the automobile industry. The benefits that entry is supposed to bring have not appeared. Many of the product ideas of the would-be entrants of the 1940's eventually were installed on American production cars, but it is doubtful that their faltering entry attempts had any influence on the eventual adoption of these ideas. Kaiser-Frazer, far from bringing new blood into the industry, mostly hired the old blood away from established firms. Kaisers and Frazers were essentially conventional cars and left no innovational marks on the industry.[67] The Kaiser-Frazer manufacturing operations were equally unexceptional. Kaiser-Frazer may have been a bit more active in its research efforts on new uses of light metals, particularly aluminum (the existence of Kaiser Aluminum in the Kaiser industrial empire may have been a spur to these efforts), but none of this came to fruition while Kaiser-Frazer was still operating. The Willys Aero and the Kaiser Henry J did not leave lasting marks on the industry; the small car influence came from the imports and from the Rambler, a product of an existing Independent. The Edsel certainly brought nothing new to the industry. Detroit may have been a bit more on its toes during the late 1940's as it found itself surrounded by a barrage of entry announcements. It seemed to have become more complacent in the 1950's after having successfully warded off all entry.

6

Integration and Diversification

Vertical Integration

Until now, we have been assuming that a fair amount of vertical integration was necessary for automobile production without really explaining why this was so. Of the manufacturing processes described in Chapter 3, only final assembly could be considered absolutely essential to a company's identity as an automobile manufacturer. In theory, an auto producer might be just an assembler of parts, all of them purchased from suppliers, perhaps designed by the assembler but produced outside. In fact, the current producers are highly integrated, owning all of the assembly and most of the stamping, machining, and casting facilities involved in manufacturing automobiles, plus other facilities for making items like glass, upholstery, steel, batteries, and spark plugs. What benefits do the companies derive from this vertical integration? Are there differences in the degree of integration among the companies, and, if so, how can these differences be explained? How do risk considerations bear on the extent of vertical integration?

There are a number of reasons for integrating backward into one's suppliers' areas. Almost all of these reasons revolve around the problems of imperfect markets and imperfect forecasts of the future and the fact that to change suppliers is often very costly in terms of both time and money.

The first reason would be economies of joint production of the two vertically integrated items. Often, these are economies of the entrepreneurial function. An assembly plant is really one large vertically integrated unit. In theory, there could be separate firms handling each station in the assembly process. In fact, the shipping costs — if the stations were geographically separated — would be astronomical, and the coordination problem, even if they were under one roof, would be enormous.[1] The American construction industry presents just such a picture today, and it has never been noted for its high efficiency.

The advantages of unified coordination and control extend beyond just one plant. The complex process of designing, producing, testing, and modifying an automobile requires a high degree of coordination. Engine, transmission, frame, body, brakes, windshield, and other components all have to perform well with each other and have to be in the right place at the right time and in the right quantities. A failure in the supply of any component can spell disaster.

Similar considerations hold for the desire to emphasize product differentiation and the uniqueness of one's own product. To the extent that components of the product (for example, engines, transmissions, sheet metal) require special, nonstandardized design to maintain this uniqueness, then close control and perhaps secrecy will be required to design, develop, and coordinate the components.

In such situations, coordination and control on an in-house basis is simply easier than the arm's-length negotiations that take place between independent companies. If a company wants to design a new car that will require a new engine (which, in turn, may require new manufacturing techniques), it feels more confident that the problems of developing the engine and integrating it with the body will be given full attention and solved in time if the efforts are all in-house. A customer company is never quite sure that its suppliers' goals and its own goals are closely enough attuned. It is never entirely certain that the supplier will not at some point say "Sorry, but we can't supply that item." Substitutes cannot always be found instantly; new tooling cannot be obtained overnight. Even matters such as scheduling meetings to coordinate projects are easier in-house than at arm's length.

Note that the problem is not just one of guaranteeing a future price, which could be arranged simply through futures contracts. Rather, it is one of guaranteeing future *delivery* of an item whose technical characteristics are somewhat uncertain. A suit for breach of contract would be cold comfort to a firm whose production lines were idle because a supplier at the last minute announced that it could not deliver a particular component.

It is worth mentioning at this point the one postwar instance in which a major auto manufacturer went outside for its engines. In its eagerness to get into production in 1946 (and also because of capital and raw materials shortages), Kaiser-Frazer contracted with Continental Motors to supply it with engines. The relationship was entirely unsatisfactory. Continental was continually slow in delivering engines, and in the end Kaiser had to take over the engine plant.[2] Though the whole 1946–1948 period is one of "special circumstances," this experience would certainly make a manufacturer pause before thinking of going outside for his engines.

A second reason for vertical integration would be to avoid exploitation by a monopolistic supplier. Beside the risks of doing business with a single supplier in terms of the interruption of supply, a customer company would also face the likelihood of its profits being taxed away by a supplier on whom it was solely dependent.

A third reason revolves around labor relations. If strikes in a supplier's plant can halt a customer company's operations, the customer would feel more confident about the situation if it had control over the collective bargaining arrangement. It is at the mercy of someone else's judgment about the wisdom of incurring or ending a strike. The greater the size of the investment in facilities, the greater the anguish as production lines stand idle because of someone else's strike. Again, substitutes are not always instantly available. One way for the customer to substitute his own judgment and protect his investment is to manufacture the item himself. This seems to have been the response of the auto companies after the 1946–1948 period, when supplier strikes repeatedly disrupted production lines.

A fourth reason for integration would be to enter a potentially profitable field that has not yet been exploited (for example, integrate into parts production and sell the parts in the replacement market) or integrate so as to reap larger profits from goods that are jointly consumed by purchasers. This latter argument has been developed by Robert Crandall.[3] He points out that autos and spare parts are jointly consumed goods and that an oligopolist who produces both can juggle prices in the two areas, so that the combined profit is greater than if prices for autos and for parts were set independently. There are externalities to auto sales, in that they set up a demand for replacement parts; there are also externalities to replacement part prices, since they affect the costs of car ownership and therefore the demand for cars.

There are a number of other possible reasons for integration. Managers may become better decision makers, even in one area of expertise, if they are given exposure to a wider range of activities. The "fall out" from basic and applied research may be better appropriated, the wider the range of the firm's activities. Similarly, the use of related patents may be easier if the firm is actually in the related fields.

The logical extension of the justifications for integration we have mentioned, particularly that of coordination and control, would mean the development of self-contained industrial empires: mining their own coal, generating their own electricity, shipping their own goods, and so forth. Though the elder Henry Ford seems to have been after this goal,[4] in fact nothing like this exists today.

First, no firm or management team has the expertise to do *every-thing*. Any wholly self-contained empire would surely collapse of its own weight (as Ford's nearly did). At some point, the lower cost offered by suppliers outweighs the risks of doing business with it, particularly when quickly available substitute supplies exist. For most firms, with limited capital and management resources, the make-or-buy question is usually decided easily in favor of "buy." For auto manufacturers, with usually overabundant capital and great confidence in their managerial capabilities, the question is less easily decided.[5] Still, none of the auto companies currently owns a railroad or makes its own aluminum or manufactures its own machine tools or presses. Lines can be drawn.

Second, integration is a two-edged sword. Though it reduces the risks of supply failure, it also converts variable costs into fixed costs — it commits that much more capital toward the success of the firm. More money is at stake, and though the probabilities of loss may not be changed, the financial penalties of losses (that is, risks) have increased.

A way of reducing the risks of vertical integration is through partial or tapered integration: a company can produce a portion of its needs of an item and buy the fluctuating remainder. This has the advantage of providing full utilization for its own equipment and allowing the supplier to absorb the risks of fluctuations in demand. The company has to pay a premium to get someone else to absorb the risks, but the risk transfer is achieved. In the case of a supplier failure, production of the final good does not have to cease and may not even slacken if extra output can be squeezed out of the in-house supply; though the extra output may be high cost, it may be a superior temporary alternative to allowing final production to slacken. Tapered integration can also serve to check any exploitation by a supplier, making very credible a threat by the customer to produce 100 percent of his own needs. Of course, the technology of production has to be such that the customer can fully exploit the economies of scale of the process, and the leftover demand for the supplier is sufficient to allow him also to get reasonably close to minimum efficient scale.

Another simple alternative to the risks of relying on one supplier is to have two or more suppliers for an item. Again, the economies of scale have to be small enough to permit multiple manufacture. If both supplier firms deal with the same labor union, however, the strike threat to supply may not be eliminated.

All of the bargaining power does not lie on the side of the suppliers. A credible threat to integrate or to seek a second source may well induce the supplier to offer price concessions in order to retain a monopoly of supply. This ought to be true when the supplier thereby retains a dominant position in a different market; for example, by being the sole supplier of spark plugs to an auto company, a supplier would have an inside track on the replacement market. In 1947 the Champion Spark Plug Company was charging Ford only $0.06 for spark plugs installed as original equipment and selling the same spark plugs for $0.22–$0.29 as replacement parts.[6] It has been claimed that in such cases the original equipment prices were $0.10–$0.11 per spark plug under Champion's manufacturing costs.[7] This type of arrangement may well explain the auto companies' willingness to rely on single suppliers for their electrical components for many years.

One other practice in this area ought to be mentioned. Though they may rely partially or fully on suppliers for some items, the auto companies frequently provide the tools for a supplier's production of an item in order to retain some control over supply. The companies can refuse the use of the tools for the replacement market, reserving this market for themselves and forcing the supplier to tool up anew if he wants to produce for that market.[8] The companies can also pull their tools out in the event of a strike. This was done a number of times in the 1946–1948 era; in 1965 a strike at a supplier plant was settled two days after General Motors and Chrysler started to move out their tools.[9] Through this practice, the companies can take advantage of, say, the lower labor costs of a supplier and still retain some of the advantages of in-house production.

Overall, it is hard to predict on a priori grounds exactly what the pattern of integration and supplier relations will look like in the auto industry. In areas presenting extensive coordination and control problems, we should expect to find complete integration. Beyond that, it is difficult to tell whether a company should choose a single supplier, multiple suppliers, tapered integration, or complete integration without knowing the price that a single supplier is willing to offer, the probabilities of supply disruption envisaged by the buying company, the economies of scale of the manufacturing process, and the utility function of the firm's management. Consequently, in the following pages we can only look for some historical clues and make some reasoned guesses as to the particular patterns that are found.

Actual Integration

All four of the firms currently in the auto industry assemble their cars, produce their own bodies and most of their stampings, and machine their own engines. All employ their own designers and do their own developing and testing of their models. All but American Motors cast their own engine blocks and cylinder heads and make their own automatic transmissions.

This level of integration can be explained by the coordination and control considerations mentioned above, reinforced by the fact that many of these activities are closely tied to the public's identification of the companies' cars: design and power train. Here is where a company's money and reputation is really at stake. Here is where a company wants to make sure it is in control.

There have been exceptions to this pattern. Studebaker hired industrial designer Raymond Loewy to design its 1947 models and its 1953 models. The former design was an unqualified success; the latter was held partially responsible for Studebaker's sales difficulties of that year. Some of the Independents hired European designers to design sports cars in the early 1950's. Most of these cars never saw the light of day. Chrysler used to design the bodies for its Plymouth models and have the Briggs Manufacturing Company make its bodies; Packard did the same for all of its bodies. A new Chrysler management team bought out Briggs at the end of 1953; since then Chrysler has produced all of its own bodies. Packard rented a Briggs plant from Chrysler and produced its own bodies also. As automatic transmissions spread through the industry in the later 1940's, the Independents (with the exception of Packard, which developed its own), lacking the volume or the funds to build their own transmissions, bought them from General Motors and outside suppliers. This policy has continued for American Motors to the present; it currently buys its automatic transmissions from Borg-Warner. American Motors closed down its foundry in 1961, for reasons that have never been made public.[10]

Once one gets beyond these basic facilities, the picture varies among companies and over time; the reasons for much of the integration become a mixture of history and economics. The elder Henry Ford saddled his company with a steel mill and a glass plant, beside the Brazilian rubber plantations and the soy bean processing factories. The latter projects were clearly not vital to auto manufacturing, and the decision to sell them was an easy one for Henry Ford II and Ernest Breech to make in 1946. But, in that era of steel and raw materials shortages, a decision to close down even an inefficient steel mill or glass furnace would have been truly courageous and perhaps foolhardy. Since then, both facilities have been expanded and modernized. This author suspects that the steel mill is still more costly to operate than other mills in the steel industry. For example, MacDonald cites Ford claims that its steel division wages were 34 percent above the average for the steel industry, along with a Ford denial that these cost differences were offset by higher efficiency.[11] But the "sunk cost fallacy" has probably precluded any decision to scrap the mill.[12]

Many decisions to integrate into items like plastics, upholstery, and electronic components appear to have been made at least partly as a consequence of the 1946–1948 episode, when repeated strikes in suppliers' plants, even on trivial items, were able to bring assembly lines to a halt. Again, it is no coincidence that Chrysler's decision to build its own glass plant in 1959 quickly followed a crippling 135-day strike at Chrysler's lone glass supplier, Pittsburgh Plate Glass Company.

The profitability of the replacement parts market has been another spur behind integration, influencing Chrysler's and Ford's development of their own electrical equipment capabilities in the 1950's. It appears to have been the primary reason behind Ford's purchase of the Electric Auto-Lite Company in 1961. General Motors seems to have absorbed this lesson earlier; its Delco division has supplied most of General Motors' electrical requirements since the 1920's.

Tapered integration plays a large role in the industry. Ford buys

50 percent of its steel; Chrysler buys 50 percent of its glass; all the companies have bought varying percentages of their frames, wheels, brakes, gears, valves, and clutches. Even on items like high volume stampings, companies may produce only part of their requirements. For example, in recent years a percentage of Chevrolet's fender stampings have been farmed out to the Budd Company.

Reliance on a single supplier has generally been avoided. The exceptions have been (1) cases in which economies of scale required it and/or funds limitations precluded in-house production, and (2) cases in which a replacement market supplier was willing to offer large price concessions on original equipment. The Independents' purchases of automatic transmissions were an example of the first. Ford's and Chrysler's purchases of electrical equipment from single suppliers were an example of the second. Also, a supplier firm will occasionally hold a key patent on an item. If this is an optional item for car buyers, the absence of which would not hurt production or sales very much, the companies may tolerate a single supplier situation. The Dana Corporation has been the sole supplier of nonslip differentials, on which it holds the key patent. But more frequently, and especially if the item is an important one, the auto companies will insist that the patent holder license other suppliers or license the auto companies themselves to produce part of the required supply.

Glass, though, presents a somewhat mysterious exception to this pattern. Until 1959 Chrysler relied solely on the Pittsburgh Plate Glass Company, while General Motors bought its glass exclusively from the Libby-Owens-Ford Glass Corporation.[13] Only after the 1958–1959 Pittsburgh Plate strike did Chrysler decide on 50 percent self-supply. General Motors at the same time decided that a second supplier would be a good idea and started ordering part of its glass needs from Pittsburgh Plate. It is unlikely that the replacement market was large enough for the glass companies to offer below-cost prices on original equipment, and no key patents were involved. One possibility is that the economies of scale had originally been so large that reliance on one supplier was necessary and it took the 1958–1959 strike to jolt the auto companies into realizing that the market had grown sufficiently and/or the technology had changed so that a second source of supply was possible. Another possibility is that the single suppliers had grown increasingly inefficient while producing for their captive markets and that the strike served as a stimulant or a convenient excuse for the auto companies to seek second sources to provide competition. This latter explanation, though, does not offer a satisfactory rationale for the companies' unwillingness to expose themselves to the risks of reliance on a single supplier for as long as they did.

More common is the practice of multiple suppliers, even in cases of tapered integration. All of the auto companies buy their steel from a number of steel companies; all buy their tires from all of the major tire companies; General Motors buys its frames from four suppliers. Chrysler and Ford buy their crankcase ventilator valves from two suppliers; Ford also makes some of its own requirements. Chrysler buys its carburetors from three suppliers.

On some components, there has been a tendency to let suppliers develop a product, purchase it for a while, and then either purchase the plant or build one for in-house production. This, of course, shifts the risks of development on to the suppliers. Ford initially bought its automatic transmissions from Borg-Warner but soon switched to producing its own. Chrysler originally bought its power steering from the Gemmer Manufacturing Company, and Ford bought its power steering from Bendix and General Motors. Both auto companies soon began producing their own.

General Motors has had a greater tendency to initiate such projects in-house. This seems to be due primarily to a greater willingness on General Motors' part to absorb risk in these areas; that is, General Motors seemingly has had a greater amount of confidence in its own management and engineering and in the success of any projects undertaken.[14] On items like automatic transmissions, power steering, and power brakes, this willingness paid off handsomely. On items like transistorized ignition, fuel injection, air suspension systems, and aluminum engines, all of them "hot" items at one time that subsequently fizzled out, General Motors rushed in while its rivals hung back and allowed suppliers to take the risks. General Motors surely incurred losses on these projects, the size of which remains hidden in the consolidated accounts.

Overall, with some variation over time as technology and supplier bids change, there is the tendency for the Big Three to produce some or all of their requirements in the following fields:

engines, transmissions, casting, stampings: all three
valves, gears, clutches: all three
wheels: all three

brakes: all three

manual and power steering: all three

plastics and upholstery: General Motors and Ford

carburetors: General Motors and Ford

frames: Ford (General Motors made part of its requirements until recently; Chrysler's unitized construction does not require frames)

air pollution control equipment: General Motors and Ford

electrical equipment: all three[15]

glass: Ford and Chrysler

steel: Ford

Traditionally, General Motors has been considered the most integrated of the firms in the auto industry (despite Ford's steel and glass), producing more of its major components than did its rivals. Chrysler's and Ford's development of their own manufacturing capabilities in these lines, aided by Ford's 1961 acquisition of Auto-Lite) has largely closed this gap, at least at the components level. Nevertheless, General Motors remains more integrated than its rivals: in 1966, only 47.0 percent of every General Motors sales dollar went to suppliers, compared to 56.8 percent for Ford and 58.4 percent for Chrysler.[16] This has been due to General Motors' greater willingness to produce the "parts of parts" — the small clutches, valves, and subassemblies from which the larger components are made — and to forego tapered integration and to produce 100 percent of its requirements in many areas, absorbing more risk but also keeping a tighter control over the lucrative replacement market.

American Motors, with its smaller volume and more limited capital resources for much of the postwar era, has remained much less integrated. Only a detailed analysis of the confidential accounts of all the companies could determine if this has put American Motors at a serious cost disadvantage. This author would tend to agree with American Motors' claim that it has not.[17] In any event, American Motors current difficulties are caused by a lack of sales, not by a few extra dollars in supplier costs.

The route to integration is not necessarily a one-way road. General Motors has always claimed that its divisions were free to purchase parts from outside suppliers rather than in-house, and there have been instances when this has occurred.[18] The most recent major action of this sort was the decision by the Chevrolet and Pontiac divisions to give up frame production and buy their entire supplies from outside frame suppliers.[19]

What effect does integration have on the structure and behavior of the industry? To the extent that the vital areas of integration are larger than, say, just one assembly plant, the capital investment required for entry is increased and the barriers to entry are raised. As was seen in the previous chapter, integration into just the key areas of stamping, casting, machining, assembly, and design and development would require a $1 billion investment for an efficient, viable producer. A single assembly plant would cost only $50 million. One can conceive of the possibility of a number of separate assemblers, engine builders, foundries, and stamping plants (economies of scale would probably limit the numbers at this stage), making up a nonintegrated automobile industry, with the lower barrier to entry for each specialty serving as a check on each segment's behavior. The internal advantages of coordination and control have ruled out this possibility.

Second, to the extent that the "optional" integration into items like electrical components reduces the possible market for these items and thereby reduces the number of suppliers, nonintegrated producers face a smaller selection among suppliers and face greater risks of failure of supply or of monopsonistic exploitation. The nonintegrated producers face the unwelcome choice of enduring these risks or of devoting some of their limited management and monetary resources to integrating into these areas. Prospective entrants would face the same choice.[20]

Finally, the increased coordination and control achieved by integration should permit a faster pace of model changes and product changes in general than if the industry were composed of nonintegrated units. Integration should basically make such changes easier. On the other hand, it might be argued that with fewer numbers of supplier firms, the number of sources of independent ideas would be reduced and the pace of "true" technological change would slacken if most of the effort is put into the design aspects of the product. We shall return to this aspect of product change in the discussion on product behavior.

Diversification

The extent of, and reasons for, the diversification of the auto companies' activities have not always been clearly understood. For example, one often hears claims that defense sales provide a vital prop to auto company fortunes. Yet during the 1960's, defense sales were only 2–3 percent of total Big Three sales, and even the conflict in South Vietnam has not raised this percentage appreciably. A more serious example would be the Senate Antitrust Committee's charge in 1958 that General Motors had more "leverage" to exert in nonautomotive areas than did Ford because only 65.2 percent of General Motors' revenues came from automotive pursuits as compared to 82.5 percent for Ford.[21] In fact, the committee was comparing United States car and truck revenues to worldwide revenues for General Motors and comparing United States car and truck revenues to just United States revenues for Ford. Actually, a smaller proportion of Ford's worldwide sales come from American cars and trucks than in the case of General Motors. This section will attempt to set the record straight on the extent of diversification; it will also try to provide some of the reasons that lay behind the diversification that has taken place.

The consolidated accounting methods of modern corporations serve to hide the details of their diverse activities. The auto companies are no exception in this respect. They have, however, revealed the dimensions of some of their activities in their annual reports, and other sources can help us fill out the picture somewhat. Unless otherwise noted, the data come from the annual reports.

In 1967 General Motors had total sales of $20,046 million. Defense sales were 3.5 percent of the total. Nonautomotive civilian sales were 7.6 percent. The automotive remainder — cars, trucks, and parts — accounted for $17,723 million, or 88.6 percent of the total. In 1957 American cars and trucks sales alone accounted for 65 percent of total General Motors revenue.[22] That same percentage would yield around $13 billion in 1967.

In the automotive category, beside American automobiles, General Motors produces American trucks (678,939 units, factory sales, in 1967), Canadian cars and trucks (385,827 units), and overseas cars and trucks (1,086,881 units), primarily German Opels, British Vauxhalls, and Australian Holdens. Total overseas sales revenue, most of it automotive, came to $2,781 million in 1967. The company, of course, sells replacement parts in all of these markets. The truck and Canadian operations extend back to the early days of the company before 1920. Opel and Vauxhall were acquired in the 1920's. Australian operations had been confined before the war to partial assembly of

American- or British-made vehicles; in 1948 General Motors introduced the Holden, Australia's first domestically built car.

General Motors also owns the General Motors Acceptance Corporation (GMAC), which finances a large proportion of General Motors cars and trucks at wholesale and retail. In the 1950's GMAC financed 41–46 percent of General Motors' retail automobile time sales.[23] GMAC, in turn, has a subsidiary, the Motors Insurance Corporation, which offers fire, theft, and collision insurance (but not liability insurance) on cars that GMAC finances. GMAC was established in 1919.

In the nonautomotive category, General Motors produces the Frigidaire line of home appliances, diesel locomotives, industrial and marine diesel engines, heavy earth-moving machinery and off-the-road dump trucks, and gas turbines and heavy-duty transmissions. Frigidaires entered the General Motors line in 1918, when General Motors President William C. Durant bought the Guardian Frigerator Company, hoping to provide his dealers with something to sell if war production cut off the supply of cars. Diesel locomotives were developed by General Motors in the 1930's, after buying a diesel engine manufacturer and an engineering firm interested in diesel locomotives in 1930. Heavy earth-moving equipment came into the firm in 1953 with the purchase of the Euclid Road Machine Company. The Justice Department filed suit to prevent the acquisition and in 1968 obtained a consent decree in which General Motors agreed to sell the original Euclid plant but was allowed to retain the heavy earth-moving machinery plants it had subsequently built.[24] The turbines and heavy transmissions were developed in the Allison division, formed by the purchase of the Allison Engineering Company, in 1924.

General Motors formerly had wider interests and holdings — in the Bendix Aviation Corporation (23 percent of outstanding shares), North American Aviation (29 percent), Greyhound Corporation (3 percent), Kinetic Chemicals (49 percent), Ethyl Corporation (50 percent), and Hertz Drivurself Corporation (100 percent) — but has disposed of them at various times since the war. A policy of unloading minority holdings, plus a possible fear of Clayton Act antitrust proceedings, appear to have been the guiding forces behind these disposals.

Ford sales revenue in 1967 was $10,516 million, down from $12,240 million in 1966 because of a strike in the fall. Defense sales were 4.1

percent of the 1967 total (3.1 percent in 1966). Nonautomotive sales by Ford's Philco subsidiary were 5 percent of total sales in 1965,[25] so that a figure for automotive sales somewhere over 90 percent would probably be a good guess.

In addition to American cars, Ford sells trucks (488,407 units, factory sales, in 1967), Canadian cars and trucks (225,133 units), and overseas cars and trucks (1,069,892 units) — primarily English Fords, German Fords (Taunus), and Australian Falcons; Ford also sells tractors (85,026 units), two-thirds of them overseas. Replacement parts, of course, are sold in all of these markets. All of the above activities date back to the early days of the company. Ford of Canada is 79 percent owned by the parent company, and a number of the overseas Ford companies have minority interests. In late 1960, in a major acquisition, the parent company bought out the 45.4 percent minority interests in Ford of England for $368 million. Ford of France was sold to Simca in 1955 for 15 percent of Simca's stock. This, in turn, was sold to Chrysler in 1958.

Ford had formed a finance subsidiary, the Universal Credit Corporation, in 1928 but sold it in 1933. In 1959 a new finance subsidiary, the Ford Motor Credit Company, was formed, along with an insurance subsidiary. In 1960 a car leasing subsidiary was formed.

In 1961 Ford purchased two plants and certain other assets, along with the brand name, from the Electric Auto-Lite Company to broaden its parts line. A recent antitrust decision against Ford in 1968 on the Justice Department's suit to forbid the acquisition now puts the future of the Auto-Lite division in doubt.[26]

Ford had very little activity in nonautomotive lines (aside from tractors) until it acquired the Philco Corporation in late 1961. Through Philco, it now sells home appliances, computers, and sophisticated electronics systems.

Chrysler's sales in 1967 came to $6,213 million. Its defense sales came to 3.4 percent of the total. Unfortunately, no other break-down of Chrysler's revenues have been given; but from the nature of Chrysler's nonautomotive activities, it is clear that vehicle and parts sales are well over 90 percent of the total.

In addition to American cars, Chrysler sells American trucks (142,172 units, factory sales, 1967), Canadian cars and trucks (204,345 units), and overseas cars and trucks (528,692 units) — primarily British Rootes cars, French Simcas, and Australian Valiants and Dodges. Parts are sold for all of these markets. All of Chrysler's North

American vehicle operations extend back to the formation of the company in the 1920's. In 1964 Chrysler tried to expand its truck line by acquiring the Mack Truck Corporation; the Justice Department filed suit to stop the acquisition, and the venture was canceled. By comparison with its rivals, Chrysler was late in expanding across the ocean. In 1958 it bought Ford's 15 percent interest in Simca Automobiles, Société Anonyme, and another 10 percent on its own; by 1967, it had extended its ownership in Simca to 77 percent. During 1964 and 1965 Chrysler acquired 45 percent of the voting shares and 65 percent of the nonvoting shares of Rootes Motors. It now holds 77 percent of Rootes voting shares. In 1964 Chrysler entered the car finance business for the first time, forming a subsidiary, the Chrysler Credit Corporation; an insurance subsidiary was also formed. Nonautomotive sales consist primarily of air conditioning units and marine and industrial engines. Both were built up internally, although the latter was aided by two small acquisitions in 1965.

American Motors currently produces only automobiles and parts. The last nonautomotive division, Kelvinator home appliances, was sold in June 1968 to White Consolidated Industries. In fiscal year 1967 (ending Sept. 30, 1967), American Motors had sales of $778 million, of which approximately $125 million were by Kelvinator.[27] In calendar year 1967 American Motors sold 23,789 cars (registrations) in Canada.

During the 1950's and 1960's, as American Motors struggled for survival, the company performed the financial equivalent of "the dance of the seven veils." One after another, parts of the company, often profitable ones, were sold so that the company could acquire ready cash to keep its creditors from the door. In 1955 and 1956 it sold the Hudson body plant, the West Coast assembly plant, and its interests in Ranco, a manufacturer of thermostatic controls. In 1959 the company, though a bit more prosperous than a few years earlier, liquidated its controlling interest in Altorfer Brothers, a manufacturer of laundry equipment. As hard times again overtook the company, its appliance finance subsidiary, Redisco, was sold to Chrysler in 1967; finally, Kelvinator was sold in 1968.

Studebaker, before it left the auto industry, had embarked on a wide diversification program, buying companies involved in, among other fields, plastics, floor finishing equipment, tractors, and oil additives. These activities, supplemented by newer ones, are currently maintaining the company nicely.

7

The Structure
of Demand

The demand for new automobiles can conveniently be divided into two categories: (1) private consumer demand, and (2) business and fleet demand. The former category needs little descriptive explanation. The latter includes cars bought individually and in fleets by businesses, rental and leasing firms, and various governments — national, state, and local.

The two categories of demand exhibit many similar characteristics, but more is known about consumer demand than about business and fleet demand. The following discussion will deal with consumer demand, except where otherwise noted. Table 7.1 gives the relevant figures on the relative sizes of consumer and business and fleet demand since 1955. There has been no discernible trend in the division of sales between the categories, with the average of business and fleet sales reaching 16 percent for the years shown in the table.

The fact of overwhelming importance in the new car market is that the demand for new cars, by both consumers and owners of business and fleet vehicles, is essentially a replacement demand. In *Look* magazine's 1965 survey, 90.4 percent of new car buyers owned a previous car; of this latter group, only 12.3 percent kept their previous car or cars, so that 87.7 percent of those with a car or 78.3 percent of all new car buyers either traded, sold, or scrapped a car when buying their new car.[1]

The proportion for business and fleet replacement was probably very similar, since it has been estimated that the total number of cars in fleets of four or more rose by only 190,000 cars a year between 1962 and 1967, while new car sales to businesses and fleets were averaging 1,250,000 units per year over those same years.[2]

Purchasers usually have the option of buying a new car or retaining the old for a while longer.[3] Since the latter decision carries with it no necessary likelihood that future replacement purchases will be made more frequently, a delayed purchase is effectively a lost sale to the automobile manufacturers. Consequently, it is always in the manu-

Table 7.1 **Estimated Division of New Car Sales to Consumers and Businesses and Fleets** (in millions of units)

Year	Total new car sales (including imports)	Consumer sales	Business and fleet sales[a]	Business and fleet as a percentage of total
1955	7.2	6.2	1.0	14
1956	6.0	5.3	0.7	12
1957	6.0	4.5	1.5	25
1958	4.7	3.9	0.8	17
1959	6.0	5.2	0.8	13
1960	6.6	5.4	1.2	18
1961	5.9	4.6	1.3	22
1962	6.9	5.9	1.0	14
1963	7.6	6.0	1.6	21
1964	8.1	7.2	0.9	11
1965	9.3	7.9	1.4	15
1966	9.0	7.6	1.4	16

Source: *Automotive News Almanac, 1968*, p. 45; University of Michigan, Survey Research Center, *Survey of Consumer Finances, 1967*.

[a] Derived by subtracting consumer sales from total sales.

facturer's interests to hasten a purchase and quicken the pace of replacement demand.

Even the nonreplacement demand is frequently of a deferrable nature. The number of multiple-car households rose from 9,500,000 in 1960 to 14,700,000 in 1967; the latter figure is 25.1 percent of all households and 32.0 percent of car-owning households.[4] The purchase of a second or third car in a household cannot, in most cases, be labeled as a "vital" purchase.

Thus, although automobiles may be a necessity in modern American life — 46 million households, or 78.1 percent of all households, owned at least one car in 1967,[5] *new* cars are for the most part in the luxury good category. And, as we shall see, most consumers have

Table 7.2 Studies of the Demand for New Cars

Author	Years covered	Dependent variable	Price variable and price elasticity	Income variable and income elasticity	Other variables in the model
Roos and Von Szelski	1920–1938	New car sales	Average unit values of low price 3; −1.5	Disposable personal income less subsistence living expenses; 1.5–2.5	Stock of cars on road; maximum ownership level; replacement pressure
Atkinson	1925–1940	New car sales per 1,000 households	Deflated BLS new car price index; −1.359	Real disposable income per 1,000 households; 2.536	Ratio of current income to previous year's income; average scrapping age of cars
Chow	1921–1953	New car sales per capita	Price index constructed from newspaper ads; −1.2	Real per capita disposable personal income; 3.0	Stock of cars per capita weighted by average used car prices
Suits	1929–1956	New car sales	Complex price and credit terms; −0.59	Personal disposable income; 4.16	Stock of cars
Suits—Senate Antitrust Subcommittee Staff	1929–1956	New car sales	Deflated BLS new car price index; −1.22	Personal disposable income; 4.16	Stock of cars; credit terms
Nerlove	1922–1953	New car sales per capita	Chow's newspaper series; short run: −0.9 long run: −1.2	Chow's income series; short run: 2.8 long run: 3.8	Lagged dependent variable

	Period	Dependent variable	Price	Income	Other variables
Dyckman	1929–1962	New car sales per capita	Newspaper price series; −0.748 Deflated BLS new car price index; −1.2	Real "discretionary" income per capita; 1.749 Real disposable income per capita; 3.951	Stock of cars; state of credit conditions (dummy variable)
	1948–1962	New car sales per capita	Newspaper price series; −0.980	Real discretionary income per capita; 1.096	State of credit conditions
Houthakker and Taylor	1929–1961	Real per capita consumption of new cars	Price deflator for the consumption series; short run: −0.9578 long run: −0.1525	Real per capita consumption of all goods; elasticity not given	Lagged dependent variable
Hamburger	1953–1964 (quarterly)	Consumption of automobiles and parts	Implicit deflator for series; −1.17	Real personal disposable income; 4.32	Interest rates; lagged dependent variable

SOURCES: C. F. Roos and Victor von Szelski, "Factors Governing Changes in Domestic Automobile Demand," in General Motors Corp., *The Dynamics of Automobile Demand* (New York, 1939); L. Jay Atkinson, "Consumer Markets for Durable Goods," *Survey of Current Business* (April 1952); Gregory C. Chow, *Demand for Automobiles in the United States, 1929–1956*," *Review of Economics and Statistics* 39 (Nov. 1958); Daniel B. Suits, "The Demand for New Automobiles in the United States, 1929–1956," *Review of Economics and Statistics* 39 (Nov. 1958); *Administered Prices*, part 7, pp. 3998–3999; Marc Nerlove, "A Note on Long-run Automobile Demand," *Journal of Marketing* 22 (July 1957); Thomas R. Dyckman, "An Aggregate Demand Model for Automobiles," *Journal of Business* 38 (July 1965); H. S. Houthakker and Lester D. Taylor, *Consumer Demand in the United States, 1929–1970* (Cambridge, Mass., 1966), p. 112; Michael J. Hamburger, "Interest Rates and the Demand for Consumer Durable Goods," *American Economic Review* 57 (Dec. 1967).

treated them as such. True, over time cars will be destroyed in accidents and others will age and sustain astronomical repair costs to keep them running; this would generate a "necessity" replacement demand. But at any given moment in time, most consumers are able to defer their demand for new cars and get along with their old ones for a while longer.

The studies of the demand for new cars that have been made tend to support this view of new cars as a luxury good. Table 7.2 summarizes these results. The income elasticity estimates fall in the 1.0–4.0 range, with 3.0 as a rough center point. The price elasticity estimates are in the −0.5 to −1.5 range, with −1.0 as a rough center point.

Not too surprisingly, those who buy new cars display different characteristics from those who own cars in general; that is, new cars are not bought by a random selection of car owners but, instead, tend to be bought by a smaller group who buy new cars comparatively frequently and sell their used cars to the general public to hold. Of those new car buyers in 1965 who already had a car, two-thirds had bought the previous car new.[6] We have sample figures on how long new-car buyers held their previous cars before buying a new one. If the new-car buyers who had bought their previous car new had been drawn from the car-owning population at random, we should expect to see the age structure of previous car ownership approximate the age structure of the car population as a whole. In fact, the previous car ownership age structure is a good deal younger, implying that new-car buyers are a special group who buy new cars frequently. Table 7.3 offers the figures on car age structure. The drawback to the use of the table is that the figures in the right-hand column also include those new-car buyers who bought their previous car used. For that year, that percentage was 33 percent. But even if we make the extreme assumption that all of those new-car buyers who had bought their previous car used had held that previous car for the shortest possible time, the median for the remaining 67 percent would be somewhere in the 49–60 month category, below the 60–61 months median for the car population as a whole.

The special group of new-car buyers hypothesis tends to be supported by the cross-section analysis of the Michigan Survey of Consumer Finances sample made by David S. Huang. Huang found that among purchasers of all cars (new and used), the probability of purchasing new is larger, the younger the age of the car currently held. The highest probability was among those who had bought new less than three years previously; the next highest probability was among those who had bought new but more than three years previously; and the lowest probabilities were among those who had bought their previous car used.[7]

We can use the figures in Table 7.3 to arrive at a rough estimate of the size of the new-car buying group. Suppose the last column in the table accurately reflects the previous car age structure of those who

Table 7.3 Age Structure of Car Population and Number of Months New Car Buyer Held Previous Car, 1965 (percent)

Months	Age of car population as of July 1, 1965	Months	Number of months new car buyer held previous car
0–9	9.3	0–12	6.8
10–21	11.4	13–24	12.4
22–33	10.6	25–36	19.9
34–45	9.6	37–48	19.2
46–57	7.8	49–60	13.4
58–69	8.7	61–72	8.8
70–81	7.8	73–84	4.7
82–93	5.3	85–96	4.5
94+	29.5	97+	10.3
Total	100.0		100.0
Median	60–61 months		43 months

SOURCE: Look Magazine, *National Automobile and Tire Survey, 1965;* Automobile Manufacturers Association, *1967 Automobile Facts and Figures*, p. 24.

bought their previous car new, and the pattern is consistent over time. Suppose, further, that in each of a number of years, 1,650 cars represented the entire new car market. If 90 percent of the purchasers already had a car and two-thirds of those had bought their previous cars as new cars, then about 1,000 cars a year are sold to the repeat new-car buyers.

Of these 1,000 cars a year, 68 will be bought by consumers who buy a new car every year. Another 124 will be bought by consumers who buy a new car every two years; there will be two such groups, each buying every other year. There will be three groups who buy 199 cars each on a rotating basis once every three years, and so forth. Summing all of these groups up to eight years (and dropping the last open-ended sector), we see that approximately 900 cars a year over a number of years are sold to a group of 3,568 buyers.

What about the other 750 purchases a year? Each year 100 cars are bought by purchasers with cars that were bought new more than eight years previously. Another 500 are bought by purchasers with cars bought used. And the final 150 are bought by first-car consumers.

Thus, of 1,650 new cars sold each year, about 900, or just under 60 percent would be sold to a rotating group of about 3,600 buyers. If we were to blow these figures up to the actual size of new car sales to consumers, we should find that, say, taking 7.5 million as the level of new car sales to consumers, 4.5 million a year would be sold to a group of about 20 million households, with the other 3 million going to those who regularly buy at greater than eight-year intervals, those who had a previous car bought used, and those who bought new for the first time. Since there were 46,000,000 car-owning households in 1967 (44,400,000 in 1965), this is a comparatively small group that is doing most of the buying.

The above estimate is, of course, very rough. It would have been different had we used a different set of figures for length of time car is held, but these have, in fact, been basically similar for the middle 1960's.[8] Over time, though, there has been a trend toward quickening the pace of replacement buying. In the middle 1950's the median car to be replaced had been held over four years. In 1965, it had been held only three years and seven months.

If we look at the income per household for new car buyers and for the entire car-owning population, we again see a significant difference. As seen in Table 7.4, new-car buyers' incomes are higher than are car owners' incomes, with the median income at $8,042 for the former group and at $6,762 for the latter.

Thus we can think of the market for new cars as being composed of a comparatively small group of repeat buyers, supplemented by buyers who trade in used cars and first-time buyers. A good car sales year will mean that the regular buyers have been induced to replace their cars sooner than otherwise, more families have become two- and three-car families, more owners who had originally bought used cars will be induced to trade in for a new car, and more first-time buyers will be attracted. A poor year will mean less replacement, and fewer families will become multiple car owners. The growth of the new car market will consist largely of additions to the repeat group and any permanent quickening of the replacement pace within that group.

The type of new car actually purchased indicates considerations in consumer preference functions that extend beyond just those of minimum cost and the utility of transportation. As a glance at the appendix will show, not everyone buys American Motors' Ramblers or even just Fords, Chevrolets, and Plymouths. Even within the traditional low price makes, most buyers avoid the less expensive models. In 1967, only 26 percent of American Motors buyers chose the bottom of the line Rambler American models; the rest preferred the higher priced models. Among buyers of the full-sized Chevrolet (excluding station

Table 7.4   Income Distribution of Car Owners and New Car Buyers, 1965 (percent)

Income (dollars)	All car owners	New car buyers
Under 4,000	17.3	8.1
4,000–4,999	8.0	4.7
5,000–6,999	28.0	25.1
7,000–7,999	11.3	11.8
8,000–9,999	14.4	16.4
10,000–14,999	13.9	20.2
15,000 and above	7.1	13.7
Total	100.0	100.0
Median	$6,762	$8,042

SOURCE: Look Magazine, *National Automobile and Tire Survey, 1965*, pp. 10, 18.

wagons), only 9 percent chose the bottom of the line Biscayne; only 9 percent chose the bottom of the line Custom model among full-sized Fords; only 15 percent chose the bottom of the line Fury I among full-sized Plymouths. This type of pattern repeats itself for almost all car lines and has remained true consistently year after year since the war.

Not only do buyers shun the bottom of the line models for the top of the line models but they prefer the more expensive body styles within each series and take increasing amounts of optional equipment. In 1967 only 30 percent of United States factory sales were standard two-door and four-door sedans. The other sales were hardtops (56 percent), station wagons (10 percent), and convertibles (4 percent).[9] In that same year, 87 percent of buyers of United States-produced cars ordered automatic transmissions; even 55 percent of Rambler American buyers ordered them. Further, 85 percent ordered radios, 75 percent ordered power steering, 41 percent ordered power brakes, 38 percent had air conditioning, 24 percent took bucket seats, 23 percent ordered vinyl tops.[10] In 1966, according to the Survey Research Center, consumers spent an average of $3,250 per new car.[11] A stripped Rambler American two-door sedan listed for $2,017 and probably could have been bought for under $1,800.

Yet, there is a sizable minority — 10 percent in 1968 — who buy smaller, less expensive imported cars, of whom three-fifths choose the comparatively spartan Volkswagen. Most of these buyers seem to be after the lower initial cost and running costs (and extra handling ease) of the smaller car and prefer the reliability and warranty of a new car, rather than rely on a used car for their transportation.

Overall, the market for new cars appears to be a somewhat segmented one, with the segments overlapping. The segments do not necessarily involve separate consumers, since the first car bought by one household might fit into one category and the second into another. At the bottom of the price scale are those after basic, cheap transportation with new car reliability. These consumers are interested in imports, inexpensive compacts and intermediates, and bottom of the line, full-sized cars if their needs require a larger car (for example, a large family). At the top of the market are the luxury or specialty cars — Cadillacs, Lincolns, Imperials, Thunderbirds, Buick Rivieras — whose buyers are after comfort and prestige and seem relatively unconcerned with initial cost or parking-space worries. In the middle are the bulk of consumers, seeking convenient transportation but willing to indulge their wallets and/or their egos for fancy models and optional equipment. Styling considerations will play an important role in this market.

Business and fleet buyers appear to fit mostly into the first and third categories. Most business and government agencies will provide their salesmen and personnel with basic transportation, "no frills" American cars; some rental firms buy stripped models for the frugal rental customer. But most rental firms seem to be interested in top of the line models, hardtops, and optional equipment, since competition among the large rental agencies seems to have been along quality lines, reflecting the relatively price-insensitive nature of the bulk of their market, for example, business executive accounts.

Though there is some overlapping at the edges of these market segments, one suspects that the cross-elasticity of demand between a Cadillac and a Volkswagen, or even between a Chevrolet Impala and a stripped Ford Falcon, is very low. Also, within the segments, there are niches, like sporty cars, station wagons, compact sedans, and inter-

Table 7.5   Median Income of New Car Buyers by Make, March 1954

Make	Income
Low-price	
Willys	$ 5,808
Plymouth	5,837
Chevrolet	6,308
Ford	6,538
Middle-level	
Studebaker	6,752
Dodge	6,766
Kaiser	6,883
Pontiac	6,978
Nash	7,080
Hudson	7,194
Mercury	7,969
Buick	8,438
DeSoto	8,442
Oldsmobile	9,063
Chrysler	9,977
Luxury	
Packard	10,707
Lincoln	17,738
Cadillac	23,306
Median income for all new car buyers	$ 7,528

SOURCE: U.S. News and World Report, *The People Buying New Automobiles Today* (June 1955), p. 17.

mediate hardtops, that would exhibit greater cross-elasticity within the niche than across niches.[12] That these segments and niches within segments appeal to different groups tends to be supported by the data on median income of new-car buyers by make collected in 1954. (See Table 7.5.) Makes at that time tended to be more homogeneous and exhibit less overlapping in price between the middle level makes and the low price makes. It is clear that Buick, say, was addressing itself to a different set of buyers than was Plymouth; and both groups were yet different from the Cadillac or Lincoln buyers. Unfortunately, there do not appear to be any more recent comprehensive studies that have been published; but any such study, if broken down by car lines and models, would surely show similar results.

Table 7.6 shows the breakdown of 1967 United States production by list price groups. Unfortunately, these list price figures understate the actual outlays by new car purchasers for these cars. Though most

Table 7.6   1967 Model Year Production by Price Class

Price range	Number	Percent
$1,700–1,799	25,742	0.3
1,800–1,899	15,536	.2
1,900–1,999	77,738	1.0
2,000–2,099	168,207	2.2
2,100–2,199	202,863	2.7
2,200–2,299	378,679	4.9
2,300–2,399	744,845	9.7
2,400–2,499	899,404	11.7
2,500–2,599	690,189	9.0
2,600–2,699	1,333,750	17.5
2,700–2,799	675,912	8.8
2,800–2,899	457,710	6.0
2,900–2,999	464,432	6.1
3,000–3,099	235,000	3.1
3,100–3,199	264,108	3.5
3,200–3,299	170,418	2.2
3,300–3,399	91,544	1.2
3,400–3,499	32,238	0.4
3,500–3,599	33,295	.4
3,600–3,699	14,875	.2
3,700–3,799	47,136	.6
3,800–3,899	26,927	.4
3,900–3,999	77,191	1.0
4,000–4,099	121,149	1.6
4,100–4,199	46,568	0.6
4,200–4,299		
4,300–4,399	17,337	.2
4,400 and above	345,690	4.5
Total	7,658,383	100.0

SOURCE: *Ward's Automotive Yearbook, 1968*, p. 34.

new cars are bought at below list price, the figures in the table neglect freight charges paid (over $100 to West Coast cities) and optional equipment bought (automatic transmissions averaged $200 in 1967; power steering, $95; radios, $65). The net effect would be to push actual outlays significantly above the figures shown in the table. Also, the inclusion of import purchases would swell considerably the below $2,000 categories. Still, the table gives a general idea of the nature of the division of the market.

A few other characteristics of the auto market ought to be mentioned. New-car buyers make extensive use of installment credit, with an average of 61 percent of new car buyers financing their cars in the 1960's. Only 45–50 percent of used car buyers finance their cars.[13] New car purchases are somewhat seasonal in nature. The new model introduction date in late September or early October inspires a wave of buying that lasts through December. At the first appearance of good weather in the spring, buyers again flock to the dealers' showrooms. The late winter and summer months are the lull periods. For the 1963 through 1967 calendar years, the first quarter sales averaged 23 percent, the second quarter 28 percent, the third quarter 23 percent, and the last quarter 26 percent of the annual totals.

Finally, the auto market is one in which brand loyalty is important. Repeat buying of makes ranges from 40–70 percent for different makes in different years.[14] This range is, of course, far above the figure that random behavior among makes with none over 25 percent of the market would predict. With the automobile as an expensive, complicated item about which the average buyer has very little expertise, previous experience and reputation can count for a great deal.

Consequences for Industry Behavior

The durable good replacement nature of automobile demand and the willingness of much of the American public to treat cars as special objects of pride and status stand as crucial elements in the structure of the automobile industry. Automobiles are highly visible and durable items. They are complex and multifaceted, capable of extensive technological and design changes. Most car owners can distinguish a new car from its older brothers, and this distinction often is important to them. Autos have acquired much more importance as objects of pride and status in our society than have other consumer durables like refrigerators and stoves. To own a new or recent model car can mean a great deal in many parts of America.

As elements of market structure, these demand characteristics can lead us to expect certain forms of product and price behavior by the industry. The high visibility of automobiles, their importance as symbols in our society, their intermediate durability and their multi-faceted nature all point toward the attractiveness of product behavior that stresses design change. Design change and efforts toward design distinctiveness also maintain and enlarge brand loyalty, reducing the price elasticity for each company's own product. Further, these demand characteristics indicate that extensive advertising should appear worthwhile. They also provide incentives toward offering consumers a bigger and more luxurious product. On the other hand, consumers' lack of technical expertise would discourage product behavior that emphasized technological change. The fact that most technological changes are hidden beneath the sheet metal, where they cannot be easily displayed by proud owners, would also argue against this type of product behavior. Finally, the lack of interest by new car buyers in "basic transportation," combined with the indicated low elasticity of demand, would argue against extensive price competition by the members of a well-organized oligopoly. Chapters 8 and 10–13 will discuss in greater detail these aspects of market behavior.

8

Prices and Pricing Policy

Automobile prices and the pricing policies of the auto companies have been frequent subjects of public interest and inquiry, particularly during periods of rising prices. The highly concentrated oligopoly of the auto industry makes it obvious that the invisible hand of competition is no longer setting automobile prices. "Villains" in a price rise can be identified; public pressure can be brought to bear.

This chapter will try to develop a theory of pricing in the auto industry and try to offer explanations of the pricing patterns that have occurred in the postwar period. We shall argue that a hypothesis of price leadership by General Motors fits the facts of the postwar period very well. We shall also argue that, contrary to the impression gained from the widespread use of the term "administered prices," automobile prices at the retail level have been a good deal more flexible than most observers have recognized and that automobile prices are far from the rigid downward, always traveling upward phenomena that have frequently been described. Nevertheless, this flexibility has been held within certain limits by the recognized mutual interdependence of the automobile companies.

The Nature and Structure of Automobile Prices

Although list prices get all of the publicity in any discussion of auto prices, in fact they are only symbolic. Few sales actually get made at list prices, and they exist only because they serve as convenient

105

bench marks for haggling to begin between dealer and buyer and because federal law requires them.[1]

Wholesale prices are the key prices to the manufacturer. They determine how much revenue he gets per car. The wholesale price plus the retailer's margin — the latter influenced by the manufacturer, since he has the power to force cars on the dealer and force down margins — determines the actual retail price and thus the number sold in the market.

List prices are determined by the following formula from wholesale prices: Start with the wholesale price. Add a nominal dealer margin that is calculated so that the margin is 25 percent of the sum of wholesale price plus margin for full-sized cars,[2] 21 percent of the sum for compacts and intermediates, or 17 percent for the new subcompacts. (This 17–25 percent is the "dealer discount" in the industry terminology.) Add to the wholesale price and nominal margin the federal excise tax levied on the wholesale price (7 percent in 1968; between November 1951 and May 1965, it was 10 percent). Add a dealer preparation and delivery charge of $40–$50, which is supposed to cover the dealer's costs of righting any malfunctionings that slipped past factory inspectors. The sum of these four components — wholesale price, dealer nominal discount, excise tax, and preparation charge — is the list price for an automobile. Added to this will be any transportation charges and local taxes.

The smaller dealer discount on smaller cars had its origin in the Big Three's desire, in the fall of 1959, to price their new generation of compact cars at list prices of under $2,000. Since dealers never got their full margins anyway, the smaller discount really affected nothing, but the list price under $2,000 was important symbolically. This smaller discount has stuck as newer compacts and intermediates have been introduced. The still smaller discounts on the subcompacts have again been the result of the symbolic importance of having list prices under $2,000.

Automobiles are not and never have been fair-traded. Though dealers are urged not to exceed list price, there is no prohibition on cutting list prices, and in fact the dealers are "strongly urged" to do so.

The retail market seems to be one of imperfect information and as much price discrimination among buyers by dealers as the latter think they can get away with. Although, given the nature of the product and the nature of the bargaining process, this might seem intuitively reasonable, it is reassuring to have some hard evidence in support. In a series of articles in the *Journal of Business*, beginning in 1959, Allen F. Jung described the new-car shopping experiments that he had supervised. Test shoppers were sent out to Chicago dealerships to price standard models of new cars. The shoppers told the dealers they were interested in buying a new car and named the specific model. No trade-in was involved.

Jung first experimented with differing approaches to the dealer, which involved timid-unknowledgeable, medium-knowledgeable, and forthright-knowledgeable approaches. He found that these different approaches did not significantly affect the initial price quoted by the dealer. But subsequent bargaining (according to a standard pattern that could be followed by all of Jung's shoppers) did tend to lower quoted prices by another $50–$75.

But the striking results of Jung's studies are the range of prices offered. For a Ford in February 1959, with a list price of $3,034, the mean price among thirty dealerships was $2,590, with a range of $2,425–$2,875. After bargaining, the mean price fell to $2,514, with a range of $2,400–$2,625. Table 8.1 summarizes Jung's findings. It is clear that in this type of environment, it pays to shop around. Jung computed the expected savings to be had from shopping at multiple dealers, as shown in Table 8.2.[3]

Even more striking was Jung's results when he repeat-shopped dealerships. In one study, Jung sent sets of two shoppers to price twenty-eight Ford dealers, the second shopper following shortly after the first. In only two cases did the same dealer offer identical prices. Nine dealers offered prices that differed by $50 or more. Two dealers quoted prices that differed by more than $135.[4]

When trade-ins are involved, it appears likely that the possibilities for price discrimination grow even greater. The real price to the customer is the retail price less the trade-in value, and consumers may have more difficulty in judging the correctness of such a price. Many dealers are convinced that consumers are more sensitive to the size of the offer on the trade-in than to cuts in the retail price. Consequently, the dealers overallow on the trade-in. In the 1950's this behavior reached a peak in which dealers were wildly overallowing on trade-ins and raising list prices by "price packing" to compensate for this. There was no evidence that significant numbers of consumers were being

Table 8.1   Retail Prices among Chicago Automobile Dealers

Year and make	Number of dealers	List price (including freight)	Before bargaining		After bargaining	
			Mean price	Range	Mean price	Range
1959 Ford (Feb. 1959)	30	$3,034	$2,590	$2,425–2,875	$2,514	$2,400–2,625
1959 Chevrolet (Feb. 1959)	28	2,969	2,497	2,400–2,600	2,436	2,350–2,515
1960 Falcon (Feb. 1960)	11	2,370			2,080	2,033–2,142
1960 Corvair (Feb. 1960)	11	2,430			2,108	2,036–2,175
1960 De Soto (June 1960)	7	4,025			3,393	3,275–3,457
1960 Mercury (June 1960)	12	3,710			3,178	3,060–3,393
1960 Oldsmobile (June 1960)	17	3,855			3,220	3,140–3,356
1960 Cadillac (June 1960)	8	5,490	4,793	4,643–4,900	4,706	4,635–4,832
1960 Imperial (June 1960)	13	5,455	4,562	4,400–4,900	4,476	4,300–4,600
1960 Lincoln (June 1960)	7	5,500	4,710	4,513–4,867	4,534	4,420–4,640

SOURCE: Allen F. Jung, "Price Variations among Automobile Dealers in Chicago, Illinois," *Journal of Business* 32 (Oct. 1959); Jung, "Compact Car Prices in Major Cities," *Journal of Business* 33 (July 1960); Jung, "Pricing Policy and Discounts in the Medium- and High-priced Car Market," *Journal of Business* 33 (Oct. 1960).

Table 8.2   Expected Savings from Shopping Multiple Dealers

Dealers shopped	Total saving	Marginal saving
Ford		
1	0	0
2	$ 42.92	$42.92
3	64.38	21.46
4	78.31	13.93
5	88.50	10.19
6	96.42	7.92
7	102.89	6.47
8	108.37	5.48
Chevrolet		
1	0	0
2	$ 29.55	$29.55
3	44.33	14.78
4	53.92	9.59
5	60.94	7.02
6	66.39	5.45
7	70.84	4.45
8	74.62	3.78

SOURCE: Allen F. Jung, "Price Variations among Automobile Dealers in Chicago, Illinois," *Journal of Business* 32 (October 1959).

harmed by this practice, but the dealers convinced Congress that this was not a healthy practice for the new car market. A price labeling law was passed, requiring each car to carry a label containing the list price of the model, the list price of any optional accessories included in the car, and the point of assembly and transportation charge.

The Determination of Automobile Prices

The general problem of price determination in an oligopoly resolves itself into two subproblems:[6] (1) How are prices set? Once the invisible hand of competition is gone and oligopolists recognize their mutual interdependence, the setting of prices is a matter of conscious decision and choice and speculation about the reactions of rivals. At what levels, relative to costs, will prices settle? (2) How do prices change? When underlying conditions in the market change, how can oligopolists coordinate their decisions to adjust prices so as to avoid price wars and rivalries that can prove mutually damaging to all?

On the first point, among the various theoretical solutions to the problem of oligopoly price setting that have been offered by economists, the one that appears most reasonable to this author is the suggestion by Chamberlin[7] and Fellner[8] that there is a tendency for oligopolists to aim toward a maximization of joint profits and to set their prices and outputs accordingly. There are a large number of important qualifications to this hypothesis — differing cost structures among the oligopolists, differing views of the profit-maximizing price, differing views of the proper division of the joint profits, differing views of the likelihood of entry — but its basic idea appears very sound.

If one accepts this hypothesis with its qualifications, one is still left with the second problem, how are price changes coordinated and price wars avoided when there are differing views (as there almost always will be) as to the proper new price levels after market conditions change? There is a strong incentive for oligopolists to develop some sort of coordinating institution to avoid the "destructive" price warfare that could develop at such times. Even the oligopolist who had a differing view of the proper price would be willing to go along with a price that gave him less profits than he otherwise "deserved" if he were assured that by doing so he would avoid setting off a spree of price uncertainty, warfare, and retaliation that would leave him even worse off.

Price leadership, the explicit or implicit acceptance by all firms that one firm's price changes are those that all will follow, provides one convenient mechanism for achieving this price coordination. All follower firms avoid independent action on prices in the knowledge that, by doing so, price competition will be avoided. The price leader sets his prices with the understanding that others will follow and thus keeps his "social" function in mind when setting his prices. In the event of a change in the environment warranting a price change, the industry knows that it will be able to effect a smooth transition and avoid triggering a destructive downward spiral.

Which firm will assume the role of price leader? From a theoretical standpoint, it does not really matter; as long as all agree to follow, any firm can lead. Still, as Schelling has pointed out,[9] in cases of implicit maneuvering, points of obvious recognition on the landscape can assume large importance. One such point would be the largest firm in the industry. Because it does stand out in this way, the largest firm may "naturally" become the price leader. The largest firm may also gain this position because it has the largest economic muscle with which it can intimidate would-be price cutters: "if you want to start a price war, I can outlast you at any destructive level that *I* choose." If the largest firm should have the lowest cost structure and thereby prefer the lowest prices, its leadership potential will be that much strengthened.[10]

This model of price leadership is not applicable to all cases of oligopoly price behavior. Price flexibility does exist, price wars occasionally do break out, firms seeking low prices sometimes can win out in the implicit bargaining that goes on among oligopolists. But it does appear to describe adequately a good deal of oligopoly behavior. And specifically, it does appear to be applicable to the automobile industry.

The pricing pattern in the automobile industry is, in fact, one of price leadership by the largest firm, General Motors. Before the war, and particularly in the 1920's, the price leader was Ford, the largest firm in the industry and also the low-price seeker. But in the postwar period, the role has been assumed by General Motors, as has been demonstrated by a number of pricing incidents and testimony before congressional committees. But, as we shall see, this set of prices is not a rigid phenomenon, determined once a year by General Motors and then followed by all throughout the year. Rather, it provides a bench mark, a general guide from which all prices vary as the state of demand fluctuates over the year but which keeps price competition from getting too far out of hand and provides a convenient point of reference for determining the next year's set of prices.

Another qualification to add to the model of price leadership in automobiles is that, rather than one price, there is a large set of prices that have to be determined. Models have to be priced in relation to each other within a company, and each company's makes have to be priced in relation to those of other companies. Since even makes that directly compete, like Ford, Chevrolet, and Plymouth, are not identical products, price differentials can and have persisted over time.

How are prices actually set within the firms? For all of the auto companies, a general price target is set while the car is still in its design and development stage.[11] A Ford will not be expected to cost $5,000 nor a Cadillac, $2,000. The particular quality aspects to be standard on the car are expected to be kept within the cost targets.

As development proceeds, cost targets and model quality aspects will be revised in the light of inflation, changes in the car market, and other factors.

Final prices are not set until a few days before new models appear in late September. With the design, development, and tooling costs already sunk, the short-run marginal costs (which are probably constant over most ranges of output) of producing the cars are somewhere between one-half and two-thirds of the eventual wholesale price. On top of short-run marginal costs will be a varying margin to cover fixed costs and earn profits. There appears to be a range of $40–$60 of possible last minute flexibility in this margin; thus, the exact level of the final wholesale price depends on last minute assessments of the market, the actual and likely prices of rivals, and, in the mid-1960s, any pressure from Washington to keep prices down.

This is the point at which General Motors' price leadership becomes clearly evident. In the fall of 1956 and again in the fall of 1966, 1967, and 1968, price differences appeared initially in published prices. Ford or Chrysler appeared with its prices first. General Motors followed with prices that, except for 1956, were lower. Within a week, the other two had closed whatever gap existed between their prices and General Motors' for comparable models. (More detail on these incidents will follow later in the chapter.)

Testimony before the Senate Antitrust Subcommittee makes clear the different environments in which General Motors and the other companies set their prices. General Motors appears to be concerned mainly with its profit targets and the overall state of the market. What the competition is doing is taken into account, but, it appears, almost as an afterthought.

MR. (ALBERT) BRADLEY (General Motors Executive Vice President): In the early 1920's, I think I can say that Donaldson Brown, who was then vice president of the finance staff, he and I pretty much worked up, in cooperation with the divisions and the other executives, our pricing procedures upon a fundamental line. We published several articles dealing with that, and we reviewed them from time to time. And the principles we established at that time still govern.

MR. BURNS (Committee Counsel): I would like to ask you some questions with respect to those principles, and the source of my information is the articles by Donaldson Brown, which I believe were published in 1924, entitled "Pricing Policy in Relation to Financial Returns." You are familiar with those articles?

MR BRADLEY: Yes.

MR. BURNS: And do they express in broad terms the pricing policies which have been used by the corporation since that time?

MR. BRADLEY: That is correct.

MR. BURNS: Now, in this article, Mr. Brown makes this statement: "An acceptable theory of pricing must be to gain, over a protracted period of time a margin of profit which represents the highest attainable return, commensurate with capital turnover and the enjoyment of wholesale expansion with adequate regard to the economic consequences of fluctuations in volume. Thus, the profit margin translated into its earliest characteristic rate of return on capital employed is the logical yardstick with which to gage the price of a commodity with regard to collateral circumstances affecting supply and demand." Now, is that the basis for General Motors' pricing policies today?

MR. BRADLEY: That is a long sentence, sir, but it pretty much covers the policy . . .

MR. BURNS: Well, now, what profit margin or attainable returns have you used in pricing policy in recent years?

MR. BRADLEY: Well, actually, in the back of our minds we have a standard, but one of the factors referred to there was competition. So we do have to do our pricing in relation to competition. And the net profit may be below standard or what we hope to have — the economic return attainable may be bigger in one business — one activity or one division than another. But we can always compare with what we expected.

We have not changed our general sights in a period of over 20 years.

MR. BURNS: What have been the general sights?

MR. BRADLEY: Ours is a fairly rapid turnover business, and our operations will yield between 15 and 20 percent on the net capital employed over the years . . .

MR. BURNS: I wondered from that whether the 20 percent figure was the figure which was used by the Finance Committee on making its projections.

MR. BRADLEY: Well, actually, what we have done is establish our prices which have to be established in relation to competition, as I mentioned, and then we see what the indicated return is, and then we compare that with what we have in mind. And, generally, we are close enough to what we have in mind, so it has not been a major problem. It would be a major problem if we could not earn half of that, or something like that.[12]

Compare this with the testimony two years later of Theodore O. Yntema of Ford:

In the case of an automobile manufacturer, the range of discretion in setting prices on a car line is small. We have not found it possible to price much above the most nearly comparable models of competition; to do so would entail heavy loss of sales volume. We have found it impossible to price substantially below competition and still make a reasonable profit.

One of the things that you take into account before you establish a price . . . is what the prices of all your competitive products are.

What is General Motors charging for each item all the way across the board, and these are literally hundreds of items because of all the accessories and so on and hundreds of combinations.

You see what Chrysler is charging. And then what you do is to look also at what has happened to your costs: What happened last year? How much higher are your wage rates? How much are the costs of materials?

As I show later on, in our own particular company we do not have a simple, cost-plus formula . . . We do not have any simple way in which you go just from cost to price.

We have to look at our competitive situation. Ordinarily, what we find is this: We have very little leeway. If we would reduce the price very substantially to meet competition, we would not make a very respectable profit.

SENATOR O'MAHONEY: Do you have a goal of a certain profit on invested capital or net worth?

MR. YNTEMA: We are not in the fortunate position — we would like to be doing better than we are doing . . . No, we do not have a goal (of 15% to 20%). We just like to do better than we are doing.[13]

Or the testimony of L. L. Colbert of Chrysler, following a discussion of the cost elements in pricing:

We estimate, for example, what consumers will be paying for competitive cars. In doing this, we rely heavily on our knowledge of the prevailing prices and specifications of current competitive models, our knowledge of periodic design cost changes in competitive products, and the knowledge we have gained through analysis of economic changes as they relate to our own new model costs, so far as our competitors' design cost changes are concerned, we rely on rough calculations, but we know that price changes in basic commodities and changes in wage rates will have an effect on unit costs of competitive products similar to the effect on our own.

Having estimated the probable competitive prices, we then pay careful attention to differences in value between our new model and those with which it will compete.

Having done all of this, and in light of all competitive information, we establish our final prices.[14]

Thus, among the Big Three, General Motors clearly sees itself as a price leader and the other two see themselves as price followers. As we shall see, their postwar behavior has borne out these roles.

An important consideration in the pricing process is the positioning of one firm's models relative to its rivals. This is clearest among the low price makes, Ford, Chevrolet, and Plymouth, which are actively competing for the same basic market. Chevrolet had been the traditional low price brand, with Ford charging an extra $20–$30 for comparable models (that is, bottom of the line, top of the line) and Plymouth charging $100 or more over the Chevrolet price.[15] In a price cut in the middle of the 1953 model year, Plymouth prices were brought down to $60–$70 over Chevrolet's. By the 1956 model year the margin had been lowered to $40–$45. At the beginning of the 1957 model year, this margin was eliminated, and Plymouth for the first time had models carrying list prices that were lower than for comparable Chevrolets. Also, the 1957 model year marked the first time that Ford was willing to match Chevrolet's prices. This rough equality held until the 1965 model year, when Plymouth raised its full-sized car prices $40–$50 over Chevrolet. At the beginning of the 1967 model year, Ford raised its full-sized car prices $10–$20 above Chevrolet's. Similar spreads have reappeared on comparable compacts and intermediates.[16]

The Independents have traditionally had a bit more freedom in their pricing policies. Often aiming their products at niches in the market where they did not have to confront the Big Three head-on, the Independents have rarely entered into a direct price-jockeying contest with the Big Three. They are definitely aware of the Big Three prices and to a certain extent constrained by them, but the Independents on the whole appear to have worried less about the specific effects of their own prices on those of the Big Three.

Once the wholesale and retail list prices are finally set in September or early October, the list prices will rarely change during the year. Changes in the excise tax or freight rates or, recently, the installation of required safety equipment as of January 1, will bring about changes in list prices, but competitive conditions per se will usually not cause changes in them. In the automobile environment of strongly recognized interdependence among the Big Three and a not very elastic market demand curve, price competition has not been seen as a potent competitive weapon. Price cuts are too easily met and no one gains. Price cutting is seen as a last resort measure. L. L. Colbert described for the Senate Antitrust Subcommittee the troubles that Chrysler had had in selling its 1953 cars:

> We put on intensive advertising campaigns. We did all the talk we could that people needed shorter cars to go into their garages, the parking facilities were crowded.
> We used every argument known to man to impress on the American public they needed a smaller car rather than larger cars . . . Then we reduced the price and announced we were reducing the price to increase volume.
> We had been running those cars from October, 1952, about six months, and finally, as I said, after we tried everything else, we tried price reduction.[17]

Similarly, in the face of falling sales, American Motors' lowering of its Rambler American prices in February 1967 appeared to have been a "we've tried everything else" measure. Parenthetically, in both cases, the other auto producers did not lower their prices to meet the price cuts ($14–$274 for Chrysler, $169–$234 for the Rambler American), apparently not fearing great harm.

Not too surprisingly, the only pricing innovations have come from the Independents, American Motors and Studebaker-Packard, who are less bound to the mutual interdependence network. In June 1960 Studebaker-Packard offered a $100 discount on the purchase of a new car to stockholders of the corporation. In December 1960 American Motors offered all buyers a $25 United States Savings Bond for each 10 percent that the company's sales from December 1960 through March 1961 rose above the company's sales of the same period in the preceding year (with a maximum of $150). Sales, in fact, fell during this period below the previous year's mark (these months marked the low points of the 1960–1961 recession in the United States); American Motors never had to make good on its offer.

Retail Price Flexibility

Despite the persistence of list prices through the model year, actual retail prices have been quite flexible. The usual pattern has been for actual retail prices to reach a peak in October and November[18] and then slide downward for the rest of the model year. By September, new car prices can be anywhere from 3–10 percent below their October–November peak (see Figure 8.1).

There are a number of reasons for this pattern. First, the October and November buyers are a special group within the larger group of habitual new car buyers.[19] They are eager, often for prestige reasons, to have the new model while it is still a comparatively uncommon item, and they are willing to pay a higher price for it. The demand of this group is more inelastic than that of new car buyers as a whole. As the model year progresses, buyers with greater elasticities of demand enter the market, and prices slide in response. Second, since the future trade-in value of a car is largely determined by its model year and only secondarily by its mileage, new car buyers who make their purchases late in the model year lose relatively more in future depreciation than do buyers earlier in the year. This reduces the value of the new car to them. Effectively, their demand curves shift downward as the model year progresses, and, at any given price, their demand curves have become more elastic. Finally, on the supply side, excess inventory late in the model year may induce price cuts, since the inventories will sharply decline in value after the next model appears.

The manufacturers achieve these price reductions by holding sales-incentive contests and giving rebates on the wholesale price. The sales contests are sometimes of the "best salesman gets a trip to Hawaii" variety. This sort of contest should shift a salesman's or dealer's leisure-profit trade-off point and should not affect retail prices. But most of the "contests" are, in fact, schemes to spur dealer sales by offering rebates on the wholesale price. The usual schemes involve a quota arrangement. Thus, for example, in August 1966, General Motors had in effect a rebate program on its full-sized cars (except Cadillac) that offered a rebate of $50 for every car sold from 0–50 percent of the dealer's quota, $75 for every car sold from 51–75 percent of the dealer's quota, and $100 for every car sold above 75 percent of the quota.[20] Other manufacturers have had similar programs in effect at various times since the buyer's market returned to automobiles at the end of the Korean War. These rebate programs have sometimes started as early as December and are usually in full swing by March or April. Rebates of $200 by August are not unheard of. The rebates are often on selective car lines (for example, there will be a different set of rebates in effect on Ford Galaxies than on Ford Fairlanes) and often even on particular, slow-moving models. Also, ever

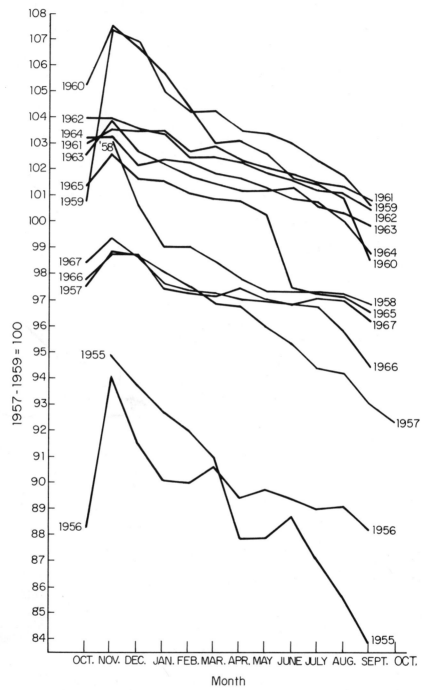

FIGURE 8.1   BLS New Car Price Index, Monthly, by Model Year, 1955–1967

since the dealer relations reforms of the middle 1950's, the manufacturers have been offering their dealers an automatic 5 percent rebate on the list price for any old model still in the dealer's hands when the new model year cars are announced. It is clear from the BLS figures that these cuts in the wholesale price have found their way through to the retail market.

❙In effect, the manufacturers are adjusting their prices to the changing conditions of the market over the model year. To a large extent they are acting as discriminating monopolists, segmenting their market over time and succeeding in this because the inelastic, high price segments are the initial buyers. The frequent presence of excess inventories late in the model year helps to reinforce this price pattern.

It is difficult to determine how much of this price cutting is competitive in origin and how much is simply adjustment to the changed state of the market. The joint profit maximization model can be thought of as flexible enough to allow for the adjustment of prices of some cars when the demand for those cars decreases without setting off a price war. Obviously, the participants in this model would need some fairly clear standards as to when a price cut was in response to a slack market and when it was a threatening, market-encroaching maneuver; but in the case of automobiles, these sorts of implicit rules of the game ought to be possible. These rebate programs have not tended to get out of hand and lead to mushrooming rebates during a model year, nor have the rebates grown appreciably over the years. It seems safe to conclude that most of the wholesale price cutting that occurs through the rebate-incentive schemes can be adequately accounted for by the changes in the joint profit-maximizing set of prices over time.❙

Why is this price cutting accomplished through wholesale price rebates rather than by straight changes in the wholesale and retail list prices? The basic reason seems to be that the companies thereby gain flexibility and escape notoriety. The rebate programs can be granted and withdrawn quickly and quietly as the state of the market changes, without having to attract the attention of the press and of Washington by changes in list prices; price cuts can be achieved on particular models with no explanations to reporters about those models that have been selling poorly, thereby avoiding the impression that there is something wrong with those models and deterring other customers. Also, at the transition from one model year to the next, the increase in list prices, if any, will be less under the current system than if list prices floated down at the end of the model year along with actual prices. The companies simply look better if list prices remain stable or rise only slightly between September and October than if they rise 8–10 percent and the company has to explain how September's prices were really 8 percent below the previous October's prices. The wholesale rebate schemes make life easier for the companies.

The fixed list price also serves as a convenient bench mark from which the companies can judge the size of rebates and mutually keep the size of rebates from getting out of hand. Further, it serves as a convenient point of reference in deciding on the following year's prices.

Finally, the price-labeling law may have eliminated any chance of varying list prices. Dealer inventories would require new labels every time a list price change was announced, which would probably not be worth the bother.

Price Elasticities and Profit Maximization

There is one inconsistent element between the analysis of this chapter and the findings on the structure of demand in Chapter 7 that is worth discussing here. The studies of the demand for new cars have found price elasticities in the area of −1.0. In this chapter we have assumed that the auto companies have acted on prices so as to maximize joint profits. But with positive marginal costs, a price elasticity of −1.0 would indicate that the companies should always try to raise prices higher than their current level. Either the estimates of the price elasticity are wrong or our assumptions about joint profit maximization are incorrect.

The error probably lies on the side of incorrect price elasticities. We can offer two arguments that support this view. First, the elasticities are usually calculated at the mean of the observations for a linear regression.[21] For prices above the mean, the elasticities would be greater (in absolute terms, for example, −2.0 rather than −1.0). Since the trend of prices has been generally upward over time, at any given time the auto companies would be operating in a price range that was above the long-run mean and thus would be faced with elasticities in excess of −1.0.[22] With short-run marginal costs in the range of one-half to two-thirds of the wholesale prices set at the beginning of the model year, price elasticities in the range of -2.0 to -3.0 would seem to be those that the auto companies confront at the margin in which they must deal.

Second, though the overall industry's price elasticity might be unity, the long-run demand curve of the Big Three, not of the industry, might well become fairly elastic at the price levels actually chosen. Threats of new entry and expansion by the Independents in the 1945–1950 period and concern about inroads by imports after 1956 may have constrained the Big Three in their pricing behavior. Effectively, long-run joint profit maximization may have called for refraining from the price increases that short-run considerations might have suggested.

Additional evidence on this point would seem to be offered by General Motors' pricing behavior at the beginning of the 1967, 1968, and 1969 model years, which is discussed in the next section. If the long-run price elasticity really were -1.0, and it was an inability to coordinate prices among the Big Three that was preventing them from charging higher prices, then the higher initial price increases suggested by Ford and Chrysler in these model years should have been gladly accepted by General Motors. Yet, in each instance, General Motors' price increases were smaller than those of its rivals. Perhaps General Motors was concerned about its public image and the possibilities of an antitrust suit and therefore wished to avoid some excess profits. But a more likely explanation would be that General Motors was reacting to a price elasticity that was a good deal in excess of -1.0.

Postwar Record on Prices
in Consumer Markets

A review of the postwar record of pricing behavior can illustrate a number of aspects of the pricing process discussed so far. Figure 8.2 shows the general pattern of new car prices from 1947 through 1967, as reflected in the BLS new car price series in the consumer price index. However, the BLS series has to be used with some care for four reasons. First, until the late 1950's, the series used only the middle of the line, full-sized, four-door sedans of Chevrolet, Ford, and Plymouth. Since that time it has widened its sample to include compacts; Volkswagen; and higher priced models in the Chevrolet, Ford, and Plymouth lines. At the end of 1967 the series sample consisted of two-

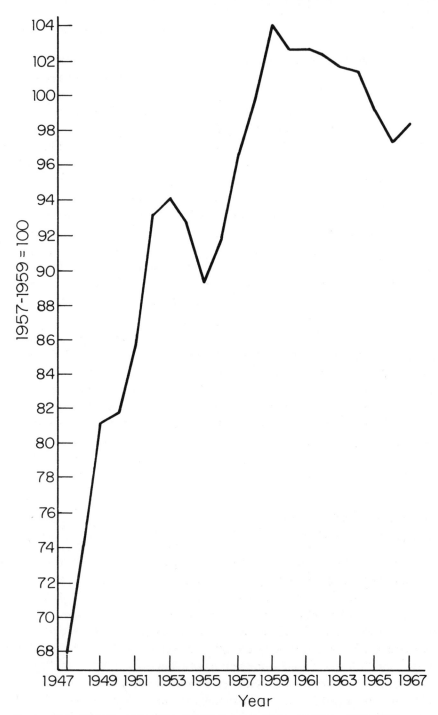

FIGURE 8.2   BLS New Car Price Index, Annual, Calendar Year, 1947–1967

door hardtops in the Chevrolet Impala, Ford Galaxie, and Plymouth Fury lines, a two-door hardtop Chevrolet Chevelle, four-door sedans in the American Motors Rebel and Pontiac Catalina lines, a Ford Mustang, and a Volkswagen. Appropriate weights are given to the models in the index. The new models have been carefully melded into the index, so that there have not been any spurious jumps in the index when new models entered, but it is clear that the index is straddling a different segment of the market than it did in the 1950's.

Second, until July 1954, the BLS relied mostly on list prices, asking dealers what their prices were but relying on the dealer to volunteer any information about the deviations from list prices. Beginning in July 1954, the dealers were specifically asked for the concessions under list price that they were granting. Thus, for the pre-1949 period, the index probably understates actual transaction prices; for 1949 and 1950, it probably overstates prices slightly; for 1951 and 1952, Korean War price controls were in effect and the index probably is reasonably accurate; and for 1953 through June 1954, the index certainly overstates actual prices. For example, between June and July 1954, the index (1957–1959 = 100) dropped from 94.9 to 88.6. This was mostly spurious, reflecting the new method of price collection.

Third, since 1959 the BLS has tried to adjust the index for changes in the quality characteristics of cars.[23] Thus changes in warranty provisions, addition of required safety equipment, and other quality changes have been systematically taken into account in figuring the relative prices of new models. Before that time, very little account was taken of quality changes. The index since 1959, then, has somewhat understated the rise in the prices of new cars per se. And, finally, the index also includes changes in freight rates and local taxes, since it is an index of retail prices. Thus not all of the variations in the index are due to changes in the manufacturer's or dealer's pre-tax prices. Fortunately, the freight rate and local tax variation have been comparatively small.

Despite these qualifications, the BLS index serves as a reasonably good guide to the general movement of prices in the postwar period. Looking at Figure 8.2, we can break the period into six major episodes: (1) the pre-1949 shortage period, (2) the 1949 and 1950 period of reasonable balance, (3) the 1951 and 1952 Korean War price controls, (4) the drop in prices after 1953 and the subsequent price rises through 1958, (5) the leveling and decline of prices between 1959 and

1965, and (6) the resumption of price increases at the beginning of the 1966 model year.

Pre-1949 Shortage Period

From the resumption of car production in 1946 until the end of 1948, a state of excess demand prevailed in the new car market. Government price controls ended in November 1946, and the companies slowly raised their prices through the next two years. Wholesale and retail prices, however, stayed below their market clearing levels. Dealers were able to earn their full profit margins and frequently more. As is seen in Chapter 9, dealers averaged an enviable 30 percent return on net worth during these years. Though the companies put pressure on the dealers to stick to list prices, the dealers were able to offer less than fair value for a trade-in, load a car with worthless extras, or even demand a kickback. A gray market in automobiles developed, in which "new-used" models were being sold for up to $1,000 over the list price.

Why were the companies reluctant to raise prices to market clearing levels? This was not an isolated phenomenon; gray markets existed in many other commodities. While we cannot offer a general explanation for the existence of these markets, we can offer some insights into the particular circumstances facing the auto companies.

Cost-oriented pricing played a role in this process.[24] Prices rose sporadically as companies acknowledged increases in the costs of labor, steel, glass, upholstery, and other materials. There was no pattern of price leadership during this period; each company raised its prices when and as it saw fit. Ford and Plymouth even lowered their prices once during 1947.[25] Only some form of cost-oriented pricing could have led to these moves.

Also, the companies may have been partial victims of money illusion. There were frequent references in the automotive press at the time to how high postwar prices seemed compared to prewar prices. Prewar Fords sold in the $800–$900 range; 1947 Fords sold in the $1200–$1300 list price range. There were fears that in the long run such "high" prices could not prevail.

But the most convincing reason lay in the companies' fears of the adverse reactions that price increases not justified by cost increases, and the consequent rise in profits, would bring. Numerous potential entrants were knocking on the door of the industry at the time; higher reported profits might encourage even more. Public and governmental reaction to such "price gouging" might be severe. A Democratic administration was in the White House, the Alcoa[26] and American Tobacco[27] antitrust cases had recently offered decisions that seemed anti-oligopoly, and market clearing prices and profits might turn the antitrust spotlight on automobiles. The UAW was sure to consider any large profit rise a justification for a large wage increase. When markets turned slack in the future, prices might be flexible downward but wages would be less so, and the companies would be caught in a cost squeeze.

For all of these reasons, it seemed better to keep prices below market clearing levels, to let the less politically vulnerable dealers make healthy profits, and to let the customers wait in queues. Not that the auto companies were without profits themselves; the industry as a whole earned a 10.9 and 13.7 percent return after taxes on total assets in 1947 and 1948, representing 16.2 and 21.0 percent on net worth. (See Chapter 15.)

Despite their reluctance to raise prices all the way to market clearing levels, prices did rise substantially between 1946 and 1948. The initial OPA-set prices for a 1946 Ford V-8, four-door sedan was $885.[28] By early 1949 the price had risen to $1,546. (A six-cylinder model, unpriced by the OPA in 1946, sold for $1,472 in 1949.) Other prices moved accordingly.

1949 and 1950 Reasonable Balance

By late 1948 or early 1949 the gray market in cars had disappeared. Dealers began to sell cars at below list prices, though the limitations of the BLS price series prevent us from determining how great the discounts were. Costs also fell for the first time, as the cost-of-living escalator clause negotiated by General Motors with the UAW in 1948 brought a temporary drop in wages in 1949 when the consumer price index fell. General Motors cut prices about 1 percent in February 1949 ($10 on a Chevrolet, $24–$42 on a Cadillac) and another 1 percent in May, with only part of the industry following. The rest of the industry did not adopt the wage escalator clause until late 1950.

Prices remained relatively stable through the end of 1949 and most of 1950, with some Independents dropping their prices for the 1950 model year, along with Buick and Cadillac; in February, General Motors cut its prices a third time by 1 percent because of escalator-clause wage cuts.

1951, 1952 Korean War Price Controls

The Korean War brought a sharp rise in raw materials prices. The Independents, introducing their 1951 models in late September and October 1950, raised their prices 5 percent. The Big Three, holding off until December for their model changeovers, announced 5 percent increases in the middle of December. General Motors and Ford announced first and Chrysler followed. The federal government instantly declared a price freeze and insisted that automobile prices be rolled back to December 1 levels. The Big Three protested but lost. They felt particularly cheated since the December 1 date favored the Independents.

For the next few years, the companies were under output and price controls. Price increases were allowed in March and September of 1951 and again in January 1952. In November 1951 the Federal excise tax on new cars increased from 7 percent to 10 percent on the wholesale value. The wholesale and retail prices were probably close to market clearing levels. But, because of production controls, the manufacturers were not able to push dealers to sell more cars at under list prices. Thus this represented a nonoptimum situation for the manufacturers. The list price of a Ford six-cylinder, four-door sedan increased from $1,472 in 1950 to $1,675 in early 1953. Other price movements were roughly comparable.

1953–1958 Price Cuts Followed by Sustained Increases

Price controls ended on March 5, 1953. Production controls had been lifted on February 13. The manufacturers immediately raced to increase their output, and Chrysler was the first to feel a sales pinch on its boxy 1953 models. In late March, Chrysler cut its prices an average of $100 on its models. Other manufacturers' list prices remained firm. But actual retail prices dropped as dealers, particularly those selling Independent makes, began giving discounts off list prices.

At the beginning of the 1954 model year, Nash, Hudson, and Packard cut their prices, Studebaker raised its prices, and the Big Three held constant. As the manufacturers' pressure for volume sales increased, larger discounts off list prices appeared, and the manufacturers began holding sales contests and offering rebates to dealers.

In the fall of 1954, list prices rose roughly 3 percent, but 1½ percent of this was offset by a lowering of freight charges to outlying areas. This marked the first of five consecutive years of list price increases at the time of the new model announcements.

In the fall of 1955, list prices rose by an average of 5–5.5 percent.[29] In one instance of particular note, Ford in the last week of September raised its prices $99 on its bottom of the line Customline models. Five weeks later, Chevrolet raised its comparable models only $85, and within two weeks Ford had cut its Customline models by $12 "to meet competition."[30] In February 1956, list prices rose another 2 percent to compensate for a second cut in freight charges.

The following year, list prices rose another 7.2 percent.[31] Once again, a clear instance of price leadership arose. Ford again announced its prices first, raising its prices by 2.9 percent on September 29, 1956, with the lowest price models getting the heaviest increases. On October 15 Chevrolet announced price increases of 6.1 percent. On four low price models, the new Chevrolet price was $5 below Ford; on one it was the same; and on nine it was $25 to $58 higher than Ford. One week later Ford announced new prices, dropping its prices on the four low price models by $5 or $6. On four other models, for which the Chevrolet price was $55 to $58, Ford made standard $45 worth of formerly optional equipment that was also standard on Chevrolet and then raised its prices by $56 to $58. On five models, for which the Chevrolet price was $26 to $43 higher, Ford simply raised its prices by $26 to $33. All but two of Ford's models were now within $2 of Chevrolet's prices.

At Senator Kefauver's Administered Prices Hearing fifteen months later, the Antitrust Subcommittee's members and staff pounced on this instance as evidence of a lack of price competition among the automobile companies. They could not understand why Ford was not willing to stick with its lower prices and challenge General Motors to come down to its level.

Theodore O. Yntema defended Ford's actions before the subcommittee with the following rationale: the Ford pricing committee was divided on the proper price increase. All recognized that costs were up considerably, but the eventually controlling opinion was that Chevrolet, in the third year of a basic model style, might shade prices considerably. Therefore, Ford had to keep its prices down to a 2.9 percent increase. When Chevrolet came out with a 6 percent increase, Ford was able to heave a sigh of relief and go along with it.[32] This is a wholly believable explanation. Implicit, of course, is the belief in a fairly inelastic demand curve for the overall product, not an unreasonable view. And it does bring out clearly the roles of price leader and price follower in the industry.

On December 1, 1956, General Motors raised its list prices another 1½ percent in return for absorbing an advertising charge that it had formerly levied on dealers on a per car basis. The net effect on actual retail prices should have been nil. In the fall of 1957, list prices rose another 3.4 percent. This time the middle-level makes, beginning to experience serious sales resistance, had lower price increases than the low price brands. This would indicate a movement away from cost-oriented pricing. Ford also masked part of its price increases by dropping its former bottom of the line model and adding a new top of the line model (thus the former middle of the line now became the bottom of the line, and so on). In the fall of 1958, list prices rose still another 2.6 percent. Again, the low price makes experienced higher increases than the middle-level makes; Ford and Chevrolet list prices rose 5.5–5.9 percent. Chevrolet and Plymouth followed Ford's example of the previous year and dropped their bottom of the line models, adding new ones at the top.

From the end of 1954 until the spring of 1959, overall list prices rose 25–30 percent. For the low price models, the rise was even steeper. The bottom of the line Ford six-cylinder, four-door sedan that had listed at $1,675 in the spring of 1953, listed at $2,273 in the spring of 1959, a rise of 36 percent. Yet, during this period, the BLS new car series rose only 15–16 percent. Why the difference? Partly, the list price increases were offset by decreases in other costs, like cuts in freight charges or advertising charges. Partly, the BLS series, sampling middle-level models of Chevrolet, Ford, and Plymouth, showed no price change when the bottom of the line model was dropped. But mostly, actual retail prices increasingly fell below list prices as the manufacturers and dealers offered sizeable discounts to the consumer. For example, Jung's shoppers, discussed above, in February 1959 found Chicago dealers willing to sell them $3,000 cars for as much as $600 below list price.

Thus, though there was a sizeable increase in the price of new automobiles between 1954 and 1958 — the 16 percent rise over these five years was almost double the rise in the overall consumer price index for these years — it was not nearly as large as a glance at list prices would indicate. Further, one could argue that, when increases in quality were taken into account, there had in fact been little or no real price change.[33]

1959–1965 Leveling and Decline of Prices

The fall of 1959 marked the introduction of compact models by the Big Three and also the beginning of a period of price stability and even price decline. As measured by the BLS series (which now began to take quality changes into consideration), new car prices fell 2.5 percent between 1959 and 1964. Aided by a drop in the federal excise tax from 10 percent to 7 percent on the wholesale value in May 1965, they fell another 2.2 percent in 1965.

The major pricing goal of the companies with respect to the compacts was to be able to price at least one model in the series at a list price below $2,000. Aided by a cut in the nominal dealer discount from 25 percent to 21 percent, they achieved their goal: the 1960 Chevrolet Corvair two-door sedan listed at $1,984, and the 1960 Ford Falcon two-door sedan listed at $1,912 (the Falcon four-door sedan listed for $1,974). The Plymouth Valiant listed for over $2,000 in 1960, but a price cut on the 1961 models brought the two-door sedan to $1,953.

List prices tended to remain constant over this period, with small shifts up or down tending mostly to balance. The major change in list prices came in the fall of 1961, when General Motors and Ford made heaters a standard item, and in the fall of 1964, when Chrysler and American Motors did the same. Since 97 percent of buyers had previously ordered heaters and since the heaters were made standard on a "delete-option" basis (the customer could specifically order the car without a heater and pay a lower price), it would be hard to argue that this action was masking a price increase.

The introduction of compact and intermediate size models by the higher priced makes tended to muddy the traditional pattern of relative pricing in the industry among the Big Three. Prior to 1960, Chevrolet, Ford, and Plymouth had occupied the lowest price rungs in the industry. Next were Pontiac, Dodge, and Mercury; then Oldsmobile, Buick, and Chrysler; with Cadillac, Lincoln, and Imperial competing for the top of the market. The Independents had sprinkled themselves in between, with American Motors concentrating on the low price field after 1955. The price ranges had usually overlapped, with the more expensive Chevrolets costing more than the cheaper Pontiacs, and so forth; a Chevrolet hard-top fully bedecked with accessories could even cost as much as a Buick.

After 1960, Dodge, Mercury, Pontiac, Oldsmobile, and Buick all offered smaller cars that had lower list prices than even the cheapest full-sized models of the low price three, though these intermediates were still more expensive than the compacts or intermediates produced by the low price three. This pattern still holds today. Though brand-price identifications have remained (Buick-high, Ford-low, and so on), the extent of price overlapping has increased considerably from the pre-1960 pattern.

As of the spring of 1965, the lowest-cost Ford six-cylinder, full-sized four-door sedan carried a list price of $2,415 (it had been $2,273 in the spring of 1959); the addition of the heater and the dropping of the bottom of the line series in 1960 accounted for almost all of this increase. Also in the spring of 1965, the cheapest Big Three compact four-door sedan, the Ford Falcon, listed at $2,082. The Rambler American bottom of the line four-door sedan carried a list price of $2,036.

How can we explain the price stability of the 1959–1965 period as compared to the 1954–1959 price rises? Demand considerations do not appear to be particularly relevant. With the exception of 1955, the earlier period was not one of particularly high demand; profit margins were falling during this period, the opposite of the normal expectation for a demand inflation.

Rather, we must look to cost considerations. First, the earlier period was one of generally rising raw materials prices, particularly 1955 through 1957,[34] whereas in the later period, raw materials prices rose only slightly. The BLS wholesale price index for the category "materials for durable manufacturing" averaged 85.7 in 1954 (1957–1959 = 100). By 1959 the index stood at 101.8 for the year's average, or an increase of 18.7 percent over the five years. By contrast, the index stood at 102.5 in 1964, for an increase of only 0.7 percent over the next five years. And second, wages rose somewhat faster in the first period than in the second. As measured by the BLS series for gross hourly wage rates for the motor vehicles and parts industry, wages went up by 23.2 percent between 1954 and 1959 and only 18.8 percent between 1959 and 1964. In the absence of any significant slackening in the pace of productivity increases during the latter period, a much slower price rise, if any, would have been expected in the latter period.

1966 Resumption of Price Increases

In the fall of 1965 list prices again began to rise. The auto companies decided to install as standard equipment on all models a number of safety items, such as padded instrument panels, back-up lights, and dual-speed windshield wipers. Chrysler led off with list price increases averaging $72.94. General Motors and Ford followed with increases of $58.68 and $67.88. American Motors, sensing sales trouble on the horizon, raised prices only $4. For the industry as a whole, list prices were up roughly $62 or 2.1 percent. After adjustment for added safety items, General Motors' prices were down $6.85, Ford's were down $9.26, Chrysler's were up $28.16, and American Motors were down $65.28.[35] For the industry as a whole, average adjusted list prices were up only $2. The BLS, deciding that there were additional quality increases, credited the companies with a 0.8 percent drop in real prices.

Though its list price increases were significantly above those of General Motors and Ford, Chrysler elected to stick with its new list prices. But as of December 1, considerably earlier than usual, Chrysler instituted a program of wholesale rebates to its dealers that effectively eliminated the price gap between the company and its rivals.

On January 1, 1966, the excise tax fell from 7–6 percent on the wholesale value, but in March Congress raised it back to 7 percent. In the fall of 1966, more safety items (dual braking systems and energy absorbing steering columns) became standard. Ford led off this time with list price increases averaging $107. Chrysler followed with an increase of $92; General Motors raised its prices $56. Within a week Ford and Chrysler cut their prices; Ford achieved this partly by making items like clocks optional rather than standard. After a second cut by Chrysler two weeks later, Chrysler's prices were up only $78.53 and Ford's prices up $82.36. American Motors' prices were up $76.00.

For the industry as a whole, prices were up $68, or 2.2 percent. After adjustment for the inclusion of the safety items, the list price increases of the Big Three were much closer. General Motors' prices were up $21.24, Chrysler's were up $28.02, and Ford's were up $29.48. For the industry as a whole, adjusted prices were up around $25, or 0.8 percent. The BLS figured that the real price increase was only 0.2 percent.

The fall of 1967 brought more safety items and still another round of price increases. Chrysler led off with an average increase of $147.94. Ford and General Motors followed with increases of $115.28 and $119.97. Within a week, Chrysler's prices were rolled back, so that the increase was only $115.82. American Motors' prices were up only $83.39. Overall industry prices were up $116, or 3.6 percent. After allowance for center seat belts and an air pollution control device, prices were up only $55, or 1.6 percent. The BLS figured an increase of 2 percent on the models in its sample.

It is clear from newspaper reports that a good deal of verbal pressure was applied from Washington at this time to discourage "excessive" or "inflationary" price increases. It is difficult to determine whether this pressure had any influence on General Motors' pricing decision. One can only say that, with the prices that it did choose, General Motors managed to earn a healthy 17.6 percent return on net worth in 1967 and a 17.8 percent return in 1968. On January 1, 1968, list prices rose another $23 to cover the cost of required shoulder harnesses. It is claimed that only governmental pressure prevented another $39 price rise at that time.[36]

In the fall of 1968, still one more round of price increases occurred. Chrysler again led off, with an increase of $89. General Motors followed with increases averaging $52, and Ford raised its prices $50. Three days after the General Motors' announcement, Chrysler reduced its prices, so that the increase came to only $55. Overall industry prices were up $52, or 1.6 percent (the addition of compulsory head restraints on January 1, 1969 added another $17–$26 to list prices). The BLS calculated a 1.2 percent price increase for its sample, as a shortening of warranty provisions offset other quality increases. Again, verbal pressure from Washington was applied in hopes of discouraging inflationary price increases; again, it is difficult to determine what influence this had on pricing decisions.[37]

The price leadership pattern of these years was unmistakable. Despite earlier price announcements by Chrysler or Ford, it was General Motors' prices that stuck, and the others rolled back their prices to General Motors' levels.

Between the spring of 1965 and the fall of 1968, list prices rose by over 10 percent. The bottom of the line, full sized Ford four-door sedan that listed at $2,415 in the spring of 1965 was up to $2,674 by October 1968. The cheapest Big Three compact, a Falcon four-door sedan, listed at $2,316 in that month. The cheapest Rambler four-door sedan carried a list price of $2,076 in October 1968, only slightly above its spring 1965 price because of a sharp slash ($169–$234) in Rambler American list prices in February 1967.

After adjustment for equipment and quality changes, real car prices were up about 5 percent for the 1965–1968 period. Again, we can look to raw materials prices and wage rates. The "materials for durable manufacturing" wholesale price index stood at 110.9 in August 1968, an increase of 8.2 percent over its 1964 level. Hourly wages in the motor vehicles and parts industry had risen 19.6 percent between the 1964 average and August 1968, a larger increase in these three and one-half years than the preceding five. A generally inflationary environment had again enveloped the American economy; the auto companies, confronted by higher costs but also by consumers with higher money incomes, raised their prices in tune with the times.

Fleet Sales Pricing

In addition to pricing the cars that go to private consumers, the auto companies have also had to determine the prices that apply to fleet customers: businesses, rental agencies, and governments. The companies are faced by knowledgeable, price-conscious purchasers, capable of playing one seller off against another. In effect, the elasticity of demand of fleet purchasers facing an individual seller is much higher than that of regular consumers. The fleet purchasers are often sizeable and present a tempting package to a company for whom short-run marginal costs are considerably below the revenue to be gained from such sales. Also, fleet sales, particularly to rental firms, provide a demonstration opportunity to potential customers who may buy the company's cars in the future because they like their rental car.

On the one hand, such sales are comparatively few, often publicized, and easily identified. The mutual interdependence pressure to maintain a joint monopoly price would appear to be great in this case. On the other hand, the gains to be had from such block sales are high, and the temptation to "chisel" on prices should be great. A priori, it would be difficult to predict whether fleet prices would be appreciably lower than the joint monopoly price for that segment of the market would warrant. We should expect fleet prices to be lower than consumer prices in any event because of the economies in administrative and selling expenses in selling to fleet purchasers. We should also expect fleet sales to be segmented from normal consumer sales, to prevent "dilution" of the high price sales of the latter by the former. This has been achieved by arbitrarily classifying block sales of ten or more units as fleet sales. Even the most extended of families can rarely muster a demand for ten cars at one time.

The pattern on pricing to fleets has been mixed. The federal government, by law, purchases all of its passenger cars for not more than $1,500 per car, well under the wholesale price for many of the full-sized sedans that the government purchases (even allowing for the fact that the 7 percent excise tax is not levied on such purchases). Ford gives a $125 rebate to the national rental agencies who buy their cars through the dealers, presumably at a price very close to the wholesale price.[38] The other manufacturers have similar arrangements. Robinson-Patman Act considerations would appear to require similar prices for all rental and lease customers.[39] By contrast, sales to state and local governments have been transacted at prices as low as $400–$800 below dealer cost.[40]

The larger rebates (lower prices) to the state and local governments, as compared to the rental agencies, fit fairly well with our a priori notions of the elasticity of demand of the two markets. Governments are under no competitive compulsion constantly to buy new cars; they always have the option of making their old cars last a bit longer. The rental firms, by contrast, compete largely on the basis of having shiny new cars at their customers' disposal. Year-old cars are an inferior substitute in this respect. Also, the demand for rental cars, emanating mostly from business accounts, is relatively price inelastic. Thus we should expect rental firms' demand to be less elastic with respect to price than that of state and local governments, and we would expect discriminating oligopolists to charge a higher price to the former.

There have been sporadic attempts by the manufacturers to close ranks and end the rebates on fleet sales. In June 1948, General Motors announced an end to a 3 percent rebate plan on fleet sales of twenty or more vehicles; Ford followed closely behind.[41] By the middle 1950's, this line was being frequently breached on sales to state and local governments, with rebates of up to $500. In June 1958 General Motors announced an end to direct bids or financial assistance to dealers on bids to state and local governments.[42] The other companies followed, but by the early 1960's Chrysler had resumed the practice of rebates, Ford followed, and reluctantly General Motors resumed them in July 1965. General Motors' share of such car sales had fallen from 37.2 percent in 1958 to 13.5 percent in 1964.[43] Ford, in February 1967, suspended such rebates in an apparent move to see if the rest of the industry would follow but quickly resumed them in March when no one followed suit.[44] On commerical fleet sales, Chrysler had been offering rebates of $125 as early as January 1961,[45] and Ford entered the fray wholeheartedly at the beginning of the 1963 model year. General Motors again held back. After watching its share of this market decline from 61 percent in 1963 to 41 percent in 1966, General Motors finally offered its dealers a fleet assistance program at the beginning of the 1967 model year.[46]

On fleet sales, then, the combination of easy identifiability of sales, tending to keep prices high, and the large benefits to such sales, tending to encourage chiseling, have led to a mixed picture of different prices to different markets. Sporadic attempts to end rebates on fleet sales altogether have usually failed. There has been no clear pattern of price leadership in these markets.

9

Dealers and
Dealer Systems

Almost all new cars sold to the public are sold through independently owned, franchised dealerships. Of all the retailing structures possible, the automobile manufacturers have settled on the franchised dealership, with direct wholesale shipments from the manufacturer to the dealer, as the preferred form. As we shall demonstrate, the franchised dealership system carries significant advantages for the manufacturers.[1]

The Origin of the Dealer System

The independent dealer as a seller of automobiles began in the earliest days of automobile manufacturing. Auto makers, short of capital, were eager to have someone else invest in retailing facilities and absorb the inventory costs of the finished vehicles. Dealers in many cases were even willing to pay for cars in advance of delivery. As much from necessity as from inclination, the independent dealer system was born.

As the industry matured, other forms of retailing, particularly factory-owned (branch) outlets, were tried. But, according to Allan Nevins

Time proved that for most companies branch marketing was a poor policy. Since branches directly represented a company's dignity, they tended to become ornate establishments, reaching an early climax in the Packard palaces erected in New York and Philadelphia at a reputed cost of $900,000 and $500,000 respectively. Salaried men were less enterprising than agents.

136

Branch managers, moreover, often gave service and repairs too freely, charging them to the company.[2]

A proper system of branch manager incentives for the successful running of a factory outlet system should have been possible. But the factory outlet system had three disadvantages: it required management personnel; it required money; and it offered no dilution of the risks of the automobile business. A private dealership system, by contrast, allowed someone else (the dealers) to provide the management and the money, and it brought in a host of second parties to share the risks of the business. These factors, particularly the last, lay behind the survival of the dealership system as the dominant form of automobile retailing. There are today a number of factory-owned outlets in Manhattan, because astronomical land prices have made it impossible for private dealers to sell cars at competitive prices. The companies, nevertheless, consider it important to have an outlet in Manhattan, for prestige purposes and as a showcase, and are willing to absorb the losses. Some sales to government units and to large rental agencies are transacted by the companies directly. But almost all of the rest of the cars are sold to the public through the private dealer system.

The franchise element has added a measure of control and supervision to the dealer system. Entry into new car retailing is not open. Only the holder of a make's franchise has the privilege of buying that make's cars at wholesale from the factory, and only a franchise holder can use that make's name on his dealership (for example, "West Side Chevrolet Co."). The franchises are granted free by the companies, but the companies limit the number given out. In return for the franchise, the dealer is expected to submit to company supervision. Facilities are to be constructed and maintained to the manufacturer's satisfaction; target levels of cars are expected to be sold. Until World War II, the manufacturers were able to specify exclusive dealing (that is, the manufacturers' make only) arrangements in the franchise.

The Forcing Model

Once one has decided on independent dealers, why choose a franchise system? Why limit the number of franchises that are granted?

In the absence of market imperfections at the retail level (sloped demand curves facing retailers) there would never be any rational reason to limit the number of dealers. Free entry into retailing would drive retailers' profits down to minimum, competitive levels; the items would be sold with a minimum retail margin added to the wholesale price. For a given wholesale price, the item would sell at the lowest possible price, and the manufacturer would achieve the largest number of retail sales consistent with that wholesale price. It would always be in the manufacturers' interest to open entry and drive down his retailers' margins. Hence we must look to retailing market imperfections as the source of the limited franchise system.

Pashigian[3] has offered two cases in which a manufacturer would wish to limit the number of dealers. The first involves a small number of oligopolist dealers behaving according to a collusive market-sharing pattern. The second involves a Chamberlin monopolistic competition model. The derivations are lengthy and do not warrant repeating here.

Unfortunately, both cases have very limited application. In the retailer oligopoly case, Pashigian's condition for the manufacturer limiting the number of retailers is

$$\frac{d^2C(q)}{dq^2} = 0$$

where C is the retailers long-run total distribution cost schedule (excluding the wholesale cost of the product) and q is the number of units sold by the retailer. The manufacturer will not wish to add new retailers if the current ones are operating at the bottom of their *marginal* cost curves. (And he will want to reduce their number if they are operating on the falling part of their marginal cost curves.) Though, a priori, one can make no predictions about where the marginal revenue and marginal cost curves will intersect, standard textbook theory leads one to expect that most firms will be operating along the rising portions of their *marginal* cost curves. Though one can construct cases in which marginal revenue curves cut downward sloping marginal cost curves from above, this does not appear to be very likely.

Similarly, for the monopolistic competition case, Pashigian's condition is

$$-2a < \frac{d^2C(q)}{dq^2} < -(2a - b)$$

where a is the slope of the demand curve facing the individual retailer and b is the effect on one retailer's price of the change in quantity by another retailer. The left-hand inequality is the standard second-order condition for a maximum; the right-hand inequality must hold if the manufacturer is to find it profitable to limit the number of retailers. But, as Henderson and Quandt, from whose analysis Pashigian has taken his formulation and nomenclature, point out, b is "numerically small" by assumption in the monopolistic competition model.[4] Accordingly, we are again in the unlikely case in which the retailer would be operating along the falling part of his marginal cost curve.

Consequently, if we are going to explain franchise limiting, we must look to a model of retail market imperfections plus "forcing," the requirement that the retailer sell a specified number of units as a condition of holding his franchise.[5] The monopolistic competition framework is the easiest one in which one can see the effects of this forcing model. In Figure 9.1, point A shows the traditional Chamberlin tangency solution. At a given wholesale price, enough retail firms will enter until the individual retailer's demand curve, D_1, is tangent to his average cost curve. He sells Q_1 units at a final retail price of P_1.

Suppose the manufacturer reduces the number of retailers so that each retailer now faces a larger demand curve, Q_2. In the absence of any forcing, the retailer will wish to charge price P_2. But if the manufacturer can simultaneously require that Q_3 units be sold by the retailer, the retailer will have to sell them at a price P_3. With the wholesale price assumed to be unchanged, the retail margin has now been cut to its smallest possible size, the final retail price is as low as it can be for that wholesale price, and the manufacturer will sell the maximum number of units consistent with that wholesale price. In effect, the combination of limiting and forcing provides a means of achieving the economies of scale in the retailing sector that the free entry tangency solution would otherwise eliminate.

This forcing model is easily applied to the retailer oligopoly situation. Again, rather than let entry create a low volume, high markup equilibrium, the manufacturer limits entry and forces the remaining retailers to sell at the bottom of their average cost curves.

The ability to force is especially valuable if the manufacturer would like to maintain a smooth flow of production. Fluctuations in final demand are met by changes in retailer inventories, rather than by frequent changes in the manufacturer's rate of production. The manu-

facturer could be doing the same inventorying himself; the manufacturer's net wholesale receipts should be the same, regardless of whether
it is he or his retailer who is paying the interest on the inventories.
Still, because of forcing, it is the retailer who has to absorb the fluc-

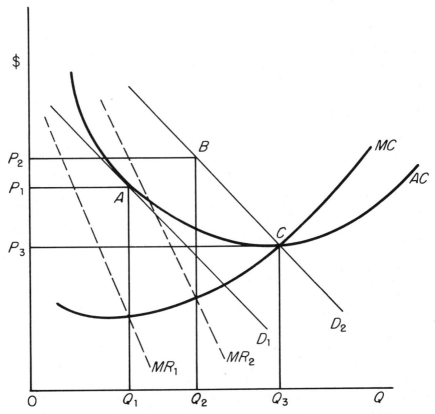

FIGURE 9.1   Individual Dealer: Monopolistic Competition and Forcing Demand
Models

tuations and uncertainties of the changing levels of inventories. By
forcing the retailer to pay the interest on the inventories, the manufacturer has created a greater incentive for the retailer to sell his cars
quickly.[6]

This type of forcing arrangement immediately sets up a conflict of
interest between the manufacturer and the retailer. The retailer, usually forgetting that it is only by the grace of the manufacturer that
he faces demand curve D_2, constantly sees more units forced upon him

than he would voluntarily wish to sell. The retailer would like to take advantage of his monopoly position and sell only Q_2 units. The manufacturer is constantly forcing Q_3 units on him. Small wonder that the dealer complains.

The manufacturer's goals in the model are not necessarily one-dimensional. True, in a riskless world, he would simply want to push his retailers to the bottom of their cost curves and nothing more. But in a world of sales fluctuation and possible dealer failures and one in which consumer loyalties are partly to a dealer rather than to a make, the preservation of a stable body of dealers may become an important goal. In this respect, the manufacturer faces essentially three choices: (1) He can drive his retailers to the bottom of their cost curves, let the fluctuations and risks come as they may, and accept the dealer turnover that accompanies those fluctuations. The fluctuations will, of course, cause retailers to demand a risk premium in addition to their normal return on capital. (2) He can offer to buffer his retailers from the fluctuations, gaining a stable dealer body and a lower risk premium to be added to retail margins, but he loses the risk-sharing properties that make an independent retailer system attractive. (3) He can offer an extra incentive to his retailers over the risk premium, exposing them to the normal fluctuations but expecting the dealer body to remain stable because of the extra premium he has offered them. Which of these possibilities the manufacturer will choose will depend, of course, on his perception of the strength of customer-dealer loyalties and on his attitudes toward risk.

Further, if consumer purchases are partly based on geographical proximity to a dealer regardless of make, there will be a great temptation for the manufacturer to expand his dealer body to new geographical locations, even though these new dealers partly take sales from the established dealers of the same make. The manufacturer faces a trade-off between having a larger number of dealers who may attract new customers but who also will sell fewer cars per dealer and thereby incur higher distribution costs per unit, and having a smaller number of dealers each selling at the bottom of his cost curve. Since the added dealers will be mostly taking sales from other makes and should have little or no effect on expanding the overall market for the product, a group of oligopolist manufacturers, recognizing their mutual interdependence, should refrain from expanding their dealer bodies as far as if they did not recognize this interdependence. Each oligopolist would reason that an extra dealer would only be met by the establishment of a rival's dealer; total sales would not expand; and the extra dealer would only dilute the sales of existing dealers of the same make. It would be better to concentrate on lowering the margins of existing dealers, which could only be met by equal actions or lower wholesale prices by one's rivals and which, at least, has the effect of expanding the overall demand for the product. Still, there is always the temptation to try to establish a new dealership and build up a local reputation and quasi-monopoly before one's rival has a chance to do the same. Also, we should expect to see the smaller manufacturers, who may be less aware of interdependent effects or less concerned about retaliation by the larger manufacturers and who generally consider themselves to be at a geographical distribution disadvantage, showing a greater tendency to expand their dealer bodies and consequently to maintain smaller sales per dealer.

The customer-dealer loyalty also gives the dealer some bargaining power vis-à-vis the manufacturer, and the dealer may be able to resist some of the forcing pressure. The manufacturer's only final recourse against a recalcitrant dealer is to cancel his franchise. If the dealer has a desirable location and can easily obtain a rival's franchise, the manufacturer may cause more harm to himself in lost sales than he would to the dealer, and the threat to cancel would not be effective. Even a threat to create more competing dealers in the area may not be effective, since the dealer can always counter with the threat to change his franchise. The stronger is this customer-dealer loyalty, the less successful will the manufacturer be in his forcing efforts.

How is the wholesale price set in this model? We can think of two extreme cases.[7] The first assumes that the dealers have the upper hand in the bargaining process. In Figure 9.2, D_D is the total final demand curve for the manufacturer's product that faces the group of dealers. If we assume that the dealers try to maximize their joint monopoly profits, they will perceive a marginal revenue curve, MR_D. If we subtract the dealer's marginal distribution cost per unit from the MR_D curve, we are left with the wholesale price they are willing to pay to sell a given quantity of goods. This then is the derived demand curve, D_M, that faces the manufacturer. This demand curve, in turn, has a marginal revenue curve, MR_M, and it is the intersection of the MR_M with the manufacturer's marginal cost curve, MC_M, that determines the quantity he will want to sell. In the diagram, Q_1 is that quantity, yielding a wholesale price P_W and a retail price P_R. The total retail markup is AC, of which BC is the marginal distribution cost and AB covers overhead and profit.

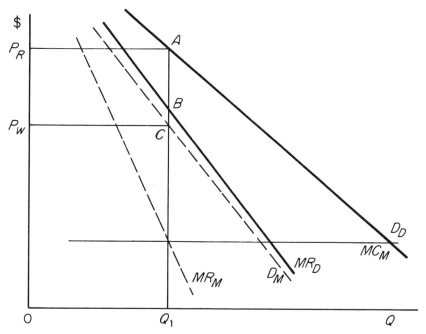

FIGURE 9.2   Total Market Demand, Dealers Powerful Relative to Manufacturers

The second extreme case is one in which the manufacturer has complete dominance over his dealers and can specify the wholesale price and the quantity that the dealers shall sell. In Figure 9.3, D_D is again the total final demand curve for the product facing the dealers. But now the manufacturer, by specifying the wholesale price and quantity, can determine the level of dealer markups. The manufacturer figures the required markup necessary at each volume to cover dealer costs and give them an adequate return on their capital. He subtracts that margin from the retail price, and he is left with the wholesale price he can charge. This is the demand curve that he faces, D_M; the intersection of its marginal revenue curve, MR_M, with the MC_M again determines the desired quantity. In this figure, that quantity is Q_2, the wholesale price is P'_W, and the retail price is P'_R, and the

retail markup is *EF*. In this latter case, by being able to force away
the dealers' monopoly profits, the manufacturer is able to gain larger
profits for himself. But he also sells more units and at a lower retail
price, so that retail customers have also benefited.

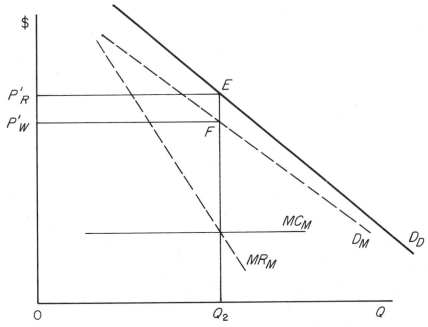

FIGURE 9.3   Total Market Demand, Manufacturers Capable of Forcing Cars on
Dealers

Oligopoly pricing uncertainties will add an element of indeter-
minateness to this wholesale pricing process but only insofar as the
position of the total final demand curve for the individual manufacturer's product, D_D, becomes less certain in an oligopoly situation.
In actual practice, the bargaining positions of the companies will be
somewhat between the two cases, and we should expect prices and
quantities also to be somewhere in the middle.

Empirical Support for the Forcing Model

Economies of Scale

One must show that there are significant economies of scale in
automobile retailing; that is, the automobile retailers average cost

curve is U-shaped or at least L-shaped, and the lowest part of the curve occurs at a significant volume.

A priori, it would seem reasonable to expect economies of scale in automobile retailing. Automobiles are not sold entirely out of a catalogue. A dealer needs to have a number of models available for customers to inspect and test drive. Though the customer may eventually have to order a car out of a "catalogue" to get the exact combination of color and accessories that he wants, he still wants a firsthand look at and a test drive of the type of car he eventually will buy. As the number of models has proliferated, the expected level of dealer inventories has risen. A thirty-day supply used to be considered normal. This has now increased to between a forty- and fifty-day supply.

The dealer requires a show room to display his cars and an area in which to store his inventories. If he decides to retail his used car trade-ins rather than wholesale them, he needs an area to store and display those inventories. Customers have come to expect dealers to provide repair and service facilities. Most of these activities are heavily land- and building-intensive, and a higher level of sales means that these expensive fixed costs can be spread over a larger number of units. Also, the high volume dealer ought to be able to experience some inventory-holding economies as compared to a low volume dealer.

Pashigian has offered some estimates of the economies of scale in automobile retailing.[8] Based on turnover rates, dealer questionnaires, and a study of confidential cost data, he estimated that the lowest unit distribution costs for metropolitan dealerships were reached at a volume of 600–800 units a year and flattened out after that point. Table 9-1 presents his estimates. In nonmetropolitan areas, with lower land costs, the minimum efficient scale would probably be lower, but the same kind of relationship would probably hold.

Imperfect Retail Markets

There is plenty of evidence to suggest the possibility of sloped demand curves for dealers. An unpublished Lincoln-Mercury study of 800 Chicago car buyers in 1955 and 1956 revealed that 65 percent of the buyers purchased their car from the dealer of that make who was located closest to their homes. Over one-third of the 800 visited only the dealer of that make closest to their home. Less than 20 percent visited dealerships further than five miles away.[9] A more recent

Table 9.1   **Estimated per Unit Distribution Cost**

Annual volume of dealership, units sold	Per unit distribution cost index	
	Low estimate	High estimate
100	130	140
200	125	135
300	115	130
400	110	125
500	105	115
600	100	110
700	100	105
800	100	100
900	100	100
1,000	100	100
1,100	100	100
1,200	100	100

Source: Bedros Peter Pashigian, *The Distribution of Automobiles, An Economic Analysis of the Franchise System* (Englewood Cliffs, N.J., 1961), p. 223.

study put the purchase from the closest dealer percentage at around 55 percent on a national basis and around 45 percent for metropolitan areas, still a very respectable percentage (see Table 9.2). Other studies have shown that over 40 percent of buyers shop from only one dealer before buying their car.[10] Pashigian, using data for 1957, has demon-

Table 9.2   **Location of Dealer Relative to Purchaser of Car, Sample 1960–1961** (percent)

	Dealer was dealer of that make closest to home	Dealer was not dealer of that make closest to home	Do not know
Metropolitan area			
500,000 population or more	42.4	41.1	16.5
Below 500,000 population	45.9	47.8	6.3
Suburbs	46.4	44.7	8.9
Outside metropolitan area, nonfarm	75.5	18.1	6.4
All farm area	62.9	25.7	11.4
Total	53.6	36.5	9.9

Source: Look Magazine, *National Automobile and Tire Survey, 1961.*

strated the probable existence of dealer-customer ties for certain makes.[11]

Customer-Dealer Loyalty

It is much more difficult to find evidence of customer-dealer loyalty irrespective of make. The difficulty with figures cited in the previous paragraph is that they do not tell us whether the consumer would have bought a car of the same make or of a different make if the particular dealer he bought from had not been there or had switched to selling a different make. Respondents in the *Look* Magazine National Automobile and Tire Surveys have mentioned dealership characteristics as influencing their choice of cars; 26.1 percent of the respondents in the 1965 survey mentioned "reliable dealer" as one of the factors influencing their choice of cars.[12] This is, however, an uncertain basis on which the case for customer-dealer loyalty irrespective of make must rest.

But the companies do appear to believe in it, as is evident from the following testimony by Paul F. Lorenz of Ford before the Senate Antitrust Subcommittee:

The termination or transfer of a franchise generally is costly to Ford. While the new franchisee is starting up his business and the former franchisee is liquidating his affairs, a large number of sales is [sic] irretrievably lost, vehicle owners are often without a convenient service home, orders are not filled properly, and costly misunderstandings with customers can arise. In short, the franchisor's goodwill, sales, and profits can suffer from a change in franchisees and it sometimes takes a long time to recoup these losses.[13]

Limiting Entry

It is clear that the auto companies have, in fact, limited the number of retailers selling their products. William T. Gossett of Ford stated this point bluntly in testimony before the House Antitrust Subcommittee:

The right to be an authorized dealer is valuable because the dealership is the only place in most communities where the consumer can buy the manufacturer's product and obtain authorized service. Although there are often a number of authorized dealerships of a given make of vehicle in the larger metropolitan areas, these dealerships, nevertheless, are limited in number compared to the number there would be if the manufacturer chose to sell to all who elected to handle its products.[14]

In 1955, a time of rising dealer dissatisfaction with their status vis-à-vis the manufacturers, a General Motors official told the Senate Antitrust Subcommittee that General Motors then had 4,976 applications for franchises.[15] Ford and General Motors have never had to advertise directly to attract dealers, though they do engage in a good deal of institutional "how fortunate are our dealers" type of advertising. Chrysler and the Independents have had a more difficult time in attracting dealers and have placed ads in the automotive press inviting prospective dealers to join the various winning teams. Still, any new dealers so attracted would not be given a free choice of location but would be guided to locations where the manufacturers felt their representation was the weakest. Finally, all the auto companies specify that franchise holders cannot open a branch location without the consent of the company. This effectively limits entry by retailers trying to encroach on one another's territory.

Table 9.3 shows the trend of new car sales per dealership from 1949 through 1967. The two Independents have had consistently lower sales per dealership than the industry average. They have favored a policy of wider geographical dispersion, as our model predicted for Independents, over one of building up the volume of their existing dealers. But the Big Three also appear to have favored geographical dispersion over volume per dealer. The industry per dealer averages, and even the highest averages, those of General Motors and Ford dealers, have been far under Pashigian's minimum efficient scale estimates. Although rural and small town dealers should have lower minimum efficient scales, the General Motors average still means that there must be a large number of dealers operating at below efficient volume. Oligopolistic interdependence has not been strong enough in this case to limit dealer bodies to a size consistent with the lowest distribution costs.

But, as the market has grown, the companies have refrained from expanding the number of dealers and have let the number of cars sold per dealership rise.[16] In fact, the companies have allowed the number of dealerships to decline, as is shown by Table 9.4. The fall in the total number of dealerships has been partly due to the elimination

Table 9.3   New Car Sales per Dealership

	U.S. industry average[a]	American Motors	Studebaker	Chrysler	Ford	General Motors
1949	101	n.a.	n.a.	n.a.	n.a.	n.a.
1950	134					
1951	108					
1952	90					
1953	131					
1954	133					
1955	175	49	47	129	225	215
1956	148	47	44	104	189	183
1957	154	56	30	130	194	169
1958	118	75	21	83	133	141
1959	158	127	53	97	199	169
1960	184	142	44	141	214	197
1961	172	125	34	104	208	193
1962	212	139	37	119	232	261
1963	233	139	33	163	243	283
1964	246	125	15	186	276	294
1965	299	115	8	213	318	351
1966	290	104		214	321	331
1967	270	99		212	259	322

Source: *Automotive News Almanac*, various years.

[a] 1949–1954 figures were obtained by dividing annual registrations by the average number of car dealers for that year, this average obtained by averaging the dealer figures for Jan. 1 of that year and the following year.

Table 9.4   Net Dealers[a] Handling United States Makes of Cars (as of January 1)

Year	Total[b]	American Motors	Studebaker	Chrysler	Ford	General Motors
1949	49,173	n.a.	n.a.	n.a.	n.a.	n.a.
1955	40,374[c]	2,791	3,146[d]	9,350[d]	8,803[d]	16,927[d]
1961	32,164	2,974	2,258	6,307	8,103	13,960
1968	27,774	2,347		6,282	7,065	12,770

Source: *Automotive News Almanac*, 1962, p. 95; 1968, pp. 75–76.

[a] Excludes multiple franchises; i.e., a dealer holding a Chevrolet and a Pontiac franchise would be counted as only one General Motors dealer.

[b] Total is less than the sum of the company dealers because of intercorporate dualing.

[c] Includes approximately 2,400 Kaiser dealers.

[d] Estimated from Table 9.3 and 1955 registration figures.

of the Independents but also due to a falling number of Big Three dealerships. One suspects that generally rising real estate costs have caused the minimum efficient scale of dealerships to rise and that the auto companies have been responsive to this in making their dispersion versus dealer volume decisions.

Forcing

The auto companies have never denied their use of forcing practices, though they prefer to talk of it in terms of sales quotas and performance targets for their dealers. Dealer performance, as judged by volume standards set by the manufacturers, has always been an important aspect of retaining a franchise. Howard E. Crawford of General Motors stated the point bluntly before the Senate Antitrust Subcommittee: "in return for the privilege and benefits a dealer receives under his GM dealer selling agreement, the dealer agrees to operate in accordance with certain requirements . . . He agrees to provide satisfactory sales performance in his area of sales responsibility. Evaluation of a dealer's sales performance is based on a formula spelled out in the agreement." [17]

W. T. Gossett of Ford euphemistically stated the manufacturer's case for forcing while testifying before the House Antitrust Subcommittee against a bill that might weaken the manufacturers' power to force:

THE CHAIRMAN: You say you will lose volume. Why will you lose volume?

MR. GOSSETT: We will lose volume, Mr. Chairman, because without the influence of the manufacturer, *the normal persuasive sales influence* of a manufacturer on the dealers, the dealers will not sell the same volume of cars that they now sell. [18]

Almost every law suit brought by dealers over wrongful cancellation of their franchises has involved manufacturer-set performance standards that the dealer has failed to meet. In two recent suits, *Kotula v. Ford Motor Company*[19] and *American Motor Sales Corporation v. L. G. Semke*,[20] explicit forcing of unwanted cars was involved. The companies would not ship some cars until other, unwanted, cars were also ordered.

Many of the companies used to distribute their cars through wholesale distributors who, in turn, dealt with the dealers. These were phased out as the companies realized that better market information and more effective pressure would be applied by direct contact with their dealers.

Though a visitor to an assembly plant will be reassured by his guide that every car being built has already been ordered by a dealer — most franchise agreements provide that cars cannot be shipped without an order — it is clear that company pressure and sales performance goals lie behind those orders.

Exclusive Dealing

Each company prefers its dealers to handle only its make of cars. Before the war, exclusive dealing clauses in automobile franchises were common, with company approval required before a dealer could handle another company's cars; similar provisions held on parts. Even if exclusive dealing were not expressly stated in the franchise, provisions such as General Motors' refusal to offer reparation in case of loss on a lease if a dealer were terminated and had been handling another make, encouraged exclusive dealing.

Though a private parts manufacturer had failed in 1936 to convince the courts to nullify General Motors' exclusive dealing in replacement parts clauses,[21] the Federal Trade Commission achieved that goal in 1941.[22] Most other manufacturers dropped their exclusive dealing clauses for cars and parts in 1949, after the *Standard Stations* case appeared to rule out most exclusive dealing provisions.[23] Still, the manufacturers have made clear their preference for exclusive dealing in cars and parts.[24]

A dealer handling only one make is in a weaker bargaining position vis-à-vis his manufacturer; the latter's forcing capabilities ought to be greater if the dealer has no other source of support to which he can immediately appeal. Also, the companies have favored this because, they claim, the dealers tend to push only the better selling of two makes and neglect the other. Pashigian rejects this argument on the grounds that it violates profit maximization conditions; if a marginal car is worth selling, it is worth selling whether the dealerhsip is exclusive or dualed. He is implicitly assuming his L-shaped cost curves for dealerships.[25] Still, this alleged dealer behavior may be credible if one assumes that there is some trade-off between dealer profits and dealer effort (or leisure) and that a dealer's preference functions may include both elements.[26]

Beside strengthening the companies' supervision and control over retailing, exclusive dealing encourages product differentiation and discourages price competition among makes. Consumers can look at only one company's cars at a time, thus hearing the virtues of only that make extolled. Comparison shopping becomes that much more difficult. Further, the preference for exclusive dealing by the Big Three may have served in the past to have helped weaken the smaller Independents and to have raised the barriers to entry, since the best dealers have probably gravitated toward the larger, better established, less risky companies. The frequent advertisements in the automotive press by Independents looking for dealers were certainly one indication of this; the frequently mentioned difficulty that Kaiser-Frazer had in attracting good dealers was another. Today, the major effect of exclusive dealing preferences is probably to limit the retailing opportunities open to foreign manufacturers considering retail operations in the United States.

Rates of Return

Last, we can look at the evidence on the rates of return earned by auto dealers to see to what extent the auto companies have been able to force away the potential monopoly profits of their dealers and thus achieve efficient retail distribution. If the auto companies have been completely successful, we should expect to see capital invested in the auto industry earning only "normal" returns, that is, earning returns close to the opportunity cost of investable funds. The long-term rate of interest is usually used as a standard for the opportunity cost of capital. We shall be somewhat less rigorous, using the average rate of return earned in all of retailing as a standard. These retailing figures probably contain some monopoly profits, but in a sense they represent the true opportunity cost for anyone interested in investing his capital in some aspect of retailing. It would be unrealistic for the auto companies to expect their dealers, other things being equal, to accept less than the average of what other retailers were earning.

Table 9.5 offers the relevant rates of return on net worth.[27] Following Pashigian's suggestions, we have also included the rate of return calculated to include net profits plus officers' compensation. The justification for this is that closely held corporations may tend to over-

Table 9.5 Rates of Return of Net Worth for Corporate Automobile Dealers and All Corporate Retailers

Year	Profits after taxes divided by net worth		Profits after taxes plus officers' salaries divided by net worth		Auto manufacturers profits on net worth
	Auto dealers	All retailers	Auto dealers	All retailers	
1946	33.49	18.34	52.28	26.44	3.25
1947	38.44	16.82	56.42	25.10	16.16
1948	29.95	14.66	47.27	23.20	20.98
1949	14.92	9.54	29.79	17.64	25.75
1950	19.33	11.82	34.57	20.11	27.47
1951	10.96	7.79	25.07	15.78	15.17
1952	n.a.	6.63	n.a.	14.48	15.60
1953	2.93	5.52	11.08	13.44	15.25
1954	0.04	5.06	11.09	12.88	16.84
1955	4.64	6.59	17.10	14.95	23.87
1956	1.47	6.33	13.79	15.12	13.24
1957	−0.10	5.11	12.83	13.27	15.33
1958	−2.20	4.92	10.36	13.76	8.87
1959	3.01	6.38	16.77	14.34	15.74
1960	−1.34	4.37	13.02	13.86	15.10
1961	3.03	4.51	17.54	14.31	13.14
1962	8.15	5.90	24.54	16.45	18.22
1963	8.34	5.33	24.90	15.91	18.22
1964	9.16	7.24	25.72	18.14	19.06
1965	12.96	7.73	29.26	18.80	21.04
Average, 1946–1965	10.38	8.00	24.92	16.90	16.72
Average, 1953–1965	3.85	5.83	17.54	15.03	15.82
Standard deviation, 1946–1965	12.04		14.07		5.35
Standard deviation, 1953–1965	4.60		6.46		5.96
S.D./avg., 1946–1965	0.86		0.56		0.32
S.D./avg., 1953–65	0.84		0.37		0.38

SOURCE: U.S. Internal Revenue Service, *Statistics of Income* and *Source Book*, various years; *Moody's Manual of Investments*, various years.

state payments to officers and understate true profits, so as to reduce their corporate income tax liability.

For the overall postwar period, the average rate of return for automobile dealers, measured by either net profits or by net profits plus officers' compensation, has been above the comparable averages for the entire retail sector. But the high auto dealer averages are due largely to the early postwar and Korean War years. As we saw in the previous chapter, these were years of limited supply of automobiles, and the companies chose for various reasons to keep wholesale prices below profit-maximizing levels (during the Korean War, government price controls forced them to do so) and to allow their dealers to make above-normal profits.

Thus the real test of the forcing model has been the years since the end of the Korean War. The average rate of return for auto dealers for 1953–1965 was below that for all retailers; but when officers' compensation is included, auto dealers came out a little ahead. Since the officers of auto dealerships may well work longer hours than the officers of most retailing establishments — most dealerships are open evenings and, where state law permits, on Sundays, and the dealer himself is often on the premises — and since a risk premium may also be included in the net profits plus officers' compensation figures, it would probably be safe to conclude that auto dealerships have earned profits roughly comparable with the rest of the retailing sector since 1953.[28]

A proper analysis of the risk elements confronting dealers would require data on failures, turnover rates, and cross-section variance of individual rates of return around the industry mean. Figures for the late 1940's and early 1950's show lower turnover rates for auto dealers than for other industries; but given the high returns that dealers were earning during those years, this result is not too surprising.[29] Conditions have changed since then; dealers have earned lower profits; many Independent dealers have fallen by the wayside. It would be surprising if the same result held true after 1954. Unfortunately, these numbers are not available for recent years.

Consequently, we must fall back on the weak proxy of looking at the variability of dealer returns over a period of time. As a general proposition, high variability should correlate with high risks.[30] Without the figures for the other individual components of the retailing sector, we cannot compare dealer risks to the risks faced by other retailers. But we can compare the variability of dealer returns with the variability of returns in auto manufacturing, to see how much of the variation has been passed on to the dealers. Table 9.5 shows the comparison between the standard deviation/average ratio for dealer returns with the same ratio for net profit on net worth in auto manufacturing. For the overall postwar period, this ratio has been higher for auto dealers than for auto manufacturing, but, again, the real test lies in the post-Korean War period. For 1953–1965 the standard deviation/average ratio for net profits on net worth was more than double the same ratio in auto manufacturing. But for net profits plus officers' compensation, the ratio for auto dealers was slightly below the net profit ratio for auto manufacturing. Still, we should expect officers' compensation to be a relatively stable component of the sum and the "true" profits component probably varied somewhat more than did the sum. Thus, from the figures in Table 9-5, we can conclude that the variability of returns faced by automobile dealers has been at least as great as the variability faced by the automobile manufacturers and is probably even somewhat higher. If this variability can stand as a proxy for risk, then the risks faced by the dealers are at least as great and are probably somewhat greater than those faced by the manufacturers. The latter do seem to have succeeded in passing on to their dealers some of the risks of the automobile business.

The Development of
Manufacturer-Dealer Relationships

In this manufacturer-dominated environment that we have just described, the dealer is likely to consider himself on the receiving end of a good deal of risk. Much of his financial fate is in someone else's hands: the designer of the car make that he sells. If the car is popular, he will have a good year. If it is not, he will suffer along with the company. He always sees himself forced to sell too many cars; the exact quantity he is forced to take may appear to rest on the whims of the manufacturers' regional sales official. He must maintain and often expand his facilities to the satisfaction of the manufacturer. There is never any guarantee that his franchise will not be revoked for what appears to him unfair causes or that the company will not flood his area with a large number of competing franchises of the same make. No dealer could have heard the following testimony of William F. Hufstader of General Motors without shuddering a little bit:

> I have described the risks and responsibilities assumed by both dealer and manufacturer under their franchise relationship. It is clear that the manufacturer assumes the greater risks and bears the ultimate responsibility to the customer. It is the manufacturer who creates the franchise in the first place. Hence he should be in a position to dispose of it, while affording reasonable protection to the dealer for his investment and his business . . .
>
> This ability to dispose cannot in any sense be shared with the dealer. The manufacturer must be in a position, based on his judgment and on his judgment alone, to retain a franchise, to grant it, or to withdraw it.[31]

The dealers may have been aware of these risks when they entered the business but found the prospective profits worth the gamble. Still, it would only be normal for them to complain about their risky state and try to improve it, particularly if they thought they could reduce the risks without reducing the levels of their profits.

The auto companies have responded slowly to dealer complaints and then only when external pressure has prompted them to do so. The companies value a contented dealer organization, but they also value selling a maximum number of cars even more. When the two are in conflict, as they usually are, there is little question as to how the companies will respond. Thus the dealer-manufacturer relationship carries with it great potential for conflict; it is at the heart of the retailing system that the manufacturers have chosen.

This section will discuss the historical development of this conflict, the issues that have come to the fore, and the behavioral responses that have been made on both sides. The concluding section will deal with the current state of dealer-manufacturer relations and the conflicts that still persist.

Dealer dissatisfaction with their status vis-à-vis the manufacturers first gained audible expression in the 1930's. Frequent complaints were that too many cars were being forced on dealers; unwanted parts and accessories were being forced on them; dealers were being loaded with too many old models and obsolete parts at the time of the new model announcements; dealers were forced to buy expensive new repair tools for the new models; dealers were forced to contribute to advertising funds. In addition, dealers felt that their franchises were being canceled arbitrarily and, in the event of cancellation, adequate compensation was not being paid for cars and parts on hand or to cover unexpired leases. Also, in the event of death, a dealer's heirs were often not given an opportunity to take over the business.

Dealer suits in the courts, usually to protest cancellations that had occurred because of one of the complaints mentioned above, were uniformly unsuccessful. The companies had drawn up the franchise agreements so as to give themselves almost a free hand. As one circuit court opinion expressed it,

It appears that the plaintiff (dealer) has been disappointed in its expectations and has been dealt with none too generously by the defendant (manufacturer); but while we sympathize with its plight, we cannot say from the evidence before us that there has been such a breach of binding contract which would enable it to recover damages. While there is a natural impulse to be impatient with a form of contract which places the comparatively helpless dealer at the mercy of the manufacturer, we cannot make contracts for parties or protect them from the provisions of the contracts which they have made for themselves. Dealers doubtless accept these one-sided contracts because they think the right to deal in the product of the manufacturer, even on his terms, is valuable to them; but after they have made such contracts, relying upon the good faith of the manufacturer for the protection which the contracts do not give, they cannot, when they get into trouble expect the courts to place in the contracts the protection which they themselves have failed to insert.[32]

Failing in the judicial branch of the government, the dealers took their complaints to the legislative branch. In 1938 Congress directed the Federal Trade Commission to "investigate the policies employed by manufacturers in distributing motor vehicles, accessories, and parts, and the policies of dealers in selling motor vehicles at retail, as these policies affect the public interest." [33] The Federal Trade Commission duly compiled and submitted *The Report on the Motor Vehicle Industry*, which chronicled the dealer complaints,[34] but nothing fundamental was done about them.

World War II effectively eliminated the conflicts between manufacturers and dealers by eliminating the source of conflict: the sale of cars. The dealers, however, were able to make respectable profits on their repair businesses during the war. The resumption of car production in 1946 did not bring a revival of the dealer-manufacturer conflicts. Cars were in short supply and the manufacturers, for reasons outlined in Chapter 7, refused to raise list prices or wholesale prices to market clearing levels. The dealers benefited from this policy, exacting the full markup from customers and often obtaining more, by underallowing on the customer's trade-in or forcing the customer to take accessories at exorbitant prices.

The Korean War continued the condition of car shortages and full retail markups. Only in 1953 did the conditions of shortage end; the manufacturers, particularly the Big Three, began to produce the quantities of cars that they really desired to sell at existing prices.

Dealers once again found themselves on the receiving end of manufacturer forcing efforts. None of the dealers had experienced truly competitive conditions in the twelve years since 1941. New dealers appointed since 1941 had never known the old competitive markets. Most had become accustomed to exploiting their local monopoly positions in the previous seven years, selling small volumes at list prices. The manufacturers' renewed emphasis on volume dealers seemed strange.

Many of the same complaints that had surfaced in the 1930's now emerged again. Forcing, parts, advertising, arbitrary cancellation were all brought forward. Many dealers complained of "stimulator" dealers, that is, high volume dealers, being established in their areas. Others complained of the companies' using allocation of best-selling models as a way of forcing dealers to accept slower moving models. A rising turnover rate in dealerships — Table 9.6 lists these figures for General Motors dealers — could not help but create a good deal of uneasiness among dealers.

Table 9.6   Turnover of General Motors Dealers

Year	Nonrenewals	Involuntary[a] termination	"Voluntary" termination	Total turnover
1951	44	120	833	997
1952	72	135	1042	1249
1953	103	153	1217	1473
1954	113	152	1534	1799
1955[b]	118	165	1277	1560

SOURCE: U.S. Senate, Committee on the Judiciary, Subcommittee on Antitrust and Monopoly, *A Study of the Antitrust Laws*, Hearings, 84th Congress, 2nd session, 1956, part 7, p. 4381.

[a] Due to death, bankruptcy, etc.

[b] First ten months only.

Many dealers had one additional complaint: bootlegging, the resale of new cars by used car dealers. Bootlegging had two sources. First, the manufacturers had been charging phantom freight on their shipments to outlying points. Cars that were assembled in regional assembly plants and which, therefore, incurred only the stacked parts freight costs to the assembly plant nevertheless were carrying a freight charge as if the assembled car had been shipped all the way from Detroit to the customer. Freight charges to Los Angeles ran $365 for a Buick and $279 for a Chevrolet; the actual shipping costs were approximately $184 for the former and $124 for the latter.[35] More importantly, tow-bar, drive-away, and even small-scale trucking costs for transporting those cars from Detroit to Los Angeles were significantly under the company-charged freight costs. West Coast used car dealers were able to buy new cars from Detroit dealers, transport them west, and undercut the franchise dealers' prices, although the cars were sometimes in less than pristine condition from the trip. The franchised dealers on the West Coast were quite unhappy over the extra competition they faced. Similar situations appeared in other outlying areas.

Second, bootlegging also took the form of dealers selling their "excess" cars to used car dealers for $50 over dealer cost, in return for the promise that the used car dealer would resell the cars in a different geographical area. Thus the original dealer was able to preserve part of his local monopoly, while dealers in other geographical areas found themselves faced by still more selling competition.

How serious was bootlegging? The market in bootlegged cars was large enough to support the services of wholesale car brokers.[36] The Department of Labor found that 18 percent of new cars bought in Houston were from other than franchised dealers.[37] Ford found that at least 5.8 percent of Ford sales in Denver and 8.8 percent of the Ford sales in Houston during the first three months of the 1955 model year were made by bootleg outlets.[38]

In 1953 and 1954, California's share of United States new car registrations was under its share of total United States registrations, a strange phenomenon for a state whose car population was growing as a percentage of the United States total. Although part of this is explained by migrants to the state bringing their own cars (which had been registered in other states), most of it was due to new cars' being bought from dealers in Detroit and elsewhere, registered there, and then shipped to California for resale. One Los Angeles dealer estimated that 20 percent of California sales were bootleg.[39]

The general dealer dissatisfaction was partly expressed in efforts to pass state administrative-licensing statutes. The statutes, some passed by state legislatures as early as 1935, typically provided for the licensing of dealers and manufacturers and the representatives of both doing business in the state. These licenses could be revoked for wrongful conduct, often defined as coercion, refusal to deliver cars to dealers who had ordered them, or unfair cancellation of franchises. The manufacturers lobbied against these laws, fought them in the courts, and for the most part managed to continue the procedures about which the dealers were objecting.

Consequently, the dealers, through the National Automobile Dealers Association (NADA), turned their efforts toward a national hearing and remedy of their grievances. Between 1954 and 1960, at least eight congressional hearings were held in which dealer grievances were aired. The brunt of dealer pressure was exerted during the hearings in 1955 and 1956. The dealer goals were usually laws to prevent manufacturer forcing and laws to legalize territorial security schemes that would allocate specific geographical areas of sales responsibility for dealers, with bonuses for in-territory sales, or fines for out-of-territory sales, so as to reduce competitive pressures generally. To end bootlegging, the dealers wanted both of the above actions plus an end to phantom freight practices.

Despite impressive factual defenses, the auto companies, particularly General Motors, were placed in a bad public light. They appeared as the giant corporations trampling the small businessman underfoot. The companies, of course, objected to any legislation that would limit their control over their dealers, but feeling that they were in an uncomfortable political position and hoping to head off legislation, they offered a number of concessions.

Since General Motors was the chief target of the complaints, it led the way in offering concessions. In a dramatic announcement on December 5, 1955, General Motors President Harlow H. Curtice, while testifying before the Senate Antitrust Subcommittee, told the subcommittee that he was sending out telegrams to all General Motors dealers extending their contracts from one-year to five-year terms. General Motors followed this action in February 1956, with franchise revisions that included:

1. The companies would reimburse the dealers on new-car warranty work at the rate of 100 percent of labor costs and the cost of parts plus 10 percent (it had formerly been 65 percent of labor costs and parts plus 10 percent; before 1953, it had been 50 percent of labor costs plus the cost of parts only).
2. Dealers were allowed to return 4 percent of parts purchased during the year (formerly 2 percent).
3. In the event of the termination or sale of a franchise, the company and dealer would each appoint a real estate representative and those two would appoint a third, and the trio would decide on the fair valuation to be paid the dealer for the sale of his property (formerly, the company's word had been dominant; the company was always interested in as low a price as possible, so as to reduce the required investment and profits of the new dealers).[40]
4. The company would grant a 5 percent rebate on the list price on all old models still in dealer inventories at the time of the new model announcements (formerly, a 4 percent rebate only on those models in excess of 3 percent of the year's sales).
5. Widows were to have a financial interest in the dealership for five years (formerly no explicit provision).
6. The company would absorb all of the costs of direct-by-mail advertising program (formerly, the dealer was charged for this).
7. There would be detailed specification of dealer performance standards written into the franchise, and the franchise could be cancelled only for cause (formerly, the contracts did not specify performance standards, and falling below the national average had often been cited as reason for cancelling franchises; the contracts had been cancellable without cause). Also, the dealer could appeal any cancellation to an impartial umpire,[41] whose decision was binding on the company but not binding on the dealer, who could still appeal to the courts (formerly, the only internal appeal was to a company dealer-relations board composed of company executives and a few hand-picked dealers).

At the end of 1956, General Motors stopped assessing advertising charges per car on the dealers. These had run $20 for a Chevrolet, $45–$60 for a Cadillac.

The other companies quickly followed with similar provisions easing the dealers' lot.[42] It should be noticed, however, that most of these concessions were relatively easy for the companies to make, since anything granted to dealers could be made up by raising wholesale prices,[43] though there might be some marginal incentive effects that would change. But, in fact, there was a general easing-up of sales pressure on the dealers in 1956.[44] The cessation of what appeared to be arbitrary and high-handed actions by the companies was perhaps the greatest gain to the dealers and cost the companies very little.

The concessions were not enough, however, to prevent legislation, and in August 1956, Public Law 1026, commonly known as the Automobile Dealers' Day in Court Act,[45] was signed into law. The key section, Section 2, of this act read:

> An automobile dealer may bring suit against any automobile manufacturer engaged in commerce, in any district court of the United States . . . and shall recover the damages by him sustained and the cost of suit by reason of the failure of said automobile manufacturer from and after the passage of this Act to act in good faith in performing or complying with any of the terms or provisions of the franchise or in terminating, canceling or not renewing the franchise with said dealer: *Provided*, That in any such suit the manufacturer shall not be barred from asserting in defense of any such action the failure of the dealer to act in good faith.

The previous paragraph defined "good faith" as

> . . . the duty of each party to any franchise, and all officers, employees, and agents thereof to act in a fair and equitable manner toward each other so as to guarantee the one party freedom from coercion, intimidation, or threats of coercion or intimidation from the other party: *Provided*, That recommendation, endorsement, exposition, persuasion, urging or argument shall not be deemed to constitute a lack of good faith.

The bill was obviously a compromise between the dealers, most of whom would have preferred stronger provisions against forcing, and the companies and the Department of Justice, who believed that any bill would increase the dealers' local monopoly position and raise retail prices.

On the subject of territorial security, the dealers and the companies were in closer harmony. Territorial security provisions had been in most franchise agreements before the war. A typical arrangement was for a dealer who sold a car to a buyer in another dealer's area to pay

$25–$50 to the dealer who had been infringed upon. In November 1949, General Motors reluctantly abandoned the provision in its franchise agreements, along with a clause that forbade a dealer's selling cars to anyone for resale, except to another authorized dealer; the company abandoned the two clauses only after receiving an informal opinion from the Department of Justice that the clauses might be illegal restraints of trade. Within the next two years, the other companies abandoned similar provisions in their franchises.

In the hearings of the middle 1950's, the dealers wanted a territorial security system of bonuses for in-territory sales.[46] General Motors also favored a territorial security scheme but one that involved penalties for out-of-territory sales. It tried to get the Department of Justice to approve a provision whereby a dealer first would have to offer the cars to General Motors before selling them to a bootlegger. But the company would not be obligated to take them, as the dealers hoped to require; this would have ended their forcing woes. The Department of Justice refused to approve the provision; General Motors, though believing in its legality, declined to put it into effect because the company's executives would thereby have submitted themselves to the risk of criminal prosecution under the antitrust laws.[47] The other auto companies were initially hostile to the resumption of territorial security; but, in hearings in 1958 and 1960, Ford and Chrysler began to favor its resumption.[48] The Independents continued to oppose it.

The gain to the dealers from a territorial security system is clear. It appears to enhance their local monopoly positions, and the mention of a bonus for sales always has a pleasant ring to it. But why should the manufacturers favor it? The answer lies in the forcing model. The effective use of forcing requires full information as to the market potential of the individual dealers. The more segmented the markets, the better the information the company can get about market potentials. The greater the ability of the companies to employ forcing, the more eager they would be to institute a territorial security system.[49] The penalty provisions would be favored over a bonus system, since the former would be self-enforcing (the infringed-upon dealer himself would have to report the infringement) and would not require an increase in the nominal wholesale price (with its unpleasant public relations effects) to make up for the bonuses.

Territorial security provisions were never enacted into law. Congress, Congressman Emanuel Cellar in particular, was never convinced of the public interest of these provisions. The companies, fearful of possible antitrust prosecutions, never instituted them unilaterally. A recent Supreme Court decision, *U.S. v. Arnold Schwinn & Company*,[50] would appear to have vindicated the auto companies' reluctance. The Court ruled that territorial restrictions, even if imposed vertically, were an illegal restraint of trade once the producer had parted title with the goods. It would now require a reinterpretation by the Court or congressional amendment of the Sherman Act to legalize a system of territorial security.

On phantom freight as a source of bootlegging, the companies' efforts to impose it can be seen as an effort at price discrimination. While maintaining a nominal national list price, they were able to maintain higher effective prices in outlying areas, where, presumably, the demand for cars was more inelastic than in the central part of the country.

The figures on total car ownership offer some support for the inelastic demand hypothesis. Despite the significantly higher prices that Californians had to pay for new and used cars, they owned 0.37 cars per capita in 1955, compared to 0.31 for residents of Ohio and 0.30 for residents of Illinois.[51] The differences in per capita income do not appear to have been large enough to explain these differences.[52]

When bootlegging effectively short-circuited their efforts to keep the two markets separated, the companies ended their phantom freight practices. Decreases in freight charges to outlying areas in 1954 and again in 1956 brought freight charges to what the companies claimed were close to the actual costs of shipment.[53] They then raised their wholesale prices in all areas to make up for the lost revenues. Effective prices (wholesale prices plus freight charge) went up in the central part of the country and down in the outlying areas, exactly what we should expect when a discriminating monopolist (or oligopolist) could no longer segment his markets.

Current State of Franchises and Dealer-Manufacturing Relations

After the flurry of activity in the 1950's, dealer-manufacturer relations settled down to a state of relative quiet. Though many of the dealer grievances were not satisfied, the dealers appeared to have succeeded in eliminating most of the apparent arbitrariness in the manufacturers' actions. Though forcing and performance goals still continue, most dealers appear to have resigned themselves to the impossibility of exploiting their local monopolies.

The majority of representatives of dealer associations interviewed by Macaulay felt that dealer-manufacturer relations had improved since the early 1950's.[54] Two statements show the current view of the majority:

The relationship between the manufacturer and the dealers is greatly improved, and this is due to the efforts of NADA. There still is a great deal of pressure to sell cars, but it is applied much differently. Today you don't get the hard beating over the head you used to get. Of course, all factories want volume, and that's a good thing.

The relationship between manufacturers and dealers is better than it was in the early 1950's. The attitude of the factory has changed. They are not as dominating and the dealer has more to say about what kinds of cars and accessories he'll take. The relationship is much more of a partnership than it was at that time. There is not as much pressure to sell quotas, but the field men will do their best to push the dealer. The dealers, however, now feel that they are in a position to talk back because they are more sure of themselves. There are not as many threats or cancellations as there were in the earlier time either, and (the association official) . . . thinks that the number of cancellations has levelled off and will stay at its present low level . . . The five-year term in the new franchises has helped a great deal.[55]

Even the negative comments show the newly acquired sophistication of the companies:

(The association official) . . . hasn't heard of many involuntary terminations recently. There's not much of this going on in his opinion. The factory gets its way by making a nuisance of itself; the dealer gets mad and is ready to quit, and the factory gets him a buyer and gets rid of the man. They don't write formal termination notices; they just get rid of the dealer. They can come in and badger him on his sales volume, criticize his service facilities, set goals that are just a little bit unreasonable and the criticism sounds all right under one interpretation, they won't get in trouble with the Good Faith Act. Moreover, they can mess around with the distribution when they don't get what they call cooperation. The dealer will get two Mustangs when he's entitled to six.[56]

The effect of the 1950's dealer efforts was more in the publicity that they gave to manufacturer's practices than in the legislation that emerged. The Dealers Day in Court Act, until very recently, has not provided any visible benefit for the dealers. The manufacturers have not had much difficulty in proving to the courts their "good faith" in canceling dealers.[57] But two recent cases, *Madsden v. Chrysler Corporation*[58] and *American Motors Sales Corporation v. L. G. Semke*,[59] have provided decisions in favor of the dealers. It is still too early to tell if these will provide significant precedents for future decisions. Also, the act may have had its most important effect in deterring manufacturers' actions that otherwise would have occurred and causing the manufacturers to settle out of court cases they previously might have won.

The franchise agreements themselves have not changed significantly since the late 1950's. Howard E. Crawford of General Motors, testifying before the Senate Antitrust Subcommittee in 1967, summarized the provisions of the current franchise:

The dealer agrees to establish a place of business adequate in size and layout.

He agrees to provide the amount of capital necessary to meet the needs of the business.

He agrees to provide satisfactory sales performance in his area of sales responsibility. Evaluation of a dealer's sales performance is based on a formula spelled out in the agreement.

He is required to have a sufficient number of trained salesmen, mechanics, and adequate equipment and tolls to provide satisfactory sales and service to owners.

He also agrees to carry an adequate inventory of parts and accessories at all times.

He agrees to use a standard accounting system and maintain records regarding the sales and servicing of motor vehicles.[60]

With much of the apparent arbitrariness of the manufacturers actions removed, the dealers' franchise agreements are probably in as favorable shape as they can reasonably expect, short of a sharp reversal in the bargaining power between dealers and manufacturer or a complete revolution in the nature of the franchise system.

But the dealers still have their complaints, as is evidenced by recent testimony by National Automobile Dealers Association officials before congressional committees.[61] The most important current complaints are: (1) the establishment of factory-owned outlets, (2) dissatisfaction over reimbursement for warranty work, (3) increased direct company sales to fleets and rental concerns, (4) favoritism among dealers as to the distribution of popular models at the beginning of a model year, and (5) the differing nominal discounts on different types of cars.

Factory-owned Outlets

In recent years, Ford, Chrysler, and American Motors have opened a number of factory-owned retail outlets in areas in which they felt their representation was weak.[62] They claim that they would have preferred to have attracted private risk capital but were unable to do so and that these dealerships are up for sale to private buyers at all times. These factory outlets are not yet in significant numbers. Ford, as of October 1967, had only 66 or 67 such outlets out of a total of over 7,000 automobile dealers.[63] But the NADA, always concerned about any new competition and the setting of a trend, has objected.

Why should the companies be willing to invest their capital when potential dealers refuse to invest? Two possible reasons come immediately to mind: lower borrowing costs or discount rates by the companies and a lower assessment of the risks involved in the new dealership by the company. But a more fundamental reason is more likely. Repeat buying is an important element in the market. Once a consumer buys a company's car, there is a high probability that he will buy the same brand or another brand in the company's list the next time. Thus a "conquest" sale is worth more to the company than if future purchases were entirely random. The company should be willing to accept a lower profit on the initial sale in return for having to expend a smaller selling or advertising cost to influence the customer on his next purchase; or, because of his brand loyalty, the company may be able to raise its price on the next purchase above what it could have charged if future purchases were random. Note that the company does not want to lower its wholesale prices generally but only wants to lower them for conquest sales. The companies have sometimes achieved this effect by offering special bonuses or rebates on sales in which a car from a different company is taken as a trade-in. But it is not a common practice, since its general use by all companies wipes out its usefulness. Oligopolistic interdependence is again evident.

In setting up a dealership in a new location where, presumably, most sales will be conquest sales, the company would like to be able to lower its wholesale price just for the new location. But Robinson-Patman Act considerations, plus the likelihood of general dissatisfaction among other dealers, prevent this practice. The company can achieve the same effect by operating the new location itself and accepting a less than competitive return on its retail operations as such. In the long run, though, the expected repeat sales should make the dealership profitable according to normal competitive standards, and private individuals should be willing to purchase the dealerships.

Note that this is not simply a matter of differing time horizons between dealers and companies. If a dealer initially invested in this location, he would have to accept below-normal profits for the first few years. If the strength of consumer loyalty to dealers is less than that of consumers to a car brand, as it probably is,[64] then the dealer will not be able to gain as much future benefit from the initial sales as the company can. Consequently, a dealer would prefer to wait until the company developed the local market before buying the franchise.

Since these factory outlets should appear only in underrepresented areas, and since they should eventually revert to private dealer hands, the NADA's fears of a trend toward factory outlets are probably groundless. The auto companies have repeatedly expressed their support of the franchise system.[65] The analysis of this chapter has demonstrated the advantages of the franchise system for the companies. There have been no recent changes in the retail environment that would alter the conclusion of this analysis.

Reimbursement for Warranty Repairs

As new car warranties have grown longer and more complicated, consumers have come to expect more free service from their dealers. Explaining that the fine print in the warranty excludes the customer's particular claim may send away an angry customer and lose a future sale, yet the company will refuse to reimburse the dealer on such a repair. Also, the dealers have claimed that the companies have been slow or neglectful in reimbursement on legitimate warranty repair work. The Federal Trade Commission has conducted an investigation of warranty practices, but nothing substantial has changed as a result.

The decreased warranty provisions on the 1969 models may ease this source of conflict.

Direct Sales to Fleets and Rental Customers

The companies sell cars to fleet customers — businesses, government, and rental agencies — usually at prices below dealer cost. These sales are often negotiated directly by the company. If they are conducted through a dealer, they leave him with only a nominal margin, and he receives a lower price for these sales.

The dealers' objections are, of course, partly based on envy; they would always like to see more sales conducted through their premises on a profitable basis. But their objections have a deeper base than that. Dealers are not unaffected by sales outside of dealerships, since these cars eventually find their way into the used car market and thereby compete with future new-car sales by dealers. The time lag is not very long. Most rental agencies resell their cars after one year. Thus the dealers prefer a situation in which as many cars as possible are sold within the dealer system and none are sold outside of it.

The companies, on the other hand, are indifferent as to how the cars are sold. Though the companies would probably prefer to sell fleet cars at higher prices, competitive bidding for fleet contracts has prevented this. They figure that the selling and administrative costs for such sales are much lower per car than for normal sales and are either easier to arrange directly or require much less effort by the dealer, therefore requiring less remuneration to him than for normal sales. As long as the companies find bulk sales profitable, this source of conflict is likely to continue.

Favoritism

Rationing car models among dealers does not make sense for a manufacturer as a long-run policy. The logical response to an excess demand for a particular model is to raise the price and produce more.[66] But at an early stage in the model year, before a manufacturer has had an opportunity to rationalize his production plans, he may well have to ration certain models. He can use this rationing as a supplement to forcing, favoring those dealers who have pushed for high volume. Again, this source of irritation is likely to continue.

Differing Nominal Discounts

Currently, list prices are such that most full-sized cars carry a 25 percent dealer discount, most compacts and intermediates carry a 21 percent discount, and the new subcompacts carry a 17 percent discount. (See Chapter 8 for an explanation of these terms.) The dealers would prefer to see a uniform discount structure, preferably at 25 percent. Though few of them ever realize their full margin on sales, the notion of having a higher nominal margin is always a pleasant one. The fact that it will be competed away or forced away is not considered. Perhaps dealers somehow believe that the larger margin will come at the expense of lower wholesale prices rather than higher list prices.

Also, some dealers complain that the differing discounts inhibit their selling behavior. Many believe that buyers are more sensitive to the size of the offer on their trade-ins than to cuts in the list price. Consequently, they prefer to sell cars at list but overallow on trade-ins or offer a "cash bonus" for customers without trade-ins. They claim that it is difficult to explain to customers why their trade-ins should have a lower value when they trade it for a compact or intermediate rather than for a full-sized car.[67] One would think that, if this dilemma became too great, the dealer could easily switch to convincing his customers about the advantages of buying at less than list price.

10

Product Behavior:
A General Summary

Product behavior in automobiles encompasses a wide area. Styling, model proliferation, improved performance, durability, accessories, warranties, and advertising are all important aspects of product behavior. This chapter will try to establish some general principles of product behavior in the automobile industry. The following chapters will illustrate these principles with specific examples of behavior in the postwar period.

Structural characteristics ought to be dominant in determining the form and directions that product behavior will take. The character of demand will be one strong influence. As has been mentioned earlier, the replacement nature of demand will loom importantly in product behavior. The high degree of variability of consumer tastes in the automobile market, creating high risks, will also be important. The inherent nature of the product may suggest some likely forms of product behavior. Some products seem less susceptible to packaging efforts than do others; it is unlikely that automobiles with bows or wrapped in cellophane will sell better than those without (though all cars in showroom windows do carry whitewall tires).

The supply characteristics of product strategies should also influence the pattern of product behavior, and it is on these elements that the discussion will focus. The costs of particular strategies, the length of time necessary for development of the strategy, its flexibility, and the perceived likelihood and speed of response by rivals should all enter into the calculus of a firm's behavior choices. The last element, of course, is directly related to concentration in an industry.

171

It is, however, the risks connected with product strategies that make these supply characteristics important. In a world of perfect forecasting of the future, the high costs or inflexibility of a product strategy would be relatively unimportant; the future would be known, the profit-maximizing strategy could be calculated and implemented, and that would be the end of it. Allow uncertainty to enter the picture, however, and the various characteristics of the different product strategies quickly attain significance.

The risks of a product strategy are, of course, due to uncertainty about future sales and costs that are attributable to the strategy. The uncertainty about sales, in turn, is generated from two sources: uncertainty about future consumer tastes and incomes and uncertainty about the future product strategies of rival firms. There are measures that a firm can take to lessen these uncertainties: market surveys to get a better idea of consumer tastes, studies of past and projected cost trends to get a better estimate of costs, explicit or implicit agreements with other firms to share information or licence patents. Still, these measures can only reduce uncertainty, not eliminate it, and any product strategy, even that of persisting with the status quo, will necessarily carry risks.

But some product strategies will carry more risks than others, and here the supply characteristics become important. Other things being equal, the riskiness of a product strategy will be greater as its fixed costs become larger. More money is at stake; the general condition of the firm may be put to the test; significant changes may appear on the profit and loss statement for stockholders to observe. Given an equal state of uncertainty about consumer receptivity, a project to launch an entirely new model such as an Edsel or a Mustang would be considered much more risky than a project to try a new color paint on existing models.

Similarly, the risks of a strategy will increase as the delay between a strategy's formulation and the final outcome is increased. In a world of changing consumer tastes, a product strategy that has to be planned three years in advance, such as a new model, would definitely carry more risk than one that could be planned three months in advance, such as an advertising campaign.

The ability to modify the strategy in mid-effort should also affect risk. The risk of a strategy should increase as the ability to modify it in response to changes in consumer tastes decreases. Again, the new model, with a design that is largely unchangeable, or at least very costly to change, within two years of the date of the first sale, is more risky than an advertising campaign, the nature of which can be changed almost at will.[1]

Finally, the increasing likelihood of counterstrategies by rivals should increase risks. There is always the risk of a possible coup by a rival, that is, a breakthrough in some area of product variation that cannot be easily or quickly duplicated. And there is also the risk that a rival will duplicate one's own product strategy, thereby making unprofitable a strategy that would be profitable in the absence of this type of retaliation. The larger the fixed costs associated with a strategy and the fewer the number of firms in the industry, the greater will be these risks.

It is worth stressing that we are directly suggesting the possibility of recognized mutual interdependence among oligopolists in this area of market behavior. Traditional oligopoly theory has usually maintained that mutual interdependence and lack of competition is most prevalent in the area of prices and pricing policy. Competition, therefore, is usually channeled into the areas of advertising and product development, with an absence of the recognition of mutual interdependence in these areas often the case. The reasons given for the willingness to compete in product development rather than in price are clear: the delayed and often unequal response by a competitor to a product development, as opposed to the exact and rapid response possible on price changes, and a tendency to believe that one's own product development really is what consumers want (or will want, after suitable advertising) and that one's rivals really cannot equal it.

Need this be so? If the members of an industry are few enough, it seems altogether likely that each member would consider the possible response of his rivals before embarking on a product strategy. The auto industry would certainly appear to qualify on fewness of members. Even if the product strategy could not be duplicated exactly by rivals, the likelihood and possible effect of rough duplication of product strategies should be taken into consideration. Thus, although no firm would ever duplicate exactly a model produced by a rival, the likelihood that a rival would bring out something similar surely would affect a firm's decisions on bringing out a new model.

This combination of cost, length of gestation, flexibility, and risk has important implications for product behavior in the automobile industry and for oligopolistic product behavior in general. For example, low capacity utilization or unsatisfactory profits are often seen as spurs to product variation by disadvantaged firms. But the long lag between design and production of an entirely new model, plus the high costs and generally high risks of a new model, would seem to rule out this particular type of response to low capacity utilization in the auto industry. By the time the new car actually saw the light of day, the economic position of the firm might be quite different. The same would be true for new types of engines or accessories or other product variations that required a long gestation period. Rather, these types of product variations should be related to long-run strategies by firms and not to short-run considerations. Thus Ford's development of the Edsel was part of a long-run strategy to improve its weak position in the medium-level market. By contrast, advertising and warranty changes would seem to offer highly flexible means of product variation (though, in the case of an improved warranty, the manufacturing changes that would be necessary to prevent a warranty improvement from becoming excessively costly might require extensive preparation).

More generally, this author would argue that in cases in which the product variation is expensive and carries high risks and in which the mutual interdependence among the oligopolists is strong and is recognized as such, there will be a tendency for product competition to be limited. This is *not* to say that all product competition will cease and that the industry will become a virtual cartel. Rather, we should expect to see competition channeled into areas in which the oligopolists feel themselves more in control of the risks that are present and feel safe from the risks of breakthroughs by rivals. It seems likely that this is one of the reasons why the auto industry has chosen styling, rather than fundamental technological change, as the basic area of competition and why the free exchange of information has been so great in the industry.

Further, under some circumstances we should expect the members of an oligopolistic industry to refrain from developing a new product that might be profitable for one producer alone to develop. Suppose that an oligopolist sees a profitable market niche for a product. The development of the product and tooling-up for production require a large investment, and a significant scale of production relative to the size of the market is required to recoup this investment. Under these circumstances, a single oligopolist might well refrain from developing this product until he was sure that enough room existed for himself *and his rivals* to produce it at a reasonable profit. Plunging in without this room for expansion might result in all of the oligopolists' struggling in an uncomfortably small market.

Why would his rivals follow the oligopolist into a market that was too small to support all of them? They might simply miscalculate. Alternately, they might put a high value on not being excluded from a successful market that a rival had already developed. Consequently, though the probability of success might be small and the expected monetary value of entering the market might be negative, the utility value of entering would still be positive. But they would put a higher utility value on a state of the world in which all had refrained from entering this particular market. This situation is similar to game theory's familiar "prisoner's dilemma." Finally, they might wish to "discipline" the original developer of the product to show him that he will never be allowed to get ahead of them all. This type of retaliation, and the consequent hesitancy in entering, is likely for major segments of a market in which oligopolists might fear that a failure to react could have unsettling consequences for the future.

Effectively, we are proposing a "spatial" theory of product behavior in which one oligopolist will not enter an expensive new product line until there is room for all of his fellow oligopolists to enter successfully. The less strongly is their mutual interdependence recognized, the more likely it is that a member of an industry will plunge into what may be only a small market. We shall argue in the next chapter that this has been the case in the development of small cars by American manufacturers.

Also, oligopolists should be more aware of the problem of "spoiling their own market" with the introduction of new products to supplement old ones. An atomistic competitor would see new products as taking sales from its rivals, and that is as far as his reasoning would go. An oligopolist, however, has to visualize the possibility of retaliation. If he were the only one to bring out the new product, he would largely take sales from his rivals and would not decrease the sales of his existing products very much. But if his rivals also brought out a similar product, then, except for any wholly new customers, the new group of products could expand sales only at the expense of sales of the existing product of the industry. If the new product is seen as a less profitable item for the industry as a whole, then even though it would be highly profitable for one firm alone to introduce it, the product is not likely to be introduced. Strong interdependence is strategic here, of course. Again, we shall argue that this aspect of behavior was important in the development of the small car.

One other aspect of product behavior ought to be mentioned. The *timing* of product behavior should be somewhat related to perceived positions of relative disadvantage by individual firms in the industry. Most product behavior will occur by firms who are trying to anticipate changes in consumer tastes, regardless of perceived disadvantage, but we should expect to see some product behavior related to this condition. The behavior could be part of a long-run strategy to strengthen product lines in weak areas (for example, Ford's Edsel adventure or the Independents' development of small cars in the 1950's), or a short-run effort to regain lost market shares and increase capacity utilization (for example, Chrysler's radical expansion of warranty provisions in the fall of 1962).

11

The Small Car Story

For the entire postwar period the subject of small cars — cars smaller and cheaper than the standard six-passenger sedans that Detroit considers its "basic" car — has been one of active concern to the auto companies. A case study of the origin and development of small cars can serve to illustrate a number of the structural and behavioral problems of the industry: rapidly shifting consumer tastes, long development lag times, the tendency toward cost-oriented pricing in the early postwar period, the recognized interdependence of the Big Three, the problems of product behavior in a replacement market. It will also provide an opportunity to expand on the interaction between costs, flexibility, risks, and interdependence that can create parallelism of behavior among the auto companies.

We shall argue that the auto companies were deliberately slow in entering the small car market. This delay was largely due to the recognized interdependence among the Big Three. This interdependence had its effect in two ways. First, the companies were concerned with "room for all" considerations, refraining from entering the small car market until they were convinced that the market was large enough to support all three. With the high costs and high risks of developing wholly new models, the companies did not want to find themselves jointly in a market that could not support all three.

Second, each company saw the small car as a less desirable, less profitable item to produce and as one that would, to some extent, shift sales from their own larger, more profitable cars. Essentially, they viewed consumers favoring small cars as a minority who, though preferring small cars over large cars, would buy large cars if there were no alternative. Thus, in the absence of an alternative, the Big Three could safely ignore the wishes of this segment of the market. In this behavior, the Big Three definitely recognized their mutual interdependence. In the absence of retaliation by rivals, a single firm contemplating the production of a small car should have expected to gain more profits from absorbing the dissatisfied customers from other firms than he would lose from dissatisfied customers of his own large cars buying the less profitable small cars. But the Big Three mutually contemplating a small car could only see lost profits from reduced sales of large cars. Only after consumer tastes changed so that this minority became larger *and* imports began satisfying these customers did the Big Three finally respond to this segment of the market. Low profit customers were better than no customers at all. By contrast, it was the smaller companies, the Independents, less worried about interdependent effects, that entered the small car market much earlier.

The Light Car Episode and the Independents' Small Cars

America came out of World War II with what might be called a *volkswagen* ("peoples' car") attitude. There was general agreement that the low price cars of the Big Three had passed into the semi-luxury stage; they were larger, better outfitted, and more expensive than a "basic transportation" vehicle required. A new generation of smaller, lighter, cheaper cars was necessary, many claimed, so that new-car ownership could be expanded in a new wave comparable to that which engulfed America at the time of the Model T. From the discussion in newspapers and magazines, it appeared that the American public was clamoring for this new generation of cars.

In response to this apparent demand, General Motors and Ford in May 1945 separately announced their intention to build lightweight cars. Chrysler a year later, in what would become typical follower behavior in this area, announced that "if the market exists and if other companies have a low priced car, Chrysler will be ready with something competitive." [1]

Through the middle of 1946, work on the small car proceeded at a fast pace. General Motors obtained the Federal Government's approval (many war production controls were still in effect) to build the car in Cleveland and ordered the structural steel for the Cleveland factory. Then, in September, both General Motors and Ford announced the cancellation of their light car projects. There were a number of reasons for the cancellation. Raw materials and parts were hard to get; it was not clear that materials could be found for constructing the factories, not to mention building the cars. General Motors, particularly, was worried that the light car could be built for only $100 under a Chevrolet and that this was not a large enough differential to induce people to buy it. Most importantly, the companies found that although people might be talking volkswagen they were indeed trying to buy Chevrolets, Fords, and Plymouths in larger numbers than the companies could produce. Despite their talk of cheap cars, a sufficient number of consumers were not willing to give up the luxury elements in their cars to which they had become accustomed, and they were willing to pay for those luxuries. Even in the tightest car market ever known, Crosley's bantam-size car was not selling well. Though this was not a real test, since the Crosley was a good deal smaller than the proposed lightweight cars, still it was instructive.

The development work on the small cars was not a total loss for the companies, however.[2] The General Motors light car eventually appeared in the fall of 1948, in a largely unchanged form, as the Australian Holden car produced by General Motors' Australian subsidiary. The Ford light car appeared also in the fall of 1948 as the French Ford Vedette. This international transmission within a company of designs that would otherwise not have a market value constitutes the main economic argument (aside from the usual "better management" contention) for the existence of the American-owned foreign subsidiaries. As long as foreign consumers do not object to "hand-me-down" designs, foreign subsidiaries reduce the risk of developing unsalable products at home.[3] In America, the light car projects were put on the back burner in the research departments, to be stirred occasionally but not to be seriously looked at for another ten years.

Curiously, Chrysler appeared with short wheelbase versions of their full-sized Plymouths and Dodges in 1949. No explanation of these models was ever offered, but it seems likely that Chrysler had decided to hedge against the possibility of a small car market's blossoming forth by offering these "shortie" models, as they were called. These models were essentially stripped-down versions of the standard cars, with 8-inch shorter wheelbases obtained at the expense of back seat and trunk space. Only two-door models were offered. The Plymouth two-door "shortie" was priced only $27 under the comparable full-size, two-door sedan. The Dodge "shortie" two-door sedan was $93 under the lowest price full-sized Dodge, a four-door model. But the normal differential between two-door and four-door models was $30–$50, so that the real cost saving was only around $50. These small cost savings were not substantial enough to attract customers; after three years of poor sales, these models were quietly dropped at the end of the 1952 model year, another victim of cost-oriented pricing.

In 1950, the Independents began to enter the small car field. Apparently believing that a market for these cars did exist, and undeterred by the possibility that too many producers might enter this limited market, four Independents — Nash, Kaiser, Willys, and Hudson — offered compact cars to the public between 1950 and 1954.

Nash was the first to enter this market with its 100-inch wheelbase Rambler convertible in April 1950. The car was priced at $1,808, only $40 below Chevrolet's convertible ($140 under Ford's), but the Rambler carried a radio, heater, turn signals, and other accessories as standard equipment. In June, a Rambler station wagon, also priced at $1,808, was introduced; in June 1951, a two-door hardtop was introduced at $1,846, both models carrying many accessories as standard. Nash evidently was hoping to find a special niche in the market, buyers who wanted luxury options but who were willing to accept a smaller package in return for a smaller price than for the same options and models on a full-size Big Three car. Though a 108-inch wheelbase, four-door sedan was introduced for the 1954 model year, only at the beginning of the 1955 model year did Nash drop all of the accessories on the Rambler and concentrate on the low price section of the market. Separate Rambler sales figures are not available for earlier years, but in 1953 Rambler sales were only 40,000 units, and in 1954 they were 36,000 units. These disappointing sales may have led to the decision to concentrate on the cheaper section of the market.

Kaiser entered the small car field in the fall of 1950 with its 100-inch wheelbase Henry J. The car was definitely aimed at the low price market, with a four-cylinder, two-door sedan priced at $1,299, the cheapest car (aside from Crosley) in the market. Its six-cylinder model, however, sold for $1,429, a price that was $26 above the list price of the cheapest full-sized Chevrolet two-door sedan. Customers complained of poor workmanship on the car, and it suffered a tremendous drop in resale value in the used car market; this latter phenomenon was spurred by Kaiser's general "orphan" image at the time. Only 107,000 Henry J. cars were sold over the three years that it was in production. This was not enough to make the venture profitable, and Kaiser ceased Henry J. production at the end of the 1953 model year.

Willys reentered the car market with its 108-inch wheelbase Aero models in early 1952. As was pointed out in Chapter 5, the Aero was overpriced for the quality attributes that it offered, and it never sold well; production ceased in 1955.

Hudson introduced its 104-inch wheelbase Jet models at the beginning of the 1954 model year. Jet prices were about $200 over comparable full-sized Chevrolet models. The Jet was a victim of the 1954 Nash-Hudson merger, the new management preferring to concentrate on the Rambler as their single compact car. Jet production ceased at the end of the 1954 model year. At the prices that Jet models were carrying, it is unlikely that the car would have been a long-run success in any event.

As one looks back at these efforts to establish small car lines by the Independents, it is tempting to conclude that these cars were really seven years before their time. If they had only survived until 1958, one might argue, these models — and the companies that produced them — might still be around today. The difficulty with this argument is that it ignores the prices that the Independents were charging for their compacts. With the exception of the four-cylinder Henry J., these cars carried price tags that did not offer "bargain transportation." It is unlikely that these cars would have sold well even in a booming small car market. The Independents, apparently practicing cost-oriented pricing, refused to price the cars in such a way that they would have had a chance to sell in high volume. The cars may have been ahead of their time in concept; they were seriously lacking in price considerations.

By 1955, only the Rambler and the 85-inch wheelbase Metropolitan that American Motors was importing from England were left in the small car field. Sales were a disappointing 72,000 units in 1955 and 71,000 units in 1956.

The First Import Wave and the Big Three Response

American car market and consumer tastes were, however, beginning to change. Cars were growing bigger and more expensive. The 1955 Chevrolet had a wheelbase of 115 inches and an overall length of 195 inches; by the 1958 model, these dimensions had grown to 117.5 inches and 209 inches, respectively. The price rises of this period have already been chronicled. By the second half of 1957 the American economy had lost its expansionary luster and was beginning to go into a recession. Consumers began to look for smaller, cheaper, more maneuverable cars. At the same time, European producers began to enter the American market for the first time. Small, inexpensive European cars looked like what the new American market wanted.

From 58,000 units in 1955, import sales rose to 207,000 units in 1957. In 1958, they reached 379,000 units, 8.1 percent of the market. Rambler sales also benefited, rising to 91,000 units in 1957 and 186,000 units in 1958. The combination of Ramblers and imports held over 12 percent of the 1958 automobile market.

Rambler's sales resurgence was not due solely to its size. Unlike the early 1950's, Rambler's prices were under those of the Big Three low price models. Exact model for model comparisons are difficult because of lack of exact model correspondence, but American Motors had the cheapest six-cylinder, two-door sedan at a list price of $1,788, compared to $2,030 for the cheapest Ford. American Motors' cheapest six-cylinder, four-door sedan was priced at $2,047, compared to $2,084 for Ford. American Motors' cheapest six-cylinder, four-door hardtop was $2,287, compared to $2,372 for Plymouth. Observers were quick to point out that most American Motors' customers were buying the more expensive models, but the important point is that many were attracted to the American Motors' dealer showrooms by the economy image, in operating costs *and* in initial cost, of the Rambler.

Studebaker-Packard, the only remaining Independent, quickly jumped on the cheaper car bandwagon. For the 1958 model year, it brought out the Scotsman, a stripped version of the full-sized Champion models that listed for $400 less than the Champions and provided the cheapest four-door sedan in the industry at a list price of $1,874. For the 1959 model year, the company introduced its own 108.5-inch wheelbase compact, the Lark, which sold well enough to give Studebaker-Packard its first profits in five years.

The year 1959 brought still a higher surge of imports and compact car sales and convinced the industry that small cars were more than a temporary fad. Import sales were 609,000. Rambler sales were 363,000 and Lark sales were 133,000, the total of these three segments coming to 18.4 percent of the market. These figures undoubtedly would have been higher if the Big Three had not brought out their own compact cars in the fall of 1959.

The behavior of the Big Three in the face of the small car threat is instructive. Sometime in late 1955, Ford and General Motors took their small car projects off the back burner and began the advanced styling work on a compact car. As the small car trend had not yet appeared, this activity seems to have been one of risk hedging, since both Fords and Chevrolets were planned to increase appreciably in size by the 1959 model year.[4] Chrysler started planning shortly after. As small car sales began to swell in late 1956 and early 1957, the pace of development does not appear to have been appreciably quickened. Bringing out a small car immediately, of course, was impossible; tooling lead times prevented it. But had they chosen to do so, the Big Three could have embarked on a crash program to bring out their compacts in the fall of 1958, at the same time as the Studebaker Lark was actually introduced. The problem of tooling lead times would have prevented any earlier date, but the fall of 1958 was feasible.

The companies, in fact, chose to continue development on a leisurely basis. They had been somewhat fooled by the phantom small car boom of ten years earlier, and they were not eager to repeat their mistakes. They were concerned that their own small cars might simply divert customers from their more expensive, more profitable models. The investment in the new cars would be substantial, and the companies wanted to assure themselves that the market was large enough for all three firms. Edward N. Cole, then head of the Chevrolet Division, stated that the small car market would have to reach a size of 500,000 units before General Motors would be interested in entering.[5] Since General Motors fully expected its rivals to enter also, Cole was implicitly stating a "room-for-all" proposition.

As a holding measure, General Motors in June 1957, announced plans to import the German Opel and the British Vauxhall, made by its overseas subsidiaries.[6] Ford, with less fanfare, stepped up its imports of English Fords and began importing German Ford Taunus models. After Chrysler bought into Simca in 1958, it began to import Simcas. At the same time, the companies, particularly General Motors, tried to play down the small car boom. "Of all Detroit auto makers, G.M. has been the most scoffingly skeptical of the prospects of the small car in the U.S. market. If G.M. has said it once, it's said it ten thousand times: 'a good used car is the answer to the American public's need for cheap transportation.' " [7] General Motors also discouraged the idea that it would build a small car in the United States, reviving the claim that such a car could sell for only $100 under a Chevrolet.[8]

By early 1958 the Big Three had already placed their tooling orders and thus were firmly committed to the introduction of the compacts, barring a total collapse of the small car market. Yet the companies continued to be vague and skeptical about the small car in their public statements. Before Senator Kefauver's Administered Prices Hearings on January 30, 1958, General Motors President Harlow H. Curtice testified as follows on the subject of building a small car:

SENATOR O'MAHONEY: Do you plan to build a small car here in the United States to compete with imported smaller cars?

MR. CURTICE: For over the years that has been the subject that we have constantly studied. Thus far it has not been practical from the standpoint of the economics to offer the small car, on the basis that because you take the value out so much more rapidly than you can take the cost out.[9]

A few days later, President L. L. Colbert of Chrysler testified on the same subject: "Up to this point all I can say is we at Chrysler have not given up, but we have not found a way yet to engineer, style, and build one of these smaller cars for enough difference in price to justify what we believe the American market demand for it is . . . It may come, and when it does, we are going to try to be ready, but that is the situation on the small car, and also on the American small cars as we see it today . . . We are studying it very carefully." [10]

In December 1958, General Motors' new president, John F. Gordon, claimed that the company was still "weighing the pros and cons" of building a small domestic car.[11] As late as March 1959, Chrysler's Colbert would only acknowledge that Chrysler would introduce a small car if the other manufacturers led the way.[12] Yet, it was an open secret in the automotive press as early as April 1958 that the Big Three would introduce their compact cars in the fall of 1959 and that the General Motors' car, despite elaborate secrecy efforts by the company, would have a rear engine with a unitized body and swing axles.[13]

Why were the Big Three so reluctant to reveal their intentions to build a small car? Basically, they were concerned that many of their customers might refrain from buying 1958 and 1959 model cars and instead wait for the new compact cars. In a replacement-cycle market, any delayed sales are the equivalent of lost sales; the companies wanted to minimize their sales losses by not showing their hands until as late as possible.

The Big Three's compacts were a success. They sold well, taking some sales from full-sized models,[14] but also pushing back the import tide. From a high of 609,000 sales, or 10.1 percent of the market in 1959, import sales fell to 339,000 units, or 4.9 percent of the market in 1962. This decline occurred at two levels. First, the imports of the Big Three's overseas subsidiaries withered away to almost nothing. Second, those foreign makes that had relied largely on novelty buying and had not bothered to build up a solid dealer and service-repair system also fell by the wayside. Renault was probably the best known example of this. By contrast, Volkswagen, which had spent a good deal of effort on its dealer system, continued to increase its sales year after year. The inherent quality of the automobile was probably the dominant factor in this process, but the importance of the parts and service aspect should not be overlooked.

After the Big Three introduced their compacts, two trends developed. One was Ford's intention to develop a still smaller car that would compete directly with the imports. The first round of Big Three compacts had wheelbases of 106.5–109.5 inches and list prices of $1,900 or above. A Volkswagen had a wheelbase of 94.5 inches and a list price of $1,595. The price difference was not as great as it looked, since the Big Three compacts were being sold at discounts of up to $400, whereas Volkswagens were sold only at list price. However, Ford felt a smaller car might provide a better rival to the small imports. The Cardinal, as it was provisionally called, was to have a 96-inch wheelbase and an overall length only 5 inches longer than a Volkswagen, a front-mounted, four-cylinder engine, and front-wheel drive. It was to carry a list price of $1,650–$1,700.[15] The transmission and engine were to be built in Germany, with the rest of the car made in the United States and assembled at Ford's Louisville assembly plant.

The car was tentatively scheduled for introduction in the fall of 1962. General Motors was rumored to have a "Fisher" model in preparation as a rival to it.[16] Then, on April 11, 1962, after the advertising brochures had even been printed, Ford canceled the project. Ford's reasons were never made public, but it seems likely that the public's preference for larger cars in the 1962 model year, combined with the continuing decline in import sales, convinced Ford that the small car boom was over; seeing a downward trend, Ford probably felt there would be little room for its car and those that its rivals might produce. Once again, however, the discarded design was not a total loss. The Cardinal eventually appeared in Germany as the Taunus 12M.

The Cardinal was definitely a victim of the development lag time problem of the industry and of unlucky timing. Planned in 1959 when imports were 10.1 percent of the market, it could not reach the market until 1962 and was dropped in that year when imports fell to only 4.9 percent of the market. But, in fact, imports had reached their low point in that year. They have risen steadily ever since and have more than doubled their relative and absolute shares of the market. Had Ford gone ahead with its decision to produce the car, it could have capitalized on this rise.

The second trend in compact cars was toward the introduction of slightly larger compact models by the middle-level maker. Even before the compacts had been introduced, the auto companies had noticed that many small car buyers were willing to pay a premium for deluxe interior and exterior trim;[17] this was later confirmed when 60–70 percent of compact car buyers ordered the deluxe versions (extra trim) of their cars.[18] Perhaps these buyers could be induced to buy a somewhat more expensive compact. Giving a compact to the middle-level make dealers would boost the morale of these dealer bodies. Perhaps the buyers of these middle-level compacts could be eventually attracted back to buying full-sized, middle-level makes. The middle-level compacts seemed likely to fulfill all of these goals; they were introduced in the middle and latter parts of 1960. They also sold well and by 1965 had been increased in size to an "intermediate" status between the full-sized cars and the low price compacts. The low price makes also introduced intermediate-sized cars to fill out their lists.

At the bottom of the market, there was a tendency for the Big Three low price compacts to grow in size and cost. By 1968 the compacts had grown by about two inches in wheelbase and four to five inches in overall length. More importantly, compact car prices had increased by $300 or more between the spring of 1961 and the spring of 1968. The cheapest Big Three compact in the spring of 1968 listed at $2,252 (a Ford Falcon two-door sedan), compared with $1,912 for a Falcon two-door sedan in the spring of 1961. Part of this rise was due to the addition of safety equipment, but Volkswagen, facing the same safety equipment requirements, had risen in price from $1,595 to only $1,695 over the same period.

The New Import Wave and Big Three Response

Import sales began to rise again in 1963. After their low point in 1962, import sales rose to 386,000, or 5.1 percent of the market in 1963, and climbed steadily to 781,000 sales, 9.3 percent of the market in 1967. In 1968 they passed the 10 percent mark, reaching 986,000 units, 10.5 percent of the market. This rise was spearheaded by Volkswagen sales; but other importers, learning the lessons of the first import sales collapse, spent more money and effort on strong dealer systems and saw this pay off in terms of rising sales.[19]

The reaction of the Big Three to this renewed import boom was almost identical to their reaction eight years earlier. They disparaged the small car sales. They stepped up imports of their overseas subsidiaries' makes. They again claimed that it would be impossible to build a small car for under $2,000. Finally, in 1968, convinced that the market indeed was large enough to support their collective entry,

General Motors, Ford, and American Motors announced their plans for a new generation of small cars that would cost under $2,000.[20] The Ford Maverick (103-inch wheelbase) appeared in the spring of 1969 and the American Motors Hornet (108-inch wheelbase) appeared in the fall of 1969. Still another set of "subcompacts," under 100-inch wheelbase, appeared in 1970: the American Motors Gremlin, the Ford Pinto, and the General Motors Vega. Chrysler was far behind its rivals in preparing a small car for this market. Its subcompact was scheduled for 1972, and in the interim Chrysler was expected to try to sell small cars produced in Japan by Mitsubishi Heavy Industries and sold under a Chrysler nameplate.

At least as early as 1967, the evidence on import sales indicated that the market for a new generation of small cars was large enough to support all of the domestic producers. Ford, making the first expensive commitments on tooling for the Maverick in mid-1967, was the first to recognize this. This was consistent with its role as an ambitious seeker of new market niches that it could exploit profitably before its rivals caught up. (See Chapter 12.) American Motors, constrained by its meager resources, was somewhat behind. General Motors, traditionally the most sceptical about the virtues of small cars and the most vulnerable to the loss of big car sales to the new small cars, lagged even further behind in development of the subcompacts. Chrysler, guessing wrongly about the size of the small car market, was last.

In any event, none of the producers was publicly committed to enter this market until late 1968, when the first three companies made public their preparations at about the same time. Before this time, all could have quietly dropped their plans, as Ford had done with the Cardinal six years earlier. Only after the announcements were they irrevocably committed. By late 1968, the market was clearly large enough to support all the domestic producers.

Why were the companies willing to announce their intentions so far in advance this time? Because this round of small cars would be more directly aimed at the small foreign car and the companies were more confident this time that the customers they would attract would be from import sales and not from their own sales. An advance announcement would deter mostly import sales, not their own.

12

Product Behavior:
Durability, Styling, Models,
and Model Proliferation

"Last year a Yale University physicist calculated that since Chevy offered 46 models, 32 engines, 20 transmissions, 21 colors (plus nine two-tone combinations), and more than 400 accessories and options, the number of different cars that a Chevrolet customer conceivably could order was greater than the number of atoms in the universe. This seemingly would put General Motors one notch higher than God in the chain of command. This year, even though the standard Chevrolet never accounts for less than two-thirds of Chevy's sales, Chevy is offering still more models (a total of 50), and options, indicating that while they may not be increasing their lead over Ford, they are pulling away from God." [1]

In a market in which replacement demand is the dominant element, there are always great incentives to try to speed up the pace of the replacement cycle. Any acceleration of the cycle means increased annual sales. Even a temporary acceleration, which then recedes to the previous pace, means a one-shot increase in sales.

An example will help to clarify this point. Suppose that cars lasted perfectly for ten years and then collapsed, like the one-horse shay, and that owners held on to their cars for the full ten years. Then, if 40 million people wished to own cars, there would be (if they distributed themselves randomly) sales of 4 million cars each year, each cohort returning to the market every ten years. If these 40 million owners could be induced to replace their cars every five years, then the auto industry could sell 8 million cars each year. Even if only one cohort were induced to replace its car after five years and then that cohort settled back to a ten-year cycle, there would still be a net gain in sales. Thus, even if a monopolist controlled the industry, it would be in his interests to attempt to quicken the pace of replacement. As we shall see, oligopolistic rivalry may lead to even greater efforts in the areas that affect the replacement cycle.

The Theory of Decreased Durability

How can the replacement cycle be shortened? One possible strategy would be to make cars less durable. Interestingly, this strategy will only work if used in conjunction with some other strategy for quickening replacement.

Suppose that new car buyers keep their cars until scrapping time. Then, if buyers are fully aware of the decreased durability of the cars that they are buying, any advantages to the company from decreasing durability could be better gained by simply raising prices and keeping durability unchanged. For example, a company's cars last ten years and sell for $3,000; it envisions cutting car life to five years and keeping the price at $3,000. Whatever benefits are to be gained from this policy could be better gained by keeping durability at ten years, raising the price to $6,000, and allowing consumers to pay it off in two equal installments in year one and year six. Consumers should presumably be indifferent to buying two identical five-year-lasting cars each costing $3,000, or to buying a ten-year-lasting car costing $6,000, payable in two installments. In the latter case the company saves itself the expense of building the second car. Only if decreased durability offers sizable reductions in manufacturing costs would a decreased durability strategy be rational. But the potential cost savings are probably not large for an automobile manufacturer. A manufacturer would have to find areas for cost-cutting that did not seriously impair car performance as the buyer drove his new car out of the show room but did cause earlier scrapping.[2] Thinner steel, less rust-proofing, and fewer welds are ways of decreasing durability in this manner, but the potential savings here do not appear to be large. Thus, in a one-owner market, auto companies should not be interested in decreasing durability.

But suppose through some other strategy (for example, model changes, which will be discussed later) new-car buyers trade in their vehicles long before they physically wear out and a second group of consumers buy these used vehicles. Again, our company considers cutting durability from ten years to five years and plans to continue charging $3,000 per car. If new-car buyers trade in after

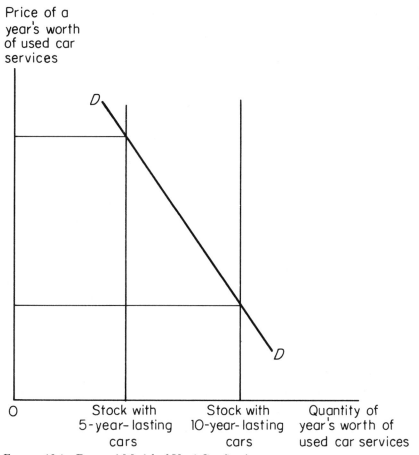

FIGURE 12.1   Demand Model of Used Car Services

three years, they should be unaffected, except as this affects the trade-in value of their cars. Initially, knowledgeable used car buyers should be offering to pay less for these used cars. But very quickly, the available stock of years' worth of used car services would fall drastically (see Figure 12.1), and the price of a single year's worth of used car services would rise. If the price rise were more than proportionate to the decrease in the stock (that is, if demand were inelastic), then the price paid for used cars would actually rise, even though the cars did not last as long. New car buyers would thus receive higher prices for their trade-ins, and they would be in a position to buy more expensive cars and buy cars more frequently. This would be in addition to any increased sales, occurring because of the substitution effects between new cars and the higher priced yearly services of used cars. The auto company would clearly stand to gain from this decreased durability.[3]

The inelastic demand for used car services (and thus for used cars) would appear to be significant here. This does not seem to be an unreasonable assumption, in that used cars would more likely be in the "necessity" category than would new cars. Chow found that the price elasticity of demand for the entire stock of cars on the road was between -0.6 and -1.0.[4]

Although a tacit industry agreement to decrease durability jointly would make a decreased durability strategy for a single company easier, it is not necessary. As long as there is a fairly inelastic demand for the company's used cars, the company should be able to gain the benefits of a moderate decrease in durability by itself without losing too many used car customers to its rivals' longer lasting cars. Through successive steps by individual members, an entire industry could thus achieve a decrease in durability even though there had not been any tacit agreement. This process would continue only until the profit-maximizing level of durability was achieved: the level that reduced the stock of cars to the point at which the used car buyers' price elasticity was just equal to -1.0. But because of the tentative, small-step nature of the oligopoly process, the gradual decrease in durability might persist for a lengthy period before durability stabilized.

Do we have any a priori reasons for suspecting an actual decrease in automobile durability during the postwar period? If the companies have followed a decreased durability strategy, this would imply either that the optimal (profit-maximizing) level of durability has decreased since 1946 or that durability was not at its optimal level in 1946. Both are possible. If the income elasticity for new cars is greater than that for used cars, then the demand for new cars has grown faster than the demand for used cars since the war. To prevent these new cars from eventually glutting the used car market, which would have had unpleasant reverberations for the new car market itself, a decreasing durability strategy might have been employed to reduce the effective stock of used cars. Also, the war might have disrupted any equilibrium that had existed, and it could have taken the companies some time to grope their way to a new equilibrium.

Evidence of Decreased Durability

Is there any evidence to indicate that car lives have been shortened because of decreased durability? We have figures on the age distribution of all cars on the road as of July 1 each year, collected by R. L. Polk & Company. The relevant figures, of course, are not the average or median age of cars, since those would be influenced by the pattern of recent sales, but, rather, the percentage of cars built in a certain year that are still on the road n years later. Since some production may get exported, a better number to use as a base is the number of cars of model year X that are registered as on the road as of July 1 in year $X + 1$. Any scrappage in the interim should be miniscule and inconsequential. Consequently, then, we are looking at the percentage of cars of model year X that are still on the road in year $X + n$, this fraction having as its numerator the cars of vintage X still on the road as of July 1, year $X + n$, and as its denominator the cars of vintage X on the road as of July 1, year $X + 1$.[5]

Cars do not begin to fall by the wayside in significant numbers until they are five or six years old. Consequently, we shall look at the groups of cars that are seven, eight, and nine years old. Table 12.1 gives the survival percentages for these groups of cars over time. The survival rates for all three groups have clearly declined. To make sure that this was not simply a result of the cars of Independents' makes that are no longer produced being junked abnormally early, survival rates for Big Three makes only (excluding Edsel and De Soto) were also calculated and included in the table. They also show a decline, ruling out the hypothesis that the Independents' cars were being junked.

Are these declines evidence of decreased durability? Not necessarily. Since consumers' incomes have gone up over time, they might well decide to scrap their cars earlier than physical durability would

Table 12.1   **The Number of Seven-, Eight-, and Nine-Year-Old Cars, as a Percentage[a] of Their Original Production, Still on the Road as of July 1 of the Year Listed**

Year	Seven years old		Eight years old		Nine years old	
	All[b]	Big Three only[c]	All[b]	Big Three only[c]	All[b]	Big Three only[c]
1953	92.86	93.90	—	—	—	—
1954	91.81	91.96	88.89	89.74	—	—
1955	92.84	93.05	85.40	86.16	79.07	80.70
1956	89.52	90.10	83.51	84.74	71.25	72.84
1957	89.34	90.16	78.35	79.55	68.73	70.93
1958	86.57	87.64	79.33	80.76	64.37	65.89
1959	88.58	89.40	79.54	81.17	69.55	71.49
1960	89.29	89.83	79.00	80.49	67.08	69.17
1961	89.46	89.86	80.23	81.21	66.56	68.41
1962	90.27	90.42	81.56	82.26	68.91	70.27
1963	88.64	88.91	81.73	82.08	71.95	70.64
1964	85.31	85.60	78.81	79.18	70.09	70.59
1965	87.01	85.13	75.24	75.79	66.78	67.20
1966	86.23	86.48	72.89	71.51	60.19	60.83
1967	84.47	86.36	73.84	74.34	56.12	55.23

SOURCE: R. L. Polk figures, from *Automotive Industries, Annual Statistical Issue*, various years.

[a] Really, as a percentage of the cars registered as of July 1 of the year following production or as of July 1 of the second year following production.

[b] For reasons of consistency, imports, Willys, and Kaiser-Frazer vehicles have been subtracted from the R. L. Polk totals.

[c] Excludes De Soto and Edsel.

require in favor of new cars. (Or they might decide to use that extra income to purchase and keep second and third cars and, thus, would try to stretch out the life of their cars. There is no good a priori prediction on which way the income effect should go.) Also, repair costs, for both labor and parts, have increased faster than the consumer price index or the BLS series for new cars.[6] Increasing repair costs should lead consumers to scrap their cars earlier. Other factors affecting perceived survival rates would be a larger car population causing a possible more-than-proportional increase in the number of accidents that created unrepairable ("totaled") cars and, offsetting this, an increasing proportion of the nation's cars residing in warmer climates where the weather is not as severe and where cars should physically last longer.[7]

How can these various influences be sorted out? Ideally, one would like to set up a demand and supply model for, say, seven-year-old cars of the following form:

$$Q_7^D = f(Y, R, P_7, P_u)$$
$$Q_7^S = g(P_7, P_s, Q_7^o, t)$$

where

Q_7^D, Q_7^S = quantities of seven-year-old cars demanded and supplied
Y = personal disposable income
R = repair costs
P_7 = price of seven-year-old cars
P_u = price of all other used cars
P_s = price of scrap metal
Q_7^o = original production of the particular vintage car
t = time trend

The time trend term should include the time trend in the supply of seven-year-old cars after the other influences have been taken into account; presumably, this should be related largely to the trend in inherent durability. Unfortunately, preliminary efforts at estimating these equations for seven-, eight-, and nine-year-old cars were un-successful. Hopes of separating out individual demand and supply curves from the overall used car market were probably utopian.

Consequently, a rearrangement of the model was attempted, focusing on scrapping behavior. An alternative way of expressing the decreasing survival rates of Table 12.1 would be in terms of increasing scrapping rates. Between July 1 of year 7 and July 1 of year 8 of a car's life, an increasing number of cars, as a percentage of the number in existence in year 7, have been scrapped over time. Table 12.2 shows these scrapping rates for the postwar years. Can we sort out the various influences on scrapping behavior and isolate a time trend that might represent decreasing durability?

The model looks as follows:

$$\frac{Q_{i,7} - Q_{i,8}}{Q_{i,7}} = f(P_i, P_s, t)$$

$$P_{i,7} = g\left(\frac{Q_{i,7} + Q_{i,8}}{2}, Y, R, P_u\right)$$

$$P_u = h(C, Y, R)$$

where

$Q_{i,7}$ = quantity of vintage i cars in existence in year 7
$Q_{i,8}$ = quantity of vintage i cars in existence one year later in year 8
$P_{i,7}$ = price of vintage i cars between years 7 and 8
C = stock of all cars on the road

All other symbols are as given for the previous equation.

The first equation was specifically estimated with the two-price terms in a relative price form. The estimation was done on a two-

Table 12.2 **Scrapping Rates for Cars** (as a percentage of cars of that vintage in existence at ages six, seven, and eight respectively)

Year	Ages 6–7	Ages 7–8	Ages 8–9
1952–53	2.60		
1953–54	3.36	4.27	
1954–55	3.50	6.98	11.05
1955–56	12.46	10.06	16.57
1956–57	6.33	12.37	17.69
1957–58	7.62	11.20	17.83
1958–59	3.22	8.12	12.33
1959–60	6.21	10.81	15.67
1960–61	3.59	10.15	15.76
1961–62	4.86	8.83	17.10
1962–63	6.46	9.46	11.79
1963–64	8.45	11.09	14.25
1964–65	8.34	11.80	15.26
1965–66	7.71	16.22	20.01
1966–67	6.18	14.37	23.04

stage least squares basis. The BLS series for auto repair costs was used for R; personal disposable income in 1958 dollars was used for Y; National Automobile Dealers Association used car prices were used for P_i (they are only available for eight- and nine-year-old cars through 1966 and the regressions had to end there); the BLS wholesale price index for scrap iron and steel was used for P_s; and R. L. Polk data was used for the Q's and C. Regressions were run for scrappage between years 6 and 7 (for 1953–1967), between years 7 and 8 (for 1954–1966) and between years 8 and 9 (for 1955–1966). The results are as follows:

$$\frac{Q_{i,6} - Q_{i,7}}{Q_{i,6}} = 0.1011 \quad - 0.1280(P_{i,6}/P_s) + 0.0041t \qquad R^2 = 0.4136$$
$$\phantom{\frac{Q_{i,6} - Q_{i,7}}{Q_{i,6}} = } (.0243) \quad\;\; (.0526) \qquad\qquad (.0015)$$

$$\frac{Q_{i,7} - Q_{i,8}}{Q_{i,7}} = 0.1242 \quad - 0.1784(P_{i,7}/P_s) + 0.0080t \qquad R^2 = 0.7116$$
$$\phantom{\frac{Q_{i,7} - Q_{i,8}}{Q_{i,7}} = } (.0190) \quad\;\; (.0575) \qquad\qquad (.0016)$$

$$\frac{Q_{i,8} - Q_{i,9}}{Q_{i,8}} = 0.1830 \quad - 0.2142(P_{i,8}/P_s) + \;.0070t \qquad R^2 = 0.3356$$
$$\phantom{\frac{Q_{i,8} - Q_{i,9}}{Q_{i,8}} = } (.0219) \quad\;\; (.1057) \qquad\qquad (.0035)$$

The results of these regressions indicate that, after the relative price effects have been taken into account, there has been an increase in scrapping of 0.41 percent per year between years 6 and 7; 0.80 percent per year between years 7 and 8; and 0.70 percent per year between years 8 and 9. Unfortunately, time trend residuals are just that. They tell us that there is an unexplained trend, without identifying it. Still, this trend may well be representing the results of a decreased durability strategy by the automobile industry.

An interesting side result of the study of durability was the findings of the durability of individual car makes. Among Chevrolets, Fords, and Plymouths, for example, Chevrolets have usually had better survival rates than have its two rivals, as is indicated in Table 12.3.

Table 12.3 Survival Rates for Chevrolets, Fords, and Plymouths

Year	Seven years old			Eight years old			Nine years old		
	Chev.	Ford	Plym.	Chev.	Ford	Plym.	Chev.	Ford	Plym.
1953	95.23	96.37	93.04						
1954	94.55	87.03	94.43	92.21	92.01	89.13			
1955	96.79	83.02	96.34	90.91	80.66	89.78	85.18	82.32	81.30
1956	94.32	86.41	93.49	90.66	72.08	89.94	80.76	66.75	78.33
1957	92.72	88.10	91.69	86.64	72.82	86.06	78.98	57.74	77.74
1958	92.03	85.32	88.62	85.66	77.41	83.75	75.27	56.99	75.46
1959	93.88	89.73	86.00	87.80	77.72	82.84	78.30	67.41	76.17
1960	93.36	91.11	87.05	87.50	80.57	77.43	78.22	64.52	72.20
1961	93.79	89.53	88.89	87.73	82.48	77.72	78.37	68.09	65.71
1962	93.03	88.63	87.64	89.02	81.15	80.62	79.94	71.20	66.49
1963	92.64	86.48	85.12	87.04	79.03	77.10	81.28	68.40	68.73
1964	92.75	83.61	77.59	85.82	74.87	72.96	78.48	66.25	63.43
1965	91.07	81.79	79.78	88.98	72.02	60.46	77.04	60.98	58.91
1966	89.34	85.00	80.36	80.61	65.87	61.48	79.99	54.87	42.83
1967	89.52	82.35	82.19	78.83	71.88	64.34	65.48	48.96	43.17

[a] The percentage of seven-, eight-, and nine-year-old cars still on the road, as a percentage of the cars registered as of July 1 of the year following production or as of July 1 of the second year following production.

This has held true generally, for General Motors cars vis-à-vis its rivals, with the exception of the Chrysler make. Are General Motors cars better made? Or do General Motors owners take better care of their cars? Or do the higher used car prices that General Motors cars bring in the market make it less likely that they will be scrapped? But do they command higher used car prices because consumers recognize superior inherent durability? Efforts to sort out these effects have not been successful.

Another strategy for increasing the pace of new car replacement demand would be to shorten the *economic* life of a car by raising the price of repair parts. If the substitution effects (substituting new cars for old cars that require expensive repair parts) exceed the income effects of the repair parts price increase, the price increase should quicken the pace of replacement. There is some evidence to suggest that the auto companies have kept repair parts prices high.[9] The real test of this proposition, however, would require a demonstration that the repair parts prices of the auto companies were higher than profit-maximizing conditions for that market alone would dictate, an almost impossible test.[10]

Styling and Model Change

The alternative to decreasing directly the physical or economic life of a car is to create in consumers' minds the belief that the economic usefulness of their cars has diminished before actual physical usefulness ends, so that they will be willing to replace their cars sooner. If one can, at the same time, create a demand for used cars in a second group of consumers so that the new-car buyers do not have to suffer so great a loss when they dispose of their old cars, and therefore are financially better able to buy a new car, so much the better.

This inducement to replace before the end of the physical life of the car could come from two directions. The auto companies could rely on engineering advances to induce replacement, and major new advances in automotive technology every few years might achieve this result. But the research and development expenses necessary for this strategy could be very large, with a great deal of uncertainty as to the results. The technological room for major advances every few years may simply not exist. Consumers, most of them technically incapable of evaluating the advances, may not respond to them.

The alternative to frequent technological advances is frequent styling changes, coupled with some moderate engineering changes, to create the image of a new and different ("improved") product each year. This approach has advantages in that there is no uncertainty over the ability to develop new designs. The risks lie instead in the desirability of these designs compared to the designs of rivals. Also, there is no necessity for the consumer to be technically sophisticated; he need only have the desire (inherent or created) either to "be the first one on the block to own . . ." or to "keep up with the Joneses" (who were the first ones on the block). This is, of course, the strategy that the auto companies have chosen, and the annual model change has become an established part of the automobile market. The auto companies may offer various euphemistic rationales for this practice,[11] but, fundamentally, it sells cars.

The contrast with the truck industry is worth making at this point. Truck demand is also largely a replacement demand, but truck buyers are technically more sophisticated than car buyers and are relatively more interested in performance than in appearance or prestige. Also, there have traditionally been a larger number of Independent truck manufacturers than Independent car manufacturers, with a larger share of the market. In this field, the industry, taking its lead from the smaller truck manufacturers who have been technologically very aggressive, has largely foresworn an annual model change approach, relying more on engineering advances. It is interesting to note that automatic transmissions, power brakes, and power steering were originally developed for, and first commercially applied to, trucks and buses. Diesel engines, as an alternative to four-cycle spark plug (Otto) engines have been developed for trucks but not for American cars. (Mercedes, though, does have an automobile diesel engine.) Currently, turbine engines may well find commercial application on trucks before they are used on cars. Though there may be many inherent characteristics of trucks that would warrant developing these items for them first, still the nature of the market structure (more small producers more willing to take the risks of a technological change strategy) and of the buyers in that market have probably been influential in this process.[12]

Oligopolistic rivalry may spur the pace and extent of design changes. For a firm faced by oligopolistic rivals, styling changes are not only a way of quickening the replacement pace of its "loyal" customers, but also a way of attracting new customers away from other firms. With price competition largely eschewed, rivalry for customers has centered on a styling strategy rather than on a major technological change strategy for the same reasons as were advanced for a styling strategy to speed replacement. Detroit is basically convinced that it is styling that sells cars. Consumers Union may complain about inconveniently shaped trunks or rear seats on two-door sedans that require a contortionist to enter and exit, but the auto companies seem to ignore this. If the car looks good, it will sell; if it does not look good, conveniently shaped trunks are not going to make much of a difference.

Risk plays a role in oligopolistic styling strategies. If a monopolist controlled the auto industry, a poor model or two would simply temporarily slow the pace of replacement. Present sales would be lost, but future sales should be unaffected. But with brand loyalty an important factor in the oligopolistic auto market, a poorly received model can have serious consequences both for the present and the future. Not only is replacement delayed when current sales are lost, but potential customers are lost to rival firms' products and may not return in the future. The same effect may occur if a firm simply holds too long to a basic model shape, while its rivals introduce new models; its previous customers, desirous of obtaining a new model, may desert. New customers may feel that they want an "all-new" model, not a modified version of a car that was new a few years ago. Consequently, with styling seen as the major battleground of competition and brand loyalty producing consequences extending into the future, we should expect the effort and attention given to styling to exceed that which would exist if replacement were the only concern.

Another strategy encouraged by a replacement market is that of "trading-up." Efforts to get customers to buy more expensive, more profitable versions of a product exist in all industries, but replacement markets offer a unique opportunity to convince the customer that he has outgrown his present model and that he ought to trade-up to a more expensive car. This is frequently done within a make by advertising and direct sales efforts (getting the bottom of the line owner to trade-up to the top of the line, the sedan owner to buy a hardtop, and so forth); but also between makes by advertising ("Move up to a Mercury").

Turning to the actual pattern of car model behavior, we find that there has indeed been a great deal of emphasis on model changes and speeding the pace of replacement.[13] This was held in abeyance through the early postwar years, as consumers sought to replace their prewar models without any extra urging from the auto companies. The auto companies still seemed to be feeling their way slowly into the replacement market in the 1949–1951 period; the Korean War, limiting production to less than that which the auto companies would have preferred to produce, dampened whatever tendencies there would have been to rush ahead with widespread model changes. The end of the Korean War, however, ushered in a period of active styling competition, rapid model changes, and a proliferation of models that has continued to the present day.

Until 1959, the basic pattern in the auto industry was one of major design changes (frame and body shell) every three years, with "face-lifts" of the exterior sheet metal in the interim. This was related to the design, tooling, and production lead time of about three years discussed in Chapter 3. This was not a hard and fast rule, however. The Korean War delayed most General Motors and Chrysler changes to a four-year period; fundamental changes occurred in 1949 and 1953, or 1950 and 1954. When the occasion arose, manufacturers were willing to rush in with two-year cycles (notably Chrysler, with major changes in 1953, 1955, and 1957). But three years was considered the norm.

Of the components in the lead time structure, tooling waiting times seemed the most easily shortened. By the end of the 1950's the Big Three had acquired enough die making capacity of their own that they were less dependent on the independent tool- and die-makers and less subject to the vagaries of waiting times. The tooling order date to new car introduction lag was cut to less than two years, and managements could settle on two-year major design change cycle. They could get a look at how the previous all-new model was being received before ordering the tools for the next one. This reduced designing risks, yet avoided incurring the rush-order extra costs that this had previously entailed. Since the late 1950's, a two-year cycle has been the norm for full-sized cars, with the compacts and intermediates initially exhibiting a slower pace but speeding up as volume increased and consumer replacement demand became more important.

The new models have usually appeared in late September or early October. Early postwar materials shortages and Korean War production controls caused the new model introduction dates to be delayed somewhat, but years of unhampered production have seen the introduction date center on October 1. This timing is more than accidental. Before 1936, model years and calendar years had largely coincided, and the seasonal pattern of buying showed only one strong selling period, the second quarter.[14] The October 1 introduction date has served to smooth somewhat the seasonal variation in demand and has created two strong selling periods, the second and fourth quarters of each calendar year. This, of course, smooths production flows, reduces overtime requirements, and generally allows better use of manufacturing capacity.

In the early 1960's Ford and Chrysler began the practice of introducing some models during December through March of the model year and labeling them "1962½'s," "1963½'s," and so forth. Some outside observers mistakenly saw this as a speeding up of the pace of model changes to a semiannual basis. Rather, it was an attempt to smooth demand further by delaying the introduction of a few models (usually special hardtops or high performance engine options) until the winter months, thereby increasing consumer interest in new cars during these slack months. This tactic appears to have been unsuccessful, and it has been dropped. However, wholly new lines of cars, like Ford's Mustang and Maverick, have often been introduced in the middle of the model year, usually early spring. This timing has stemmed from the desire to give these lines a strong start by introducing them at the beginning of the strong buying season and simultaneously avoiding the competition with other new model announcements that would surround an autumn introduction.

A supplementary strategy to that of rapid model change has been one of model proliferation: the production of a wider selection of models to attract more consumers into replacing their cars sooner and trading-up to something more glamorous.[15] This has come about partly through the provision of more optional extras such as bucket seats or power steering, which can be installed on standard cars, and partly through the production of additional models as standard (though often it is just extra trim that distinguishes one model from another). Greater assembly line flexibility, as described in Chapter 3, and better inventorying practices have been the technological advances behind the proliferation. Greater overall volume in the market has also been an important factor in preventing economies of scale from being eroded away. Table 12.4 shows the increase in

Table 12.4   Number of Models Offered and Average Output for Model Offered

Year	Number of models offered at end of model year	Model year production divided by number of models offered
1949	205	21,400
1950	243	26,700
1951	243	24,700
1952	224	17,000
1953	210	29,000
1954	240	20,200
1955	216	33,500
1956	232	27,100
1957	245	25,300
1958	263	16,100
1959	239	23,300
1960	244	24,600
1961	260	20,800
1962	296	22,600
1963	336	21,900
1964	336	23,500
1965	348	25,400
1966	368	23,400
1967	370	20,700

SOURCE: *Automotive News Almanac, 1968*, pp. 57, 62.

the number of models that have been offered by the auto companies.[16] This increase is all the more striking when one realizes that five Independent makes had dropped out of the market between 1952 and 1958. The table also shows that the average volume per model offered has not changed appreciably since 1949. Though many models, in fact, sell at much higher volumes than the average, still the table gives a rough idea of the constancy that has held. One should probably also credit the wave of import buying in the late 1950's as influential in the process of proliferation, jolting the Big Three out of their tendency to produce only one basic kind of car (big) and spurring them to provide more varied forms of automobiles. If the imports had not been available to show the trends in consumer tastes, the Big Three might well have continued to sell only the big cars to consumers, who would have bought them but who might have preferred smaller cars.

The costs per vehicle produced of the annual tooling expenses for the Big Three are presented in Table 12.5. These figures can only be used in a general way, since they represent total company wide tooling divided by total companywide vehicle sales, including trucks,

Table 12.5   Tooling (Amortization) **Expenses per Car, Big Three Producers**

	General Motors[a]		Ford[b]		Chrysler[c]	
Year	Expenditure per vehicle (1)	Expenditure per vehicle in constant dollars[d] (1949 = 100) (2)	Expenditure per vehicle (1)	Expenditure per vehicle in constant dollars[d] (1949 = 100) (2)	Expenditure per vehicle (1)	Expenditure per vehicle in constant dollars[d] (1949 = 100) (2)
1949	$ 48	$48	n.a.	n.a.	$ 39	$39
1950	37	34			8	8
1951	60	50	—	—	25	21
1952	66	55	50	42	27	22
1953	99	81	30	25	49	41
1954	82	66	35	28	42	34
1955	82	62	45	34	70	53
1956	99	70	64	45	47	35
1957	110	73	92	61	91	60
1958	134	86	143	92	100	64
1959	110	69	88	55	94	59
1960	120	73	64	39	145	88
1961	116	70	62	37	116	70
1962	101	60	50	30	75	44
1963	101	59	51	30	62	37
1964	97	56	59	34	53	31
1965	102	58	60	34	71	40
1966	127	69	71	38	81	43
1967	134	70	92	49	73	39

SOURCE: *Moody's Manual of Investments*, various years; Annual Reports, various years.

   [a] Opel and Vauxhall sales and tooling costs are not included, 1949–1953.

   [b] U.S. sales and tooling costs, 1949–1960; worldwide, 1961–1967.

   [c] U.S. and Canada sales and tooling costs, 1949–1962; worldwide, 1963–1967.

   [d] Column (1) deflated by BLS wholesale price index for "metalworking machinery and equipment."

overseas cars, and other vehicles. Nevertheless, they offer a general idea of the trend in tooling costs. When, as in column 2 of the table, the tooling costs are corrected for inflation, we see that the real amount of tooling per vehicle has not changed appreciably since the end of the Korean War. This tends to confirm the finding that the trend toward model proliferation has been offset by production volume increases.

When we look at the specific styling and product strategies in the automobile industry, we see that the Big Three have pursued a blanket strategy, covering as broad a spectrum of the market as possible with multiple makes. General Motors currently has five makes. Ford has three; the Edsel was an attempt to establish a fourth. Chrysler also has three; De Soto, an ailing fourth, was dropped in late 1960. The multiple makes serve an import risk-diluting function. By offering cars to different segments of the market and enjoying separate identification in the minds of consumers, multiple makes act as a buffer to company fortunes if consumer tastes change from one segment to another. The multiple makes also give a company a better chance of retaining the trading-up customer.

Cars of different makes but of similar size within a company often use the same body shell: the full-sized Chevrolet, Pontiac, Oldsmobile, and Buick use the same shell;[17] the intermediate size cars of these makes also use one body shell. Using the same basic shell means using many of the same internal stampings, the same windshield and back-window frames, and sometimes, but not always, the same wheelbase measurements. This sharing effects some economies on internal stampings,[18] but more importantly it eases the problems of mixing different makes along a common assembly line. The different makes, though, usually have different engines and transmissions and often have different suspension systems, so they effectively are separately engineered cars.

Cars using a common body shell usually resemble each other. This is a bit puzzling. Risk reduction principles would seem to call for styling that was as dissimilar as possible among makes. Though the common body shell may dictate some similarity, the amount that in fact occurs seems to exceed this level. This is confirmed by the fact that "family resemblances" are maintained even on cars that share no structural features at all such as a full-sized Ford and a Ford Fairlane. Perhaps immediate public recognition of a car as "a

General Motors car" is worth more than the gains from risk dilution. Perhaps, also, managements simply do not want to function on the assumption that some of their designs may fail.

Short-run tactics by the Big Three have usually been to meet and try to equal the styling innovations or special product niches that one of their rivals has introduced. Thus, when General Motors introduced the two-door hardtop models for the 1949 model year and four-door hardtops for the 1955 model year, Ford and Chrysler were quick to follow with similar models. The Chevrolet Corvette in 1953 and the original Ford Thunderbird in 1954 were aimed at a somewhat similar sporty market, though they were very different cars. The unsuccessful $10,000 Continental (Ford's Lincoln division), introduced in the fall of 1955, was met with a similarly priced Cadillac. The four-passenger Thunderbird, introduced in the fall of 1957, was followed a few years later by the Buick Riviera. All three brought out compacts in the fall of 1959 and followed with somewhat larger compacts for their middle-level makes. Ford's Fairlane, an intermediate-sized car introduced in the fall of 1961, was followed by the Chevrolet Chevelle in the fall of 1963 and the Plymouth Belvedere in the fall of 1964. The Mercury Meteor, also of intermediate size, was soon followed by General Motors and Chrysler middle-level intermediates. The Ford Mustang was met in the same year (1964) by the Plymouth Barracuda and by Chevrolet converting its Corvair into a sporty, hardtop-only line. This last tactic failed, and in the fall of 1966 Chevrolet brought out the Camaro and Pontiac brought out the Firebird, while Ford brought out a second sporty car, the Mercury Cougar.

On a more frequent year to year basis, Chevrolet, Ford, and Plymouth have usually tried to offer similar models (top of the line, bottom of the line, station wagons, hardtops, and so on) to similar segments of the market. A similar process has taken place among middle-level makes. This "conscious parallelism" of offerings serves an important risk-reducing function. If a firm is unsure of the future state of consumer tastes, offering models similar to those of its rivals will reduce the risks of introducing models that are relatively less popular than those of rivals.

If the behavior of the Big Three was to be categorized, one would have to say that General Motors has generally been the styling leader. It has introduced the two major styling innovations of the postwar period, the two- and four-door hardtop models,[19] and many of the styling themes that its competitors have followed. Some of these are tailfins, wraparound windshields, and the "Coke bottle" automobile shape introduced in the mid-1960's. Otherwise it has been staid in its product behavior, meeting the product challenges of its rivals but rarely initiating challenges of its own.

Ford, while usually a follower on styling, has been a leader in seeking out product niches. Ford's public relations rhetoric has indicated that the company sees itself as a disadvantaged firm, dissatisfied with its market share and constantly seeking ways of increasing that share. This niche seeking behavior can be directly related to this self-image.

Chrysler has largely been a follower firm. Styling themes that led to disastrous results in 1954, 1958, and 1962 have led its management to proclaim that, in the rhetoric of the industry, it would stick to evolutionary rather than revolutionary styling advances in the future. The firm has not been particularly active in seeking product niches to expand its market share. Most of its energies seem to have been directed inward, toward improving management, lowering costs, and solving the short-run problems of recovery after three styling failures.

In introducing new models and new lines, the Big Three have been conservative in their styling and model change behavior. The compacts, introduced in the fall of 1959, seem to have been aimed for a low volume market that would not be interested in fast replacement. All three had largely unchanged styling for the first three years, with Plymouth Valiant changing its styling for the 1963 models, Ford Falcon for 1964, and Chevrolet Corvair for 1965. When the volume of this segment of the market exceeded initial expectations and the possibilities of replacement became important, the amount of annual styling changes increased. A similar pattern followed the introduction of the compact cars of the middle-level makes.[20]

Unlike the Big Three, the Independents have not had the resources to attempt a blanket strategy. Rather, they have usually concentrated on one segment of the market. For Packard, it was the luxury segment; for the rest it was the broad, middle-level, medium price market. Sporadic attempts were made to widen their market coverage. Kaiser, Hudson, and Nash introduced lower priced compact cars, but the first two failed and the third required seven years before it gained success. The 1954 mergers were attempts to gain the risk-diversifying benefits of multiple-make companies, but, since the companies were already in financial trouble, this approach did not have an opportunity to succeed. The Nash, Hudson, and Packard brand names faded from the scene in 1957; from that time on, American Motors and Studebaker-Packard concentrated their efforts on the economy segment of the market. Since 1965, however, American Motors appears to have been attempting a blanket strategy, keeping its economy models but also pushing sporty and semiluxury models. The success of this strategy has yet to appear.

With a few exceptions, the Independents' contribution to styling has not been noteworthy. The 1947 Studebaker was a bold styling effort that influenced the trend of postwar design, with its elongated trunk, curved rear windows, and generally lower, longer look. The 1953 Studebaker was another bold attempt, this time less successful. The 1948 Hudson featured the "step-down" design: the sinking of the floorboards around the drive shaft tunnel to allow the body to be lower without reducing the road clearance. This was eventually copied by the rest of the industry, to the everlasting discomfort of middle-seat passengers. But aside from these few examples, the Independents have generally been followers in the field of styling.

Implications of Market Structure

A replacement market places a premium on product strategies that will accelerate the pace of replacement. It is more than by chance, then, that the auto companies have chosen the strategies of styling, model changes, and model proliferation as their major areas of rivalry. These are strategies that also encourage replacement, and they may well have been supplemented by a tendency to decrease durability, a strategy that also encourages replacement because of the presence of a used car market and inelastic demand by the second owners.

Has the structure of the industry affected these forms of behavior? Suppose the auto industry were consolidated into a monopoly. Presumably, a monopolist would feel more secure in his market share (100 percent) than would an oligopolist and would not have to engage in efforts to win away market shares. Still, he would be interested in ways to induce faster replacement, like model changes, but probably not at the rivalry-generated levels that emerge from the present oligopoly; on the other hand, he would probably be able to achieve a faster rate of deterioration of the product toward the profit-maximizing level of durability.

Suppose the oligopoly were loosened, with more firms of roughly balanced size in the industry. They would still be interested in replacement-inducing strategies, although some might be willing to engage in the more risky area of technological change as a way to encourage replacement. Only when the numbers in the industry grew so large that each firm's incentives were directed much more toward attracting the customers of rivals than on inducing its loyal customers to replace faster, would the attention to replacement-inducing strategies diminish. One can imagine that a strategy of stressing better dealer service might overshadow replacement strategies, though the latter might still be used to a limited extent to attract the customers of rivals. Of course, the technology of the industry effectively rules out these large numbers. Yet, it is interesting to note that one of the points that Volkswagen has stressed is good dealer service. One wonders if the Independents did not make a serious mistake in trying to match the Big Three in their expensive replacement strategies, instead of stressing contributions like good dealer service or mechanical dependability that might have had broad appeal to customers.[21]

Overall, then, it appears that the current structure of the industry tends to encourage devoting a maximum or near-maximum amount of effort to styling, model changes, and model proliferation. A monopolist would probably spend less in this area, though his product would probably deteriorate faster; an industry of large numbers would probably be less concerned with replacement strategies in general. A somewhat less concentrated oligopoly than now exists would be highly interested in replacement strategies and might spend as much as or possibly more than does the current industry on replacement efforts, but it is likely that more of the effort would be channeled into the area of technological change.

What is the "proper" amount of resources that ought to be devoted to these areas of styling, model changes, and model proliferation? Presumably, this is a question that should be left to the market. If consumers have their choice among cars that change more frequently or less frequently and the prices of these cars accurately reflect (or at least arc proportional to) their costs, consumer choices should lead us to the proper resource allocation.[22] If, though, a sizable minority of buyers were being denied cheaper, unchanging cars through some set of circumstances comparable to that which surrounded the Big Three's delay in providing small cars, as described in the previous chapter, then the allocation found in the market might not be optimal. But it is doubtful that this last argument would be found to be operational in the case of model changes. Consequently, this author believes that the market allocation, stressing model changes, probably reflects accurately consumer preferences.[23] We shall return to this point in our discussion of performance in Chapter 15.

13

Other Aspects
of Behavior

Product Technology

Perhaps the most striking thing about automotive technology in the postwar period has been the lack of fundamental change or advance. Cars built in 1968 are not fundamentally different from cars built in 1946. A good 1946 auto mechanic would have little difficulty understanding a 1968 automobile. Even in the areas in which modern cars do differ from their early postwar predecessors, such as the widespread application of automatic transmissions and power-assisted equipment, the basic technology had been developed before the war, and postwar developments represented achievements in refining this technology rather than in any fundamental change.

Consequently, in describing the behavior of the auto companies with respect to technological progress, we are dealing with refinements of the technology, innovational advances to bring basic inventions to a marketable state, rather than with the basic inventions themselves. This process of refinement should not be taken too lightly. Significant progress often comes in a series of small steps. Still, the absence of fundamental technological changes does indicate an industry whose major efforts have been focused elsewhere. This should not be too surprising, since, as discussed in Chapter 12, the auto companies have concentrated on model changes rather than on fundamental technological advances because it appears to be a more profitable, less risky strategy.

The auto industry has tended to rely a great deal on its suppliers

211

for advances in technology. Effectively, the auto companies have allowed their suppliers to take the risks and absorb the initial costs of developing new technology. This pattern of behavior reinforces the impression that the auto industry's main attention has been directed elsewhere.

The raw materials suppliers — steel, aluminum, copper, plastics, paints, and others — have constantly pushed their materials and provided technological advances. For example, the aluminum companies (and the Doehler-Jarvis division of the National Lead Company, which builds aluminum die casting equipment) continually pressed for the adoption of aluminum components and especially aluminum engines. The technological problems of aluminum engines — excessive wear, corrosion, porosity in the castings, machining difficulties — were gradually solved by the aluminum industry, and the auto industry finally adopted aluminum engines on some models in the early 1960's. A few years later they were discarded on all but the Corvair. Their advantages, less weight and superior heat transfer, were not qualities for which consumers were willing to pay the price that the higher cost aluminum engines required. The development of thin wall casting, meaning lighter weight iron engine blocks, also speeded the demise of aluminum engines.

Similarly, the fiber glass plastic manufacturers have been improving the technology and urging the adoption of fiber glass bodies for low volume models.[1] They succeeded in the Chevrolet Corvette and the short-lived Studebaker Avanti but have yet to break through on standard passenger cars where the volumes are higher and where a rival's claim that "our cars are made of steel, theirs are made of plastic" might well prove very damaging. The paint companies provided the technology behind the new acrylic lacquers and enamels, and the glass companies, the technology behind curved glass, tinted glass, and the newer, thicker laminated safety glass. International Nickel provided the technology, the addition of magnesium to cast iron, that lay behind ductile iron, the lighter weight, stronger iron used in most castings today.

In the area of components, the pattern of reliance on suppliers is similar. The Gemmer Manufacturing Company and Bendix controlled the key patents on power steering. Kelsey-Hayes and Bendix developed power brakes, and Bendix and Budd, disc brakes. The Dana Corporation controlled the key patents on nonslip differentials;

Motorola made the principal breakthrough on a silicon rectifier for alternators. Ball joint front suspensions were developed by Thompson Products, and the first automatic speed control, by the Perfect Circle Company. Bendix and American Bosch did the basic development work on the short-lived fuel injection systems. The use of teflon for front suspension joints was developed by du Pont and the American Metal Products Company. Motorola and Electric Auto-Lite, before its absorption by Ford, did much of the advance work on transistorized ignition systems. U.S. Rubber developed the toothed, glass-fiber reinforced nylon and rubber timing belt that made Pontiac's overhead camshaft engine possible. This list is incomplete, but it offers a general idea of the role of suppliers.

When we turn to the behavior of the auto companies themselves in developing new technology or in introducing into production the ideas of their suppliers, we do not find one technological "pioneer" with the others as followers. Rather, there has been a mixed pattern of each company "leading" the way on some items (though many items such as air-cooled engines or disc brakes had long been used in Europe) and following on others. Table 13.1 lists some of the postwar innovations in which one or two companies clearly led in the introduction of an item. Several items, like aluminum engines, in which a number of companies adopted the item simultaneously, are not included.

The Big Three clearly seem to have introduced the lion's share of the postwar innovations, with the Independents introducing a moderate but not overwhelming number. This is in contrast to prewar behavior, when the Independents appear to have been more important in introducing innovations.[2] It is difficult to offer a satisfying explanation for this decreased activity by the Independents. Sheer decrease in numbers may be part of it; a complacent attitude until 1953[3] and financial woes after that are all that can be offered to explain the rest.

The auto companies have generally acted in a manner so as to minimize the risks of being left out of any technological advance. Though a formal royalty-free patent licensing agreement among the companies was allowed to expire on January 1, 1957 (the last extension of this agreement only covered patents obtained before 1940), there has generally been a policy of licensing patents for moderate royalties or sometimes exclusive use of a patent for two or three years

Table 13.1   Cases in Which One or Two Companies Clearly Led in the Introduction of an Innovation

General Motors
Torque converter (1948 Buick)
Bonded brake linings (1948 Chevrolet)
High compression V-8 engine (1949 Oldsmobile and Cadillac)
Fiber glass body (1953 Chevrolet Corvette)
Rear engine (1960 Chevrolet Corvair)
Air-cooled engine (1960 Chevrolet Corvair)[a]
Independent springing of rear wheels (1960 Chevrolet Corvair)[a]
Rear transmission (1961 Pontiac Tempest)
Flexible drive shaft (1961 Pontiac Tempest)
Dual brakes (1962 Cadillac)
Simplified overhead cam engine (1966 Pontiac Tempest)
Front wheel drive (1967 Oldsmobile Toronado)[a]
Collapsible steering column (1967 GM cars)[b]
Side beams to resist side impact (1969 GM cars)

Ford
Cast crankshaft (1952 Ford)
Ball joint front suspension (1952 Lincoln)
Lifeguard safety package (1956 Ford)
Deep-dish steering wheel (1956 Ford)
True hardtop convertible (1957 Ford)
Extensive use of galvanized steel (late 1950's Fords)
Thin wall, cast engine block (1960 Ford Falcon)
Peg-type safety door latch (1962 Ford Fairlane)
Dual-action station wagon tailgate (1966 Ford)
Energy-absorbing front end (1968 Ford)
Skid control braking system (1969 Thunderbird and Continental Mark III)

Chrysler
Use of powdered metal parts (late 1940's Chrysler cars)
Power steering (1951 Chrysler)
Power brakes (1952 Chrysler)
Automatic speed control (1958 Chrysler)
Alternator (1960 Plymouth Valiant)

American Motors
Deep-dip, rust-proofing (1958 Rambler)
Ceramic muffler (1961 Rambler)
Dual brakes (1962 Rambler)

Studebaker-Packard
Self-adjusting brakes (1946 Studebaker)
Power brakes (1952 Packard)
Torsion bar suspension (1955 Packard)[a]
Nonslip differential (1956 Packard)
Disc brakes (1962 Studebaker Avanti)[a]

Kaiser-Frazer
Padded dashboard and seat back (1952 Kaiser)
Pop-out windshield (1952 Kaiser)

SOURCE: *Automotive News, Automotive Industries*, and *Ward's Automotive Reports*, various years.
  [a] Previously used in Europe.
  [b] Developed by General Motors, though all companies introduced it in 1967.

and then licensing at nominal or zero royalties.[4] On some developments, especially those concerned with safety (for example, headlights, doorlocks, seat belts) the companies have banded together through committees of the Automobile Manufacturers Association to set a uniform standard. On a more informal basis, continuous "spying" by the companies on each other's plans (often the easiest way to do this is to hire away a rival's engineer or designer) is accepted by all. In all of these areas, a company gives up the opportunity of scoring an exclusive coup and putting its rivals at a serious disadvantage, but it also avoids the risk that a rival might do the same. This type of arrangement, though, may dampen incentives for a company to innovate.

In cases of engineering developments that appeared to be the wave of the future and/or offered great potential for advertising and attracting interested customers into the showrooms, the companies (especially the Big Three) were usually quick to jump on the bandwagon and avoid the risk of being left out in the cold. Thus high compression overhead valve V-8 engines, power steering, power brakes, and air conditioning were usually offered by all companies a short time (allowing for tooling times) after they were first introduced. In the late 1950's and early 1960's fuel injection, air suspension systems, aluminum engines, and transistorized ignition systems were the special items. Though none of this latter group in fact enjoyed long-term commercial success, this was impossible to determine ahead of time. And all of the companies were eager to have at least a few of their cars equipped with these items.

All of the above-mentioned items were of the nature of optional devices that the consumer could easily see (if not evaluate) and for which he presumably would be willing to pay a premium. By contrast, on internal engineering items, which seemed less fundamental, less obvious to the consumer, and thus less capable of attracting or deterring his attention, the pace of adoption was a good deal more leisurely. This occurred, for example, on items like ball joint front suspensions, self-adjusting brakes, 12-volt electrical systems (European cars had had these for a long time), and alternators.[5] All of these were eventually standard on American cars, but the companies seemed to be in no hurry to adopt them or make them widespread at any one time.

The major exception to the above pattern — what was obvious

and optional was quickly adopted, what was hidden and standard was slowly adopted — was the development of automatic transmissions. It is a puzzling exception. Even before the war, General Motors had developed a commercially feasible automatic transmission, its Hydra-Matic, and had offered the item in the fall of 1939 on its Oldsmobiles. After the war, interest turned to torque converters which had been successfully applied to prewar buses and to wartime tank destroyers. While continuing production of Hydra-Matics, General Motors developed a torque converter and offered it on the 1948 Buick under the name Dynaflow. Packard offered its Ultra-matic in early 1949. The rest of the industry was caught without them. Kaiser, Nash, Hudson, and the Lincoln division of Ford in 1949 arranged to buy the Hydra-Matic from General Motors. In late 1950, Studebaker and Ford offered their own automatic transmission (produced by Borg-Warner); finally, in mid-1953, Chrysler offered its own automatic transmission.

It is possible to make some guesses about the reasons for this long lag between the fall of 1939 and the actual introduction of the devices by General Motors' rivals.[6] Ford's lag may have been due to the elder Henry Ford and the organizational disarray he left in his wake. Chrysler had developed a semiautomatic transmission (Fluid Drive) before the war and mistakenly thought that it would be sufficient to counter any competitive threats from automatic transmissions. The Independents probably assumed that they lacked sufficient volume to utilize fully an automatic transmission plant and that their suppliers would develop the item for them; if so, then part of the blame for the delay must rest on the supplier industry. Overall, the 1946–1948 period of tight supply and raw materials shortages may have reduced the pressure to think about the need to develop an automatic transmission. Thus bad decision making by managements seems to be the general explanation for the lags in automatic transmission adoption. It is not an entirely satisfying explanation, but, in an industry of few rivals and less than perfect competition, perhaps it is not too surprising.

Size and Power

When we look at the overall product trends in the market, it is clear that, in addition to the trend to diversity of models after 1949, discussed in Chapter 12, the long-run trend has been to larger, more luxurious cars with more power and more luxury options. The important moves toward larger size were taken in the middle and late 1950's, especially by the low price makes, when it appeared that the bulk of consumers desired larger, heavier cars. When the minority of consumers wanting smaller cars found it had other alternatives, such as Ramblers and imports, the Big Three reluctantly brought out smaller cars. (See Chapter 11.)

After the small car trend had seemed to pass its peak in 1961 and 1962, cars again began to grow larger. Table 13.2 indicates the rough

Table 13.2   Growth in Car Dimensions

Dimensions	1949	1959	1968	1968
				Ford Fairlane 6
		Ford V-8		
Wheelbase (in.)	114.0	118.0	119.0	116.0
Length (in.)	196.8	208.0	213.3	201.1
Width (in.)	71.7	76.8	78.0	74.5
Weight (lbs.)	3030	3485	3596	3083
				Oldsmobile F-85, 6
		Oldsmobile V-8		
Wheelbase	119.5	123.0	123.0	116.0
Length	202.0	218.4	217.8	205.6
Width	75.2	80.8	80.0	76.8
Weight	3615	4130	3873	3108
		Cadillac V-8		
Wheelbase	126.0	130.0	129.5	
Length	215.1	225.0	224.7	
Width	78.9	80.2	79.9	
Weight	3950	4770	4640	

SOURCE: *Automotive Industries, Annual Statistical Issue*, various years.

outlines of car-size trends. Between 1949 and 1959, low, medium, and high price makes grew in all relevant dimensions. After 1959 the high and medium price makes tended to remain about the same size or shrink slightly, while the low price makes continued to grow. The table also shows that the current intermediate-sized cars, represented by the Ford Fairlane and Oldsmobile F-85, are larger than was the full-sized Ford of 1949.

The increase in luxury options needs little discussion, except for their mention. Automatic transmission, power steering, power brakes, power seats, air conditioning, and bucket seats, to mention the major items, have become an important part of the automotive market.

The trend toward increased power took the form of what has been called the "horsepower race." A description is valuable, in that it brings out a number of important points discussed above: the step by step nature of the technological advance in the industry, the slowness of the Independents to respond on innovations, and the bandwagon type of behavior by the Big Three.

In the middle of 1947, Charles F. Kettering of General Motors delivered a technical paper, describing the feats of what later came to be called the Kettering engine:[7] a V-8 engine with overhead valves operating at a 7.5:1 compression ratio and capable of 12:1 with suitably high octane gas. (Common at this time was 6.50:1). The Kettering engine caused a great stir in the industry and essentially pointed the way to the future development of automotive engines.

It is difficult to determine what was so revolutionary about the engine. The V-8 designs had been around for over thirty years; the standard Ford had a V-8 engine. Overhead valves (or valve in head) had also been around; the Buick straight-eight engine had them at the time of Kettering's paper. Everyone knew the effects of high octane gas in permitting high compression (more efficient) engines. But somehow the combination of these elements excited the industry and started it down the path of the horsepower race: bigger engines with more horsepower.[8]

The V-8 overhead valve engine was originally seen as simply a more efficient engine capable of delivering somewhat more power with greater fuel economy. The V-8 engine offered compactness and torsional rigidity; the overhead valves offered better combustion and more efficient, higher compression compared to the then standard L-head (valve-on-the-side) engines. The 1949 Cadillac V-8 engine (7.50:1) offered 160 horsepower on 331 cubic inches of displacement,[9] as compared to the 150 horsepower, 346 cubic inch Cadillac engine (7.25:1) the year before.

Other manufacturers, sensing a challenge, began work on their own V-8's, offered higher horsepower by increasing the displacement, and offered optional aluminum cylinder heads to increase the compression and performance of their engines. Ford, Chrysler, and Studebaker undertook to build overhead valve V-8's; Hudson, Nash, Packard, and Kaiser elected to remain with L-head sixes and straight eights. General Motors offered larger, more powerful V-8's in its Buick and Oldsmobile lines; Ford made plans to replace its old V-8's with the new V-8's on its Ford automobile and to develop overhead valve sixes. All of the Big Three followed suit on the other's strategies; the horsepower race was on. Advertised engine power had become an important arena of competition.

The Korean War retarded the introduction of the new engines, as production controls limited the companies' ability to acquire new engine manufacturing capacity. By 1955, though, all of the Big Three's makes had V-8's. Chrysler and Cadillac at the top offered 250-horsepower engines, Chevrolet and Ford offered 162-horsepower V-8's and 120-horsepower sixes, compared to 90-horsepower sixes, and a 100-horsepower Ford V-8 in 1949. Packard finally offered a modern V-8 in 1955, but Nash and Hudson (American Motors) did not offer one until 1957. Common compression ratios were in the 7.50:1 to 8.50:1 range, compared to a 6.30:1 to 6.70:1 range in 1948.

The push for higher horsepower continued through the middle of 1957. Cadillac and Lincoln in that year offered 300-horsepower engines, Chrysler offered one at 375 horsepower. The low price three offered V-8's in the 190-horsepower range, and their sixes had reached nearly 140 horsepower. A number of compression ratios were over 10.00:1; none of the Big Three had compression ratios under 8.00:1. Power and performance were being actively pushed in advertising. A typical 1956 Chevrolet advertisement read: "This year the hot one's even hotter."

Then, in June 1957, in response to Congressional concern and pressure over the attention given to speed and horsepower, the auto companies, through the Automobile Manufacturers Association, pledged themselves to forswear participation in auto racing and speed and acceleration tests and ". . . to encourage owners and drivers to evaluate passenger cars in terms of useful power and ability to afford safe, reliable, and comfortable transportation, rather than in terms of capacity for speed." [10] In fact, this was a comparatively costless pact, since consumer tastes by this time had turned to smaller cars and operating economy. Some engines were "tuned down" to offer more economy in 1958 and 1959, and the new generation of compact cars brought with them a new generation of small engines.

But, by 1962, consumer tastes had again returned to an interest in larger cars and more power. Larger engines were again offered; power began to be stressed in advertising; and the auto companies again began to appear at auto races. Ford formally broke the AMA pact in June 1962, and it has not been revived since. In 1968 the low price three offered V-8's in the 200 horsepower range on their full-sized cars, sixes in the 150 horsepower range, with optional engines offering up to 400 horsepower. The minimum compression ratio in the industry was 8.25:1, with most standard engines falling in the 8.50:1 to 10.50:1 range; compression ratios as high as 11.00:1 were offered.

Warranties

One other trend in product behavior ought to be discussed. The companies, particularly since 1961, have been offering longer warranties on their cars. Before October 1960 the standard warranty in the industry had been for three months or 4,000 miles, whichever came first. Factory-caused defects would be repaired by the dealer, with both parts and labor costs covered by the factory. In October 1960 Ford led the industry in announcing the extension of warranties to a twelve-month or 12,000 miles basis for the 1961 model cars.

The next major extension was made in the fall of 1962. Chrysler, in a bold attempt to regain its market share that had deteriorated in the disastrous 1962 model year, announced a five-year or 50,000-mile warranty on the power train (essentially engine, transmission, and differential). The company promised to repair any factory-caused defects but required normal servicing (for example, changing spark plugs) from the owner. The 12/12,000 warranty was still retained for the rest of the car. The other companies were only willing to follow with 24-month/24,000 mile guarantees on the entire car.

In September 1966 the other companies finally extended their power train warranties to 5/50,000. Chrysler followed by extending its warranty on the rest of the car to 24/24,000 to meet the terms of its rivals and extended the 5/50,000 warranty to steering, suspension, and wheels. The other companies quickly equaled Chrysler's extension, and warranties were once again largely uniform across the industry.

The fall of 1967, though, marked the beginning of a retreat on warranties, as limitations on the applicability of the warranties to subsequent owners were imposed by all companies. The fall of 1968 saw further retreat, as the industry reverted to a 12/12,000 warranty on the components that had previously been covered by the 24/24,000 warranty. The 5/50,000 warranty was left largely unchanged. It is not clear why, after five years, the 24/24,000 warranty should have been considered too burdensome by the auto companies. One suspects that the competitive extension that had been spurred by Chrysler's growth of market share efforts may have extended the warranties too far and that, after developments had settled down, some sort of recognized interdependent behavior had reasserted itself to allow the industry as a group to shorten the warranties.

The insurance value of the extended warranties to consumers has always been clear, though the detailed provisions of what is and is not covered have often escaped consumer attention. The warranties have some value to the companies, in that they encourage consumers to continue servicing their cars at the companies' dealerships, rather than at independent service stations; often a dealer's certification of normal upkeep is required before warranty work can be authorized. This increases the sales of company-made replacement parts and perhaps increases customer loyalty. The misunderstandings of the warranty provisions have been a headache, however, and the companies have also had the problem of trying to encourage dealers to correct defects in cars before they leave the showroom (which is what the dealer preparation charge is supposed to cover) rather than after, when the company would have to make good on the warranty. The incentive structure here has been difficult to manipulate toward the ends that the companies seek.

Manufacturing Technology

A detailed recounting of the development of manufacturing technology in the postwar period would be too lengthy for the purpose at hand, but some general comments can be made. As in the case of automotive technology, progress largely has been in the form of steps rather than large technological leaps. Improvements in dies, presses, machinery equipment, and assembly techniques have been brought about partly through the efforts of the auto companies themselves and partly through the efforts of their suppliers who supply improved materials and equipment.

When there have been new fundamental processes developed, however, as in the area of cold extrusion of metals, cold rolling of splines on shafts, electrical discharge machining of dies, and numerical control of die cutting, the initial development of these processes has usually taken place outside of the automobile industry. The industry has usually been fairly prompt in adopting and adapting these processes, but, again, as in automotive technology, it appears to have let others take the risks of initial development. The major exception would seem to be Ford's early postwar development of the shell molding process for casting (replacing sand molds with a sand-resin baked mold) and the thin wall casting techniques (depending on hotbox cores of sand and resin) that logically followed. But even here the basic idea of shell molding had been developed earlier by a German foundry.[11]

In nonautomotive manufacturing areas, like steel and glass, the auto companies do not appear to have made any special contributions to new technology and appear to have been somewhat slow in adopting the major technological developments of these industries. Ford did not convert its steel mill to the basic oxygen process until the mid-1960's, after many steel companies had already made the change. Ford converted its glass plants to the float glass process in 1965, again lagging behind the major producers in the field. Chrysler, as of 1968, still had not converted its plants to the float glass process.

Advertising

For firms of equal size, advertising offers an area that is halfway between price behavior and product behavior in its susceptibility to mutually acknowledged quasi-agreements to limit competition. Advertising expenditures are easily capable of being met by equal dollar amounts by a rival. Thus there would seem to be a great incentive for mutually interdependent firms to agree implicitly on a joint limitation of expenditure, just as they might agree to avoid price-cutting. On the other hand, each management probably believes in the superiority of its own advertising campaign and may doubt that its rivals can quite equal it for an equal cost; in this case, advertising may be used as an aggressive, sales-expanding weapon. Thus, a priori it is difficult to predict what the pattern on advertising will be.

For firms of different sizes, a further problem arises. The smaller firm faces the choice of matching either the larger firm's total advertising expenditures or the larger firm's expenditures per unit of sales. In the former case, the smaller firm will suffer a higher per unit advertising cost disadvantage; in the latter it suffers from less quantitative advertising coverage. Large firms may then see advertising as a way of putting their smaller rivals at a disadvantage and may not be interested in arriving at implicit agreements to place limits on advertising.

There may, however, be a threshold beyond which a smaller firm does not suffer a very serious disadvantage from proportionately smaller quantities of advertising. If Chevrolets are advertised four times a month on television and Fords (with three-fourths the volume in 1967) only three times a month, Ford may nevertheless be able to hold its own. But a firm with one-sixteenth the sales of Chevrolet might find that advertisements once every four months were simply not sufficient for it to hold its market share. The exact location of this threshold is an empirical question; as we shall see, for nonluxury cars this threshold seems to be reached by car makers of somewhere between 300,000 and 500,000 units volume per year.

According to *Advertising Age* estimates, the auto companies were the second, fifth, eleventh, and one-hundred and fifth largest advertisers in the United States economy in 1967; Procter and Gamble was the first largest. General Motors spent $184,000,000 (0.9 percent of worldwide sales), Ford spent $106,500,000 (1.0 percent of worldwide sales), Chrysler spent $78,328,000 (1.3 percent of worldwide sales), and American Motors spent $13,412,000 (1.7 percent of worldwide sales).[12] Although these figures are large in absolute amounts, in terms of a percentage of sales the auto companies are relatively moderate spenders. The leading advertisers in the soap, cigarette, drug and cosmetics, and food industries frequently spend over 5 percent of sales on advertising; advertising budgets of over 40 percent of sales are not unknown.

Not all of the above amounts are spent on car advertising. Home appliances, repair parts, car finance plans, and institutional advertising are also included. *Advertising Age* has tried to separate the amounts specifically spent on the individual car makes. For 1967, this total came to $280,244,000 or approximately $36 per car; if one includes the value of the institutional advertising, a figure of $40 per car would not be unreasonable.[13]

To get an overall figure for advertising in the car market, the advertising by car dealers should be included. *Automotive News* estimated that franchised new car dealers spent $380 million on advertising in 1966.[14] Much of this advertising is for the used cars that the dealers take as trade-ins. In 1966, franchised dealers sold 1.2 used cars for every new car they sold.[15] If we make an arbitrary division of advertising expenditures according to that ratio, then slightly more than $200 million was spent by dealers on new cars. With 8.3 million American cars sold in that year, dealer advertising comes to approximately $25 per car. A roughly similar amount per car probably was spent in 1967.

The advertising figures by individual make allow us to look at the competitive strategies by the companies in this area. Though these figures for individual makes go back to the mid-1950's, only in recent years have they become consistent or complete enough to permit worthwhile comparisons. Table 13.3 offers the advertising, sales, and advertising per car figures by make for 1965–1967. Ford and Plymouth have been content roughly to equal Chevrolet's per car expenditures, despite the latter's higher volume. Rambler, though, with volumes of 325,000 units or less, has chosen to spend $20–$40 more per unit. In the medium price range, the strategy seems to have been, again, roughly to equal the per car advertising of the low price makes. The major exceptions have been Mercury, with sales in the 300,000 units range; and Chrysler, with sales in the 225,000 units range. Both have chosen to spend appreciably more per unit than their rivals. Thus there does seem to be a break between 500,000 units and 300,000 units, with makes in the latter group spending appreciably more per unit than their rivals.

It appears to be impossible to obtain a consistent, believable series on advertising for the entire postwar period. *Advertising Age*'s series begins in the mid-1950's; *Printer's Ink*'s series runs from 1951 through 1961; and neither is internally consistent nor consistent with the other; their coverage and completeness vary over time, posing a

Table 13.3 Advertising, Sales, and Advertising per Car

Make of car	1965 Adv. (thousands)	1965 Unit sales (thousands)	1965 Adv. per car	1966 Adv. (thousands)	1966 Unit sales (thousands)	1966 Adv. per car	1967 Adv. (thousands)	1967 Unit sales (thousands)	1967 Adv. per car
General Motors									
Chevrolet	$62,732	2,424	$26	$75,583	2,159	$35	$74,452	1,979	$38
Pontiac	18,417	831	22	20,101	831	24	20,853	836	25
Oldsmobile	18,769	609	31	17,735	581	31	16,127	552	30
Buick	16,138	607	36	19,474	469	34	17,784	566	32
Cadillac	9,000	190	47	9,500	196	48	8,548	210	41
Ford Motor Co.									
Ford	58,130	1,998	29	74,000	1,992	37	58,721	1,522	39
Mercury	17,504	331	53	19,180	308	63	16,434	296	56
Lincoln	3,008	43	70	3,217	49	65	2,155	35	62
Chrysler Corp.									
Plymouth	22,467	625	36	20,551	598	34	23,356	628	39
Dodge	27,277	522	51	20,795	544	38	18,984	492	39
Chrysler-Imperial	12,850	220	58	12,355	245	50	10,890	222	50
American Motors									
Rambler	21,190	325	65	17,393	266	65	12,850	234	56

SOURCE: *Advertising Age*, Aug. 28, 1967 and Aug. 26, 1968; *Automotive News Almanac, 1968*, p. 24. Material from *Advertising Age* reprinted with permission. Copyright 1967 and 1968 by Crain Communications, Inc.

difficulty for anyone interested in true trends. The Internal Revenue Service's *Statistics of Income* gives figures on advertising for the motor vehicles and equipment industry, but these should include advertising by the parts manufacturers, yet the Internal Revenue Service's figures are below those reported by *Printer's Ink* or *Advertising Age* for the auto companies alone. What to believe is a significant problem.

Consequently, we can talk only in very general terms about the time pattern of advertising expenditures. Advertising expenditures seem to have been restrained during the late 1940's and early 1950's, not a surprising pattern for a period of general excess demand and production limitations. After the Korean War, though, advertising increased steeply. Between 1951 and 1955, auto advertising expenditures probably tripled on a gross basis and doubled on a per-unit basis. *Printer's Ink* figures show total Big Three advertising, including nonautomotive, rising from $76 million in 1951 to $231 million in 1955.[16] Since the mid-1950's, overall advertising expenditures have probably grown only slowly, if at all, and per-unit expenditures have probably declined slightly. *Advertising Age* figures — these are larger than *Printer's Ink* figures — show Big Three advertising rising from $312 million in 1955 to $369 million in 1967, and better reporting may account for most of this apparent rise.[17]

Have the auto companies by implicit agreement limited their advertising to a level close to the joint profit-maximizing level? There are a number of forms a limitation could take: a limit on gross expenditures, a limit on advertising as a percentage of profits, or a limit on advertising as a percentage of sales revenues or on advertising per vehicle. An agreement to limit gross advertising expenditures does not seem to have occurred. The period immediately after the Korean War offers a test of this proposition. Though the optimum amount of advertising was probably higher in 1955 than during the Korean War, it is unlikely that this optimum amount was three times as high as Korean War levels. Even if the 1955 levels were indeed the optimum levels, it is likely that the participants in an implicit agreement would have had to grope their way toward the higher level much more slowly than the rapid rise that in fact took place. Further, since 1955, expenditures by individual makes have not stayed in any set relation to each other, again seeming to indicate the lack of an agreement.

An agreement to limit advertising as a percentage of profits would not seem to be practical. Since relating United States car advertising to worldwide reported profits would be senseless, each company would have to know its rival's profits on each make of American car for an agreement to be workable. Yet there have been times when Chrysler has barely known its own profitability by make. In times of poor profits or losses, Ford and Chrysler have not felt required to reduce advertising by proportionate amounts. In 1966, Ford's advertising was 21 percent of after-tax profits; in strikebound 1967, advertising was 127 percent of after-tax profits.[18]

A limit on advertising as a percentage of sales would again run into the problem of relating United States car advertising to worldwide sales. On the other hand, a limit on advertising per car would seem to be feasible. Yet it would be hard to distill the essence of an agreement from the expenditure per car figures of Table 13.3. There have been relative movements of the figures for the individual makes; one suspects that, if we had better figures to allow a longer period to be studied, still greater relative movements would be found.

Consequently, in this author's opinion automobile advertising has not been subject to an implicit agreement among the auto companies. Rather, perceived marginal productivity or other internal considerations have most likely been the controlling factors. Also, it might not have been in the industry's interests to limit advertising appreciably, since large advertising expenditures could create high barriers to entry to deter foreign manufacturers from retailing in the United States. The other possible barriers to entry, the economies of scale and high capital requirements, have not been applicable to foreign-based producers.

A more rigorous test of the agreement to limit advertising hypothesis would require a better series on advertising expenditures, good estimates of the sales revenues and profits from United States car operations alone, and the development of a complete model of the relationship between advertising, sales, and profits. Such a model would have to include a resolution of the problem of causality between advertising and sales. Are advertising expenditures the independent variable in the relationship, or are advertising expenditures at least partly dependent on sales or profit levels, as statements emanating from corporations have often implied? Unfortunately, these projects are beyond the resources of this study and will have to await further research.

14

Air Pollution and
Automobile Safety Issues

The air pollution and automobile safety issues are currently the areas in which public policy affects the auto industry to the greatest extent. These issues share two basic and related features: they involve economic externalities, the incurring of uncompensated costs by second parties as a consequence of first party vehicle use; and the auto companies have been slow to move in these areas in the absence of governmental prodding.

Air Pollution

The internal combustion engine is a cheap, durable, compact, versatile, reasonably efficient source of power. With surprisingly few fundamental changes, it has provided the motive power for automobiles for the past seventy years. The major failing of this engine is the tendency to burn its fuel incompletely and spew the residue into the surrounding atmosphere, which is harmful to individuals in the neighborhood. Motor vehicles are the major source of air pollution in the United States. In terms of total tons per year of pollutants discharged into the atmosphere, motor vehicles in 1966 contributed an estimated 86 million tons of pollutants out of an estimated total of 142 million tons.[1] Private industry and public and private power plants were the other major source of air pollution. Motor vehicles were the major sources of carbon monoxide, hydrocarbons, lead compounds, and nitrogen oxides in the atmosphere, contributing in only a minor way to sulfur oxide and particle pollutants. The typical uncorrected car in 1963 discharged 520 pounds of hydrocarbons, 1,700 pounds of carbon monoxide, and 90 pounds of nitrogen oxides, while traveling 10,000 miles during the year.[2]

All would agree that air pollution is a problem. The difficulty is that there have been no clear estimates about the real costs of air pollution, not to mention the specific costs of automotive air pollution. It is easy to mention the possible costs — health impairment, crop damage, faster weathering of buildings, more frequent building cleanings, increased laundry bills, general unpleasantness in the smell of city air — but it is difficult actually to estimate these costs. The figure most frequently cited for the 1960's has been $11 billion a year for economic losses excluding health effects. According to Allan V. Kneese, the figure of $11 billion was obtained by multiplying $60 per capita by the 1958 United States population; the $60 was based on a 1950 extrapolation of Pittsburgh smoke damage, the original data having been collected in 1913.[3]

Laboratory tests can easily demonstrate the deleterious effects of carbon monoxide or nitrogen oxides on the lungs of mice or men. It is easy to demonstrate that smoke in the air makes laboratory swatches of cloth turn gray faster than smoke-free air.[4] The difficulty is in duplicating these findings in actual city environments. Ronald G. Ridker, through the use of multiple regression cross-section analysis, tried to measure the differential effects of air pollution across a number of cities.[5] He was not able to find any significant relationships between pollution levels and per capita cleaning and laundry bills, office and apartment house cleaning expenditure, or household expenditures on cleaning items.[6] There appeared to be no significant relationship between pollution levels and mortality rates due to lung diseases;[7] on a small sample in St. Louis, he could not find worker absentee rates related to local neighborhood pollution levels.[8] He was, though, able to discover a relationship between property values in St. Louis neighborhoods and the local level of sulfur compounds in the air.[9]

The absence of evidence, with the exception of Ridker's St. Louis property values, on the costs of air pollution leaves us in a bit of a quandary. The laboratory findings are convincing; the physical evidence on air pollution is all too evident to us every day. But our data are not good enough and our research has not progressed sufficiently to yield any estimate of the costs of pollution. Some costs, like the pyschic costs of a general deterioration of the quality of urban air, may not even be capable of being fully captured in comparative property values or comparative wage rates. In such cases, we are forced to fall back on a squeaking-wheel-gets-the-grease theory of public action. If the public clamor has been such that Congress is moved to pass a law to curb air pollution, then citizens must feel strongly enough about it, even though an exact dollar amount cannot be placed on their feelings. This theory, of course, does not consider the possibility of special interest legislation; but in the present case this seems justified, since no special industry or powerful small group has benefited from the legislation.

To understand the pollution control measures that have been passed, a short discussion of pollution sources is necessary. An automobile without control equipment emits pollutants from three sources: (1) exhaust, (2) crankcase blowby, and (3) evaporation.

Exhaust

Exhaust is the discharge of the burned gases from the engine. About 55 percent of the hydrocarbons, 100 percent of the carbon monoxide, 100 percent of the oxide of nitrogen, and 100 percent of the lead compounds are emitted from this source.[10]

Crankcase Blowby

Engines have been designed so as to allow them to "breathe" with a ventilation system and an exhaust port designed to clear the crankcase of fumes and gasoline vapors that might have slipped past the piston rings. This system has worked exactly as it was supposed to, so that 25 percent of hydrocarbon emission comes from this source.

Evaporation

Evaporation of gasoline into the air occurs from the gas tank (an airtight filler cap is not possible because air must be let in to avoid a vacuum as gas is pumped to the engine) and from the carburetor. About 20 percent of hydrocarbon fumes are from this source.

Despite the increasing recognition in the 1950's of motor vehicles as a major source of air pollution in California, the auto companies dragged their feet in attempting solutions. It was clearly not in their interest to move quickly. Pollution control devices would be an extra cost item that would not add anything to the sales appeal of the car; they could only mean fewer cars sold. In late 1953 the auto companies formed a joint committee through the Automobile Manufacturers Association to study the problem; a year later they signed a cross-licensing agreement to provide for the royalty-free use of any patents in the pollution control field. In the interests of risk minimization for all, no one was going to be allowed a competitive edge in the development of control devices that might subsequently be required on all vehicles. One suspects that this also tended to slow the pace at which research was undertaken.[11]

The compiled correspondence between Kenneth Hahn, Los Angeles County supervisor, and the auto companies from 1953–1967 on the subject of automotive air pollution seems to be an accurate reflection of the companies' attitudes.[12] While assuring Hahn of their sincerest interest in the subject, they tended to take refuge behind the AMA committee and behind the issuance of technical papers; more information was needed, they said, more research required. And, besides, better maintenance of vehicles would probably solve most of the problems.

Finally, in 1959, as pressure mounted on the companies, the blowby vent was "discovered" as a major source of hydrocarbon discharge.[13] The companies announced their voluntary adoption of "positive crankcase ventilation" devices, which would recycle blowby air back into the cylinders, on all 1961 and later model new cars sold in California; approximate cost was $8–$10 per car. These devices were made mandatory in 1963; subsequent legislation made their installation mandatory whenever a used car changed owners. To ward off federal legislation in this field, the companies voluntarily installed the devices on all new cars sold everywhere in the United States, beginning with the 1963 model year. Despite some initial maintenance problems (Ford removed the devices during the 1964 model year on all new cars, except those sold in California and New York, because of maintenance problems), these devices have worked reasonably well, ending the blowby vent as a source of pollution.

California kept up the pressure on the companies in the early 1960's to solve the exhaust problem. Four main approaches seemed likely: (1) afterburners to oxidize the pollutants, (2) catalytic converters to chemically convert the pollutants, (3) air pumps to increase the oxidation of the pollutants in the exhaust, and (4) engine modification schemes to reduce the original discharge of pollutants. The catalytic converters, originally the most promising approach (and even now capable of reducing the pollutants far below current systems), had to be discarded because of lead compounds in the exhaust. The elimination of lead from the gasoline refining process would be a costly operation for the oil companies.[14] In the absence of specific pressure on them, they would, of course, decline the opportunity to change their refineries. With all of the specific pressure being put on the auto companies, the structure of markets thus prevented the thorough exploration of the unleaded gasoline–catalytic converter approach to pollution control.

The California legislature, fearful of relying solely on the good intentions of the auto companies to develop the pollution control devices, provided that exhaust control devices would be required on all new cars one year after two devices had been approved by the State Motor Vehicle Pollution Control Board. The legislature thus opened up the field to the competitive efforts of any parts manufacturer that wished to enter. This strategy produced positive results. In March 1964 the auto companies announced that they would have exhaust devices ready by the 1967 model year. (The original date in the early correspondence with Supervisor Hahn was the 1958 model year.) In June the control board approved four exhaust devices developed by parts makers, thus requiring the devices on the 1966 model cars. In August the auto companies announced that they would, after all, be able to provide their own exhaust devices by the 1966 model year. The companies chose to meet the requirements through engine modifications (Chrysler) or air pumps (Ford, G.M., American Motors). The Chrysler system cost $18–$25; the air pressure system, approximately $50. For the 1968 model year, most of the industry went over to engine modification system for all but manual transmission cars.

Meanwhile, national interest in automotive pollution control was growing. Appearing before congressional committees, the auto companies opposed any legislation but assured the committee of their sincere interest and the need for more information and more research. Even after exhaust devices were made mandatory on California cars, the companies rejected the idea of installing the devices on a nationwide basis in testimony in the summer of 1964.[15] But events were moving rapidly. The federal government was going to require the devices on its 1967 model cars; it became increasingly apparent that, once the industry had the technology to install the devices on California cars, there were no logical reasons for not installing them nationally. Public pressure was mounting. In the spring of 1965 the companies announced that they would indeed be able to install the devices if Congress so desired. In the fall of that year, Congress passed the Motor Vehicle Air Pollution Act of 1965,[16] instructing the secretary of health, education, and welfare to issue standards and require installation of pollution control devices. The secretary set standards similar to those of California and made January 1, 1968, the installation date. Exhaust devices identical to those on California vehicles were installed on all 1968 model cars.

The exhaust standards set by California and followed by the federal government allow an average of no more than 275 parts per million hydrocarbon emissions and a 1.5 percent carbon monoxide emissions. An uncontrolled car produced 900 parts per million hydrocarbon fumes and 3.5 percent carbon monoxide gas, so that air pollutants are being cut to 25 percent for hydrocarbons and 40 percent for carbon monoxide.[17] California is raising its standards to 180 parts per million hydrocarbon and 1.0 percent carbon monoxide by the 1970 model year, and the federal government again has followed California's lead with identical requirements.[18] Controls to eliminate gasoline evaporation will be required in 1970 on California cars and in 1971, nationwide.

Thus by the early 1970's automotive pollution should be reduced considerably on new cars. It will take several years, however, before most of the cars on the road have pollution control devices. Blowby and evaporation emission should be eliminated, and exhaust hydrocarbons should be reduced to one-fifth of the uncontrolled levels so that overall hydrocarbon emissions should be only one-ninth of their original levels. Carbon monoxide emissions should be less than a third of the original levels. It should be remembered that these levels will be attained only if the control devices continue to work properly during the life of the car. The approximate cost is $50–$60 per vehicle ($10 blowby, $30–$40 exhaust, $10 evaporation devices).

Is it worth it? The answer is a probable "yes." An extra $600 million a year ($60 × 10 million cars) expenditure on pollution control does seem to be well under the probable benefits to be gained from easing air pollution, even allowing for the fact that automobiles are not the sole cause of pollution, nor will all automotive pollution have been eliminated. The elimination of about half of the gross tonnage of pollutants, even if one recognizes that pollutants are not linear in their effect,[20] should bring benefits (probably unmeasurable) that may exceed those costs by a wide margin.

Is the current system of controls the most efficient or the most equitable method of achieving these benefits? Here the answer is not so clear. From a legislative standpoint, the auto companies were the easiest target for remedial action on pollution. "It is their product that is directly causing the pollution; let them clean it up," seemed to be the general attitude. This attitude neglected the role that gasoline modifications could have played in reducing pollution. In addition to lead, most gasolines contain substances that cause deposits to form in cylinders; the deposits in turn increase the level of hydrocarbon emission. Removing the lead and these substances might have been the most effective and lowest cost approach to reducing pollution. The possibility of more stringent state inspection and maintenance requirements as an alternative or supplement to other measures was similarly not considered. However, a political assault on the oil companies and the auto companies jointly was probably not feasible, and the amount of coordination necessary to impose a joint gasoline modification–engine modification solution may have been impossible. The states were not eager to incur the extra costs of vehicle inspection.[21] Thus pressure on the auto companies alone may have appeared to be the politically easiest route.[22]

A more complete approach to the automotive pollution problem is possible. Gasoline varieties, engine modifications and attachments, and levels of required maintenance would be components in an overall automotive control system. Standards, prohibitions, fines, and differential taxes would be ways to achieve a given level of control.[23] An efficiency frontier, composed of the lowest social cost system for every level of pollution control, could be constructed. In the absence of measurable dollar benefits attributable to these control levels, it is not possible to calculate a maximum net benefit solution. Consequently, we should have to rely on legislators to choose among the alternatives according to the strength of the signals from their political antennae. While the current control system might in fact be on that efficiency frontier, it is unlikely. The current approach of seeking marginal adjustments from the vehicle manufacturers only, largely to the exclusion of other possibilities, implies a strong preference for moral over least cost solutions.[24]

Electrical vehicles and urban mass transit systems are often seen as long-run solutions to the problems of air pollution. In this author's opinion, the proponents of these systems have not made realistic appraisals of consumer demand for transportation.

The current state of electric car technology is uncertain. What is needed is a small, cheap, lightweight power source that can be used for cruising at 60 miles per hour, has a range of at least 200 miles, and is capable of quick recharging. Unfortunately, not many of the currently proposed electrical power sources look promising.[25] Currently available lead-acid batteries are clearly incapable of meeting the above requirements. Also the supply of lead may be too inelastic for the demand that a better lead-acid battery would generate. Proposed alternatives, like nickel-cadmium, silver-zinc, sodium-sulfur, or lithium-chloride batteries have a variety of drawbacks: either their raw materials are too expensive, they require too high starting and operating temperatures (250–600° C), they cannot be quickly recharged, or they simply do not have the power and/or range capabilities. The current state of the art in fuel cells presents an equally bleak picture. It will take a major breakthrough, not just the "normal" marginal improvements over time, to bring electrical power packages to the point at which they are roughly competitive with internal combustion engines.

A more immediate possibility, however, would be a small (two to four occupants), lightweight (2,000 pounds or less) electric car with a top speed of about 40 miles an hour and a range of 50 miles, capable of recharging overnight. The vehicle would cost in the range of $2,000 and be powered by currently available or soon to be available battery sources. Such a vehicle would appear to meet the "needs" of the second and third cars of a family, fulfilling the commuter, errand, and shopping trip functions. The proponents of such vehicles, naturally, are convinced that the public is eager to own such a vehicle.[26]

Consumer reaction to small, lightweight, cheap cars in the past does not bear this out. Even during the height of the import boom in the 1950's, the very small, lightweight cars never sold as well as the somewhat larger imports (for example, Volkswagen or Renault). The failure of Crosley's bantam-size car has been mentioned a number of times in this study. The Rambler Metropolitan, with an 85-inch wheelbase, 55-horsepower motor, room for two occupants, plus a small back seat, and a list price of $1,673 in 1961 — in short, a car that offered all that the proposed electric cars offer, plus a higher speed and longer range and instant "recharging" at any gasoline station — never sold more than 15,000 units a year and, after eight years of poor sales, was dropped in 1962. Despite the apparent transportation "needs" of American families, they seem to prefer large, relatively expensive automobiles with versatile characteristics. Unless a radical change in consumer tastes occurs or until the financial penalties of owning and operating such vehicles become very severe, Americans are likely to continue to prefer such vehicles over the currently proposed electric cars.

Similarly, urban mass transit systems planners appear to be arguing that commuters yearn for such systems and that the combination of shiny new mass transit vehicles, "reasonable" fares, and convenient service is expected to attract them away from their cars. Implicit is the assumption that commuting in one's own car has no value beside its transportation value.

Much could be said about the extra convenience and flexibility that a car provides or the short-run low marginal costs per trip that a car provides (though high parking rates are eliminating this). But what if the basic assumption is false? What if commuters actually like driving to work? A car perhaps represents one of the last bastions of privacy in modern America, where a man is away from his family and his boss and colleagues. He can sing, shout, scratch his ears, turn the radio on loud, and make threatening gestures and shout obscenities at other motorists, all without fear of social rebuke. Is it a coincidence that most transportation studies find average commuter car occupancy rates only slightly higher than one per car? A car is responsive to the driver's wishes; it is he who is actually controlling 4,000 pounds of steel and complex machinery. He has control over his immediate environment to a degree probably not equaled anywhere else in his daily routine.

We are arguing that automobile transportation may well provide a great many psychological satisfactions that mass transit cannot provide. Private auto transportation may have to become quite expensive in relation to public transit before consumers begin to substitute the latter for the former. Astronomical downtown parking rates do not seem to have deterred commuters or even to have encouraged car pools. The provision of mass transit systems may be equally ineffective in reducing appreciably the amount of automobile transportation and the pollution therefrom.

In the late 1960's, steam-propelled automobiles were proposed as a solution to the air pollution problem. Though enthusiasm for them outside the automobile industry has been high, problems in development have been large. The key one seems to be an inability to develop a small condensor of adequate potential horsepower. With William Lear's decision in October 1969 to drop his development efforts, steam automotive technology is not likely to progress rapidly in the near future.

Automotive Safety

Four thousand pounds of steel, rubber, and glass going 60 miles an hour, or even 20 miles an hour, can do a lot of damage upon hitting something else. Therein lies the problem of automotive safety.

Increased auto safety, a reduced number of accidents, is effective at two levels: (1) reduced costs to first parties — the driver and the occupants of his car, and (2) reduced costs to injured second parties and their property. Though liability insurance is usually applicable, there are often delays in settlements and incomplete or disputed payments. It is arguable whether deaths can even be compensated for. In the long run, reduced injuries to second parties should reduce insurance costs to first parties.

The first element ought to enter directly into a car buyer's preference function (though, apparently, as we shall see, it has not). Collision and medical insurance can somewhat ease the first-party costs of accidents, but there are uncertainties about payment and delays and inconveniences in making repairs, so that the incentive to reduce first-party accidents and costs still ought to be strong. The second element is a bit more complicated. Despite liability insurance, it is always in a driver's interests to avoid accidents with second parties, since first-party damage usually cannot be avoided in an accident and insurance premiums tend to rise after an accident. But the *amount* of damage caused to second parties, once there has been a reportable accident, is not really of financial concern to a first party covered by liability insurance. Here, then, is a serious externality. The imposition of uncertainty, inconvenience, and delay on the second party may not be fully compensated for by the first party's insurance, again creating an externality. Further, there may be many cases in which a second party will be legally liable for damages, and therefore his liability insurance will have to pay the first party, even though some action by the first party could have avoided the accident. Perhaps the clearest example of this is the case in which a dark car, at night, which has its headlights and taillights shielded so they cannot be seen from the side, is hit from the side by a second driver who could not see the car. The second driver is likely to be held legally liable, yet a light on the side of the first car (as has been required on all 1968 and subsequent models) could have prevented the accident. Though the uncertainty and delay costs should still be operating to encourage the first driver to add a light on the side of his car, the incentive is not as great as if he himself were liable for the damages. Again, there is an element of externality involved here.

The economic magnitudes of the safety problem are somewhat easier to obtain than are those of air pollution. Automobile accidents, injuries, and deaths are reasonably accurately reported to police departments and insurance companies. These, in turn, are compiled by the National Safety Council. According to the council, in 1967 there were 13.7 million auto accidents involving 24.3 million drivers. Approximately 53,100 deaths were attributed to these accidents. The council estimates that the economic loss due to auto accidents was $10.7 billion in 1967, of which $2.7 billion was in lost wages (including the discounted future wages of those who died), $0.7 billion in medical expenses, $3.4 billion in property damage, and $3.9 billion in insurance administration.[27] Another rough estimate of the economic loss due to accidents is the annual amount of premiums paid on automobile insurance policies.[28] In 1967, motorists paid $10.6 billion in premiums.[29]

There are a number of areas in which an attack on accidents could be made. Better design of roads, better street lighting, higher driver physical qualifications, and so forth, would all tend to reduce accidents. In the area of automobile manufacture, with which we are concerned, there are three types of action that could reduce accidents:

1. Greater reliability of components. This might mean more rigorous factory inspection, manufacturing to finer tolerances, or redesign of systems, as in the case of dual brake-cylinder systems replacing single-cylinder systems.
2. Redesign to reduce injury to second parties and perhaps to eliminate some accidents. This would include redesigning bumpers and grilles to reduce injury to pedestrians. It would also include cases like the requirement of a light on the side of a car.
3. Redesign and the addition of components to reduce injuries to first parties in the event of an accident. This involves better "packaging" of a car's occupants and includes seat belts, padded dashboards, nonprotruding instrument knobs, better safety glass, impact-reducing frames and sides, and other interior and exterior equipment.

Again, one would like to be able to ask, what are the costs and expected benefits from a particular safety measure? Unfortunately, there do not appear to be any clear answers. This author is not aware of any large scale statistical studies of accident types, their frequencies, and the potentialities of particular safety features in reducing the accidents or the damage caused. The effectiveness of particular safety features in particular instances has been demonstrated. Safety researchers at the Cornell Aeronautical Laboratory, studying samples of actual accidents, have been able to demonstrate the injury-reducing capabilities of items like seat belts, safety door latches, padded dashboards, and safety-glass windshields with an extra thick layer of plastic.[30] Still, one would have to know the frequency of such accidents, and the probability and costs of injuries, before making an overall evaluation.

When we turn to the behavior of the auto companies in respect to the safety issue, we find that generally, until 1965, they dragged their feet, behaving as if safety did not enter into the preference functions of consumers and as if the mention of safety considerations might well deter consumers. The major exception here was the 1956 Ford effort to stress safety features ("Lifeguard design"): a deep-dish steering wheel, padded seatbacks, swingaway rearview mirrors, and safety door latch as standard equipment; seat belts, padded dashboards, and padded sunvisor and rearview mirror as options. The 1956 Ford sold only moderately well; Ford dropped the safety campaign in mid-year and declined to renew it for the following model years. The 1956 Ford was largely unchanged from the previous year, whereas Chevrolet, which outsold Ford, had undergone a major "facelift" and had a new V-8 engine. This may have contributed to the 1956 Ford's mediocre sales record. Nevertheless, "safety doesn't sell" became the accepted byword in the auto industry.

Why should consumers shy away from safety? Why should it not be a positive component in their preference functions? We can offer some possibilities. Few consumers would like to be reminded that the 4,000 pounds of steel for which they have just paid $2,500 or more might become a death trap. Few wish to visualize a smashed forehead as a reason for preferring a padded dashboard. Accidents always happen to "other people," whereas the purchaser "knows" that he will be able to steer clear of any serious accidents.[31] Further, few consumers have the technical competence or the information to judge the merits of particular safety devices. But if he somehow comes to believe that the car is "unsafe" (and that is why the safety device is being offered), he may well shy away from buying it in the first place.

This view of consumer motivations seems to have been that on which the auto companies operated. According to a *Fortune* author, General Motors executives were furious at Ford over the 1956 safety efforts, fearing that Ford's efforts would frighten buyers away from everyone's cars.[32] For the next few years, nothing was said or done about auto safety. If one looks at the list of items involving safety features that the manufacturers offered voluntarily before 1965 — better brakes, easier steering, automatic transmission, better headlights, better doorlocks, deep-dish steering wheels — all but the last two involved simply better performance of components without really implying that there was any danger of accidents involved. Safety doorlocks were installed in 1955, but nowhere was there any mention that their real value was in keeping doors closed in accidents; pre-1955 doors had opened in 42 percent of serious accidents.[33] The new locks basically consisted of an extra steel plate to prevent longitudinal displacement of the door in an accident; this was a relatively low cost way to avert what could have become a minor scandal. On deep-dish steering wheels (designed to reduce the chances of a driver's being injured by the steering column), the other companies quietly followed Ford's lead after 1956. The new steering wheel probably cost no more than the old and it did not conflict with design considerations, so that this was a relatively low cost action for the companies.

Up before congressional committees, company executives professed their sincere interest in safety matters but claimed that more research and better information were needed; they did not, however, seem to be interested enough to collect that information themselves.[34] They stressed the importance of consumer education to the merits of safety but did not undertake that task themselves. They stressed the need for better highways and better vehicle inspection to reduce accidents. They discouraged the setting of any federal standards in the area of vehicle safety, emphasizing that the current system of state-set standards was performing satisfactorily.[35] At the same time, however, they were discouraging the states from setting any new standards by complaining that 50 separate state standards on items would mean the end of mass production economies.

The companies' behavior with respect to seat belts is typical of their behavior on the safety issue. Until the early 1960's seat belts were not offered as a factory-installed option except by Ford and Studebaker.[36] The other companies, beginning in 1955, provided seat belts to the dealers, to be installed if customers so requested. The latter was usually a more expensive operation than the former, especially since special seat belt anchorages were not being provided; anchorage installation costs for mass production were estimated at $0.50 per car; retail service outlet installation was estimated to cost $8–$12.[37] The seat belts were never advertised or merchandised vigorously (with the exception of the 1956 Ford). As political pressure mounted, the companies slowly gave ground. At the beginning of the 1962 model year, they began installing the anchorage as standard equipment and about the same time began offering seat belts to their dealers at cost. New York State Senator Edward J. Speno's efforts were quite influential in this process. In February 1963 Studebaker began installing front seat belts on a delete option basis; as of January 1, 1964, front belts became standard on all American cars. All but General Motors included rear belts as standard on the 1965 models, with General Motors following on its 1966 models.

After seven years of hearings, Congress finally became active in setting federal standards for automotive safety in 1962. In that year, the secretary of commerce was directed to set standards for hydraulic brake fluid. The following year, standards for seat belts were set. Expressing its increasing dissatisfaction with the auto companies' safety efforts, Congress, through Public Law 88-515,[38] in 1964 directed the General Services Administration (GSA) to prescribe safety standards for the automobile bought by the government. De jure, this changed very little, since the GSA had always had the power to specify the requirements of the items that it bought. De facto, however, it placed the initiative in the hands of the GSA. Previously, the auto companies might have replied to a GSA request with "sorry, but we don't produce those kinds of cars." Now, it was clear that Congress expected them to add safety equipment for cars used by the government.

The first seventeen standards were issued by the GSA in June 1965 for the 1967 model cars it would buy. They provided for the following items:

1. anchorage for seat belts assemblies
2. padded dash and visors
3. recessed dash instruments and control devices
4. impact-absorbing steering wheel and column displacement
5. safety door latches and hinges
6. anchorage of seats
7. four-way emergency flashers
8. safety glass
9. dual operation of braking system
10. standard bumper heights
11. standard automatic transmission gear arrangement
12. sweep design of windshield wiper and inclusion of washers
13. glare reduction surface
14. exhaust emission control system
15. tire and safety rim
16. backup lights
17. outside rearview mirror

One through six and eight were better passenger packaging requirements. The rest were items to reduce the likelihood of driver-caused accidents, with the exception of fourteen, which was the federal government's effort toward reducing air pollution.

The auto companies quickly saw the coming trend. In July 1965 they announced that all but three of the GSA items would be made standard on all 1966 model cars (implying, of course, that they had made these preparations at least a few months before the June standards were issued). The items left out were the four-way flasher (which Ford in fact did make standard), the dual braking system, and the exhaust devices. Also, a thicker plastic layer safety-glass windshield was offered. The following model year (1967), the flasher and the dual brakes (which had been on Cadillacs and Ramblers since 1962) were made standard. A collapsible steering column and frontseat latches (to prevent injuries in a sudden stop) on two-door models were also introduced.

Meanwhile, the companies were fighting against proposals to give the secretary of commerce power to set safety standards on all cars. They preferred (naturally) to have the initiative in their own hands and wished to limit the federal government's role to one of supporting research and supporting the safety activities of state and local governments.[39] Having shown "good faith" by making most of the GSA items standard on their 1966 cars and announcing their intention to make the rest standard by 1967 or 1968, the companies probably could have succeeded in thwarting any efforts to impose federal standards for all cars. But then a minor scandal broke over the Corvair, Ralph Nader, and General Motors. Nader, a lawyer, had written a book, *Unsafe at Any Speed*, that was critical of the auto industry's behavior on the safety and pollution issues and was specifically critical of the alleged unsafe oversteering properties (the tendency for the rear wheels to slide sideways as a car moves around a turn) of the 1960–1963 Chevrolet Corvair.[40] Nader was also encouraging and assisting damage suits concerning accidents involving Corvairs. General Motors assigned some detectives to investigate Nader's background. The detectives apparently subjected him to considerable harassment. These facts came out; General Motors had made itself look like the giant corporation tramping on the rights and privacy of the individual; and the corporation had to apologize for its actions before Senator Ribicoff's Subcommittee on Executive Reorganization on March 22, 1966. Four years later, General Motors settled out of court for $425,000 an invasion of privacy suit by Nader.

Meanwhile, on March 2, 1966, a major bill, endorsed by the president, which authorized the setting of national safety standards for motor vehicles, was introduced into the Senate. After the Nader incident, passage became assured. The bill passed the Senate unanimously in June and became the National Traffic and Motor Vehicle Safety

Act of 1966 in September.[41] The legislation set up a new agency under the secretary of commerce (it is now the National Highway Safety Program and under the Department of Transportation). The agency issued a proposed set of standards in November; by the end of January 1967 most of the standards for the 1968 model cars had been set.[42] The standards included most of the GSA items, plus a number of additional features like lights on the side and shoulder harnesses.[43] Standards have since been issued for the 1969 model year and subsequent model years. The GSA, in September 1967, decided to suspend its special standards and henceforth to follow the standards of the National Highway Safety Bureau.

The net effect of the legislation and the National Highway Safety Bureau has been positive.[44] Not only have the standards gone into effect (though some critics have charged that the standards simply codify existing practice, rather than break any new ground),[45] but the companies have been spurred to develop safety features on their own. Ford in its 1968 model cars introduced an energy-absorbing frame; General Motors in its 1969 cars introduced special side reinforcements to reduce the penetration of a vehicle by another vehicle hitting it from the side. These were both clearly after-the-crash safety items and publicized as such, yet the companies were no longer afraid of such items. Ford has also introduced a skid-control braking device on some 1969 models. "Safety" is no longer an unmentionable word in the automobile industry.[46] Also, more publicity has been given to the call-back campaigns aimed at correcting possibly defective cars, thus increasing the likelihood that owners of defective cars will be contacted and their cars repaired; the publicity may also spur the companies to tighten their quality control and improve their testing procedures.

As one appraises the overall safety issue, one is struck by three basic problems: (1) information for the consumer, (2) safety-feature education of consumers, and (3) consumer sovereignty.

Information for the Consumer

If the companies have ever had information relating to accident rates or car performance in general, they have been most reluctant to release it.[47] Most consumers, even if they wished to, have not been able to get adequate information about the safety aspects of cars.

Private publications, such as *Consumer Reports* and many car magazines, often publish reviews of new cars, but there are difficulties. The information is not always complete; the *Consumer Reports* automobile buying guide issue does not appear until April, when more than half the model year has passed; and the car magazines have sometimes taken too enthusiastic an approach to anything that Detroit has produced. The recent proposal by the National Highway Safety Bureau that the companies themselves provide performance data in a booklet accompanying each new car is a welcome step in the right direction. The companies, not too surprisingly, have objected to many aspects of the proposal,[48] but the prospects that this sort of information will eventually become required look promising.[49]

Safety-Feature Education of Consumers

It takes more than the quiet issuance of safety studies to convince consumers of the worth of safety features. Such findings must be heavily publicized before their message is accepted. Until 1966, the auto companies obviously did not consider it in their interest to fulfill this function. Was it in anyone's interest to push safety, provide information, publicize safety studies? Or was this a role that only society as a whole, acting through its government, could fulfill?

The logical candidate for this role would have been the automobile insurance companies. Though the liability principle meant that companies paid damages to the *other* driver and therefore were indifferent to most of the safety features that their own insured driver did or did not have, still there were enough incentives that should have moved the insurance companies to a leading safety role. Some companies were large enough so that a significant number of accidents would have involved drivers who were both insured by the same company. Some safety devices, like dual brakes or nonglare surfaces, would have reduced accidents by their own insured drivers. Collision and medical insurance, though they involved a smaller volume of business than liability insurance, were still sizable enough to warrant insurance company interest in safety. Further, a competitive industry might well have offered differential rates according to the safety records of particular cars or of particular features. Liability insurance should have been cheaper if one had a dual brake system or nonglare surfaces on one's car; collision insurance should have been cheaper if one had a padded dashboard. The industry could have created incentives for consumers to become interested in safety.

Unfortunately, no such action was forthcoming, with the exception of Liberty Mutual Insurance Company's building of two "survival cars" in the 1950's. The reasons for this general lack of safety orientation are not quite clear, but one can guess that the state-regulated price fixing arrangements that dominate the industry may bear a good deal of the responsibility. Price competition has not been one of the automobile insurance industry's strong points. The incentives seem to be to get as large a premium flow as possible and keep it as long as possible, investing the proceeds at high rates of return. With insurance contracts renegotiated annually and policy rates set roughly according to accident frequencies, reduced accidents would quickly be translated into lower premiums, an unenticing proposition for an industry that may be able to think of itself in joint profit-maximizing terms.[50]

The producers of safety equipment, of course, might have pushed safety. "Be sure there's an XYZ brand padded dash on your next car," would have been the type of advertising campaign that a parts manufacturer could have sponsored. But most of the smaller parts makers were not accustomed to aiming their advertising at consumers, concentrating instead on dealers and auto equipment retailers. The parts manufacturers may well have feared incurring the wrath of the auto companies by trying to push safety. Thus the two most likely candidates to educate the public on safety declined the role; it was left to government, mostly state government, to assume this function.

Consumer Sovereignty

Suppose that, in the presence of adequate information and strenuous efforts to push safety, consumers still prefer not to buy the items or use them. One can make a respectable case for still insisting on items (for example, dual brakes and side lights) that prevent accidents on grounds of externality: the uncertainties, delays, and inconveniences caused to second parties even in cases in which insurance covers the physical damages.

But what about the better packaging items, like padded dashboards, seat belts, and shoulder harnesses? Should a man be forced to buy seat belts, even when he chooses not to use them? Since most occupants of cars are usually the owner and his immediate family, are there really externalities here? To defend these items, one would have to use the argument that a man does not have the right to subject his children to danger any more than he can keep them out of school or that society is likely eventually to have to foot the bill on many accident costs. Perhaps, if seat belts are standard equipment for long enough, people will eventually get used to wearing them. This case can be made, but in the author's opinion, it is somewhat weaker than the straight externalities argument.

Generally, in the area of government efforts on safety, there has been a more balanced approach than on the pollution problem. Vehicle safety standards have been only one of the government's programs. Better vehicle inspection, increased driver education, tighter licensing standards, better emergency medical services, and better highway design and maintenance have all been encouraged, although Congress has been reluctant to grant funds to the states for the first two items. There is no guaranty that the socially optimum combination of measures has been chosen, but the wide range of measures is encouraging.

The costs of the automotive safety items that have been installed on cars, beginning with seat belts on January 1, 1964, through head restraints on seatbacks on January 1, 1969, reach somewhere between $150 and $200 per car.[51] For an 8-million car year, this is $1.2–$1.6 billion a year. Are the benefits worth the costs? Probably, but until detailed analyses of accident rates are made, the question must remain largely unanswered.

15

Performance:
An Evaluation

Rate of Return

Table 15.1 offers the postwar record of profitability of the auto companies in terms of profits after taxes plus interest divided by total assets. Table 15.2 shows the profitability record in terms of net profits on net worth. Table 15.1 offers a view of the profitability of all capital invested in the industry; 15.2, a view of the profitability of equity capital. As long as debt capital is earning only normal returns (that is, close to its opportunity cost), the profits on equity figures should offer the better picture about the excess profits being made in an industry. Still, the rate of return on total assets does offer a convenient base mark for indicating how serious any overall distortion of capital allocation has been. As is seen in the two tables, the auto industry has averaged an 11.51 percent rate of return on total assets and 16.67 percent on net worth for the postwar period. General Motors has been the outstanding performer in this respect; all other companies' profitability figures are below the industry average. If we exclude General Motors, the industry average comes to 7.76 percent on total assets or 11.41 percent on net worth.

As a first approximation, we can say that, in the absence of serious externalities, capital is being efficiently allocated if it is just earning its opportunity cost — earning a return close to the long-term rate of interest. A good guess about the long-term rate of interest in this period would be somewhere in the range of 5–6 percent. By this measure, the auto industry has clearly been earning excess profits. Even if we exclude General Motors from the figures, the remaining companies still have earned, on the average, profits in excess of the

Table 15.1   Annual Rates of Return: Profits before Interest after Taxes Divided by Total Assets

Year	General Motors	Ford	Chrysler	American Motors	Nash	Hudson	Studebaker-Packard	Stude-baker	Packard	Kaiser	Crosley	Total auto industry[a]	Total excluding G.M.[a]	All nonfinancial corporations	All manufacturing corporations
1946	4.59	− 0.73	6.87		3.74	4.36		1.55	5.97	−39.94	n.a.	2.53	0.00	5.83	8.54
1947	11.94	6.39	13.93		13.73	7.41		9.53	4.75	6.39	8.71	10.90	9.60	7.90	9.65
1948	15.15	8.91	16.52		13.66	12.43		15.23	14.09	8.91	17.86	13.73	11.87	7.87	9.70
1949	23.56	14.66	20.78		17.24	11.07		19.87	5.50	−31.83	−13.71	19.40	14.56	6.10	7.55
1950	24.26	17.62	17.19		15.56	10.96		14.67	5.54	− 9.69	−11.91	20.23	15.43	7.61	9.64
1951	13.83	7.97	9.50		8.84	− 1.07		7.98	5.59	− 6.38	−20.84	10.92	7.38	5.88	7.10
1952	14.01	6.68	8.61		6.43	8.26		7.49	4.13	− 0.21	−39.13	10.70	6.86	4.99	5.80
1953	13.64	8.78	8.33		6.72	− 9.10		1.87	4.08	−14.23		10.44	6.50	4.87	5.84
1954	15.94	10.93	1.90	− 3.32			−10.43			−38.91		11.30	4.88	4.46	5.44
1955	18.99	16.74	7.60	− 1.86			−12.36					15.85	11.49	5.54	6.99
1956	13.17	8.05	1.99	− 7.67			−69.43					9.14	3.39	5.21	6.31
1957	12.67	9.21	8.56	− 5.10			− 7.77					10.71	8.08	4.71	5.70
1958	9.41	4.03	− 1.83	13.13			−10.01					6.56	2.45	4.06	4.58
1959	12.20	13.33	0.29	21.35			18.16					11.49	10.51	4.78	5.78
1960	12.39	11.66	3.04	14.34			0.99					11.15	9.41	4.10	4.96
1961	11.01	8.23	1.46	7.14			1.96					9.02	6.67	4.17	4.85
1962	16.19	9.09	4.86	9.16			1.62					12.50	8.02	4.54	5.36
1963	16.69	8.38	8.09	8.58			−45.62					12.22	7.25	4.86	5.72
1964	17.00	7.97	9.22	6.23			7.69					12.79	8.21	5.37	6.24
1965	18.69	9.40	8.27	1.14			11.13					13.82	8.78	5.99	7.10
1966	14.91	7.87	6.29	− 2.92								11.05	7.02	n.a.	n.a.
1967	12.53	1.78	5.53	−17.36								7.67	2.38	n.a.	n.a.
Avg.[b]	14.67	9.85	7.59	3.12	10.62	5.33	− 9.50	9.77	5.53	−12.42	− 9.83	11.51	7.76	5.44	6.64

SOURCE: Moody's Manual of Investments, various years; U.S. Internal Revenue Service, Statistics of Income, various years.
[a] Weighted average.
[b] Arithmetic average.

long-term rate of interest. Another rough test would be to compare auto industry profits to the profit rates of all corporations or of all corporations engaged in manufacturing. These figures, particularly the latter set, probably include some monopoly profits, but they indicate the alternative opportunities open to owners of capital. These figures also are included in Tables 15.1 and 15.2, and, again, even by these much less rigorous standards, the auto industry is shown to be earning excess profits.

The drawback to the figures used so far is that they do not explicitly take into account risk. Presumably, risk-averse investors will demand a risk premium before investing their money in a risky industry. Such high risk industries should presumably earn higher returns than the average of all industries. We have previously characterized the automobile industry as a high risk industry. Can its profit record be attributed solely to risk considerations?

It would be hard to argue that an investment in General Motors or Ford was a very risky proposition. Since 1947 General Motors' rates of return have consistently been above the averages for all corporations or for all manufacturing corporations. The same has been true for Ford since 1947 with the exception of 1958 (the year of the Edsel fiasco) and 1967 (a major strike). These two companies have been able to overcome or avoid the risks of the industry through dominant market positions, multiple brand structures, and the various types of action described in the previous chapters. Still, Chrysler has been less successful in avoiding these risks, and the Independents surely have been a risky proposition. A potential investor might well decide that "if it can happen to Chrysler, it can happen to anybody" and conclude that the potential risks, even to General Motors or Ford, were high. Is there any way of measuring this risk aspect and taking it into account in our profit calculation?

Fortunately, just this sort of calculation has already been done. Using a sample of 783 companies grouped into 59 major industries, Gordon R. Conrad and Irving H. Plotkin have tried to estimate the relationship between rates of return and risk.[1] For each industry they obtained the weighted average of rates of return (net profit after tax plus interest divided by total assets less current liabilities) for each year from 1950 through 1965 and summed these annual figures to get sixteen-year average rates of return for each industry. For their risk measures, they took the weighted variance around the average for

Table 15.2 Annual Rates of Return: Net Profits after Taxes Divided by Net Worth

Year	General Motors	Ford	Chrysler	American Motors	Nash	Hudson	Studebaker-Packard	Studebaker	Packard	Kaiser	Crosley	Total auto industry[a]	Total excluding G.M.[a]	All corporations	All manufacturing corporations
1946	6.14	− 1.13	5.30		5.22	5.83		2.34	8.22	− 56.05	n.a.	3.25	− 1.34	9.90	10.30
1947	18.34	8.27	20.67		28.00	12.55		19.02	6.46	32.62	12.84	16.16	13.65	11.31	13.35
1948	24.47	11.49	23.18		25.76	23.00		30.07	21.61	15.67	28.65	20.98	16.96	11.40	13.35
1949	31.38	17.98	28.05		26.58	15.61		32.33	10.98	− 84.75	24.94	25.75	19.26	8.85	9.80
1950	34.97	22.53	24.86		25.17	16.67		22.54	6.85	5.88	25.81	27.47	19.58	11.34	13.43
1951	20.00	10.11	13.81		13.54	− 1.61		12.10	7.32	− 12.04	63.55	15.17	9.71	7.68	10.16
1952	20.49	8.78	14.37		10.19	10.91		12.67	7.21	− 8.56	−5,502.78	15.60	9.88	7.23	8.02
1953	20.05	11.46	13.12		10.94	−16.08		2.48	6.56	−168.48		15.25	9.32	7.23	8.11
1954	24.14	14.30	3.16	− 6.79			− 17.69			c		16.89	7.05	7.11	7.39
1955	27.95	22.75	15.34	− 4.83			− 24.98					23.87	17.87	8.53	9.87
1956	18.50	11.67	3.09	−15.89			−661.87					13.24	4.98	7.92	8.85
1957	17.20	12.78	16.38	−10.64			−248.83					15.33	12.42	7.10	7.65
1958	12.63	5.02	− 4.89	18.97			− 22.16					8.87	2.97	5.53	5.84
1959	16.26	17.26	− 0.80	31.62			31.86					15.74	14.96	6.46	7.78
1960	16.49	14.86	4.56	21.61			0.72					15.10	13.03	5.53	6.41
1961	14.82	13.10	15.65	10.45			2.45					13.14	10.72	5.72	6.31
1962	21.94	14.06	8.50	13.73			2.18					18.22	12.80	6.00	7.07
1963	22.35	13.14	17.55	13.84			−214.52					18.22	12.26	6.11	7.76
1964	22.83	12.61	19.05	9.41			17.49					19.06	13.81	6.96	8.65
1965	25.81	15.66	14.75	1.95			20.61					21.04	14.90	8.36	10.28
1966	20.55	12.99	11.12	− 6.17								16.74	11.79	n.a.	n.a.
1967	17.57	1.83	10.92	−39.44								11.61	3.24	n.a.	n.a.
Avg.[b]	20.67	12.34	11.98	2.70	18.18	8.34	− 60.55	16.69	9.40	− 35.94	929.91	16.67	11.41	7.90	9.02

[a] Weighted average.

[b] Arithmetic average.

[c] Losses incurred on a negative net worth.

each year for each industry and summed these over sixteen years to get an average risk level for each industry. They then regressed the average rates of return on the average risk levels for the 59 industries and obtained the following relationship:

$$\text{Rate of return} = 8.6 + 0.08214 \text{ (risk)}$$
$$R^2 = 0.46$$
$$F = 49.80$$

The relationship is not unreasonable. The 8.6 percent return implied for a riskless investment is probably on the high side, but this result is probably due to Conrad and Plotkin's sample. Their 783 companies are among the largest in the economy and often enjoy positions of market power; thus the profit figures of these companies include some measure of monopoly profits. Accordingly, the 8.6 percent figure is really the return on a riskless investment in an industry in which some monopoly profits are likely to be earned.

Nevertheless, even by this admittedly weak standard, the auto companies are shown to have excess profits after allowing for risks. This sample includes five auto companies: the Big Three, Studebaker, and American Motors. For the 1950–1965 period, these 5 companies had an average rate of return of 17.9898, and an average variance of 58.127; the auto industry was eighth highest of the 59 industries on this latter measure. If we insert this variance figure into the equation, we get an expected average rate of return of 13.4 percent. Thus the actual rate of return was a good deal higher than the expected return, or, in other words, excess profits were being earned over and above a risk premium. Of the 59 industries, the auto industry was second only to the cosmetics industry in the size of the margin between the actual rate of return and the risk-adjusted expected rate of return.[2] Thus it is safe to conclude that the automobile industry has been earning excess profits, regardless of how it is measured. This result should not be too surprising for an industry with such high rates of concentration and such high barriers to entry.

A number of provisos should be offered on the use of these profit figures. First, the auto company figures are all on a consolidated company basis, and the rates of return represent profits on all of the companies' activities, not just automobile manufacturing. It is impossible to determine what the rates of return in each sector have been. Unless the Securities and Exchange Commission radically changes its financial reporting requirements, we are unlikely to get any better figures. Nevertheless, United States automobiles do constitute the bulk of auto company receipts; if only normal profits were being earned in auto production proper, the companies would be earning phenomenal profits in their other activities. In any event, when faced with the charge of excess profits, the burden of proof to show that only normal profits are being earned in the activity in question should rest on those who have chosen to hide behind a consolidated balance sheet.

Second, the profit figures given above may well underestimate the true potential profitability of the auto industry because of static production inefficiencies. Through most of the postwar period Chrysler has had a reputation for being a very poorly managed firm.[3] The Independents' reputations have not been much better in this respect. MacDonald cites numerous instances in labor relations matters in which poor management decisions by Ford, Chrysler, and the Independents led to higher labor costs than General Motors incurred.[4] Kilbridge, writing in 1960, stated that "it is common knowledge that Chrysler for years had a slower work pace than either Ford or General Motors . . . An industrial engineer familiar with the Detroit automotive industry states that the Chrysler work pace was until recently about 30 percent slower than that of General Motors and that the Ford work pace was about midway between the two." [5]

One suspects that what was true in labor relations was true in other areas of management. Chrysler has gone through a number of management reorganizations in the postwar period in efforts to increase efficiency. That these efforts had not entirely succeeded by 1968 is indicated by the fact that Chrysler was not able to take advantage of the import boom in 1968 with imports from its overseas subsidiaries. It had failed to design these cars so that they could meet United States safety standards. The oligopoly market structure in the automobile industry has surely played an important permissive role in the continuance of this inefficiency. Thus, if the companies had been able to use more efficiently their resources at hand, costs would have been lower and profits would have been higher.[6] Also, if in efforts to reduce risks, the auto companies have devoted "excessive" resources to activities like advertising, styling, or model proliferation, true profits would be understated. (This will be discussed below.)

One could also ask what would profits be if somehow the auto industry did not have to bargain with the United Automobile Workers? Since recent econometric studies have shown industry profits to be an important determinant of industry wage rates, one can speculate that part of the excess profits in the auto industry may have been siphoned off as higher wages for its workers. A thorough test of

Table 15.3 Average Hourly Wages in Manufacturing in Certain Cities, Early 1967 and Early 1968[a]

Category	Detroit	Pitts-burgh	South Bend	Cincin-nati	Indian-apolis	Dayton
	Early 1967					
Machine tool operator	$3.94	$3.45		$3.58	$3.84	$3.72
Machinists, maintenance	3.95	3.77	$3.35	3.58	3.55	3.78
Tool and die maker	4.11	3.71	3.79	3.78	3.85	4.09
Male accounting clerk, Class A[b]	3.71	3.30	3.30	3.00	3.36	3.24
Female secretary[b]	3.48	2.81	2.85	2.76	2.91	2.99
	Early 1968					
Machine tool operator	4.33	3.64		3.89	4.20	4.32
Machinist, maintenance	4.33	3.88	3.56	3.77	3.64	4.15
Tool and die maker	4.54	3.87	3.91	4.03	4.13	4.40
Male accounting clerk, Class A[b]	3.98	3.42	3.22	3.16	3.42	3.41
Female secretary[b]	3.68	2.88	2.69	2.94	3.20	3.15

SOURCE: U.S. Bureau of Labor Statistics, *Area Wage Surveys*, Bulletins 1530 and 1575.

[a] Indianapolis figures are for the previous December; Detroit, Pittsburgh, and Dayton are for January; South Bend and Cincinnati are for March.

[b] The clerk and secretary wages were originally expressed as weekly salaries. They have been divided by average weekly hours worked.

this proposition would require a complete study of the labor markets in which the auto companies operate and a comparison between UAW wages and the wages for jobs of similar skills in non-UAW areas with similar unemployment rates. Still, a rough estimate can be made. Table 15.3 shows the straight-time hourly wage rates reported by the BLS for certain types of jobs in Detroit and other industrial cities in the mid-West for early 1967 and early 1968.[7] The Detroit wages should be heavily influenced by the UAW; the other cities' wages should be influenced only slightly, if at all, by the UAW. Other unions are influential in other cities (for example, the Steelworkers in Pittsburgh), but any hopes of getting a competitive wage totally free of union influence, to use as a base, are probably doomed. Thus we are looking at wages influenced by the UAW, as compared to wages influenced more or less by other unions. The clerical and secretarial wages are included because these have traditionally been adjusted in line with union wage increases.

The auto companies probably pay wages somewhat above the Detroit averages; in 1967 General Motors reported average wage payments of $4.12 per hour plus fringes.[8] They also pay higher fringe benefits, so a figure of $0.50 per hour as the average premium the UAW was able to extract from the auto companies in 1967 would not be unreasonable. In 1967 General Motors employed 406,000 hourly rated workers in the United States, and they worked for an average of 39.5 hours per week.[9] For the year, then, the $0.50 per hour premium comes to $417 million, or 12½ percent of pre-tax profits. (It would be somewhat larger if the higher wages paid to white-collar workers could also be included, but the company does not list its United States white-collar employment.) Thus General Motors' profits in 1967 might have been 12½ percent higher, or it might have earned 19.8 percent on equity instead of 17.5 percent if somehow it could have paid the wages that prevailed in cities in which the UAW was not a dominant force. Similar results for other years and other companies are likely.

Finally, the finding of excess profits in automobile manufacturing does not necessarily lead to the conclusion that insufficient resources were being devoted to auto production if one uses the test of social, rather than private, marginal product. Many have argued that *too many* resources have been devoted to auto production. Though this argument sometimes is simply a criticism of the path that consumers' preferences have taken, it can be stated to include the external costs that automobile owners create but do not pay for. Pollution, noise-accidents, urban congestion, and ugly, neighborhood-destroying freeways would be examples of the detrimental effects more or less caused by auto owners. Though pollution and accidents may be correctable by changes in the cars themselves, the other externalities remain. These are largely connected with use rather than ownership, and the socially optimal allocation of resources would call for car *use* to be limited to the point where the divergence between the price and private marginal costs of car use was just equal to the marginal social costs caused by car use. Still, a "second best" argument could be made that a limit on car production short of the point of optimal private allocation (that is, where the price paid equals long-run private marginal costs) could, in an all-or-nothing fashion, effectively limit car use to socially desirable levels.[10]

But auto production has in fact been limited. The federal excise tax (7 percent currently) has limited auto production somewhat, and the record of excess profits shown above indicates that production has been limited even more. What are the magnitudes of this limitation? If the auto company had earned only normal profits on equity during the postwar period, its profits would have been only half of what they actually were. Since profits on sales have averaged around 7 percent for the industry, normal profits would have meant wholesale prices that were 3½ percent lower. The absence of the excise tax would drop wholesale prices another 6½ percent. This combined 10 percent drop in wholesale prices would probably mean a drop of about 9 percent in retail prices. Then, in an 8-million unit year, car output has been limited by at least 720,000 units (assuming a price elasticity of -1.0) and possibly by as much as 2,160,000 units (assuming an elasticity as high as -3.0) per year.

Thus the excise tax and the excess profits have restricted auto output and use below the point of optimal private allocation, but the existence of externalities justifies some restriction. Has the point of optimal social allocation been reached?[11] In the absence of better information about the magnitudes of the externalities, we cannot make any judgment. But the presumptive cases for either expanding the resources in auto production (because there are excess profits) or contracting them (because there are externalities) can no longer be made.

Progressiveness

In trying to evaluate the past progressiveness of an industry, we enter the realm of the might-have-been. What was the potential for technological progress in the automobile industry, and how well did the industry measure up to that potential?

We can divide the question of progressiveness into two parts: manufacturing technology and automotive technology. In manufacturing technology, the companies' record of progressiveness seems fair to good. Though they have originated very little of the new technology in this area, they have usually been reasonably prompt in assimilating it. It would not appear to be possible to charge the auto companies with the kind of technological delay that Adams and Dirlam claim has occurred in the steel industry.[12]

One measure of the speed of technological progress would be the rate of increase of labor productivity through the postwar period. Auto company employment and output figures could not be used to measure this, since nonautomotive employment and changing degrees of vertical integration by the companies could seriously affect the results. A rough measure of labor productivity, though, can be gained by dividing the Federal Reserve Board (FRB) index of industrial production for the motor vehicles and parts industry by the number of man-hours devoted to that industry.[13] Though this measure would probably be too crude for measuring just one year's change, it should give us a reasonably good idea of the long-run trend. The logarithm of this fraction was regressed against a time trend for the years 1949 through 1967, the coefficient on this time trend showing the compound annual increase in labor productivity. Both production worker man-hours and total employment man-hours were tried as denominators for this fraction.

The results of these regressions are shown in the following list of average annual labor productivity increases from 1949–1967.[14] (The figures in parentheses indicate the standard error of these coefficients in the estimating equations.)

Automobiles

FRB index for motor vehicles and parts divided by production and related personnel man-hours: 4.33 percent (0.35)

FRB index for motor vehicles and parts divided by total employee man-hours: 3.96 percent (0.34)

All manufacturing

BLS series, output per man-hour in manufacturing: 2.80 percent (0.11)

FRB index for manufacturing divided by wage and salary workers in manufacturing man-hours: 3.19 percent (0.16)

FRB index for manufacturing divided by total employment in manufacturing man-hours: 3.33 percent (0.07)

As a standard for comparison, the increase in labor productivity in manufacturing as a whole was chosen. According to the figures, the motor vehicles industry has out-distanced the rest of manufacturing in its labor productivity gains, particularly on the production worker productivity basis. Since the national income category "gross automobile product" has accounted for about 15 percent of the manufacturing output figures, the exclusion of motor vehicles from manufacturing as a whole would have made the productivity differences appear even sharper. Of course, one can always ask about the potential for progress in auto manufacturing, as compared to manufacturing as a whole, but that is unlikely to lead to a fruitful discussion. Overall, again, it would be hard to accuse the auto companies of slow motion in this area. Thus incorporating our previous argument on the static inefficiency of many of the auto companies, we are arguing that they have been able to move along to new technologies reasonably rapidly, while never being able to utilize the maximum amount of efficiency of their resources at any given point in time.

When we look at the area of automotive product technology, the picture changes. The auto industry can be described as a technologically stagnant industry in terms of its product. Cars are not fundamentally different from what they were in 1946; very little new technology has been instigated by the industry. The product has improved over the last twenty years, but these have been small improvements with no fundamental changes. The sources for these improvements have often been the components suppliers, rather than the auto companies themselves; and the auto companies have often been slow to adopt these improvements.

The potential for more fundamental change does seem to be present. The German auto firm NSU has developed and produced commercially a rotary piston engine. Citroen does have a working pneumatic suspension system. Volkswagen has perfected a commercially feasible fuel injection system for its larger (1600-cubic centimeter) models. Mercedes has adapted a diesel engine for automotive use. Domestically, turbine engines and electric vehicles appear to be the most likely candidates to embody fundamental change. Yet turbine engines seem to be no closer to commercial adoption than they were fifteen years ago, and the auto companies did not become active in electric car and steam technology until the mid-1960's, when concern over air pollution and the competitive efforts of other industries spurred the auto companies into action.

If the large size of the auto companies had any special value for research and development, it should surely be in these areas of fundamental change. Yet the auto companies' postwar record is woefully lacking. Perhaps a more competitive environment, with more independent centers of initiative, would have spurred technological progress. This seems to have been true for the period before the war.

Responsiveness to Changes in Consumer Tastes and to Public Concerns

The auto companies' record on responsiveness to changes in consumer tastes has been mixed. They responded rapidly to consumer desires for large cars, greater horsepower, and more power equipment in the 1950's and for sporty cars and optional equipment in the 1960's. By contrast, the Big Three were slow in responding to the compact car boom of the late 1950's, and all four companies were slow in responding to the subcompact boom of the late 1960's.[14] In the former cases, the changes coincided with the industry's notion of jointly increased profits; in the latter, the changes did not.

Their record on responsiveness to issues of public concern is not very impressive. Their response to state and federal government concerns over air pollution and automotive safety was far from rapid. Even their response to the complaints of dealers was delayed until the companies were exposed to the glare of congressional inquiry.

Throughout the postwar period, one gets the impression that the Big Three were a tight oligopoly, convinced that they and they alone knew what kinds of cars the American public wanted.[15] Not too surprisingly, those kinds of cars also appeared to be the most profitable for them to produce. They recognized the problems involved in air pollution and automotive safety and saw responses in these areas as carrying only costs and little or no benefits in terms of increased sales. On safety, further, they saw the issue as one that might well scare away potential customers. On small cars, they were reluctant to move while consumers only had the choice of buying their larger cars or going without, and slow to move until they were convinced there was room enough in these new markets for all three companies to enter profitably.

Thus it is not surprising that it was the small companies that moved most rapidly to meet the small car market in the 1950's or that Studebaker was the first to install seat belts on a standard basis or that American Motors was the first to install dual brakes on nonluxury cars or that only after parts suppliers had developed air pollution control exhaust devices did the auto companies respond to California's air pollution control program.

It is important to see this lack of response by the Big Three not as a conspiracy "to do the public in" among a handful of men,[17] but rather as the result of a tight oligopoly that was constantly looking for the joint profit-maximization solution in the auto market. Auto safety was not seen by them as a profitable venture, and that is why they were slow. Unless we expect altruistic behavior from companies (and, if so, we must be willing to accept the bad along with the good), this is as it should be. The task of public policy in such cases should be to change the environment, if possible, so that social and profit-maximizing goals are in accord. Along these lines, one can again wonder whether, with a less tight oligopoly, the response on these issues by the industry as a whole might have been faster. With more centers of initiative and a smaller likelihood of joint profit solutions being agreed upon, more companies might have found it profitable to produce small cars earlier, some companies might have seen safety as a competitive area that it was in their interests to try to exploit, and competitive pressure might have led the companies to try to meet California's goal of air pollution control earlier.

Some Subjective Measures

There are a number of further questions we can ask about the auto industry: inflation has been a major concern of public policy during much of the postwar period, and price stability has been a major goal. How has the auto industry performed in this area? Have consumers been offered a sufficient variety of cars? Is there too much variety? Have too many resources been devoted to styling and model changes? Have too many resources been devoted to advertising?

On prices and inflation, the numbers are easy to obtain, but properly interpreting them is a good deal more difficult. Table 15.4 shows the relevant price figures for the 1949–1967 period.[18] The Consumer Price Index has increased by 40.1 percent over this period; the new car component has increased by only 20.8 percent. But since 1959, the BLS has been adjusting the new car components for quality adjustments, so that despite a rise in list and retail prices, the component has shown a drop of 5.6 percent. Griliches has argued that adjustments for quality increases for the pre-1960 period would show "real"

Table 15.4   Prices and Price Increases

	Consumer price index (1957/1959 = 100)	New car component CPI (1957/1959 = 100)	Full-sized Ford 6 4-door sedan		Ford Fairlane 6 4-door sedan	
			List price[a]	Probable mid-year retail price	List price[a]	Probable mid-year retail price
1949	83.8	81.2	$1,474	$1,474		
1959	101.5	103.9	2,273	1,923		
1967	116.3	98.1	2,496	2,096	$2,339	$2,000
Percent increase:						
1949/1959	22.3	28.0	54.2	30.5		
1959/1967	14.4	−5.6	9.8	9.0		
1949/1967	40.1	20.8	69.3	42.2	58.7[b]	25.7[b]

Source: *Monthly Labor Review; Automotive Industries,* and *Annual Statistical Issue,* various years.
[a] List price for bottom of the line model, including federal excise tax but excluding transportation and local taxes, as of spring of the year in question.
[b] Increase from 1949 Ford to 1967 Fairlane.

automobile prices falling during the 1954–1960 period and rising much less than the CPI showed for the entire 1950–1960 period.[19] Unfortunately, we do not know how similar quality adjustments would change the overall CPI, either before or after 1959. Consequently, we are left in somewhat of a quandary.

We are on somewhat firmer ground if we look at the increase in retail prices for a typical car and compare that to the increase in the (presumably, largely unadjusted) CPI. A bottom of the line Ford six-cylinder, four-door sedan increased in retail price by 42.2 percent over this period, roughly in line with the CPI rise. If we look at the rise in retail price from a 1949 Ford to a 1967 Ford Fairlane, a car of roughly the same dimensions as the 1949 Ford, we see a rise of only 35.7 percent. The two 1967 cars were clearly superior to their 1949 predecessor. The full-sized Ford, of course, was a good deal larger. Both had higher horsepower engines (yet around the same gasoline mileage); around $150 in safety equipment; more glass area; 12-volt electrical system (rather than 6-volt); turn signals; alternators; a longer warranty; better upholstery; and the opportunity (certainly worth something) to add automatic transmissions, power equipment, and higher horsepower engines, all of which the 1949 Ford was lacking. A similar price and quality pattern would be found for other makes.[20]

By this measure, it is clear that the auto industry over the postwar period has at least done no worse than to equal the general rate of price increase, and, when quality changes are taken into account, has probably enjoyed a slower rate of "real" increases. But this should not be too surprising from an industry that has shown the rapid rate of manufacturing technological progress that was demonstrated earlier in this chapter. It would be surprising if it were otherwise.

Have consumers been offered an adequate variety of cars to choose from? Here it is necessary to define what one means by "adequate." One test of adequacy would be to close one's eyes, try to imagine all of the possible types of cars that consumers might buy in commercially feasible quantities, and then see if that selection is being offered. By this test, the author would conclude that the consumer has been offered an adequate choice, with a wide range of size, price, and shape, though it has not always been the Big Three that have offered that choice to the consumer. The role of the Independents and especially of imports has been important here. Since 1959 the selection available from the Big Three has widened considerably in terms of size and price, though they have been slow in offering Volkswagen-size cars to the market. Thus in this area, the United States industry should receive only a fair mark for their performance; in the absence of imports, consumers would be faced with a far too limited selection.

Has the proliferation of models by the domestic industry since 1959 proceeded too far? "Too far" is also a phrase that needs qualification. One measure would be whether a fewer number of different models could be produced at lower unit costs; whether consumers would be better off with this hypothetical solution is another question. But there is no evidence that the increase in the number of models offered has affected overall costs or prices. Larger volumes sold combined with modern assembly and inventorying techniques seem to have kept this potential problem under control. Purchasers of low volume cars with production appreciably under 400,000 a year (for example, Ford Thunderbird, Buick Riviera, and Chrysler Imperial) may be paying a premium because of the cost penalties of low volume, but these purchasers always have the alternative open to them of high volume standard models that are produced at efficient scale.

What about model changes? In 1962, Fisher, Griliches, and Kaysen, in an article titled "The Cost of Automobile Model Changes since 1949," [21] argued that these costs have averaged $4,843 million per year in the late 1950's, or somewhere over $800 per new car.[22] Their costs consisted of the following items: (1) the difference between actual prices paid for cars and the price that would have been paid for a car with average 1949 specifications (the latter determined by econometric techniques); (2) the added costs of automatic transmissions, power brakes, and power steering; (3) extra advertising expenses; (4) extra tooling costs; and (5) the extra gasoline consumed by the larger cars.

But only categories 3 and 4 should really qualify as the added costs of model changes, and these were only slightly more than one eighth of the total.[23] The rest of the "costs" are simply the result of consumers preferring to buy Buicks with automatic transmissions, rather than Fords without them. That this is an increased use of resources is certainly true, but to label this as "the costs of model changes" is quite another matter. Even if models had remained unchanged from the 1949 specifications and consumers had simply switched their preferences toward the larger cars within the 1949 selection, many of these same "costs" would have appeared in the Fisher-Griliches-Kaysen calculations. Consequently, from their figures, about $110 per car in tooling costs and advertising might be called the costs of model changes. And it is not clear even that the increased advertising was a consequence of model changes rather than of the general speedup of auto selling efforts after the end of the Korean War.

A better approach to the costs of model changes would be to look solely at the tooling and development expenses per car. As we saw in Chapter 4, in the mid-1960's, these costs have been approximately $100 per car for tooling plus another $100 for design and development plus an unknown amount for tooling by suppliers. It is difficult to know how much of this $200-plus per car would have occurred even in the absence of model changes. Most of the tooling wears out and has to be replaced anyway; much of the engineering and development costs probably would continue as technological improvements were made to the cars.[24] The figures in Chapter 12 indicated that the real costs per car for tooling (that is, tooling costs corrected for inflation) have not risen appreciably since the mid-1950's. Even if we take the tooling costs per car in 1949 or 1950 as a standard, the real costs have risen since then only by $30–$35 per car in 1949 dollars or $60–$70 per car in 1967 dollars.[25] Perhaps a doubling of this figure to allow for the increase in supplier tooling costs[26] and for development expenses would be a good guess about the costs of model changes.

Is this $130 per car "excessive?" Would consumers be happier with cars that had fewer wrinkles and curves and that changed styles less frequently (allowing more complete use of dies and less development expenses) but cost $130 less per car? As we argued at the end of Chapter 12, this is a question that is usually left for the market to determine. The absence of these simple, cheaper cars is probably indicative of the absence of adequate demand for them. It is interesting to note that American Motors' announcement in February 1967 of a $169–$234 cut in the price of its Rambler American models, combined with the statement that these price cuts were reflecting the cost cuts that would be achieved by not changing the design in the future, seemed to arouse very little consumer interest.[27] Rambler American sales fell in absolute number between 1966 and 1967 and its share of all American Motors sales rose only from 28.5 percent in 1966 to 28.9 percent in 1967. The vast majority of new car buyers do foreswear "basic transportation" in favor of fancier cars with varying degrees of extras. It is not surprising that they would favor paying an extra $130 for newer styles and more wrinkles.

What about advertising? Approximately $40 per car is spent by the auto companies, and approximately another $25 per new car is spent by the dealers. The latter seems to play largely an informative role, giving prices, locations, and so forth. The former also often offers information but more frequently seems to be of "The Hot One's Even Hotter" or "There's a Ford in Your Future" variety. There probably is no way of separating the information type from the blandishment type. It is clear, though, that this advertising is not providing all consumers with an adequate amount of information, as is indicated by the large number of car-enthusiast magazines in existence. The total of $65 per car, or about 2 percent of the average retail price of cars, seems low by soap, cigarette, or breakfast cereal company standards; advertising in these areas can easily run over 5 percent of sales. In the absence of absolute standards of judgment for advertising costs, it is difficult to say more than that.

General Motors' Profitability and Behavioral "Restraint"

Next, we can attempt to answer a few frequently asked questions: Why does General Motors make so much more money than its rivals? In the absence of antitrust restrictions, could it (would it) cut prices so as to drive out its rivals? Has it behaved so as deliberately to keep its rivals, particularly the smaller companies, in business?

As we saw earlier in this chapter, General Motors has consistently earned a higher rate of return on capital than has any other company in the automobile industry. Can this record be explained by General Motors' size, as is frequently claimed? The company itself, not too surprisingly, has denied that this is so,[28] and this author is inclined to agree with it. With the major technological economies of scale extending only up to annual volumes of 400,000 units, General Motors' profit record, particularly vis-à-vis Ford and Chrysler, cannot be explained by its size.

Rather, General Motors' superior profitability must be attributed to its superior management: a superior ability to utilize efficiently the resources at hand and to make decisions under conditions of uncertainty.[29] References have already been made to General Motors' lower labor costs. General Motors has not made a major styling error that was comparable to Chrysler's three major postwar flops. It has not made a product error comparable to Ford's Edsel. Perhaps the worst mistake it has made was to underestimate the attraction of Ford's Mustang and delay two and one-half years in bringing out a sporty model of its own.[30] True, as the dominant firm in the industry, it could afford to sit back and let its rivals take greater chances. Still, it was the leader in developing high compression V-8 engines, automatic transmissions, and hardtop styling, all three of which developed into major trends in the postwar period. It has not been a dormant firm. It has taken risks along with the rest; in producing new styling each year, it could not avoid doing so. It has had a superior record in dealing with those risks.

Superior management is not an entirely satisfying explanation; it does not have the hard, rigorous ring to it as do explanations of

Table 15.5   Auto Company Sales, Profits, Assets, 1966 (millions)

	General Motors	Ford	Chrysler	American Motors
Sales	$20,208.5	$12,240.0	$5,649.5	$870.4
Assets	12,213.5	8,090.4	3,148.5	459.5
Gross profits (before taxes, before interest)	3,297.4	1,182.2	364.4	−30.9
Gross profits, as a percent of assets	27.0	14.6	11.6	
Gross profits, as a percent of sales	16.3	9.7	6.4	
Gross profits, as a percent of sales after a 6 percent return on assets has been deducted	12.7	5.7	3.1	
Gross profit on a $2,500 car (wholesale price)	407.50	242.50	160.00	
Gross profit on a $2,500 car (wholesale price), after 6 percent return on assets has been deducted	317.50	142.50	77.50	

SOURCE: *Moody's Manual of Investments*, 1967.

profitability based on more "objective" factors, such as concentration ratios and economies of scale. Nevertheless, all firms are not identical in their ability to manage their resources efficiently, and, particularly in an oligopoly where the competitive pressure to maintain efficiency is absent, it should not be too surprising that one firm should have a superior "track record."

In the absence of antitrust restrictions, would General Motors have the power to drive out its rivals, if it were willing to engage in a long enough price battle? Table 15.5 reproduces some balance sheet figures for 1966; 1967 was not chosen because of the distorting effects of the Ford strike in the fall. When the profit figures are transformed into the gross profit (pre-tax) earned on a $2,500 (wholesale price) car,[31]

General Motors' potential economic clout becomes apparent. General Motors grossed $407.50 on that car; Ford grossed $242.50; Chrysler grossed only $160.00; and American Motors lost money that year. Even if we allow for the differing capital/sales ratios of the companies and look at the gross profits after a 6 percent return on assets has been deducted, the picture does not change. General Motors' grossed $317.50 on that car; Ford grossed $142.50; Chrysler grossed only $77.50. If General Motors wished to cut prices far enough and hold them there long enough, it could surely drive American Motors and Chrysler to the wall and would most probably outlast Ford.

Would General Motors wish to do this? The key determinants would be (1) the length of time that General Motors would have to keep its prices and profits low, (2) the size of the reduction in profits during the price war, (3) the size of the increase in profits after the price war was over,[32] and (4) the discount rate at which General Motors would evaluate its future gains and losses. It would probably require a not very large price cut, held for not very long, to drive American Motors, in its present state, out of business. But the prize to be gained would not be very large; American Motors' small market share would be divided among the Big Three and import sales. The gains might not be worth the losses. Driving Chrysler to the wall would require steeper price cuts that would have to be held longer. Shubik[33] has argued that it would take so long to drive Chrysler out of the market that, at a discount rate of 4 or 5 percent, the whole attempt would not be profitable for General Motors;[34] at a discount rate of 6 percent or higher, applicable to the late 1960's, this project would be even less worthwhile. Similarly, an attempt to drive out Ford would require still larger price cuts and a longer price war; again, the discounted benefits might not be worth the costs. Thus it is not altogether clear that General Motors would choose to drive out its rivals, though it has the power to do so. Since, however, any such attempt would be seen by the Department of Justice as an attempt to monopolize in violation of Section 2 of the Sherman Act, the point is essentially a moot one.

Has General Motors restrained its behavior so as to keep its market share below 50 percent and thus ward off a possible antitrust suit? The company has stepped across the 50 percent line in six years during the postwar period, and it seems likely that it will do so again in the future if its rivals give it the chance. The company has disavowed any policies of limiting its own market share,[35] and these disavowals ought probably to be taken at their face value. There is no evidence to show that the company is doing anything but trying to maximize profits. A company that has led the industry for three straight years in keeping prices low can hardly be said to be afraid of expanding its market share.

Has General Motors restrained its behavior so as to keep its rivals, especially the Independents, in business, again to ward off a possible antitrust suit? As we argued above, predatory pricing behavior probably would not be in General Motors' interest anyway, so the absence of such action is no real test here. But General Motors did arrange to buy stampings from Kaiser in 1951; it has agreed to sell a number of its components to its rivals at various times; and it did refrain from meeting American Motors' price cuts in February 1967. A company bent on driving its rivals from the market might have acted differently. But these actions were profitable for General Motors (and the perceived cross elasticity between the Rambler American models and General Motors' models may have been small), and it is not clear that the alternative actions would have driven its rivals from the field appreciably faster. When Kaiser and later Studebaker actually did leave the market, there is no evidence that General Motors made any direct attempts to try to induce them to stay in the market. While General Motors' behavior has been exemplary in this nonpredatory sense, it is not clear that any other type of behavior would have been more profitable for the company.

An Analysis of Current Company Size

Finally, as part of an evaluation of the automobile industry, we can combine the elements of history, structure, and behavior to offer an explanation for the current number, sizes, and concentration of firms in the auto industry.[36] As we saw in Chapter 4, a minimum-size efficient firm would require a volume of 800,000 units annually through two makes. Thus an 8-million-unit car market could theoretically support ten efficient firms. In fact, there are only four, with one, American Motors, currently in the 250,000-unit category. How can we explain the current sizes and concentration of the Big Three?

Mergers account for, at best, only a part of the concentration. General Motors was put together by William C. Durant in a series of mergers that, for motor vehicles, ended before 1920. In 1919, total General Motors sales were 344,000 units for 20.8 percent of total automobile sales by American producers.[37] Ford sales were originally built on the Model T, which was followed by the Model A and the Ford V-8. Ford's purchase of Lincoln in 1922 added less than 0.1 percent to the company's sales. The Mercury was introduced in 1938 as a company-created make. Chrysler was put together in the 1920's by Walter P. Chrysler. His purchase of Dodge in 1928 was the last merger to affect the Big Three. Chrysler's sales in 1929 were 375,000 units, 8.2 percent of the total market.

General Motors and Chrysler, then, at the completion of their mergers, were far smaller in sales and market shares than they are today. True, if the individual components had not merged, they might have grown equally as fast as did the merged firms, but the high risks for single-make firms make this a problematical statement; a number of merged General Motors makes did fall by the wayside in the 1920's. In any event, current market shares for General Motors and Chrysler are double what they were at the end of merger period for each, indicating that they have been able to grow faster than has the overall market. Ford's fortunes waxed and waned wholly on the strength of company-developed cars. Mergers are far from the whole answer.

The 1920's were time for consolidating the assembly line techniques that had been developed by Ford a decade earlier. Automobile bodies were still largely made of wood, and engine transfer lines were still in the future. The assembly line was fundamental. If 100,000 units a year were sufficient for Paul Hoffman in 1939, then somewhere around 50,000 units probably would have been sufficient in the 1920's.[38] But retail distribution was also important. With national highways being built, trips of longer distance became possible, and the desire for parts and service "out of town" became important. National distribution was now a factor. Finally, in the 1920's the first-time owner market became somewhat saturated. Though population growth and rising income would continue to provide first-time owners, replacement purchasing provided the bulk of the market. The company that could induce consumers to replace their cars earlier would succeed. In this market, consumers had the choice not only of how soon to trade in their old-models but also how much extra luxury to demand on their new models. A company with a full line of makes could better match the whims of the market and reduce the risks of getting caught in a disappearing niche.

In this environment small companies that before 1920 had sold their cars mostly on the basis of the public's fascination with automobiles in general were now doomed. They lacked the volume for efficient assembly and effective national distribution; they did not have the resources for annual model changes; and they could not afford a diversity of models. The larger companies, particularly General Motors and Chrysler, sensed their advantages and exploited them. General Motors' market share grew to 40 percent by the mid-1930's, as it mastered the techniques of mass production and national distribution, developed the new management techniques of Alfred P. Sloan, Jr., stressed annual model changes, and pursued a policy of "a car for every purse and purpose." Walter Chrysler, buying Dodge in 1928 and bringing out the De Soto and Plymouth makes that same year, pursued the same policies, though not quite so successfully. Henry Ford, though an early master of mass production and national distribution, was more obstinate on the subject of marketing techniques. His excessive attachment to the Model T cost his company the leadership of the automobile industry. Though the Model A and the V-8 were popular, high volume cars, it was only in the 1930's, as Henry's son Edsel gained a greater role in making policy, that the model change and model diversification strategies took hold.

The Great Depression, by shrinking the overall demand for autos, further weakened the remaining small companies. Some of the stronger Independents tried to diversify. Studebaker introduced the Rockne; Hudson tried the Terraplane; Nash tried the Lafayette; and Packard tried the Packard Clipper, but the 1930's were not propitious years for introducing new models. Finally, the 1930's development of the all-steel body, with its appreciably higher economies of scale, caused all but a handful of Independents to leave the automobile business.[38] By 1941, only five Independents[39] were left of the over 1,000 manufacturers who at some time over the previous forty years had produced an automobile.

Briefly, the return of postwar competition in 1953 placed the surviving Independents under strain. Production volumes below those necessary to achieve the full economies of scale, higher labor costs, and delay in adopting the major new innovations of the postwar era — high compression V-8 engines and automatic transmissions —

placed them at a disadvantage. Mergers, born of necessity and designed to gain production economies and diversify product lines, failed to keep Kaiser-Willys or Studebaker-Packard afloat in the long run. Only American Motors survived. But import sales soon filled the gap, so that the Big Three market share today, at 88 percent, is just under what it was in 1941 when the five Independents were still alive.

Thus, the present position of the Big Three can best be explained by their successful exploitation of the changed market conditions of the 1920's and 1930's. Walter Chrysler was the last man to recognize and exploit successfully the strategies of size and multiple makes that those conditions required. Since then, as the market has grown, the Big Three have grown with it. The high barriers to entry in the automobile industry have precluded the permanent establishment of new domestic producers to challenge their positions.

Decline and Fall of the Independents

The decline and fall of the Independents in 1953 and 1954 is worth some further attention. At the beginning of 1953 there were six Independents in the market: Nash, Hudson, Studebaker, Packard, Kaiser, and Willys. By the end of 1955, there were only two, Studebaker-Packard and American Motors (Nash-Hudson); by 1958 both of these remaining companies had settled on only one make each.

It is fairly easy to find specific reasons for the decline of each make. The difficulties involved in these companies' high cost, small cars have already been described in earlier chapters. As of 1953, only Studebaker had a high compression V-8 engine; the rest were relying on straight-sixes and straight-eights, mostly of prewar design. Only Studebaker and Packard had their own automatic transmissions; the rest bought Hydra-Matics from General Motors. Since Hydra-Matics did have a strong public identification with General Motors, this was not the sort of behavior that was designed to encourage an image of strength by the Independents. When Korean War production controls ended and the Big Three began to expand production rapidly (with largely new designs and new engines), these and other weaknesses rapidly enlarged. Kaiser, lagging since 1949, was in no condition to compete with anybody. Willys' small car was overpriced. Packard's luxury image had been tarnished during the 1930's, and it had not been able to regain that image. Studebaker simply was unlucky in its 1953 styling. Hudson stressed a "hot car," race-winner image, but the 1953 model was almost identical in appearance to the 1948 model. Nash had no image, was underpowered, and handled poorly. A tailspin pattern for all quickly set in. Only a change in consumer tastes to small cars saved American Motors and provided a few years' profitable respite for Studebaker.

But a more general explanation for the weakness of the Independents can be offered. Fundamentally, the Independents had been saddled with the status of "off-brands": brands that were less well advertised,[41] carried a connotation of "inferior" in the eyes of many consumers, and were expected to sell for less than the "major" brands. The clearest example of this was in the used car market, where Independents' cars perennially sold at larger discounts relative to original list price than did those of the Big Three. Yet, because of volumes too low to exploit fully economies of scale and because of higher labor costs,[42] the Independents' new cars carried list prices equal to or above the prices of roughly comparable Big Three cars. When production restrictions were removed, only especially good styling or product advance would have saved them, and both were lacking.

A Summary on Structure and Performance

With a discussion of performance behind us, it would now be useful to review the lines of development from structure to performance in the automobile industry.

The salient characteristics of the technology of the industry are the high economies of scale in sheet metal stamping (around 400,000 units per year); the flexibility in assembly that allows many different optional features to be offered at little or no cost penalty; the long lag (two to three years) required between design and sale of a new model; and the large costs of designing, developing, and tooling a new model (approximately $200 per car, or $80 million for a volume of 400,000 units). The important demand characteristics are that the demand for new cars is a replacement demand, with the stock of used cars always existing as a short-run alternative for potential new car buyers, and that the demand is income sensitive (and therefore cyclical in nature) and subject to large swings in consumer tastes regarding styling and size.

The combination of the long lag in model development, the large size of investment in new models, and the variability in consumer tastes have meant that auto producers face large risks. The most important means of surmounting these risks has been to dilute them through multiple-make production and retailing structures. Also, retailing their product through a franchised dealer system has served to allow the manufacturers to transfer some of the risks to a host of second parties, while still allowing the manufacturers to retain a large degree of supervision and control to achieve efficiency in the retail sector.

The large economies of scale and the vagaries of consumer tastes have caused a large number of smaller, single-make firms to fall by the wayside, so that only four producers remain in the market: General Motors, Ford, and Chrysler, all of them multiple-make producers, accounting for 88–90 percent of United States sales; and American Motors, a single-make firm, accounting for 2–4 percent of United States sales. Imported makes, with Volkswagen the most prominent of them, have accounted for the remainder. Very high barriers to entry — the large economies of scale, strong product differentiation, and extremely high capital requirements ($1 billion for an efficient two-make firm) — have prevented the successful establishment of any domestic producers to challenge the position of the established firms in the industry.

This highly concentrated oligopoly has largely avoided price competition, instead adhering to a pattern of price leadership by General Motors. Product performance has been reserved as the main arena for competitive efforts, but even here the recognized mutual interdependence of the auto companies has channeled this action into limited areas. The replacement nature of the demand for new cars has placed a premium on product strategies that would induce faster replacement by new car buyers. The auto companies have chosen a styling and model change strategy to induce replacement, rather than a strategy relying on fundamental technological change; the latter strategy would involve greater risks and uncertainties and probably require extensive education of unsophisticated car buyers to the benefits of the new technology. The flexibility of assembly line techniques has allowed a proliferation of models and styles that has supplemented the model change strategy and has also served to reduce the risks of being caught with a small number of unpopular models.

The short-run tactics of the Big Three have been to blanket the market with cars in all price ranges and (since 1959) most sizes. The Independents, with more limited resources, have usually had to concentrate on one segment of the market. The long lags, large costs, and high risks of new model development have meant that behavior in this area has been keyed to long-run strategies rather than to short-run considerations like capacity utilization.

The auto companies have pursued a policy of moderate technological change to accompany their styling strategies but have relied largely on their materials suppliers and components suppliers for this new technology. None of the auto companies has been a particularly outstanding pioneer in the introduction of innovations, but the Big Three have introduced the lion's share of innovations in the postwar period, with the Independents lagging far behind in this respect.

Trends in consumer tastes toward large cars, more horsepower, and more optional equipment were encouraged by the auto companies. Selling "more car per car" always seemed like a profitable undertaking. Trends toward smaller cars were less warmly greeted by the Big Three, who dragged their feet until the inroads made by Independents and imports forced them to respond. Interdependent behavior among the Big Three seemed especially prominent in this area. The industry was predictably laggard in its response in the areas of air pollution and automotive safety. These areas involved economic externalities, and the companies jointly saw that rapid responses could not directly benefit the industry.

The performance of the industry has followed predictably from the behavior described. The absence of price competition has led to profits clearly in excess of a normal rate of return, even when risk considerations are included. The strategy of concentrating on model changes has meant an absence of fundamental technological change in the product the industry has produced. The industry, though, has been reasonably prompt in adopting new manufacturing technology and has had a high rate of increase of labor productivity. This, in turn, has permitted a record of price increases that have been below the general average of price increases in the economy. Styling and advertising expenditures have probably been greater than "basic transportation and informational needs" would warrant, but it would be hard to argue, particularly with respect to styling, that car buyers have regretted the resources that have been devoted to this area.

Has this performance been "good," "bad," or "fair"? The industry clearly has performed better in some areas (for example, manufacturing technology) than in others (for example, automotive technology) and the weighting that would go into an overall rating will vary among individuals; consequently, the reader will be left to make his own appraisal. But this author believes that there is potential for better performance; this will be the topic of the concluding chapter.

16

Recommendations for
Public Policy

What is to be done?

The automobile industry has a high concentration and high barriers to entry and is dominated by three firms with large market power. There are only four firms in the industry, which has a theoretical capacity for ten viable firms. Strict price leadership is followed. Cars are distributed through a retail system that is designed for maximum efficiency but which leaves the retailer feeling powerless and put-upon. Model changes are stressed as a way of inducing rapid turnover of cars in a replacement market. The industry has earned excess profits; it has made rapid technological progress in manufacturing operations but has been slow in developing automotive technology; it has hesitated in responding positively to the questions of safety and pollution; it has been slow to respond to some of the changes in consumer tastes.

There would seem to be room for public policy actions. And after a review of public policy from 1945 to the present, some recommendations for the future will be offered.

A Review of Public Policy

Public policy has affected the automobile industry in a number of areas. Some policies, like the Korean War price and production controls and the Regulation W credit controls of the late 1940's and Korean War periods, are strictly historical relics. They are unlikely to be revived in the future, and a discussion of these policies will be left to economic historians. Public policy with respect to automobile

276

retailing has already been discussed in Chapter 9 and need not be repeated here. Similarly, the safety and air pollution issues were discussed in Chapter 14.

Government policy on import tariffs on automobiles can be summarized briefly. The tariff on automobiles was 10 percent in 1946. This was among the lowest of United States tariffs at the time; in subsequent Reciprocal Trade Agreement negotiations, only minor attention was given to lowering the auto tariff. Consequently, twenty years later, at the beginning of the Kennedy Round Negotiations, the tariff had only fallen to 6–½%. The Kennedy Round, however, more than halved the tariff; when the last stage of Kennedy Round Tariffs is put into effect, the auto tariff will be only 3 percent. Policy on the auto tariff does not seem to have been protectionist oriented. The auto companies have never asked for tariff protection. Rather, the 10 percent tariff in 1946 seems to have been simply a legacy from earlier times, to be used as a bargaining tool to gain tariff concessions from other countries. As these were gained, the tariff has come down.

Mention also ought to be made of the United States–Canadian Automotive Agreement of 1965. Canada had encouraged Canadian production of cars by the American companies through a high tariff policy. After a proposed scheme in the early 1960's to encourage greater Canadian production of component parts drew threats of tariff retaliation by the United States, the two countries got together and agreed on a plan for free trade in automobiles and parts intended for original production; Canada was willing to go along with the agreement after gaining assurances from the auto companies that they would increase the value-added levels of their Canadian operations. The Free Trade Agreement was put into effect by both countries in 1965.

The agreement basically allows the auto companies to rationalize their production for the entire North American market. Previously, they had produced almost as large an assortment of models for the Canadian market as for the United States market; the large number of models for this much smaller market had meant an inability to exhaust economies of scale and consequent higher costs.[1] After the agreement, the companies could more efficiently provide Canada with this large model selection, producing some models on one side of the border, some on the other, and cross-shipping. For example, in the Detroit-Windsor area, Chrysler Corporation has been producing all of its full-sized Plymouths in the Windsor plant, its other models in the Detroit plants, and cross-shipping the necessary models. The agreement should mostly benefit Canada, with prices to Canadian consumers approaching United States prices for an equally large selection.[2] Only to the extent that rationalization will bring lower transportation charges on some models built in Canada and shipped to the East Coast of the United States will American consumers benefit.

The policy on excise taxes on cars has been to change the tax level infrequently and then only as part of governmental anticyclical fiscal policies. The excise tax was 5 percent on the wholesale price until November 1951, when it was raised to 10 percent as part of a Korean War demand-restraining tax package. The tax stayed at that level until the spring of 1965, when, as part of a general expansionary tax cut, the excise tax was lowered to 7 percent with a schedule for further cuts that would eventually eliminate the tax. Congress has since delayed the schedule for further cuts as the inflationary state of the economy made tax cuts an untimely fiscal proposition.

The last major area of government policy to affect the auto companies has been that of antitrust policy.[3] As we shall see, the basic focus of government efforts in this area has been to try to prevent an expansion of market power by the companies and to attack their (primarily General Motors') supplementary activities, while avoiding a direct assault on the market power in the automobile market that the companies have maintained. To prevent an expansion of market power, the Department of Justice filed suits to prevent General Motors' 1953 acquisition of the Euclid Road Machine Company, Ford's 1961 acquisition of the Electric Auto-Lite Company, and Chrysler's attempted acquisition of the Mack Truck Company in 1964. In all cases, a decrease in actual or potential competition between the merged partners was the justification for the suits. The Chrysler acquisition was effectively deterred by the suit, and in 1968 a federal district court ruled that Ford's acquisition was in violation of the Clayton Act.[4] In 1968, the Department of Justice obtained a consent decree in which General Motors agreed to sell the original Euclid facilities it had bought but was allowed to keep the heavy earth-moving machinery plants it had subsequently built.[5]

Earlier, in the area of dealer sales-financing tying efforts, the Government had been able to obtain a criminal conviction of General Motors in November 1939, on the basis of testimony by dealers that they had been forced to use General Motors financing (GMAC).[6] But a civil suit to force a dissolution of GMAC from its parent company foundered.[7] In 1952, the Department of Justice settled for a consent decree in which General Motors agreed that its dealers should be free to deal with independent finance companies.[8] Congress subsequently held hearings to study the issue of whether auto companies should be allowed to own finance subsidiaries.[9] It declined to take any prohibiting action, and Ford and Chrysler formed finance subsidiaries in 1959 and 1964, respectively.

On the side of acquiescence, the Department of Justice gave its blessings to the mergers of Willys-Kaiser in 1953 and Nash-Hudson and Studebaker-Packard in 1954. A "failing firm doctrine" seemed to dominate here. Only through mergers did these six Independents seem to have a reasonable chance of survival in the automobile business.

In actions not directly concerned with the auto market, the most famous case was the government's suit to force du Pont to give up its 23 per cent holding of General Motors stock. Filed in 1949, the suit was eventually decided by the Supreme Court in 1957 in favor of the government.[10] The government filed criminal and civil suits charging General Motors with monopolizing diesel locomotive production, alleging that the company had used its finance subsidiary and its power as a shipper of automobiles and parts to gain unfair advantages in this market. The government eventually dropped both suits. It had more luck in a suit charging General Motors with monopolization of the bus market. In 1965, the government obtained a consent decree in which General Motors agreed to make its patents available to competitors; to sell its parts and engines to any buyer; and to make its finance facilities available to any buyer, even if the buyer used the financing to purchase a competitor's buses.[11]

Though there have been persistent rumors for the past fifteen years of an impending major antitrust suit that would attack General Motors market power directly in the auto market and force a divestiture of a number of the company's automotive divisions, this suit has yet to see the light of day.

Some Recommendations

Most recommendations on public policy are likely to confront the problems posed by the "Theory of the Second Best." [12] The theory, briefly summarized, states that once any conditions for a pareto optimum have been violated, there is no guarantee that the correction of any other violations will lead one closer to an overall optimum. The logical extension of the theory is that one cannot be completely certain of the beneficial effects of any policy recommendation until one has explored every possible ramification of the policy. Unfortunately, in an area as complex and with as many ramifications as automobiles, strict adherence to this logic would mean endless studies of ramifications and very little policy implementation. Instead, this author prefers to adopt the attitude that where the major costs, benefits, and economic externalities of a particular policy can be identified, policy recommendations should be made and, hopefully, implemented; and the burden of proof should rest on those who would argue that unnoticed ramifications cast doubt on the wisdom of the policy.

To ensure the widest possible range of choice for consumers, the tariff on imported automobiles should be completely removed. Imports have provided consumer minorities with alternatives that the economies of scale of domestic production would otherwise have made impossible. They have served as a means of registering changes in consumer tastes and have provided the fastest way of satisfying those changes. In the absence of imports, American consumers would have had a far too limited range of choice. There should be as few restrictions as possible on the exercise of that choice.

The excise tax on the sale of new automobiles would appear to have little economic justification and ought to be abolished at the earliest opportunity. If there are external costs involving automobiles, they are from auto use rather than sale, and they are more efficiently corrected through use taxes rather than sales taxes.[13] Gasoline taxes would appear to be the ideal tax for this purpose. Tax payments expand linearly with use, except for high gas consumption situations: intensive stop-go city driving and large, heavy, high horsepower cars. Both presumably create greater externalities than otherwise. City driving creates pollution and congestion; large cars create more pollution than small ones and take up more space on roads. The extra taxes paid in these situations are justifiable on efficiency grounds.

Though sizable gasoline taxes are already levied by the federal and state governments, these taxes basically cover the long-run marginal cost of providing highways.[14] Thus any diseconomies connected with automobile use would justify still higher gasoline taxes.

In the area of air pollution control, more research should be devoted to the potentials of lead-free gasoline in a pollution control system. If a system involving lead-free gasoline does prove to have the lowest social costs for the particular pollution control levels sought, a differential tax on leaded and lead-free gasoline should achieve the desired effects. Also, more consideration should be given to requiring vehicle maintenance as part of pollution control systems; current systems place sole responsibility on the manufacturer and ignore the possibility that improper vehicle maintenance may thwart pollution control goals.

In automotive safety, the major need is for better public information about the performance characteristics of new cars and about accident types, frequencies, and fatalities in general. If a new survey is required to provide accident data, government provision of this data would seem to be the easiest and fairest method. In other areas, such as detailed reports on the engineering characteristics of automobiles, the companies should be required to make this information available to the public. The companies have done extensive testing on their new models before those models appear on the market, and they can provide the data sooner, easier, and with less duplication than can anyone else. Further, some way ought to be found of urging the auto insurance companies to provide economic incentives for drivers to prefer safe vehicles. If particular models, designs, or attachments have safety value, this fact should appear in accident and injury rates and should be translatable into lower premiums. Even if drivers' preference functions are such that they are indifferent to safety features per se, they should be responsive to economic differentials in insurance rates and thus should be led to prefer safer models. Though it is unlikely that any of the current government-imposed mandatory safety standards will be discarded, perhaps better response by the insurance companies in the future will reduce the need for additional mandatory safety standards.[15]

Thus far, the policy recommendations made have largely concerned government actions to affect the environment in which the auto industry operates and effect marginal improvements in performance.

Nothing yet has been said about actions to change the fundamental structure or behavior of the auto industry. If we are concerned about the poor performance of the industry in the areas of price competition and excess profits, automotive technological progressiveness and responsiveness to changes in consumer tastes, we shall have to look to more fundamental changes involving antitrust considerations. Both behavioral and structural remedies should be considered.

What special behavior have the auto companies engaged in that might be forbidden in the interests of improved performance? The auto companies' practice of selling their cars through franchised dealers might be relevant here. What would happen if the franchise system were abolished and free entry into automobile retailing were allowed?

The analysis of Chapter 9 indicates that free entry into automobile retailing would lead to an increase in retail margins and in prices to consumers. On the other hand, dealers would be free to handle multiple makes; consumers would be confronted by more than one make on a showroom floor, and the relative prices and merits of the different makes would stand in sharper contrast to one another. Would this lead to greater price and technological competition among the auto companies and thus lead to a net gain for consumers? Perhaps. But it is difficult to believe that mutually interdependent behavior would not continue to assert itself and lead to performance much like that of the past. With so few participants in this tight oligopoly, it is unlikely that just a change in retailing practices would significantly affect performance. The companies might decide to integrate forward into retailing their own products, thus retaining the practice of one make in a showroom and thwarting any increase in competitive pressure from "comparative retailing."

Some other possible outcomes from the end of the franchise system should be mentioned. Department stores, such as Sears, might be attracted into automobile retailing. Could they sell cars at a lower cost than dealers? Nondepartment store outlets seem to have held their own in the retailing of other consumer durables. It is not clear why department stores should be relatively more efficient retailers in automobiles than in other consumer durables.[16]

Free entry might lead to the development of "catalogue stores" in which a low overhead retailer, who holds no inventory and has no showroom, would encourage customers to walk down the street to his rival's showroom, test and select the model desired, and then return. He would then order the model and sell it to the customer for less than his rival could, since he would not have inventory and showroom overhead costs. Effectively, the dealer with the inventory and showroom creates an external economy by offering free demonstration rides. Since a consumer often has to wait while the dealer orders the exact style, color, and accessories desired, buying from the catalogue store would not present very much of a disadvantage in this respect.

Would consumers prefer this form of retailing? The logical extension of this would be a situation in which all retailers in an area would operate catalogue stores and the companies would maintain central demonstration centers. However, at that point the separate catalogue operations might be redundant and we would be back at the case in which the auto companies are doing their own retailing.[17]

Free entry into retailing might also reduce somewhat the barriers to entry in automobile manufacturing, since a potential manufacturer could more readily find retail outlets for his cars. At present he would find that all the leading dealers are exclusively handling existing makes. Since the barriers to entry for domestic automobile manufacturing are very high on other grounds, the benefits to domestic manufacture would be very small. But a foreign manufacturer considering entry into retailing in the American market might find entry somewhat easier under these conditions.

Finally, free entry would reduce the level of dominance of manufacturers over retailers, since any retailer would be free to enter and to buy as many or as few cars as he wished.

In general, allowing free entry into automobile retailing appears to be an uncertain proposition. New and better forms of retailing might arise; competition among the auto companies might increase; foreign manufacturers might find it easier to enter the United States market; and retailers might experience less unhappiness over their relations with the manufacturers. On the other hand, it is likely that retail margins and prices would increase with no attendant benefits to consumers or that the companies would enter retailing, a situation that currently they wish to avoid. This author would conclude, reluctantly, that for all its strains and weak points, the franchise system probably should be left in its current form.

However, the government's prohibition of exclusive dealing practices by the auto companies should be more strictly enforced. This would allow new entrants, mainly foreign producers, to establish more retailing footholds in the American market. Through this method, it might be possible to keep the desirable aspects of the franchise system yet gain more entries by new producers and more competition at the retail level.

One other form of behavior that could be altered is the auto companies' practice of agreeing to share technological advances in particular areas, such as air pollution and safety. To forbid such agreements would be to trade the fast spread of new knowledge in return for the likelihood that the companies' pace of pursuit for new knowledge would be accelerated. Again, the existence of a tight oligopoly may mean that the presence or absence of an explicit agreement may not change actual behavior very much; despite the absence of agreements, the companies would presumably still be free to share or sell information to one another if they so chose. Still, it is probably worthwhile to forbid such agreements, though there would be no spectacular results as a consequence.

These behavioral remedies do not seem to offer much potential for improving the auto companies' performance. Fundamentally, this concentrated oligopoly is going to continue to behave and perform much as it has in the past, as long as it remains concentrated. Consequently, if we want improved performance, we must look to measures that will loosen the oligopoly and increase the number of independent centers of initiative in the industry. This can be achieved by lowering the barriers to entry or by creating more independent firms from among those already in existence. Both types of action would require structural antitrust remedies. The presumption here is that more centers of initiative would increase the likelihood of meaningful price competition, leading to lower prices, lower profits, and a better allocation of resources; more centers would also increase the likelihood of faster technological progress and faster response to changes in consumer tastes.

In this author's opinion, current judicial interpretations of the antitrust laws would not support a suit to break up the auto companies. The current standard for antitrust action seems to be one of "market power plus": market power unjustified by economies of scale *plus* some forms of predatory or exclusionary behavior by the members of the industry in question. By this standard, the auto companies would seem to be within the law. Though they have substantial market power, their behavior has been exemplary in terms of avoiding actions that could be lableled predatory or exclusionary. Still, it is worth considering the possibility of structural remedies in the event that legal interpretations change or a strict market power standard law were enacted.

How much mileage could be gotten from vertical divestiture of the parts manufacturing operations from the auto companies? Would such action significantly reduce the barriers to entry? Our earlier analysis revealed that a new entrant would not have special need to manufacture its own parts and that the capital requirements of a billion dollars for just the basic assembly, stamping, engine, and transmission plants for a viable firm would make entry nearly impossible. The auto companies do not appear to have gained increased market power in the automobile market because of their parts operations. Divestiture of their parts operations would not appear to increase the chances for an increased number of independent centers of initiative and improved performance.[18]

Could one force an even more severe vertical divestiture? An auto company could be permitted to own only an assembly plant and would have to buy its engines, stampings, and parts. This would greatly reduce the barriers to entry, since an efficient assembly plant would require an investment of only $50 million. But there would seem to be significant losses of efficiency from such an imposed solution. It is doubtful that the gains would be worth the losses, and it is not clear whether even a strict market power standard antitrust law would countenance such measures. Also one would have to guard against high concentration forming at some intermediate level, such as sheet metal stamping, thus impairing the performance of the overall auto industry.

Consequently, if there are effective structural remedies to be had, they must involve horizontal dissolution of the existing companies. Here lies the only sure way of creating the increased centers of initiative that are necessary for improved performance.[19]

Our analysis in earlier chapters indicated that a viable firm of minimum efficient size would involve a firm with two makes producing a total of 800,000 units a year. In an 8-million-unit car market, there should be room for ten viable firms.[20] What feasible ways are there for getting close to that goal?

1. The industry could simply be divided according to makes, perhaps

allowing the very low volume Lincoln to remain attached to Mercury, and Imperial to remain with Chrysler. Some appropriate division or separation of the parts manufacturing operations would also have to occur. Cases in which there are fewer parts manufacturing facilities than there are makes will present difficulties, especially if there are few outside sources of supply. This would clearly be true in the case of automatic transmissions, for example. General Motors has only one plant producing them, while Ford has two. There are obviously not economies of scale to justify this level of concentration. It is quite possible that the auto companies have recognized the dangers of a large antitrust suit and have committed themselves to single-plant supply in efforts to thwart one. In any event, the government would have to make special efforts to ensure that the smaller companies had fair access to automatic transmissions. The large companies could be required to sell at fair prices to the small companies with the courts retaining jurisdiction over this matter for fifteen years to enforce the provision. Further, special government financing could be made available to the small companies for building the facilities they lack.

These measures would convert the present Big Three into ten independent firms which, with American Motors, would make an eleven-firm industry. For long-run viability, most of these new firms would have to bring out second makes, but this might be accomplished by gradually converting some of their series or lines into second makes and modifying their retailing patterns accordingly. We could rely on the survival instincts of the managements involved to develop the optimal marketing patterns.

2. More careful pruning could be done with the antitrust knife, with more consideration given to the long-run viability of the firms that would remain. General Motors could be divided into three firms: say, Chevrolet, Pontiac-Buick, and Oldsmobile-Cadillac; Ford into two firms: Ford and Lincoln-Mercury; and Chrysler into two firms: Plymouth and Dodge-Imperial-Chrysler. One assumes that Chevrolet, Ford, and Plymouth would find it in their interests to develop second makes; Lincoln-Mercury would probably also have to develop an additional make. The Big Three would have been split into seven firms, which, along with American Motors, would yield eight firms in the industry.

3. Finally, a new start could be effected. The assembly plants,

stamping plants, and engine plants could be shuffled and dealt out so as to create ten balanced, viable firms. This would be a difficult solution, creating, among others, problems of brand identifications and loyalties. The problems probably could be overcome, but some form or modification of alternatives 1 or 2 would probably be preferable.

A horizontal dissolution antitrust policy is not entirely a benefits-only proposition. There are equity considerations here also. The excess profits of the auto companies have been capitalized by the capital markets, so that a current buyer of auto company equities receives only a normal return; most of those who benefited from the creation of the excess profits have long since sold out. Should current stockholders be penalized for the actions of others in the past? The Big Three have achieved their market power through honorable, competitive practices. They have not engaged in the predatory or exclusionary practices that one often associates with monopolies. Is it "fair" to break them up?

In summary, this author would favor antitrust action, despite these considerations. The potential gain to consumers would appear to outweigh these drawbacks. Though some form of compensation for stockholders would probably be desirable, current tax-loss provisions in the income tax code are probably the most that can be expected. Still, given the choice between antitrust action with the current, albeit inferior, compensation, and no action at all, this author would still favor antitrust action. As for "fairness," to whom else is one being "unfair" beside stockholders? Management? Does management have an independent *stake* in the company aside from their position as stockholders or as representatives of the stockholders? Are their careers or reputations affected? If not, then it is difficult to see how fairness is relevant, except as it affects stockholders.

Are there any other policies outside of antitrust that might lead to the achievement of our performance goals? Government regulation of the industry is always one possibility, but this sort of cure might well be worse than the disease. The experience of economic regulation in other industries in the United States economy does not lead this author to be sanguine about the beneficial results of regulation.

Or there is the possibility of government ownership of the entire industry. Though excess profits might be eliminated, replacing four centers of initiative with only one center would seem to be a strange way of achieving the other goals of improved performance. In general, again, the cure would seem to be worse than the disease.

A milder form of action along these lines might be for the government to develop its own line of automobiles or to buy into part of the existing industry. For example, the federal government could buy the brand name and certain assets of, say, Buick from General Motors. There are European precedents: Renault in France is government-owned, and Volkswagen until the mid-1960's was wholly owned by the West German government.[21] An autonomous government company would be still one more center of initiative and might be designed to be a spur to, and an example for, the rest of the industry, much as the Tennessee Valley Authority was seen as a spur and an example for the private electric industry in the 1930's. This possibility has some attractive aspects, but political realities would seem to rule it out as virtually impossible.

Thus, if one were to eschew antitrust action as legally, politically, or economically infeasible or unwise, the alternative would seem to be to throw up one's hands, cry "alas," and continue to endure the auto companies' poor performance in the areas mentioned. This author would prefer action.

Annual Automobile
Sales (Registrations)
1946–1967

Table A.1 Annual Sales, 1946–1950

Make of car	1946 Units	1946 Percent of total	1947 Units	1947 Percent of total	1948 Units	1948 Percent of total	1949 Units	1949 Percent of total	1950 Units	1950 Percent of total
Chrysler Corp.										
Chrysler	65,532	3.61	93,871	2.96	105,315	3.02	130,516	2.70	151,300	2.39
De Soto	54,420	2.99	72,966	2.30	82,454	2.36	103,311	2.14	115,023	1.82
Dodge	135,488	7.46	209,552	6.62	213,923	6.13	273,530	5.65	300,104	4.74
Plymouth	211,800	11.68	313,118	9.89	347,174	9.94	527,915	10.91	547,367	8.65
Total	467,240	25.74	689,507	21.77	748,866	21.45	1,035,272	21.40	1,113,794	17.60
Ford Motor Co.										
Ford	326,822	18.01	532,646	16.82	486,888	13.95	806,766	16.67	1,166,118	18.43
Lincoln	10,798	0.59	24,081	0.76	32,638	0.93	37,691	0.78	34,318	0.54
Mercury	61,187	3.37	111,198	3.51	137,512	3.94	186,629	3.86	318,217	5.03
Total	398,807	21.97	667,925	21.09	657,038	18.82	1,031,086	21.31	1,518,653	24.00
General Motors Corp.										
Buick	126,322	6.96	246,115	7.77	244,762	7.01	372,425	7.10	535,807	8.47
Cadillac	23,666	1.30	53,379	1.69	59,379	1.70	80,880	1.67	101,825	1.61
Chevrolet	329,601	18.16	640,709	20.23	709,609	20.33	1,031,466	21.32	1,420,399	22.45

	Reg.	%	Reg.	%	Reg.	%	Reg.	%	Reg.	%
Oldsmobile	93,094	5.13	180,078	5.68	175,531	5.03	269,351	5.57	372,519	5.89
Pontiac	113,109	6.23	206,411	6.52	228,939	6.56	321,033	6.63	440,528	6.96
Total	685,792	37.78	1,326,692	41.89	1,418,220	40.63	2,075,155	42.89	2,871,078	45.38
Kaiser-Frazer Corp.										
Frazer	1,873	0.10	51,158	1.62	57,994	1.66	15,827	0.33	11,884	0.19
Henry J									14,339	0.23
Kaiser	3,501	0.19	55,571	1.74	108,367	3.10	57,995	1.20	85,832	1.35
Total	5,374	0.29	106,729	3.37	166,361	4.76	73,822	1.53	112,055	1.77
Other										
Crosley	2,868	0.16	15,934	0.50	25,400	0.73	10,175	0.21	6,896	0.11
Hudson	72,484	3.99	83,344	2.63	109,497	3.14	137,907	2.85	134,219	2.12
Nash	85,169	4.69	102,808	3.25	104,156	2.98	135,328	2.80	175,722	2.78
Packard	36,435	2.01	47,875	1.51	77,843	2.23	97,771	2.02	73,155	1.16
Studebaker	58,051	3.20	102,123	3.22	143,120	4.10	199,460	4.12	268,229	4.24
Willys	2,329	0.13	23,400	0.74	21,408	0.61	28,576	0.59	33,926	0.53
Misc. Domestic	647	.04	894	.03	2,910	0.09	1,539	0.03	2,375	0.04
Total	263,357	14.51	483,107	15.25	650,695	18.64	684,578	14.15	806,577	12.75
Total U.S. makes	1,815,196	100.00	3,167,231	100.00	3,474,819	99.54	4,826,091	99.75	6,310,102	99.73
Total foreign makes					16,133	0.46	12,251	0.25	16,336	0.27
Total all makes	1,815,196	100.00	3,167,231	100.00	3,490,952	100.00	4,838,342	100.00	6,326,438	100.00

SOURCE: Data collected by R. L. Polk & Co. Published in *Automotive Industries, Annual Statistical Issue, 1947–1959*. Reprinted with permission.

Table A.2 Annual Sales, 1951–1955

Make of car	1951 Units	1951 Percent of total	1952 Units	1952 Percent of total	1953 Units	1953 Percent of total	1954 Units	1954 Percent of total	1955 Units	1955 Percent of total
Chrysler Corp.										
Chrysler	149,435	2.95	113,392	2.73	153,756	2.68	101,741	1.84	156,458	2.18
De Soto	112,643	2.23	91,677	2.20	122,342	2.13	76,739	1.39	118,062	1.65
Dodge	298,603	5.90	246,464	5.93	288,812	5.03	154,789	2.80	284,323	3.97
Plymouth	542,649	10.72	433,134	10.41	600,447	10.46	381,078	6.87	647,352	9.03
Total	1,103,330	21.80	884,667	21.27	1,165,357	20.30	714,347	12.90	1,206,195	16.83
Ford Motor Co.										
Continental									606	0.01
Ford	862,309	17.04	732,481	17.61	1,116,267	19.45	1,400,440	25.30	1,573,276	21.94
Lincoln	25,816	0.51	29,110	0.70	39,169	0.68	36,251	0.65	35,017	0.49
Mercury	233,339	4.61	185,883	4.47	287,717	5.02	269,926	4.88	371,837	5.19
Total	1,121,464	22.16	947,474	22.78	1,443,153	25.15	1,706,617	30.83	1,980,736	27.63
General Motors										
Buick	392,285	7.75	310,806	7.47	454,320	7.92	513,497	9.28	737,879	10.29
Cadillac	97,093	1.92	87,806	2.11	98,612	1.72	110,328	1.99	141,038	1.97
Chevrolet	1,067,042	21.08	852,542	20.50	1,342,480	23.39	1,417,453	25.61	1,640,681	22.88
Oldsmobile	273,821	5.40	218,189	5.25	305,593	5.32	407,150	7.35	589,515	8.22
Pontiac	337,821	6.68	266,351	6.41	385,692	6.72	358,167	6.47	530,007	7.39
Total	2,167,713	42.83	1,735,694	41.74	2,586,697	45.07	2,806,595	50.70	3,639,120	50.75

	1952		1953		1954		1955		1956	
American Motors[a]										
Hudson	96,847	1.91	78,509	1.89	66,797	1.16	35,824	0.65	43,212	0.60
Nash	140,035	2.77	142,520	3.43	137,507	2.40	82,729	1.49	93,541	1.31
Total	236,882	4.68	221,029	5.32	204,304	3.56	118,553	2.14	136,753	1.91
Studebaker-Packard Corp.[a]										
Packard	66,999	1.32	66,346	1.60	71,079	1.24	38,396	0.69	52,103	0.73
Studebaker	205,514	4.08	157,902	3.80	161,257	2.81	95,914	1.74	95,761	1.34
Total	272,513	5.40	224,248	5.40	232,336	4.05	134,310	2.43	147,864	2.07
Willys Motors[b]										
Henry J & Allstate	51,372	1.02	30,284	0.73	11,385	0.20				
Kaiser & Frazer	52,286	1.03	41,022	0.99	22,825	0.40	8,889	0.16	959	0.01
Willys	26,049	0.51	41,016	0.99	42,433	0.74	17,002	0.31	6,267	0.09
Total	129,707	2.56	112,322	2.71	76,643	1.34	25,891	0.47	7,226	0.10
Other										
Crosley	5,304	0.10	2,679	0.06						
Misc. Domestic	3,162	0.06	982	0.02	1,538	0.03	3,766	0.07	356	0.07
Total	8,466	0.16	3,661	0.08	1,538	0.03	3,766	0.07	356	0.07
Total U.S. makes	5,040,875	99.59	4,129,095	99.30	5,710,028	99.50	5,510,079	99.54	7,118,250	99.29
Total foreign makes	20,828	0.41	29,299	0.70	28,961	0.50	25,385	0.46	51,658	0.71
Total all makes	5,060,903	100.00	4,158,394	100.00	5,738,989	100.00	5,535,464	100.00	7,169,908	100.00

SOURCE: Data collected by R. L. Polk & Co. Published in *Automotive Industries, Annual Statistical Issue*, 1952–1956. Reprinted with permission.
[a] Mergers took place in 1954. In previous years, the individual makes represented independent companies.
[b] Merger took place in 1954. In previous years, Willys was a separate company, and Henry J, Allstate, Kaiser, and Frazer were all made by one company.

Table A.3 Annual Sales, 1956–1960

Make of car	1956 Units	1956 Percent of total	1957 Units	1957 Percent of total	1958 Units	1958 Percent of total	1959 Units	1959 Percent of total	1960 Units	1960 Percent of total
Chrysler Corp.										
Chrysler	106,853	1.79	106,436	1.78	58,573	1.26	64,424	1.07	79,752	1.21
De Soto	100,766	1.69	103,915	1.74	47,894	1.03	42,488	0.70	23,063	0.35
Dodge	220,208	3.70	257,488	4.30	135,538	2.91	167,277	2.76	356,572	5.42
Imperial	10,460	0.18	33,017	0.55	14,823	0.32	18,498	0.31	16,360	0.25
Plymouth	483,756	8.12	595,503	9.97	391,104	8.40	390,104	6.46	445,590	6.78
Total	922,043	15.48	1,096,359	18.34	647,932	13.92	682,791	11.30	921,337	14.01
Ford Motor Co.										
Comet									157,515	2.40
Edsel			26,681	0.45	38,601	0.83	40,778	0.67		
Ford	1,375,343	23.12	1,493,617	24.97	1,028,893	22.11	1,471,249	24.35	1,420,352	21.60
Lincoln & Continental	44,162	0.72	37,298	0.62	26,605	0.57	28,815	0.48	20,711	0.31
Mercury	274,603	4.61	260,573	4.35	136,295	2.93	157,972	2.62	150,724	2.29
Total	1,694,108	28.45	1,818,169	30.39	1,230,394	26.44	1,698,814	28.12	1,749,302	26.60
General Motors										
Buick	529,371	8.89	394,553	6.60	263,981	5.67	245,909	4.07	267,837	4.07
Cadillac	132,952	2.23	141,209	2.36	122,651	2.63	135,387	2.24	149,593	2.27

Chevrolet	1,565,399	26.29	1,456,288	24.34	1,234,414	26.53	1,419,131	23.49	1,696,925	25.80
Oldsmobile	437,896	7.35	371,596	6.21	305,566	6.59	360,525	5.97	355,798	5.41
Pontiac	358,668	6.02	319,719	5.34	229,831	4.94	382,137	6.33	399,646	6.08
Total	3,024,286	50.78	2,683,365	44.85	2,157,443	46.36	2,543,089	42.10	2,869,799	43.63
American Motors										
Hudson	11,822	0.20	4,596	0.07						
Nash	25,271	0.42	9,474	0.16						
Rambler	70,867	1.19	91,469	1.53	186,373	4.00	363,372	6.01	422,273	6.42
Total	107,960	1.81	105,539	1.76	186,373	4.00	363,372	6.01	422,273	6.42
Studebaker-Packard Corp.										
Packard	28,396	0.48	5,189	0.08						
Studebaker	76,402	1.28	62,565	1.05	47,798	1.03	133,382	2.21	106,244	1.62
Total	104,798	1.76	67,754	1.13	47,798	1.03	133,382	2.21	106,244	1.62
Other										
Total	3,866	0.07	4,329	0.07	6,057	0.13	5,696	0.09	8,910	0.14
Total U.S. makes	5,857,061	98.35	5,775,515	96.54	4,275,997	91.88	5,427,144	89.83	6,077,865	92.42
Total foreign makes	98,187	1.65	206,827	3.46	378,517	8.12	614,131	10.17	498,875	7.58
Total all makes	5,955,248	100.00	5,982,342	100.00	4,654,514	100.00	6,041,275	100.00	6,576,650	100.00

SOURCE: Data collected by R. L. Polk & Co. Published in *Automotive Industries, Annual Statistical Issue*, 1957–1961. Reprinted with permission.

Table A.4   Annual Sales, 1961–1962

Make of car	1961		1962	
	Units	Percent of total	Units	Percent of total
Chrysler Corp.				
Chrysler				
Newport	51,991	0.88	66,847	0.97
300	16,401	0.28	20,870	0.30
New Yorker	20,554	0.36	19,258	0.27
Station Wagon	5,441	0.09	7,156	0.11
Total	94,387	1.61	114,131	1.65
Dodge				
Lancer	55,500	0.95	42,266	0.61
Lancer Station Wagon	7,931	0.13	5,300	0.07
Dart (1963)			23,510	0.34
Dart Sta. Wgn. (1963)			2,161	0.03
Dart 330	57,338	0.98	47,964	0.69
Dart 440	33,250	0.57	27,031	0.39
Polara	35,129	0.60	36,520	0.53
Polara 500	13,120	0.22	11,504	0.17
Dodge Sta. Wgn.	23,677	0.41	22,943	0.33
880 & Custom 880			16,479	0.23
880 & Custom 880 Sta. Wgn.			2,375	0.04
Total	225,945	3.86	238,053	3.43
Imperial				
Custom	4,739	0.08	4,193	0.06
Crown and Le Baron	7,008	0.12	9,365	0.13
Total	11,747	0.20	13,558	0.19
Plymouth				
Valiant	105,304	1.80	109,403	1.58
Valiant Sta. Wgn.	15,491	0.26	13,590	0.20
Savoy	52,721	0.90	62,079	0.89
Belvedere	44,584	0.76	38,762	0.56
Fury	45,909	0.79	46,047	0.66
Plymouth Sta. Wgn.	35,674	0.61	31,277	0.45
Total	299,683	5.12	301,158	4.34
Total Chrysler Corp.	631,782	10.79	666,900	9.61
Ford Motor Co.				
Ford				
Falcon	345,079	5.89	246,478	3.56
Falcon Sta. Wgn.	136,883	2.34	109,408	1.57
Fairlane	5,096	0.09	85,872	1.24
Fairlane 500	15,771	0.26	239,564	3.45

Table A.4 (*continued*)

Make of car	1961 Units	1961 Percent of total	1962 Units	1962 Percent of total
Fairlane Sta. Wgn.			16,267	0.24
300			12,382	0.18
Galaxie	266,865	4.56	153,554	2.21
Galaxie 500	346,434	5.92	411,100	5.92
Ford Sta. Wgn.	131,074	2.24	122,914	1.77
Thunderbird	83,033	1.42	73,975	1.07
Total	1,330,235	22.72	1,471,514	21.21
Lincoln-Continental	31,126	0.53	31,533	0.45
Mercury				
Comet	161,423	2.76	122,217	1.77
Comet Sta. Wgn.	25,047	0.42	17,942	0.25
Meteor	2,547	0.05	73,949	1.07
Meteor Sta. Wgn.			2,188	0.03
Monterey	102,589	1.75	89,315	1.29
Commuter Sta. Wgn.	8,690	0.15	6,150	0.09
Colony Park Sta. Wgn.	8,802	0.15	10,056	0.14
Total	309,098	5.28	321,817	4.64
Total Ford Motor Co.	1,670,459	28.53	1,824,884	26.30
General Motors				
Buick				
Special	75,325	1.28	133,350	1.92
Special Sta. Wgn.	16,028	0.28	18,962	0.28
Le Sabre	106,348	1.81	131,280	1.89
Invicta	31,705	0.55	39,121	0.56
Riviera			8,108	0.12
Electra	52,452	0.89	57,504	0.83
Buick Sta. Wgn.	8,765	0.15	11,942	0.17
Total	290,623	4.96	400,267	5.77
Cadillac				
62	124,292	2.12	135,152	1.95
60-S	14,267	0.25	13,028	0.19
75	1,558	0.03	1,335	0.02
88	2,078	0.03	2,013	0.03
Total	142,195	2.43	151,528	2.18
Chevrolet				
Corvair	277,954	4.75	271,910	3.91
Corvair Sta. Wgn.	38,074	0.65	17,975	0.26
Chevy II	29,562	0.50	277,331	4.00
Chevy II Sta. Wgn.	5,688	0.10	66,362	0.96
Biscayne	187,822	3.21	169,534	2.44

Make of car	1961		1962	
	Units	Percent of total	Units	Percent of total
Bel Air	342,894	5.86	354,342	5.11
Impala	523,183	8.93	718,421	10.35
Chevrolet Sta. Wgn.	172,916	2.95	186,915	2.69
Corvette	11,641	0.20	15,239	0.22
Total	1,589,734	27.15	2,078,029	29.95
Oldsmobile				
F-85	56,680	0.97	85,541	1.24
F-85 Sta. Wgn.	14,133	0.24	9,442	0.13
Dynamic 88	133,979	0.29	171,806	2.48
Super 88	55,329	0.95	54,245	0.78
Starfire	8,624	0.14	39,224	0.56
98	45,464	0.78	64,389	0.93
Oldsmobile Sta. Wgn.	14,377	0.25	16,348	0.24
Total	328,586	5.62	440,995	6.36
Pontiac				
Tempest	89,160	1.52	123,569	1.78
Tempest Sta. Wgn.	21,028	0.36	14,575	0.21
Catalina	128,199	2.19	181,023	2.61
Star Chief	32,540	0.55	40,429	0.58
Bonneville	71,575	1.23	98,101	1.41
Grand Prix	6,556	0.11	38,686	0.56
Pontiac Sta. Wgn.	23,813	0.40	32,271	0.47
Total	372,871	6.36	528,654	6.35
Total General Motors	2,724,009	46.52	3,599,473	51.88
American Motors				
Rambler				
American	130,635	2.23	114,583	1.65
Classic	211,964	3.62	273,725	3.94
Ambassador	28,086	0.48	34,796	0.50
Total American Motors	370,685	6.33	423,104	6.09
Studebaker Corp.	72,155	1.24	77,436	1.11
Lark and Hawk			441	0.01
Avanti	72,155	1.24	77,877	1.12
Total Studebaker Corp.				
Total other	7,005	0.12	7,485	0.11
Total U.S. makes	5,476,125	93.54	6,599,703	95.11
Total foreign makes	378,622	6.46	339,160	4.89
Total all makes	5,854,747	100.00	6,938,863	100.00

Source: Data collected by R. L. Polk & Co. Published in *Automotive Industries, Annual Statistical Issue,* 1962–1963. Reprinted with permission.

Table A.5   Annual Sales, 1963–1964

| | 1963 | | 1964 | |
Make of car	Number	Percent of total	Number	Percent of total
Chrysler Corp.				
Chrysler				
Newport	61,450	0.82	74,506	0.92
300	20,289	0.27	24,798	0.31
New Yorker	23,889	0.31	28,572	0.35
Station Wagons	8,434	0.11	9,153	0.12
Total	114,062	1.51	137,029	1.70
Dodge				
Dart	143,386	1.90	169,029	2.10
330,440 & Polara (64)	164,154	2.17	161,639	2.00
Coronet			37,500	0.47
Polara (65)			12,005	0.14
880, Custom 880	25,375	0.34	24,364	0.31
Monaco			3,011	0.03
Station Wagons	46,111	0.61	54,827	0.68
Total	379,026	5.02	462,551	5.73
Imperial	15,266	0.20	21,157	0.27
Plymouth				
Valiant	159,668	2.11	167,958	2.08
Belvedere I & II (65)			30,386	0.38
Savoy (64) & Fury I (65)	65,968	0.88	52,829	0.65
Belvedere (64) & Fury II (65)	66,177	0.87	62,478	0.77
Fury (64) & Fury III (65)	79,559	1.06	108,714	1.35
Barracuda (65)			14,104	0.18
Station Wagons	54,960	0.72	56,306	0.70
Total	426,332	5.64	492,775	6.11
Total Chrysler Corp.	934,686	12.37	1,113,512	13.81
Ford Motor Co.				
Ford				
Falcon	251,483	3.33	222,874	2.76
Fairlane & Fairlane 500	265,605	3.52	211,642	2.62
Custom	68,553	0.90	95,966	1.19
Custom 500	104,102	1.38	83,799	1.04
Galaxie 500	549,178	7.27	559,734	6.94
Mustang			248,916	3.09

Make of car	1963		1964	
	Number	Percent of total	Number	Percent of total
Thunderbird	63,857	0.84	86,929	1.08
Station Wagons	256,330	3.39	239,154	2.96
Total	1,559,108	20.63	1,749,014	21.68
Lincoln-Continental	31,517	0.42	36,897	0.46
Mercury				
Comet	128,644	1.70	172,908	2.15
Meteor	29,397	0.39		
Monterey	85,826	1.14	52,834	0.66
Montclair	8,646	0.11	33,494	0.41
Parklane	5,129	0.07	21,605	0.27
Station Wagons	31,242	0.41	30,733	0.37
Total	288,884	3.82	311,574	3.86
Total Ford Motor Co.	1,879,509	24.87	2,097,485	26.00
General Motors				
Buick				
Special	128,905	1.71	150,196	1.86
Le Sabre	157,182	2.08	115,603	1.44
Wildcat	46,408	0.61	77,034	0.95
Electra 225	56,995	0.75	65,556	0.82
Riviera	36,318	0.49	34,906	0.43
Station Wagons	28,429	0.38	37,748	0.47
Total	454,237	6.02	481,043	5.97
Cadillac				
Calais	141,998	1.87	32,846	0.40
De Ville			102,578	1.28
Fleetwood	13,472	0.18	12,918	0.16
75 & 68	3,763	0.05	3,296	0.04
Total	159,233	2.10	151,638	1.88
Chevrolet				
Corvair	233,467	3.09	186,681	2.31
Chevy II	249,375	3.30	137,401	1.71
Chevelle	50,463	0.67	273,785	3.39
Biscayne	174,838	2.31	151,763	1.88
Bel Air	355,863	4.45	282,063	3.50
Impala	822,128	10.88	820,903	10.18
Corvette	21,901	0.29	20,097	0.25
Station Wagons	273,618	3.62	252,212	3.12
Total	2,161,653	28.61	2,124,905	26.34

	1963		1964	
Make of car	*Number*	*Percent of total*	*Number*	*Percent of total*
Oldsmobile				
F-85	111,506	1.47	143,484	1.78
Jetstar	18,685	0.25	68,435	0.85
Dynamic 88	173,487	2.30	158,700	1.97
Super 88	53,291	0.70	25,887	0.32
Starfire	23,005	0.31	14,277	0.18
98	67,291	0.89	62,979	0.78
Station Wagons	27,521	0.36	39,372	0.49
Total	474,786	6.28	513,134	6.37
Pontiac				
Tempest	129,427	1.71	225,224	2.79
Catalina	211,897	2.81	214,564	2.66
Star Chief	40,927	0.54	34,410	0.43
Bonneville	108,445	1.43	106,919	1.32
Grand Prix	72,642	0.97	58,933	0.73
Station Wagons	43,453	0.57	47,852	0.60
Total	606,791	8.03	687,902	8.53
Total General Motors	3,856,700	51.04	3,958,622	49.09
American Motors				
Rambler				
American	109,241	1.44	146,147	1.81
Classic	289,199	3.83	204,413	2.53
Ambassador	29,906	0.39	28,852	0.36
Total American Motors	428,346	5.66	379,412	4.70
Total Studebaker	64,570	0.86	26,073	0.32
Total Other	7,282	0.09	5,915	0.07
Total U.S. makes	7,171,093	94.89	7,581,019	93.99
Total foreign makes	385,624	5.11	484,131	6.01
Total all makes	7,556,717	100.00	8,065,150	100.00

SOURCE: Data collected by R. L. Polk & Co. Published in *Automotive Industries, Annual Statistical Issue*, 1964–1965. Reprinted with permission.

Table A.6 Annual Sales, 1965–1966

	1965		1966	
Make of car	*Number*	*Percent of total*	*Number*	*Percent of total*
Chrysler Corp.				
Chrysler				
Newport	112,052	1.20	124,401	1.39
Newport Custom			9,892	0.11
300	29,954	0.33	35,669	0.39
New Yorker	47,431	0.50	43,171	0.48
Station Wagons	13,122	0.15	17,049	0.19
Total	202,559	2.18	230,182	2.56
Dodge				
Dart	156,805	1.68	135,739	1.51
Coronet	178,254	1.91	190,492	2.11
Polara	76,428	0.82	72,961	0.81
Monaco & Monaco 500	35,292	0.38	37,063	0.41
Charger			34,720	0.39
Station Wagons	75,004	0.81	72,585	0.80
Total	521,783	5.60	543,560	6.03
Imperial				
Crown	15,210	0.16	12,789	0.15
LeBaron	2,004	0.02	1,820	0.02
Total	17,214	0.18	14,609	0.17
Plymouth				
Valiant	116,285	1.25	104,354	1.15
Belvedere	134,201	1.44	144,611	1.61
Fury I, II, III	243,209	2.61	232,458	2.58
VIP	3,626	0.04	17,472	0.19
Barracuda	50,473	0.54	28,310	0.32
Station Wagons	76,985	0.83	70,955	0.79
Total	624,779	6.71	598,160	6.64
Total Chrysler Corp.	1,366,335	14.67	1,386,511	15.40
Ford Motor Co.				
Ford				
Falcon	152,737	1.64	123,548	1.37
Fairlane & Fairlane 500	191,633	2.06	241,528	2.68
Custom	148,489	1.59	75,994	0.84
Custom 500	90,034	0.97	122,889	1.37
Galaxie 500	460,623	4.94	454,340	5.04
LTD	95,934	1.03	99,445	1.10
Mustang	518,252	5.57	540,802	6.01

Make of car	1965		1966	
	Number	Percent of total	Number	Percent of total
Thunderbird	71,046	0.76	67,392	0.74
Station Wagons	269,637	2.90	265,582	2.95
Total	1,998,385	21.46	1,991,520	22.10
Lincoln-Continental	42,636	0.45	49,324	0.55
Mercury				
Intermediate	143,311	1.54	123,977	1.38
Monterey	74,902	0.81	60,843	0.67
Montclair	43,665	0.47	34,046	0.38
Parklane	34,786	0.37	31,643	0.35
Marquis			2,385	0.03
Cougar			20,769	0.23
Station Wagons	34,703	0.37	34,386	0.38
Total	331,367	3.56	308,049	3.42
Total Ford Motor Co.	2,372,388	25.47	2,348,893	26.08
General Motors				
Buick				
Special	183,315	1.97	176,655	1.96
Le Sabre	152,869	1.64	148,105	1.65
Wildcat	98,236	1.06	71,229	0.79
Electra 225	91,960	0.98	93,138	1.03
Riviera	38,113	0.41	45,518	0.50
Station Wagons	44,127	0.48	34,486	0.39
Total	608,620	6.54	569,131	6.32
Cadillac				
Calais	33,836	0.36	27,256	0.30
De Ville	130,959	1.41	141,732	1.57
Fleetwood	20,838	0.22	19,556	0.22
75 & 68	4,028	0.04	4,142	0.05
Eldorado			3,812	0.04
Total	189,661	2.03	196,498	2.18
Chevrolet				
Corvair	209,152	2.25	88,951	0.99
Chevy II	110,682	1.19	131,396	1.45
Chevelle	312,451	3.35	376,874	4.19
Biscayne	143,911	1.55	115,704	1.28
Bel Air	275,988	2.96	228,141	2.54
Impala	1,038,400	11.15	758,660	8.42
Caprice	46,955	0.50	155,172	1.72

Make of car	1965		1966	
	Number	*Percent of total*	*Number*	*Percent of total*
Camaro			41,100	0.46
Corvette	25,889	0.28	24,978	0.27
Station Wagons	260,930	2.81	237,835	2.64
Total	2,424,359	26.04	2,158,811	23.96
Oldsmobile				
F-85	172,509	1.85	197,758	2.20
Jetstar	55,940	0.60	26,438	0.29
Dynamic	116,777	1.25	78,149	0.87
Delmont			21,070	0.23
Delta	95,767	1.03	90,030	1.00
Starfire	4,382	0.17	8,315	0.09
98	107,666	1.04	88,127	0.98
Toronado	10,881	0.11	32,803	0.37
Station Wagons	45,008	0.49	37,860	0.42
Total	608,930	6.54	580,550	6.45
Pontiac				
Tempest	297,958	3.20	351,195	3.90
Catalina	240,462	2.58	212,514	2.36
2 + 2	1,886	0.02	4,307	0.04
Star Chief	35,214	0.38	43,706	0.49
Bonneville	136,777	1.46	122,270	1.36
Grand Prix	56,810	0.61	40,173	0.44
Station Wagons	62,341	0.67	56,691	0.63
Total	831,448	8.92	830,856	9.22
Total General Motors	4,663,017	51.07	4,335,846	48.13
American Motors				
Rambler				
American	80,153	0.86	66,916	0.74
Rebel	123,018	1.32	83,715	0.93
Ambassador	47,513	0.51	54,492	0.60
Marlin	3,350	0.03	5,714	0.07
Station Wagons	70,635	0.76	54,875	0.60
Total American Motors	324,669	3.48	265,712	2.94
Total other	18,088	0.20	13,403	0.15
Total U.S. makes	8,744,497	93.89	8,350,365	92.69
Total foreign makes	569,415	8.11	658,123	7.31
Total all makes	9,313,912	100.00	9,008,488	100.00

SOURCE: Data collected by R. L. Polk & Co. Published in *Automotive Industries, Annual Statistical Issue*, 1966-1967. Reprinted with permission.

Table A.7 Annual Sales, 1967

Make of car	1967 Number	Percent of total
Chrysler Corp.		
Chrysler		
Newport	84,882	1.02
Newport Custom	40,080	0.48
300	23,283	0.28
New Yorker	40,652	0.48
Station Wagons	17,564	0.21
Total	206,461	2.47
Dodge		
Dart	134,977	1.62
Coronet	157,705	1.88
Polara	75,356	0.90
Monaco & Monaco 500	33,070	0.40
Charger	30,355	0.36
Station Wagons	61,037	0.73
Total	492,500	5.89
Imperial		
Crown	14,039	0.17
Le Baron	1,842	0.02
Total	15,881	0.19
Plymouth		
Valiant	79,262	0.95
Belvedere	136,104	1.63
Fury I, II, III	265,880	3.18
VIP	17,736	0.21
Barracuda	62,569	0.75
Station Wagons	66,136	0.79

Make of car	1967 Number	Percent of total
General Motors		
Buick		
Special	170,196	2.04
Le Sabre	151,320	1.81
Wildcat	64,952	0.77
Electra 225	108,866	1.31
Riviera	42,788	0.51
Station Wagons	28,132	0.34
Total	566,254	6.78
Cadillac		
Calais	21,169	0.25
De Ville	147,727	1.76
Fleetwood	17,009	0.21
75 & Chassis	4,089	0.05
Eldorado	19,662	0.23
Total	209,656	2.50
Chevrolet		
Corvair	24,736	0.30
Chevy II	102,434	1.22
Chevelle	344,875	4.13
Biscayne	92,910	1.11
Bel Air	175,864	2.10
Impala	670,106	8.02
Caprice	128,006	1.53
Camaro	204,704	2.44
Corvette	23,578	0.29
Station Wagons	211,967	2.53
Total	1,979,180	23.67

Total	627,687	7.51
Total Chrysler Corp.	1,342,529	16.06
Ford Motor Co.		
Ford		
Falcon	83,542	1.00
Fairlane & Fairlane 500	166,824	1.99
Custom	48,594	0.58
Custom 500	92,186	1.11
Galaxie 500	375,718	4.49
LTD	98,142	1.17
Mustang	380,136	4.55
Thunderbird	58,503	0.70
Station Wagons	218,793	2.62
Total	1,522,438	18.21
Lincoln-Continental	35,221	0.42
Mercury		
Intermediate/Montego	59,238	0.71
Monterey	46,595	0.55
Montclair	17,873	0.22
Parklane/Marquis	22,854	0.27
Cougar	119,813	1.43
Station Wagons	29,263	0.35
Tota	295,636	3.54
Total Ford Motor Co.	1,853,295	22.17
Oldsmobile		
F-85	220,863	2.64
Delmont	107,349	1.29
Delta	84,177	1.00
98	78,913	0.95
Toronado	22,094	0.26
Station Wagons	38,706	0.46
Total	552,102	6.60
Pontiac		
Tempest	284,655	3.41
Catalina	221,494	2.65
Executive	35,524	0.42
Bonneville	96,826	1.16
Grand Prix	39,806	0.48
Firebird	94,952	1.13
Station Wagons	62,425	0.75
Total	835,682	10.00
Total General Motors	4,142,874	49.55
American Motors		
Rambler		
American	61,217	0.73
Rebel	73,430	0.88
Ambassador	46,522	0.55
Javelin	10,460	0.13
Marlin	2,453	0.03
Station Wagons	40,007	0.47
Total American Motors	234,089	2.79
Total other	8,562	0.10
Total U. S. makes	7,581,349	90.66
Total foreign makes	780,579	9.34
Total all makes	8,361,928	100.00

SOURCE: Data collected by R. L. Polk & Co. Published in *Automotive Industries, Annual Statistical Issue*, 1968. Reprinted with permission.

306

Bibliography

Books and Pamphlets

Bain, Joe S. *Barriers to New Competition*. Cambridge, Mass.: Harvard University Press, 1956.

———— *Industrial Organization*. New York: Wiley, 1959.

Banner, Paul H. "Competition in the Automobile Industry." Ph.D. dissertation, Harvard University, 1953.

Brooks, John. *The Fate of the Edsel and Other Business Adventures*. New York: Harper & Row, 1963.

Caves, Richard E. *American Industry: Structure, Conduct, Performance*. Englewood Cliffs, N.J.: Prentice-Hall, 1967.

Chamberlin, Edward H. *The Theory of Monopolistic Competition*. Cambridge, Mass.: Harvard University Press, 1956.

Chandler, Alfred P., Jr. *Strategy and Structure*. Cambridge, Mass.: MIT Press, 1962.

Chow, Gregory C. *Demand for Automobiles in the United States*. Amsterdam: North-Holland Publishing Co., 1957.

Crandall, Robert W. "Vertical Integration in the United States Automobile Industry." Ph.D. dissertation, Northwestern University, 1968.

Davisson, Charles N. *The Marketing of Automotive Parts*. Michigan Business Studies 12, no. 1, Bureau of Business Research, School of Business Administration. Ann Arbor, Mich.: University of Michigan, 1954.

Denison, Merrill. *The Power to Go*. Garden City, N.Y.: Doubleday, 1956.

Donovan, Frank. *Wheels for a Nation*. New York: Crowell Collier, 1965.

Drucker, Peter F. *The Concept of the Corporation*. New York: John Day, 1946.

Duesenberry, James S. *Income, Savings, and the Theory of Consumer Behavior*. Cambridge, Mass.: Harvard University Press, 1949.

Edwards, Charles E. *Dynamics of the Automobile Industry*. Columbia, S.C.: University of South Carolina Press, 1965.

307

Fellner, William. *Competition among the Few*. New York: Augustus M. Kelley, 1965.

Galbraith, John Kenneth. *The New Industrial State*. Boston: Houghton Mifflin, 1967.

Henderson, James M. and Richard E. Quandt. *Microeconomic Theory*. New York: McGraw-Hill, 1952.

Hewitt, Charles M., Jr. *Automobile Franchise Agreements*. Homewood, Ill.: Irwin, 1956.

Houthakker, H. S. and Lester D. Taylor. *Consumer Demand in the United States, 1929–1970*. Cambridge, Mass.: Harvard University Press, 1966.

Jones, Keith A. "A Study of Automobile Dealership Location." A.B. thesis, Harvard University, 1963.

Macaulay, Stewart. *Law and the Balance of Power*. New York: Russell Sage Foundation, 1966.

MacDonald, Robert M. *Collective Bargaining in the Automobile Industry*. New Haven, Conn.: Yale University Press, 1963.

Maxcy, George and Aubrey Silbertson. *The Motor Industry*. London: G. Allen, 1959.

Meyer, J. R., J. F. Kain, and M. Wohl. *The Urban Transportation Problem*. Cambridge, Mass.: Harvard University Press, 1965.

Nader, Ralph. *Unsafe at Any Speed*. New York: Grossman Publishers, 1965.

National Safety Council. *Accident Facts*, 1968.

Nelson, Walter Henry. *Small Wonder*. Boston: Little, Brown, 1967.

Nevins, Allan. *Ford: The Times, the Man, the Company*. New York: Scribner, 1954.

Nevins, Allan and Frank E. Hill. *Ford: Decline and Rebirth*. New York: Scribner, 1962.

———— *Ford: Expansion and Challenge, 1915–1932*. New York: Scribner, 1957.

Pashigian, Bedros Peter. *The Distribution of Automobiles, An Economic Analysis of the Franchise System*. Englewood Cliffs, N.J.: Prentice-Hall, 1961.

Paton, William A. and Robert L. Dixon. "Make-or-Buy Decisions on Tooling for Mass Production." Michigan Business Reports no. 35, Bureau of Business Research, School of Business Administration. Ann Arbor, Mich.: University of Michigan, 1961.

Pearson, Charles T. *The Indomitable Tin Goose*. New York: Abelard-Schuman, 1960.

Rae, John B. *The American Automobile: A Brief History*. Chicago: University of Chicago Press, 1965.

Ridker, Ronald G. *Economic Costs of Air Pollution*. New York: Praeger, 1967.

Schelling, Thomas C. *The Strategy of Conflict*. Cambridge, Mass.: Harvard University Press, 1960.

Shubik, Martin. *Strategy and Market Structure*. New York: Wiley, 1959.

Sloan, Alfred P., Jr. *My Years with General Motors*. Garden City, N.Y.: Doubleday, 1964.

Smith, David K. "The Problems of a New Firm in an Oligopolistic Industry." Ph.D. dissertation, Harvard University, 1950.

Smith, Philip Hillyer. *Wheels within Wheels*. New York: Funk & Wagnalls, 1968.

U.S. News and World Report. *The People Buying New Automobiles Today*, June 1955.

Walker, Charles R. and Robert H. Guest. *The Man on the Assembly Line*. Cambridge, Mass.: Harvard University Press, 1952.

Weiss, Leonard W. *Economics and American Industry*. New York: Wiley, 1961.

Whitney, Simon N. *Antitrust Policies*. New York: Twentieth Century, 1958.

Articles

Adams, Walter and Joel B. Dirlam. "Big Steel, Invention, and Innovation," *Quarterly Journal of Economics* 80 (May 1966).

"Adventures of Henry and Joe in Autoland," *Fortune* 33 (March 1946).

"Advertisers' Guide to Marketing for 1957," *Printer's Ink*, 256 (Aug. 24, 1956), pp. 82–85.

Atkinson, L. Jay. "Consumer Markets for Durable Goods," *Survey of Current Business* (April 1952).

Bello, Francis. "Plastics Remold the Foundry," *Fortune* 46 (July 1952).

Chow, Gregory C. "Statistical Demand Functions for Automobiles and Their Use for Forecasting," in Arnold Harberger, ed., *The Demand for Durable Goods*. Chicago: University of Chicago Press, 1962.

Conrad, Gordon R. and Irving H. Plotkin. "Risk/Return: U.S. Industry Pattern." *Harvard Business Review* 46 (March–April 1968).

Cordtz, Dan. "The Face in the Mirror at General Motors," *Fortune* 74 (Aug. 1966).

Crandall, Robert W. "Vertical Integration and the Market for Repair Parts in the United States Automobile Industry," *Journal of Industrial Economics* 16 (July 1968).

Dyckman, Thomas R. "An Aggregate Demand Model for Automobiles," *Journal of Business* 38 (July 1965).

"The Economics of Fiberglas Reinforced Plastic in Automotive Bodies." Owens-Corning Fiberglas Corp., Toledo, Ohio, 1961.

Faltermayer, Edmund K. "The Squeeze in American Motors' Road," *Fortune* 70 (Sept. 1964).

Fisher, Franklin M., Zvi Griliches, and Carl Kaysen. "The Costs of Automobile Model Changes since 1949," *Journal of Political Economy* 70 (Oct. 1962).

"The Fortune Directory of the 500 Largest Industrial Corporations," *Fortune* 77 (June 15, 1968).

Friedman, Milton, and L. J. Savage, "The Utility Analysis of Choices Involving Risk," *Journal of Political Economy* 56 (Aug. 1948).

Griliches, Zvi. "Hedonic Price Indexes for Automobiles: An Econometric Analysis of Quality Change," *The Price Statistics of the Federal Government*, National Bureau of Economic Research, New York, 1963.

Hamburger, Michael J. "Interest Rates and the Demand for Consumer Durable Goods," *American Economic Review* 57 (Dec. 1967).

Hammer, Richard. "Welcome, Sherwood Egbert," *Fortune* 64 (Dec. 1961).

Harris, William B. "Detroit Shoots the Works," *Fortune* 59 (June 1959).

Higdon, Hal. "The Big Auto Sweepstakes," *New York Times Magazine* (May 1, 1966).

Huang, David S. "Discrete Stock Adjustment: The Case of Demand for Automobiles," *International Economic Review* 5 (Jan. 1964).

Jones, James. "The Key to Chrysler's Return to Prosperity," *Ward's Quarterly* 1 (Winter 1965).

Jung, Allen F. "Price Variations among Automobile Dealers in Chicago, Illinois," *Journal of Business* 32 (Oct. 1959).

——— "Compact Car Prices in Major Cities," *Journal of Business* 33 (July 1960).
——— "Pricing Policy and Discounts in the Medium- and High-priced Car Market," *Journal of Business* 33 (Oct. 1960).
——— "Variations in Automobile Prices: Lessons for Consumers — A Reply," *Journal of Business* 35 (April 1962).
"Kaiser-Frazer Cashes In," *Fortune* 36 (Dec. 1947).
"Kaiser-Frazer — The Roughest Thing We Ever Tackled," *Fortune* 44 (July 1951).
Kettering, Charles F. "More Efficient Utilization of Fuels," *SAE Journal* 4 (July 1947).
Kilbridge, Maurice D. "The Effort Bargain in Industrial Society," *Journal of Business* 33 (Jan. 1960).
Kneese, Allan V. "How Much Is Air Pollution Costing Us in the United States?" National Conference on Air Pollution, Washington, D.C. Dec. 1966.
Lanzillotti, Robert F. "The Automobile Industry," in Walter Adams, ed., *The Structure of American Industry*, 3rd ed. New York: Macmillan, 1961.
Lincoln, Freeman. "The $7 Billion Aftermarket Gets an Overhaul," *Fortune* 65 (March 1962).
Lipsey, R. G. and K. Lancaster. "The General Theory of the Second Best," *Review of Economic Studies* 24 (1956–1957).
Menge, John A. "Style Change Costs as a Market Weapon," *Quarterly Journal of Economics* 76 (Nov. 1962).
Modigliani, Franco. "New Developments on the Oligopoly Front," *Journal of Political Economy* 66 (June 1958).
Moore, Donald A. "The Automobile Industry," in Walter Adams, ed., *The Structure of American Industry*, rev. ed. New York: Macmillan, 1954.
"Needed: Nine Million New Cars," *Fortune* 30 (July 1944).
Nerlove, Marc. "A Note on Long-run Automobile Demand," *Journal of Marketing* 22 (July 1957).
"The Rebirth of Ford," *Fortune* 35 (May 1947).
Roos, C. F. and Victor von Szelski. "Factors Governing Changes in Domestic Automobile Demand," in General Motors Corp., *The Dynamics of Automobile Demand*, New York, 1939.
Scitovsky, Tibor. "A Note on Profit Maximization and Its Implications," *Review of Economic Studies* 11 (Winter 1943).
Sheehan, Robert. "A Big Year for Small Cars," *Fortune* 56 (Aug. 1957).
Siekman, Philip. "Henry Ford and His Electronic Can of Worms," *Fortune* 73 (Feb. 1966).
Stotz, Margaret S. "Introductory Prices of 1966 Automobile Models," *Monthly Labor Review* 89 (Feb. 1966).
Suits, Daniel B. "The Demand for New Automobiles in the United States, 1929–1956," *Review of Economics and Statistics* 39 (Nov. 1958).
Vatter, Harold G. "The Closure of Entry in the American Automobile Industry," *Oxford Economic Papers* 4 (Oct. 1952).
Ware, Peter. "The Difficulties of the Car Designer," in Graham Turner, *The Car Makers*. Harmondsworth, England: Penguin, 1964.

Government Documents

Organization for European Economic Cooperation. *Some Aspects of the Motor Vehicle Industry in the U.S.A.* Paris, 1952.

U.S. Bureau of the Census, *Annual Survey of Manufacturers, 1964 and 1965.* Washington, D.C., 1968.

U.S. Bureau of Labor Statistics. "Indexes of Output per Manhour in the Private Economy." Mimeographed. Washington, D.C., March 1968.

U.S. Congress, House of Representatives, Committee on Interstate and Foreign Commerce, Subcommittee. *Automobile Dealers Territorial Security.* 86th Congress, 2nd session, 1960.

———— *Automobile Seat Belts.* Hearings, 85th Congress, 1st session, 1957.

———— Committee on the Judiciary, Subcommittee on Antitrust and Monopoly, *Auto Financing Legislation.* Hearings, 87th Congress, 1st session, 1961.

———— *Automobile Dealer Franchises.* Hearings, 84th Congress, 2nd session, 1956.

———— Senate, Committee on Commerce, *Motor Vehicle Safety Standards.* Hearings, 90th Congress, 1st session, 1967.

———— Special Subcommittee on Automobile Marketing Practices. *Unfair Competition and Discriminatory Automobile Marketing Practices.* Hearings, 90th Congress, 2nd session, 1968.

———— Committee on Commerce and Committee on Public Works, Subcommittee on Air and Water Pollution. *Electric Vehicles and Other Alternatives to the Internal Combustion Engine.* Hearings, 90th Congress, 1st session, 1967.

———— Committee on Government Operation, Subcommittee on Executive Reorganization. *Federal Role in Traffic Safety.* Hearings, 89th Congress, 1st session, 1965.

———— *Prices of Motor Vehicle Safety Equipment.* Hearings, 90th Congress, 2nd session, 1968.

———— Committee on Interstate and Foreign Commerce, Subcommittee. *Amendments to Federal Trade Commission Act.* Hearings, 83rd Congress, 2nd session, 1954.

———— *Automobile Distribution.* Hearings, 85th Congress, 2nd session, 1958.

———— *Automobile Marketing Practices.* Hearings, 84th Congress, 2nd session, 1956.

———— Subcommittee on Surface Transportation. *Motor Vehicle Safety.* Hearings, 86th Congress, 2nd session, 1960.

———— Committee on the Judiciary, Subcommittee on Antitrust and Monopoly. *Administered Prices, Automobiles.* Hearings, 85th Congress, 2nd session, 1958.

———— *Administered Prices, Automobiles.* Report, 85th Congress, 2nd session, 1958.

———— *Auto Financing Legislation.* Hearings, 86th Congress, 1st session, 1959.

———— *Economic Concentration.* Hearings, 90th Congress, 1st session, 1967.

———— *Franchise Legislation.* Hearings, 90th Congress, 1st session, 1967.

———— *A Study of the Antitrust Laws.* Hearings, 84th Congress, 1st session, 1955.

———— Committee on Public Works, Subcommittee on Air and Water Pollution. *Air Pollution 1966.* Hearings, 89th Congress, 2nd session, 1966.

———— *Air Pollution 1967* (Automotive Air Pollution). Hearings, 90th Congress, 1st session, 1967.

———— *Clean Air*. Hearings, 88th Congress, 2nd session, 1967.

U.S. Congress Temporary National Economic Committee. *Hearings Before the Temporary National Economic Committee*. 76th Congress, 2nd session, 1940.

U.S. Department of Commerce. *The Automobile and Air Pollution: A Program for Progress*. Report of the Panel on Electrically Powered Vehicles. Washington, D.C., 1967.

U.S. Department of Health, Education, and Welfare. *The Sources of Air Pollution and Control*. Washington, D.C., 1966.

U.S. Federal Trade Commission. *Report on the Motor Vehicle Industry*. Washington, D.C., 1939.

U.S. Internal Revenue Service. *Statistics of Income*.

U.S. Interstate Commerce Commission, Bureau of Economics. *Carload Waybill Statistics*, 1955 and 1963.

Notes

1. Introduction

1. "The Fortune Directory of the 500 Largest Industrial Corporations," *Fortune* 77 (June 15, 1968) pp. 188–204. These rankings are by sales.

2. U.S. Bureau of the Census, *Annual Survey of Manufacturers, 1964 and 1965*, General Statistics for Industry Groups and Industries, 1968, p. 48.

3. Automobile Manufacturers Association, *1968 Automobile Facts and Figures* (Detroit, 1968), p. 33.

4. U.S. Federal Trade Commission, *Report on the Motor Vehicle Industry* (Washington, D.C., 1939).

5. Paul H. Banner, "Competition in the Automobile Industry," Ph.D. dissertation, Harvard University, 1953.

6. Simon N. Whitney, *Antitrust Policies* (New York, 1958).

7. Leonard W. Weiss, *Economics and American Industry* (New York, 1961).

8. Donald A. Moore, "The Automobile Industry," in Walter Adams, ed., *The Structure of American Industry*, rev. ed. (New York, 1954); Robert F. Lanzillotti, "The Automobile Industry," in Adams, ed., *Structure of American Industry*, 3rd ed. (New York, 1961).

9. U.S. Senate, Committee on the Judiciary, Subcommittee on Antitrust and Monopoly, *Administered Prices, Automobiles*, Report, 85th Congress, 2nd session, 1958.

10. Charles E. Edwards, *Dynamics of the Automobile Industry* (Columbia, S.C., 1965).

11. John B. Rae, *The American Automobile: A Brief History* (Chicago, 1965).

12. Merrill Denison, *The Power to Go* (Garden City, N.Y., 1956).

13. Frank Donovan, *Wheels for a Nation* (New York, 1965).

14. Philip Hillyer Smith, *Wheels within Wheels* (New York, 1968).

15. There is no good study of truck manufacturing. For a study of the automotive parts industry, one can look at Charles N. Davisson, *The Marketing of Automotive Parts* (Ann Arbor, Mich., 1954) or Robert W. Crandall, "Vertical Integration in the United States Automobile Industry," Ph.D. dissertation, Northwestern University, 1968.

16. The best recent work on the subject is Robert M. MacDonald, *Collective Bargaining in the Automobile Industry* (New Haven, 1963).

17. It is interesting to note that John Kenneth Galbraith, *The New Industrial State* (Boston, 1967), seems implicitly to have the automobile industry as his model for the environment in which corporations behave.

18. For a more complete discussion of the tools, see Joe S. Bain, *Industrial Organization* (New York, 1959) or Richard Caves, *American Industry: Structure, Conduct, Performance* (Englewood Cliffs, N.J., 1967).

19. The items to be included in this list will vary somewhat among economists. For example, an industry's contribution to macroeconomic stability has sometimes been considered an important performance measure. But this author believes that macroeconomic stability is the responsibility of the federal government, not of individual industries.

20. The term "Independent" appears to have originated from efforts to differentiate the makes of the smaller one-make companies from those of the Big Three, the latter makes being under some higher coordinating corporate control.

21. American Motors also produced home appliances until June 1968, when it sold its Kelvinator division to White Consolidated Industries.

22. The persistence of gambling behavior is often explained away by claiming irrationality or stressing the entertainment value of the gambling. For a different view, see Milton Friedman and L. J. Savage, "The Utility Analysis of Choices Involving Risk," *Journal of Political Economy* 56 (Aug. 1948).

2. A Brief Automotive History of the Postwar Period

1. *Automotive Industries* 94 (June 15, 1946), p. 54.

2. *Automotive Industries* 94 (May 15, 1946), p. 17.

3. Registration figures, *Automotive News 1968 Almanac*, p. 44.

4. *Ward's Automotive Reports*, May 13, 1948, p. 82.

5. Allan Nevins and Frank E. Hill, *Ford: Decline and Rebirth* (New York, 1962), p. 322.

6. "The Rebirth of Ford," *Fortune* 35 (May 1947), p. 84.

7. General Motors at the time held 19 percent of Bendix stock, and Breech was considered a General Motors man.

8. Nevins and Hill, p. 323.

9. Ibid., pp. 343, 351.

10. *Moody's Manual of Investments, 1953*.

11. Edwards, pp. 21–22.

12. Ibid., p. 41.

13. *Moody's Manual of Investments, 1958*.

14. *Automotive News 1968 Almanac*, p. 78.

15. *Ward's Automotive Reports*, April 6, 1964, p. 110. The claim was later raised to 25,000. See *Automotive News*, Dec. 7, 1964, p. 38.

16. Ironically, it was rumored that Studebaker had designed a car with a short rear deck and long hood — the Mustang's basic shape — and had wanted to put it

into production in the spring of 1964 but had lacked the money. See *Ward's Automotive Reports*, Jan. 4, 1965, p. 3.

17. Public Law 89-272, 79 Stat. 992.

18. 78 Stat. 696.

19. Public Law 89-563, 80 Stat. 718.

3. Manufacturing Technology and the Planning Process

1. A 1966 Plymouth Belvedere weighing 3,353 pounds contained 2,822 pounds of steel, iron, aluminum, zinc, etc.; 90 pounds of glass; 173 pounds of rubber; 21 pounds of plastics; and 350 pounds of soft trim, upholstery, etc.

2. A new Chrysler stamping plant in Sterling, Mich., contains 193 major presses in 32 press lines, plus 255 smaller presses in 14 lines. See *Automotive Industries* 134 (Feb. 1, 1966), p. 57.

3. Also, good press practice figures that the presses will be in use only 70 percent of plant production time.

4. Letter from Harold N. Bogart, Director, Numerical Control Office, Manufacturing Staff, Ford Motor Co., Feb. 12, 1968.

5. Exceptions are the stampings that the different makes of one manufacturer will share in common. Thus all the large General Motors cars that use the same "body shell" may have the same roof, inner-door, and underbody stampings.

6. Also, lower speed (less expensive) presses are used.

7. Some of the newer presses allow die changes in thirty minutes. See *Automotive Industries* 127 (Sept. 15, 1962), p. 74; and 128 (Feb. 1, 1963), p. 44.

8. The optimum size of dies also poses a problem. A 1.2-million-unit producer who has to buy an extra 100,000-unit life die has more original units over which he can spread this extra, higher cost than does a 400,000-unit producer contemplating the same purchase, but again, at these high volumes the difference should be quite small.

9. Chrysler's new Huber Ave. foundry. See *Ward's Automotive Reports*, Jan. 25, 1965, p. 30.

10. Also, the Huber Ave. foundry has two sets of cupolas and furnaces for regular iron, plus another set for nodular iron, so that the basic efficient unit in casting may be at a rate of only 55 tons an hour or less. In 1965, General Motors built a new foundry at Defiance, Ohio, with a capacity of only 900 tons of iron a day. See *Ward's Automotive Reports*, March 8, 1965, p. 75.

11. Greater precision casting, due to the hotbox core technology, is reducing the amount of machining that is required on many pieces.

12. The higher gross rate allows for stoppages due to breakdowns, replacing worn-out machining heads, etc.

13. The first Ford Cleveland engine plant claimed a gross rate of 140 blocks an hour on each line. See *Ward's Automotive Reports*, Sept. 17, 1951, p. 298. Also, higher engine assembly speeds are possible, but assembly is a relatively minor cost in the engine manufacturing process. It is machining that calls the tune.

14. For a more complete description of an assembly plant's operations, including diagrams and photographs, see Charles R. Walker and Robert H. Guest, *The Man*

on the Assembly Line (Cambridge, Mass., 1952). Their description is of the General Motors assembly plant at Framingham, Mass.; though the study is over seventeen years old, the basic description of the plant operations is still accurate.

15. Unitized construction eliminates a separate frame to which the body is bolted and, instead, involves a lighter frame that is welded integrally to the body.

16. For long shipment by rail or boat, cars will sometimes be given a protective waxlike outer coating, to be removed by the car dealer.

17. Union pressure seems to have been effective in preventing straight speedups. Union and management agree on an acceptable task level for sixty seconds. If a faster pace is desired, rather than increase the task level, management must hire new workers.

18. *Automotive News 1968 Almanac*, p. 73.

19. The Fremont mixture is aided by the fact that all four cars share the same body shell. But the Pontiac "home plant" in Pontiac, Mich., is able to turn out full-sized Pontiacs and intermediate Tempests — two totally unrelated cars — on the same line. Ford has been able to manufacture body-on-frame Thunderbirds and unitized Lincolns on the same line at their Wixom, Mich., plant.

20. There is an alternative to varying the speed of the line to vary output; one could keep a constant speed and vary the number of hours worked. To some extent this is done: nine-hour shifts and Saturday work is common when demand is high. But overtime at time-and-a-half rates can be costly on a continuing basis (whereas a shift in line speed is a onetime cost), and union-negotiated supplementary unemployment benefit schemes make workweeks of less than forty hours costly for the company. Employee psychology might also suffer if below forty-hour weeks persisted.

21. See *Automotive Industries* 132 (June 1, 1965), p. 23; *Ward's Automotive Reports*, Aug. 2, 1965, p. 244.

22. *Automotive Industries* 132 (June 1, 1965), p. 23.

23. For a further discussion, see *Ward's Automotive Yearbook 1967*, p. 18.

24. Charles H. Patterson of Ford, quoted in *Steel* 158 (June 17, 1966), p. 38.

25. The well-publicized recall campaigns by the manufacturers in the past few years are evidence that despite these efforts some problems remain.

26. Testimony of Theodore O. Yntema of Ford, *Administered Prices, Automobiles*, Hearings, U.S. Senate, Committee on the Judiciary, Subcommittee on Antitrust and Monopoly, 85th Congress, 2nd session, 1968, part 6, p. 2731.

27. The exception here is delays due to strikes, and even then market penetration losses are often only slowly regained.

28. The introduction of a wholly new car line (e.g., the Mustang) might be done at some other time of year, but even then an introduction date has to be specified some time in advance.

29. Peter Ware, "The Difficulties of the Car Designer," in Graham Turner, *The Car Makers* (Harmondsworth, England, 1964), appendix E.

30. The independent tool and die makers have not been happy about this development. For a reflection of these complaints, see William A. Paton and Robert L. Dixon "Make-or-Buy Decisions in Tooling for Mass Production," *Michigan Business Reports* 35 (Ann Arbor, 1961).

31. And, it appears, one can extend a model design if it is inordinately successful.

The 1969 model year will see the fifth year of the "Coke bottle" shape for General Motors large cars.

32. *Automotive Industries* 121 (Oct. 1, 1959), p. 18.

33. These amortization figures also include tooling costs for the companies' home appliance operations, General Motors' diesel engine production, etc. But these are relatively minor tooling costs and should not affect the totals by very much.

34. This would have been true until the Canadian–American Automobile Free Trade Agreement of 1965 began to take effect in 1966 and 1967.

35. American Motors' exceptionally high tooling costs per car in 1966 and 1967 were probably caused by unexpected dips in volume. Its tooling costs should fall in the future as tooling orders and car volume come into better balance.

36. "The Economics of Fiberglas Reinforced Plastic in Automotive Bodies," Owens-Corning Fiberglas Corporation (Toledo, Ohio, 1961).

37. Testimony of Forbes Howard, *Economic Concentration* Hearings, U.S. Senate, Committee on the Judiciary, Subcommittee on Antitrust and Monopoly, 90th Congress, 1st session, 1967, part 6, p. 2985.

38. In 1955 George Romney of American Motors stated that "to tool a complete body for single-plant production costs in the area of $20 million." This appears to be too high for the time. Just the year before, the American Motors Annual Report had put the cost of tooling a body shell at $10 million. Romney may have been thinking of the complete costs of tooling *and* development. Just three years earlier, Nash had claimed that the total costs of engineering, developing, and tooling the Rambler had come to $20 million. Romney may also have been a bit too eager to emphasize the savings that had been achieved by foregoing the tooling on Hudson, with which American Motors had recently merged. See *A Study of the Antitrust Laws*, Hearings, U.S. Senate, Committee on the Judiciary, Subcommittee on Antitrust and Monopoly, 84th Congress, 1st session, 1955, part 1, p. 447; *American Motors, Annual Report*, 1954, p. 13; and *Ward's Automotive Reports*, May 5, 1952, p. 142.

39. *Ward's Automotive Reports*, Sept. 14, 1964, p. 293.

40. *Automotive News*, May 25, 1964, p. 22.

4. Estimated Economies of Scale and Minimum Efficient Size

1. Joe S. Bain, *Barriers to New Competition* (Cambridge, Mass., 1956), p. 245.

2. Weiss, p. 347, Edwards, pp. 209–211; John A. Menge, "Style Change Costs as a Market Weapon," *Quarterly Journal of Economics* 76 (Nov. 1962).

3. Though "net present value" is usually a superior method of comparing investment alternatives, the internal rate of return standard is superior here because of the different sizes of the firms. If the one-year producer and the two-year producer faced the same internal rate of return on a proposed project, the former would always have a higher net present value if the interest rate is lower than that internal rate of return. This is simply due to his larger size. But the smaller firm would be earning the same return on its money as the larger, and that is what interests management and stockholders.

4. These are the annual internal rates of return. These were computed by finding

the monthly internal rates of return for the above investments and then compounding these monthly rates to their corresponding annual rates.

5. "Bootlegging" consisted mainly of used car dealers buying new cars from franchised dealers in Detroit, shipping them by truck or drive-away for less than the assessed rail rate, and thereby selling them for less than local dealers. This was especially prevalent on the West Coast, where the assessed freight charges could run as high as $279 for a Chevrolet and $365 for a Buick. See *Automotive News*, April 12, 1954, p. 1.

6. This author believes that the figures given by the manufacturers are in fact correct. They were under a great deal of public scrutiny at the time, with the possibility of court cases and evidence by subpoena always possible. Trumped-up figures would have been very risky.

7. The figures cited come from the testimony of Frederick G. Donner of General Motors in *Automobile Marketing Practices*, Hearings, U.S. Senate, Committee on Interstate and Foreign Commerce, Subcommittee, 84th Congress, 2nd session, 1956, pp. 771–787.

8. Somewhat higher increases occurred on General Motors' heavier cars.

9. The use of a truck transport might have lowered the cost slightly, but a heavier car would have cost more. The wholesale price increases for other General Motors cars were in the $50 range.

10. The trilevel rack railroad car was introduced in 1960, and its use quickly swept through the industry.

11. From figures given by Donner in *Automobile Marketing Practices*, p. 771, one can calculate that the cost of shipping a 3,100-pound Chevrolet to the West Coast in 1955 was $105, so our bias is not too pronounced.

12. A recent announcement of a Chrysler assembly plant planned for New Stanton, Pa., does not really break this pattern. New Stanton is near Pittsburgh in western Pennsylvania, no farther from Detroit than is Belvedere.

13. *Automobile Marketing Practices*, p. 767.

14. Ralph Nader, *Unsafe at Any Speed* (New York, 1965).

15. Crosley, Willys, Kaiser, Hudson, Packard, and Studebaker.

16. The orphan phenomenon is an interesting one. The basic fear is that if the company folds, servicing and spare parts for its cars will be difficult to obtain. As far as this author knows, this hypothesis has never been verified, but it remains an operational part of the used car market. For example, Edwards cites the case of the Nash and Hudson Ramblers, which were identical cars except for the nameplates; the resale value of Hudson Ramblers fell below that of Nash Ramblers, because of fears that Hudson dealerships would be closed (which they were). See Edwards, p. 68.

17. The General Motors middle-level car divisions were in the doldrums in the late 1950's after the golden years of the middle 1950's. Split off individually, they might have gone into terminal tailspins. As it is, they are currently thriving.

18. Chrysler, despite its multiple-brand list, lost money in 1958 and 1959, but this was due not only to falling sales but also to poor management. Better management might have kept it in the black. Even with the losses, there was little doubt that Chrysler had the resources to pull itself together again.

19. This author does not consider the failure of the multiple-brand operations of

Studebaker-Packard and Hudson-Nash as refutations of this position. Both mergers were born of desperation, when all four companies were losing money. A multiple-brand company in such circumstances is very different from one that begins as a healthy organization and then runs into difficulty. The multiple-brand organization was certainly one of the goals of the mergers: "Another basic reason for the merger . . . was because we felt it was desirable to have at least two major dealer bodies selling our advanced product." Testimony of George Romney of American Motors, *A Study of the Antitrust Laws*, part 1, p. 449. The testimony of J. J. Nance of Studebaker-Packard, *A Study of the Antitrust Laws*, part 2, pp. 864–872, similarly endorsed the multiple-make approach.

20. The one exception here might be the Lincoln and Mercury brands, which are identified as separate brands by consumers, even though most of the dealerships selling them are "Lincoln-Mercury" dealerships. But Lincolns and Mercurys have always had dissimilar exterior appearances, different advertising campaigns, and different price ranges, and the joint name has always appeared on the dealerships. Perhaps the joint name on the showroom window is the key element.

21. Bedros Peter Pashigian, *The Distribution of Automobiles, An Economic Analysis of the Franchise System* (Englewood Cliffs, N.J., 1961), pp. 236–237.

22. *Hearings before the Temporary National Economic Committee*, 76th Congress, 2nd session, 1940, part 21, pp. 11,215–11,218.

23. Bain, *Barriers*, p. 245.

24. George Maxcy and Aubrey Silbertson, *The Motor Industry* (London, 1959), pp. 79–82.

25. *Administered Prices, Automobiles*, p. 2851.

26. Ibid., p. 2853.

27. Paris, 1952.

28. An interview with Bernard A. Chapman by Charles E. Edwards, cited in Edwards, p. 153, n. 6.

29. Bain does mention the risks of failure but only in reference to new entry. He neglects the possibility of established firms' faltering and then cracking.

5. Entry into the Automobile Industry

1. For a more complete explanation of this point, see Bain, *Barriers;* Franco Modigliani, "New Developments on the Oligopoly Front," *Journal of Political Economy* 66 (June 1958).

2. Bain, *Barriers*, pp. 11–19.

3. Since the United States–Canadian Automobile Free Trade Agreement of 1965, the overall North American market should properly be considered the relevant market. But adding Canada's 670,000 new registrations for 1967 to the United States' total of 8,362,000 new registrations does not change the required entry percentages appreciably.

4. Even with the higher elasticities of −2.0 to −3.0, which we later argue are more reasonable for the auto market, the intrusion would still be painful for the current companies.

5. Look Magazine, *National Automobile and Tire Survey* (New York, various years).

6. See *Economist*, Sept. 20–26, 1969, p. 48.

7. Bain, *Barriers*, p. 300.

8. The only successful entry in the postwar period, that of foreign imported cars, initially had their overseas reputations working for them. Also with a foreign manufacturing base, the only scale barrier they faced was that of retail distribution.

9. Bain, *Barriers*, p. 301.

10. The divisions are supposed to regard these prices as legitimate costs and earn their expected profits on top of these costs.

11. For Chevrolet or Ford franchises, the supply curve is probably very close to horizontal.

12. Bain, *Barriers*, p. 162. He also estimates break-in losses at $200 million over ten years.

13. Roughly, a one-third expansion of the necessary plant and equipment, and a 40–50 percent inflation factor. In 1955 the Wholesale Price Index for "Metalworking Machinery and Equipment" stood at 84.1 (1957–1959 = 100). In June 1968, it stood at 128.2.

14. *Moody's Manual of Investments, 1962.*

15. *New York Times*, May 2, 1965, part III, p. 15.

16. *Automotive Industries* 128 (April 1, 1963), p. 24.

17. This was a near-capacity performance that led Chrysler to decide to expand the plant by another 273,000 square feet. See *Ward's Automotive Reports*, Sept. 7, 1964, p. 283.

18. *Automotive News*, Nov. 24, 1952, p. 2, and *Ward's Automotive Reports*, June 25, 1951, supplement.

19. *Ward's Automotive Reports*, June 8, 1953, p. 179 and Oct. 26, 1953, p. 338.

20. An automatic transmission requires much less machining and more assembly than an engine. Hence the costs of the manufacturing facilities are appreciably lower.

21. *Ward's Automotive Reports*, July 13, 1964, p. 219; *Automotive Industries* 135 (Aug. 1, 1966), p. 57.

22. Romney's estimates are $14 million for general offices and warehouses. In 1953 Chevrolet set up a testing and engineering facility at a cost of $20 million. See *Ward's Automotive Reports*, May 18, 1953, p. 157.

23. The reasoning behind these figures is as follows: In 1967, average dealer investment was $169,000, of which around $75,000 was in car inventories (35 cars at $2,200 average wholesale value) financed by a bank or finance company. Since the financing for car inventories is usually easy to arrange — the goods are there and easily sold at wholesale value — it is the $100,000 that represents the risk capital that the dealer and/or his bank is putting up.

In 1965, the industry average was 299 car sales per dealer; Chevrolet sold 365 cars per dealer that year. Hence 400 cars per dealer, or 2,000 dealers for an 800,000 units firm, is an optimistic estimate. (But Volkswagen sold over 450 cars per dealer in 1966 and again in 1967.) Any additional dealers or a higher investment per dealer needed to sell 400 cars would, of course, require a larger total investment by the dealers. But dualing with outside makes would reduce the needed investment. All figures are from *Automotive News Almanac*, 1968, pp. 75–76.

9. *1968 Automobile Facts and Figures*, p. 6.

10. *Automotive News Almanac, 1968*, pp. 69–73.

11. University of Michigan, Survey Research Center, *Survey of Consumer Finances*, 1967.

12. Casual observation of the types of advertising for different types of cars would tend to reinforce this belief in a segmented market.

13. This author is not aware of any data on business and fleet credit habits.

14. See Look Magazine, *National Automobile and Tire Survey* (New York, various years).

8. Prices and Pricing Policy

1. The Automotive Information Disclosure Act of 1958, 72 Stat. 325.

2. It is 26 percent for Cadillac, Lincoln, and Imperial.

3. One wonders if one of the attractions of buying a Volkswagen has been the knowledge in consumers' minds that there was only one fixed price and one would not suffer the psychological pain later of discovering that one might have gotten a better deal elsewhere.

4. Allen F. Jung, "Variations in Automobile Prices: Lessons for Consumers — A Reply," *Journal of Business* 35 (April 1962).

5. The Automobile Information Disclosure Act of 1958, 72 Stat. 325.

6. For a more complete discussion on this point, see Joe S. Bain, *Industrial Organization* (New York, 1959), chap. viii.

7. Edward H. Chamberlin, *The Theory of Monopolistic Competition* (Cambridge, Mass., 1956), chap. iii.

8. William Fellner, *Competition among the Few* (New York, 1965).

9. Thomas C. Schelling, *The Strategy of Conflict* (Cambridge, Mass., 1960).

10. We should hasten to add that the largest firm will not necessarily have the lowest costs. The example of U.S. Steel is all too obvious.

11. See the testimony of Chrysler's L. L. Colbert, in *Administered Prices*, part 6, pp. 2,776–2,777.

12. *A Study of the Antitrust Law*, part 7, pp. 3583–3586. It is only fair to point out that when General Motors executives returned to testify before the same committee two years later they were much more emphatic about the constraints of competition. Perhaps they were concerned about the image they had projected of being relatively unconcerned about competition. See *Administered Prices*, part 6, p. 2474.

13. *Administered Prices*, part 6, pp. 2680, 2683.

14. Ibid., p. 2777.

15. Chrysler had — and still has — the reputation for being the high cost firm in the industry. Cost-plus pricing would appear to explain the higher Plymouth price.

16. The best explanation for the reappearance of these price spreads is that Chrysler and Ford recently have desired higher prices than has General Motors, as indicated by their initial pricing and reluctant lowering to General Motors' level. The price spreads may be their way of catching at least part of the higher price they feel is warranted. They may also be a signal, vain so far, to General Motors that they would prefer high prices in the future.

17. *Administered Prices*, part 6, p. 2775.

18. The BLS new car price index figures do not measure this October peak, because their October figures usually are a mixture of the prices of the new model year cars and the leftover new cars from the past model year.

19. Compare, for example, the new car buyer profiles contained in the *Newsweek Census of New Car Buyers*, composed only of October buyers, and Look Magazine's *National Automobile and Tire Survey*, composed of a wider range of new car buyers.

20. *Ward's Automotive Reports*, Sept. 5, 1966, p. 283.

21. This would not be true, of course, for the three of the nine demand studies listed in Table 7.2 that were estimated in logarithmic form. Those three are the studies by Roos and von Szelski, Atkinson, and Dyckman.

22. Also, the variety of autos offered in one year and over time raises questions about the ability of any price index to capture adequately the price information required.

23. See Margaret S. Stotz, "Introductory Prices of 1966 Automobile Models," *Monthly Labor Review* 89 (Feb. 1966).

24. By cost-oriented pricing, we mean pricing policies that looked primarily at the cost side of the picture and largely ignored the demand considerations that would hold at the prices chosen. This notion of cost-oriented pricing need not be as rigid as the traditional cost-plus concepts, but the general idea is the same.

25. See *Ward's Automotive Reports*, Jan. 18, 1947, p. 17; *Automotive News*, April 21, 1947, p. 4.

26. *United States v. Aluminum Company of America*, 148 F. 2d 416 (1945).

27. *American Tobacco Company v. United States*, 328 U.S. 781 (1946).

28. *Ward's Automotive Reports*, Nov. 24, 1945, p. 345.

29. These figures and the price increase figures mentioned subsequently in this chapter have been taken from various issues of *Automotive News* at the new model announcement times.

30. *Ward's Automotive Reports*, Nov. 28, 1955, p. 381.

31. Although the low price makes rose only 6 percent, middle-level makes like Oldsmobile rose as much as 11 percent.

32. *Administered Prices*, part 6, p. 2693.

33. See Zvi Griliches, "Hedonic Price Indexes for Automobiles: An Econometric Analysis of Quality Change," *The Price Statistics of the Federal Government* (New York, 1963).

34. This was a period of general inflation in the United States caused, most observers agree, by excess demand generally.

35. The rough cost of the items was $70, but some of them had been standard on some models in the previous year, so that the differences between before- and after-adjustment prices were not uniform.

36. See letter from Ralph Nader to Senator Philip Hart, reprinted in U.S. Senate, Subcommittee on Reorganization, *Prices of Motor Vehicles Safety Equipment*, Hearings, 90th Congress, 2nd session, 1968, pp. 75–78. The wage settlement with the UAW in the fall of 1967, after the new model prices had been announced, was reportedly higher than had been expected.

37. General Motors denies that there was any real pressure or that it changed its

prices in response to Washington's statements. See *Automotive News*, Sept. 30, 1968, p. 69.

38. U.S. Senate, Committee on the Judiciary, Subcommittee on Anti-trust and Monopoly, *Franchise Legislation*, Hearings, 90th Congress, 1st session, 1967, p. 324.

39. U.S. Senate, Committee on Commerce, Special Subcommittee on Automobile Marketing Practices, *Unfair Competition and Discriminatory Automobile Marketing Practices*, Hearings, 90th Congress, 2nd session, 1968, pp. 25–26.

40. See Ibid., pp. 15–16; *Administered Prices*, part 6, pp. 3027–3028, 3929; *Automotive News*, May 5, 1958, p. 3.

41. *Automotive Industries* 99 (July 1, 1948), p. 18.

42. *Ward's Automotive Reports*, June 2, 1958, p. 619.

43. *Unfair Competition and Discriminatory Automobile Marketing Practices*, p. 70.

44. *Automotive News*, March 27, 1967, p. 1.

45. *Automotive News*, Jan. 30, 1961, p. 2.

46. *Unfair Competition and Discriminatory Automobile Marketing Practices*, p. 69.

9. Dealers and Dealer Systems

1. There have been three book-length studies of the dealer system: Charles M. Hewitt, Jr., *Automobile Franchise Agreements* (Homewood, Ill., 1956); Bedros Peter Pashigian, *The Distribution of Automobiles, An Economic Analysis of the Franchise System* (Englewood Cliffs, N.J., 1961); Stewart Macaulay, *Law and the Balance of Power* (New York, 1966). The first and third are legal studies; the second, as its title implies, is an economic study.

2. Allan Nevins, *Ford: The Times, the Man, the Company* (New York, 1954), p. 345.

3. Pashigian, pp. 26–32.

4. James M. Henderson and Richard E. Quandt, *Microeconomic Theory* (New York, 1952), p. 192.

5. This model is mentioned by Pashigian, pp. 33–34, 52–56.

6. Regardless of who finances the inventories, it is clear that it should always be the dealer who holds them, to reduce delivery times.

7. Pashigian presents an analysis that is similar; see pp. 54–57.

8. Pashigian, pp. 222–225.

9. Keith A. Jones, "A Study of Automobile Dealership Location," Senior honors thesis, Harvard University, 1963.

10. Look Magazine, *National Automobile and Tire Survey* (New York, various years).

11. Pashigian, pp. 130–135.

12. Look Magazine, *National Automobile and Tire Survey* (New York, 1965), p. 40.

13. U.S. Senate, Committee on the Judiciary, Subcommittee on Antitrust and Monopoly, *Franchise Legislation*, Hearings, 90th Congress, 1st session, 1967, p. 313.

14. U.S. House, Committee on the Judiciary, Subcommittee on Antitrust and Monopoly, *Automobile Dealer Franchises*, Hearings, 84th Congress, 2nd session, 1956, p. 286.

15. *A Study of the Antitrust Laws*, part 7, p. 3681.

16. The rise in sales per dealer is overstated somewhat, since a rising number of sales have been fleet sales that are either direct or are only nominally made through

the dealers. But the basic trend would still remain, even after fleet sales had been subtracted.

17. *Franchise Legislation*, p. 287.

18. *Automobile Dealer Franchises*, p. 288.

19. 338 F. 2d 732 (1964).

20. 384 F. 2d 192 (1967).

21. *Pick Manufacturing Co. v. General Motors Corp.* 229 U.S. 3 (1935).

22. *General Motors Corp.* Docket 3152, 34 FTC 58.

23. *Standard Oil of California and Station Stations, Inc. v. U.S.*, 337 U.S. 293 (1949).

24. See, for example, the testimony of L. L. Colbert of Chrysler in *A Study of the Antitrust Laws*, part 1, p. 370, the testimony of L. H. Bridenstine of General Motors in *Franchise Legislation*, p. 294, and Lyman W. Slack, of NADA, in *Unfair Competition and Discriminatory Automobile Marketing Practices*, p. 11. After this last set of hearings, General Motors denied that it had any policy of preferring exclusive dealing. But the company also indicated that "if the dealer's other business activities result in any failure of performance of the terms and conditions of the (franchise agreement), divisional representatives may discuss such failure of performance." It is not unlikely that handling another company's cars could thus become the source of any real or imagined ills that the company's field representative might find and that this may well be a deterrent to a dealer's deciding to handle another make. See General Motors' Statement, pp. 71–74.

25. Pashigian, pp. 117–118.

26. See Tibor Scitovsky, "A Note on Profit Maximization and Its Implications," *Review of Economic Studies* 11 (Winter 1943). In fact, forcing behavior would be consonant with a Scitovsky leisure profit model in which the manufacturer could force a take-it-or-leave-it, high volume, low leisure situation on the dealer.

27. For explanations of and limitations on the use of this data, see Pashigian, chaps. ii, vii.

28. These figures are only for corporate firms. Pashigian has argued that, since corporate retailers earn higher returns than do unincorporated retailers, and since corporate auto dealers are a larger percentage of total dealers than are corporate retailers of total retailers, then a finding of equality between corporate auto dealers and corporate retailers would imply higher average returns for all auto dealers. Though this is true, it is probably unrealistic to compare an auto dealer to a small family grocery store. Thus the comparison between the corporate sectors is the relevant one for us.

29. See Pashigian, pp. 21–24, 59–60.

30. This would especially be true if there is a large cross-sectional variance around the mean, as is probably the case for auto dealerships, and if the firms are small and face imperfect capital markets, so that a few bad years can wipe them out, even though in the long run average profits are being earned.

31. *A Study of the Antitrust Laws*, Part 7, p. 3681.

32. *Ford Motor Co. v. Kirkmeyer Motor Co.*, 65 F. 2d 1001, pp. 1003–1004.

33. Letter of Submittal, *Report on the Motor Vehicles Industry*.

34. Ibid., chaps. iii–viii.

35. See *Automotive News*, April 12, 1954, p. 1.; *Automobile Marketing Practices*, p. 787.

36. *A Study of the Antitrust Laws*, part 7, p. 3290.

37. U.S. Bureau of Labor Statistics 80, *Monthly Labor Review*, March 1957.

38. *Automobile Marketing Practices*, p. 1096.

39. U.S. Senate, Committee on Interstate and Foreign Commerce, Subcommittee, *Amendments to Federal Trade Commission Act*, Hearings, 83rd Congress, 2nd session, 1954, p. 106.

40. Along this line, the companies have always insisted that the dealerships be sold for book value, with nothing included for "goodwill" or monopoly power. The companies' reason that it is *their* franchise policy that has created whatever monopoly power exists, and they of course prefer the new dealer to pay as little as possible for the dealership.

41. Though the umpire is appointed by the company, the umpires have been men selected for their legal stature and apparent lack of bias toward the company. As of 1968, the General Motors' umpire was former Supreme Court Justice Charles Whittaker, and the Chrysler umpire was former Attorney General Herbert Brownell.

42. Ford had earlier (in 1955) extended special provisions to heirs in case of death.

43. This was done specifically on the advertising charges per car adjustment.

44. Macaulay, p. 182.

45. 70 Stat. 1125.

46. The dealers were not unanimous on this. Many high volume dealers saw territorial security as a threat to their operations.

47. General Motors did announce a voluntary plan whereby the dealers could offer the cars to the company, but only one dealer ever took advantage of it, and he dealt in taxicabs. Most dealers were reluctant to offer excess cars to the company because this would have been evidence that they were not performing up to volume standards.

48. See U.S. Senate, Committee on Interstate and Foreign Commerce, Subcommittee, *Automobile Distribution*, Hearings, 85th Congress, 2nd session, 1958; U.S. House, Committee on Interstate and Foreign Commerce, Subcommittee, *Automobile Dealers Territorial Security*, Hearings, 86th Congress, 2nd session, 1960.

49. Thus Ford's and Chrysler's early hostility, followed by endorsement of the system, partially reflected their varying states of confidence in their forcing capabilities. Also, Ford and Chrysler dealers in 1955 were more split in their attitudes toward territorial security than were General Motors' dealers, and Ford and Chrysler were reluctant to endorse a system that many of its dealers opposed.

50. 388 U.S. 365 (1967).

51. Automotive Industries, *38th Annual Statistical Issue*, March 15, 1958.

52. Further, despite appreciably lower per capita incomes, Florida residents owned 0.32 cars per capita. But price discrimination to the Northeast presents a bit more of a mystery. Perhaps this was a historical accident; perhaps it was considered necessary to justify the price discrimination maintained in other parts of the country.

53. Ford even claimed that it would lose $15 million on freight costs in 1956. See *Automobile Marketing Practices*, p. 1014.

54. Macaulay, p. 165.

55. Ibid., p. 166.

56. Ibid., p. 168.

57. Ibid., pp. 96–135.

58. 261 F. Supp. 488 (1966).

59. 384 F. 2d 192 (1967).

60. *Franchise Legislation*, pp. 287–288.

61. Ibid., pp. 232–264; *Unfair Competition and Discriminatory Automobile Marketing Practices*, pp. 1–44.

62. These are not to be confused with the Manhattan branch outlets, about which the dealers have no objections.

63. *Franchise Legislation*, p. 319.

64. This is not to deny that dealer loyalty is important but simply to affirm that brand loyalty is stronger.

65. See, for example, the statements of the auto companies' representatives in *Franchise Legislation*, pp. 286–354.

66. The former is precluded by the once a year price-setting policy, though it may be achieved in effect by not offering rebates on these models as the model year progresses.

67. See *Automotive News*, Feb. 7, 1966, p. 1.

10. Product Behavior: A General Summary

1. The degree of modifiability and the delay between formulation and results are related in their effects on risk, but they are separable. For any degree of modifiability, risks increase as the gestation period increases. Though changes can be made, the longer planning period increases the likelihood that changes will have to be made, and changes cost money. For any gestation period, risks increase as modifiability decreases or becomes more costly.

11. The Small Car Story

1. *Automotive Industries* 95 (July 15, 1946), p. 97.

2. General Motors reportedly spent $17 million on the light car project before it was abandoned. See *Automotive News*, Nov. 22, 1948, p. 8.

3. Since the import boom of the late 1950's, these overseas subsidiaries may have provided a potential advantage by giving the American manufacturers a better understanding of, and control over, import competition. They might also have shortened the design lead time of producing a small car by adopting designs of their subsidiaries. In fact, the companies' behavior indicates that they have not exploited this advantage.

4. William B. Harris, "Detroit Shoots the Works," *Fortune* 59 (June 1959), pp. 248–250; and *Automotive News*, Sept. 28, 1959, p. 6.

5. *Automotive News*, Oct. 14, 1957, p. 8.

6. *Ward's Automotive Reports*, June 24, 1957, p. 198.

7. Robert Sheehan, "A Big Year for Small Cars," *Fortune* 16 (Aug. 1957), p. 105.

8. *New York Times*, June 21, 1957, p. 34.

9. *Administered Prices*, part 6, p. 2483.

10. Ibid., pp. 2801, 2802.

11. *New York Times*, Dec. 8, 1958, p. 62.

12. *Automotive Industries* 120 (April 1, 1959), p. 15.

13. *Automotive News*, April 2, 1958, p. 4.

14. This appeared to be especially true of the 1960 Ford Falcon. The 1960 full-sized Ford was an unattractive car, and many normal Ford owners appeared to have bought Falcons instead.

15. *Ward's Automotive Reports*, April 16, 1962, p. 122.

16. *Ward's Automotive Reports*, Oct. 9, 1961, p. 321.

17. *Automotive Industries* 118 (June 15, 1958), p. 33.

18. *Ward's Automotive Reports*, April 25, 1960, p. 129.

19. This time, American Motors was not able to capitalize on this boom. Stuck with an "economy" image in a period of rising luxury sales in most of the market, the company, despite a dramatic price cut on its bottom of the line models in February 1967, did not seem to be able to attract import buyers. Perhaps this is because it was no longer "special" as the only American alternative to large Detroit cars, the way it had appeared in 1957 and 1958.

20. Subsequent inflation caused the General Motors Vega to have a price slightly above $2,000 when it was introduced.

12. Product Behavior: Durability, Styling, Models, and Model Proliferation

1. Hal Higdon, "The Big Auto Sweepstakes," *New York Times Magazine*, May 1, 1966, p. 97.

2. In practice, the cost-cutting efforts would have to allow good performance during the warranty period.

3. If it introduced the decreased durability slowly and gradually, the company might even avoid the initial drop in used car values.

4. Gregory C. Chow, "Statistical Demand Functions for Automobiles and their Use for Forecasting," in Arnold Harberger, ed., *The Demand for Durable Goods* (Chicago, 1962), p. 60.

5. In some cases this is not quite correct. For unexplained reasons, the R. L. Polk data will sometimes have a larger number of year X cars registered in year $X + 2$ than in year $X + 1$. In all such cases, the higher number was chosen. Also, we have excluded the "other" category, from the R. L. Polk data since these are almost entirely imports.

6. See the BLS series for auto repairs. Also, the increasing amounts of optional equipment on cars has raised the costs of repair. Automatic transmissions, power steering, power brakes, etc., are costlier to repair than their simpler counterparts and often require repairs more frequently. Maintaining an old car has become a more expensive alternative to buying a new car, irrespective of the rise in labor costs. Thus, in encouraging the purchase of these optional items, the companies may have been consciously or unconsciously pursuing a decreased durability strategy.

7. Surprisingly, the average mileage driven per car per year seems to have remained relatively constant, centering on 9,400 miles per car per year for the past

twenty years. See American Manufacturers Association, *1968 Automobile Facts and Figures*, p. 48.

8. The first stage, reduced form equations, in which the P_i's were estimated, were as follows:

$$P_{i,6} = \begin{matrix} 7.2030 \\ (1.2129) \end{matrix} + \begin{matrix} 0.0210Q_{i,6} \\ (0.0160) \end{matrix} - \begin{matrix} 0.0340C \\ (0.0640) \end{matrix} - \begin{matrix} 0.0552R \\ (0.0165) \end{matrix}$$

$$\begin{matrix} - 0.0014Y \\ (0.0031) \end{matrix} + \begin{matrix} 0.2212P_s \\ (0.1066) \end{matrix} + \begin{matrix} 0.1285t \\ (0.0975) \end{matrix} \qquad R^2 = 0.9020$$

$$P_{i,7} = \begin{matrix} 5.0504 \\ (2.7611) \end{matrix} - \begin{matrix} 0.0010Q_{i,7} \\ (0.0140) \end{matrix} - \begin{matrix} 0.0690C \\ (0.0770) \end{matrix} - \begin{matrix} 0.0250R \\ (0.0174) \end{matrix}$$

$$\begin{matrix} + 0.0024Y \\ (0.0038) \end{matrix} + \begin{matrix} 0.0553P_s \\ (0.1779) \end{matrix} + \begin{matrix} 0.1355t \\ (0.1282) \end{matrix} \qquad R^2 = 0.7094$$

$$P_{i,8} = \begin{matrix} -1.7890 \\ (1.6931) \end{matrix} - \begin{matrix} 0.0000Q_{i,8} \\ (0.0080) \end{matrix} - \begin{matrix} 0.0040C \\ (0.0370) \end{matrix} + \begin{matrix} 0.0178R \\ (0.0094) \end{matrix}$$

$$\begin{matrix} + 0.0029Y \\ (0.0015) \end{matrix} - \begin{matrix} 0.3091P_s \\ (0.0905) \end{matrix} - \begin{matrix} 0.0425t \\ (0.0686) \end{matrix} \qquad R^2 = 0.9422$$

With this large number of variables, a small number of observations, and a high degree of multicollinearity among the stock of cars, income, repair costs, and the time trend, it is difficult to say anything definitive about these equations. The signs in these equations generally agree with a priori expectations. From among the four correlated variables, the fitted P_i's presumably reflect the effects of income growth, and thus the time trend in the second-stage equations is probably not a substitute for income growth.

9. See Robert W. Crandall, "Vertical Integration and the Market for Repair Parts in the United States Automobile Industry," *Journal of Industrial Economics* 16 (July 1968), pp. 226–229.

10. Simply showing that auto company repair parts prices are higher than other manufacturers' repair parts prices is not sufficient, since the former group may have been able to create a more inelastic demand for its repair parts through advertising, dealer systems, etc.

11. See the *General Motors' Annual Report, 1960*, p. 10.

12. Or one could contrast autos with computers. Although the growth of new customers is much greater in computers, still the replacement market is important. The computer companies have chosen the route of heavy research and development expenditures and technological advances (currently the industry is in its third "generation" of computers). Again, the nature of the buyers (businesses, somewhat sophisticated, mostly interested in performance rather than appearance) and the nature of the suppliers (a surprisingly large number of technologically aggressive firms, even though IBM has a dominant position) should be stressed.

13. Encouraging a demand for used cars to ease the financial burden of the new

car buyer has been done almost incidentally as a by-product of creating the demand for new cars; e.g., advertising that stresses the wonders of car ownership and traveling by car, the auto companies lobbying in support of national highway systems, etc.

14. Bad winter weather effectively precluded strong demand in the first quarter when the cars were first presented.

15. This model proliferation also has had effects on risks. A wider selection of models involves more money at stake, but it also reduces the chances of being caught with a small number of unpopular models.

16. A model here is a separately designated car (e.g., Chevrolet Biscayne two-door sedan). Engine options are not counted.

17. This has been true since 1959; before then, the full-sized cars had three basic body shells. All of Chrysler's full-sized cars have used the same body shell since 1955. Ford and Mercury full-sized cars have usually used the same body shell, though the 1957 Mercury was given a separate body shell that was also used on some of the Edsel models.

18. This would be especially true if the individual makes had not reached the 400,000 unit level.

19. Purists may argue on the origin of the hardtop. Kaiser had a "hardtop" in the spring of 1948, but it had a glass post behind the front doors so that it did not really present the pillarless appearance that has become the mark of a hardtop.

20. The initial expectations of volume appear to have been low enough so that, to this author's eye, many of the middle-level compacts — e.g., Pontiac, Oldsmobile, Buick — appear initially to have used common outer sheet metal, disguising their similar design by different grilles and different trim. The Dodge Lancer seems to have used the same outer sheet metal as the Plymouth Valiant. Also, the Chevrolet Camaro and Pontiac Firebird, in their first two years also seem to have shared the same outer sheet metal.

21. Menge has suggested a similar strategy for Independents; see his "Style Change Costs as a Market Weapon," *Quarterly Journal of Economics* 76 (Nov. 1962).

22. It is clear, though, that product deterioration, if not accompanied by an appropriate saving in cost, is a clear loss to society. The monopolist or oligopolist who takes advantage of an inelastic demand curve by second owners through product deterioration is just as objectionable as the one who takes advantage of inelastic demand by first owners through raising the price.

23. It could be argued that model changes create external diseconomies; that the man who buys a new car reduces the utility of his neighbors, who become envious of him. In this sense, the market may not be allocating resources efficiently. This is, of course, the familiar Duesenberry "demonstration effect," and it applies as a criticism to almost all areas of consumption, not just automobiles. Further, it is not clear that policy steps are really warranted here. It would be one thing to criticize the auto companies for not producing cheaper, unchanging cars when a sizable minority wanted them. It is quite another to criticize them for model changes that create disutility because of an envy component in consumer utility functions. See James S. Duesenberry, *Income, Savings, and the Theory of Consumer Behavior* (Cambridge, Mass., 1949), chap. iv.

13. Other Aspects of Behavior

1. The tooling for fiber glass is cheaper than for steel, but the raw material itself is more expensive. Thus, for low volume runs, fiber glass is cheaper, while steel is cheaper for high volume runs. The fiber glass industry claims the crossover point is 75,000 units, but this is probably somewhat on the high side.

2. For a list of the prewar Independent innovations, see *Administered Prices*, part 7, pp. 3812–3813.

3. Their slow follower response on automatic transmissions and, as will be discussed below, high compression V-8 engines, tends to reinforce this view.

4. See the testimony of W. T. Gossett of Ford, *A Study of the Antitrust Laws*, part 2, p. 658.

5. A more efficient generator for a car that generates AC current, which is subsequently rectified into DC current to charge the battery.

6. But three and one-half years of war do not offer an adequate explanation, since they should not have stopped the thought about and advanced engineering on automatic transmissions that would have been necessary.

7. Charles F. Kettering, "More Efficient Utilization of Fuels," *SAE Journal* 4 (July 1947).

8. There had been a trend in prewar engines to larger size and more power, but the Kettering engine seemed to set off a fresh new wave of interest in this matter.

9. Horsepower ratings of an engine are usually brake horsepower. The actual power that gets to the rear wheels is a good deal less, because of power losses to drive the fanbelt, power equipment, automatic transmission, etc.

10. *Automotive Industries* 116 (June 15, 1957), p. 39.

11. See Francis Bello, "Plastics Remold the Foundry," *Fortune* 46 (July 1952).

12. *Advertising Age* 39 (Aug. 26, 1968), p. 38.

13. These figures neglect advertising for imported cars and do not include imported car sales in the denominator. The only advertiser of large scale in this category is Volkswagen, with advertising expenditures of $10 million in 1967, or $22 per car. (This was matched by another $10 million by dealers.) Ibid., pp. 212–213.

14. *Automotive News Almanac*, 1967, p. 96.

15. National Automobile Dealers Association, *Operating Averages for the Automobile Retailing Industry, 1966*.

16. "Advertisers' Guide to Marketing for 1957," *Printer's Ink* 256 (Aug. 24, 1956), pp. 82–85.

17. *Advertising Age* 28 (Aug. 19, 1957); 29 (Aug. 26, 1968).

18. *Advertising Age* 39 (Aug. 26, 1968), p. 38.

14. Air Pollution and Auto Safety Issues

1. U.S. Department of Health, Education and Welfare, *The Sources of Air Pollution and Control*, 1966.

2. U.S. Department of Commerce, *The Automobile and Air Pollution: A Program for Progress*, Report of the Panel on Electrically Powered Vehicles, 1967, part 1, p. 22.

3. Allan V. Kneese, "How much is Air Pollution Costing Us in the United States?" National Conference on Air Pollution, Washington, D.C., Dec. 1966.

4. For a review of the literature, see U.S. Senate, Committee on Public Works, Subcommittee on Air and Water Pollution, *Air Pollution 1966*, Hearings, 89th Congress, 2nd session, 1966, pp. 22–53.

5. Ronald G. Ridker, *Economic Costs of Air Pollution* (New York, 1967).

6. Ibid., chap. iv.

7. But differences in death rates have been found between rural and urban areas, though it is not clear that all other influences have been removed in such findings.

8. Ridker, appendix C.

9. Ibid., chap. vi.

10. *The Automobile and Air Pollution*, part 1, p. 18.

11. The Justice Department has so claimed, in an antitrust suit charging that the auto companies deliberately conspired to delay progress in pollution control devices. See *New York Times*, Jan. 11, 1969, p. 1. This suit was settled out of court in September 1969, with no admission of guilt by the companies. See *New York Times*, September 12, 1969, p. 1.

12. The correspondence is reproduced in U.S. Senate, Committee on Public Works, Subcommittee on Air and Water Pollution, *Air Pollution 1967* (Automotive Air Pollution) Hearings, 90th Congress, 1st session, 1967.

13. Having personally observed fumes coming out of uncorrected blowby vents, this author is a bit mystified as to why this discovery took so long.

14. Estimates hold that the incremental manufacturing cost of unleaded gasoline would be 1.8 cents to 4.7 cents per gallon, depending on refinery size, and would require an investment of over $4.24 billion. See *The Automobile and Air Pollution: A Program for Progress*, part 2, p. 46.

15. See the testimony of Harry A. Williams of the AMA in U.S. Senate, Committee on Public Works, Subcommittee on Air and Water Pollution, *Clean Air*, Hearings, 88th Congress, 2nd session, 1964, part 2, pp. 880–881.

16. P.L. 89-272, 79 Stat. 992.

17. California also set standards for nitrogen oxide pollutants, but so far the industry has not been able to meet them. One difficulty is that the current methods of reducing the other pollutants tend to increase nitrogen oxide fumes.

18. The Panel on Electrically Powered Vehicles considered standards of 50 parts per million hydrocarbon, 0.5 percent carbon dioxide, and 250 parts per million nitrogen oxide (1,500 parts per million come from uncontrolled vehicles) as commercially feasible by 1975. *The Automobile and Air Pollution: A Program for Progress*, part 1, p. 22.

19. There will, of course, be a steadily increasing car population so that the gross volume of pollutants will not be cut by as much.

20. And it is not clear which way the nonlinearity runs. Is it the last 50 percent that *really* makes pollution noisome? Or is it the first 50 percent and anything above that does not really lead to discomfort?

21. See the testimony of Louis J. Fuller, in *Air Pollution 1967*, p. 238. Recognizing this, Congress in 1967 made federal money available to aid state inspection programs.

22. In early 1970, though, the prospects for gasoline changes looked more hopeful. A number of gasoline companies have promised the production of lead-free gas, and the auto companies have promised appropriate engine modifications.

23. By themselves, differential taxes and subsidies on car use might provide the socially optimum solution to the control problem, allowing free consumer choice but forcing consumers in making their choices to take into account the externalities involved. But Congress has been reluctant to approach pollution control through the taxation route, seeing such taxes as giving the taxpayers "a license to pollute." It is conceivable that the inspection costs necessary for a differential tax system might outweigh the consumer choice losses from, say, requiring all new cars produced to have a gas tank evaporation control system (this latter requirement could be enforced at very low cost). Also, under a tax system, some owners might choose to pay the tax and continue to neglect the air pollution of their cars. Though their car use might be limited by the tax to socially optimal levels, urban dwellers would still have to endure the pollution. Requiring control systems by fiat would ensure that urban dwellers gained some benefit from the pollution control scheme. These same general comments would apply to the safety issue discussed in the next section.

24. One disturbing feature of the present system is that it is entirely based on new car installation performance averages, with no maximum allowable limit for individual cars. Thus there is no way of enforcing the standards once the car has left the dealer's showroom. Another is that the standards are mainly in terms of the proportion of exhaust; except for some easing of the standards of small foreign cars, there is no discouragement to larger engines that, with the same proportion of pollutants in their exhaust, produce a larger volume of pollutants.

25. For a nontechnical review of the current state of the art in electric car technology, see *The Automobile and Air Pollution: A Program for Progress*, part 2, pp. 62–88.

26. See, for example, the testimony of battery makers in U.S. Senate, Committee on Commerce and Committee on Public Works, Subcommittee on Air and Water Pollution, *Electric Vehicles and Other Alternatives to the Internal Combustion Engine*, Hearings, 90th Congress, 1st session, 1967, pp. 135–210.

27. National Safety Council, *Accident Facts*, 1968 ed. These statistics have come under criticism. See Jeffrey O'Connell and Arthur Myers, *Safety Last* (New York, 1966).

28. If there are excess profits by insurance companies, this is an overstatement. But since there is a sizable fraction of motorists who are not covered by insurance, and it is not clear that deaths are adequately compensated for, these figures may also contain some understatement.

29. *New York Times*, Oct. 14, 1968, p. 1.

30. For a review and references to this literature, see Robert Wolf, "Four Proposals for Improving Automobile Crashworthiness," reprinted in U.S. Senate, Committee on Government Operation, Subcommittee on Executive Reorganization, *Federal Role in Traffic Safety*, Hearings, 89th Congress, 1st session, 1965, part 2, pp. 934–948. See also *New York Times*, Oct. 23, 1968, p. 92.

31. Nevertheless, most people buy liability insurance because their state law requires it, or they think it does, or they can visualize an accident that causes injury to second parties (e.g., a pedestrian) but not to themselves.

32. Dan Cordtz, "The Face in the Mirror at General Motors," *Fortune* 74 (Aug. 1966), p. 207.

33. See the Report by the Cornell Aeronautical Laboratory, *Federal Role in Traffic Safety*, part 2, p. 684.

34. See, for example, the testimony of Charles A. Clague of General Motors in U.S. House, Committee on Interstate and Foreign Commerce, Subcommittee, *Automobile Seat Belts*, Hearings, 85th Congress, 1st session, 1957, p. 72.

35. U.S. Senate, Committee on Interstate and Foreign Commerce, Subcommittee on Surface Transportation, *Motor Vehicle Safety*, Hearings, 86th Congress, 2nd session, 1960, p. 13.

36. The outboard ends of Studebaker's seat belts, however, were attached to the doors — a very hazardous location in the event that the doors flew open (which they often did).

37. *Ward's Automotive Reports*, Oct. 29, 1962, p. 347.

38. 78 Stat. 696.

39. See the testimony of the company representative, *Federal Role in Traffic Safety*, part 2.

40. Nader was spectacularly successful, in a way. The used car prices of the particular Corvairs declined dramatically but so did the sales of new Corvairs, which no longer had the characteristics about which Nader had complained. Corvair sales, once over 250,000 units a year were under 25,000 units in 1967. The company continued to produce them, probably only because dropping the line would lead to unfavorable public relations and might be interpreted as an admission that Nader was right. Finally, in May 1969, production of Corvairs ceased. It will probably be a long time before an American producer again tries to introduce a rear-engine car. The industry's inclinations to experiment and innovate may have been somewhat discouraged by the incident.

41. P.L. 89-563, 80 Stat. 718.

42. Lead times were not much of a problem, since the industry had been able to anticipate most of the standards, and many of the interior items affected have much shorter lead times than the stampings and power-train components.

43. For a summary of the standards, see U.S. Senate, Committee on Commerce, *Motor Vehicle Safety Standards*, Hearings, 90th Congress, 1st session, 1967, pp. 22–45.

44. One negative effect, however, has been the elimination of some low volume imports from the United States market, because the low volume did not warrant the extra tooling that would be required to install the safety features. The implication, of course, is that these items would not be salable features in their home market.

45. See the testimony of William I. Steiglitz in U.S. Senate, Committee on Commerce, *Motor Vehicle Safety Standards*, pp. 154–186.

46. On the other hand, many critics (e.g., Consumers Union) claim that design considerations are still taking precedence over safety considerations.

47. This is true even of used cars that are no longer being produced. The companies fear that any stigma would be carried over to their new cars, as in fact happened to the Corvair. Also, with the phenomenon of brand loyalty, the decline in used car prices of a particular make would reduce the potential sales of new cars of that make.

48. See *New York Times*, Nov. 9, 1968, p. 29.

49. See *New York Times*, Jan. 12, 1969, p. 61.

50. The contrast with life insurance companies, who have pushed safety, is striking. In their case, though lower mortality rates will translate into lower premiums for new customers, the old customers must pay the higher premiums, and the companies make windfall gains.

51. For General Motors cars, six seat belts cost $39; the 1966 model year additions cost $70; the 1967 model year additions cost about another $30. Shoulder harnesses cost $23 and head restraints, $17. Other additions, like the penetration-reducing design on 1969 models, also added to costs, but by an unknown amount. Insofar as these items were or are being priced above long-run marginal cost, the real cost to society is lower than the simple sum of these figures.

15. Performance: An Evaluation

1. Gordon R. Conrad and Irving H. Plotkin, "Risk/Return: U.S. Industry Pattern," *Harvard Business Review* 46 (March–April 1968).

2. Another recent study of the risk-return relationship among firms is that of I. N. Fisher and G. R. Hall, "Risk and Corporate Rates of Return," *Quarterly Journal of Economics* 83 (Feb. 1969). In their study, the auto industry ranked 9 of 11 industries when profits were adjusted for risk, as measured by a firm's deviation from its trend over time, and ranked fifth of 11 when profits were adjusted for risk in the Conrad and Plotkin fashion. By contrast, in the Conrad and Plotkin study, the automobile industry ranked second of 59 industries (and ranked first of the comparable 11 industries) when profits were adjusted for risk. The contrast between the two studies in the rankings of the industries when profits are risk-adjusted is noticeable, even when the same concept of risk-adjustment is used. The rank correlation coefficient between the two rankings is only 0.60. Since Fisher and Hall use virtually the same years (1950–1964) in their study, a difference in time periods cannot be offered as an explanation.

This author believes that the Conrad and Plotkin study offers the more accurate picture of the relative position of the automobile industry in the structure of American industry. Their larger sample of firms (783, as opposed to 88 by Fisher and Hall) and larger number of industries (59, as opposed to 11) appear to offer a more complete picture of the relative positions of industries. They also include a larger number of automobile firms in their analysis, this again yielding a more complete picture.

Further, it could be argued that in oligopolies with blockaded or restricted entry, the rate of return on capital will be set by the height of the entry barriers and the degree of mutual dependence recognized, not by the supply price of capital. In this sense, both articles may be measuring managerial risk-return utility functions, rather than those of the capital market.

It is difficult to know how far to take this argument. If even barricaded oligopolies have to enter the capital market and investor returns are correlated with company returns, then oligopolies may not be wholly independent of capital market preferences. In any event, the argument does strengthen the case for using the Conrad and Plotkin article rather than Fisher and Hall, since the larger sample of the former includes more industries and firms in which oligopoly barriers and restrictions are absent.

3. Asked to assess the contention that Chrysler lagged anywhere from three to twenty-five years behind its competitors in financial control, alignment of dealers, international operations, advance planning of the product, and public relations, "(President) Townsend nodded sweeping agreement." James Jones, p. 63.

4. MacDonald, chap. vii.

5. Maurice D. Kilbridge, "The Effort Bargain in Industrial Society," *Journal of Business* 33 (Jan. 1960), p. 13.

6. One might argue that society's loss from the inefficiency at Ford, Chrysler, and the Independents may have been offset by the increased utility that workers in these companies enjoyed from not working so hard. In fact, this does not seem to be the case. The bad record on wildcat strikes that these companies have had, compared to General Motors, would seem to indicate less worker satisfaction at these companies rather than more.

7. The selection of cities had to be restricted to those for which the BLS reported wage data at about the same time of year as it reported wage data for Detroit.

8. General Motors, *Annual Report, 1967.*

9. Ibid.

10. This discussion is complicated by the fact that there are use taxes in effect already, e.g., gasoline taxes. But, according to Meyer, Kain and Wohl, these use taxes just about cover the costs of the highway facilities provided for car users. Thus, in a sense, these use taxes are covering the long-run marginal costs of providing highways and are not creating the extra margin between price and marginal costs of use that would allow for externalities. See J. R. Meyer, J. F. Kain, and M. Wohl, *The Urban Transportation Problem* (Cambridge, Mass., 1965), p. 62.

11. Discussions of optimal social allocation usually neglect the redistributional effects of externalities and of their remedies, which also ought to be considered. Suppose individual A incurs costs from the fumes of B's car. The socially optimal solution may be to impose a tax so that the difference between the price and the private marginal costs per mile of use by B just equals the marginal costs imposed on A. But nothing is usually said about actually giving the proceeds of the tax to A. Thus, though auto use has been restricted somewhat in the postwar years, urban dwellers still have had to endure the costs of smog, ugly highways, etc., generated by those cars that were still used. They have directly benefited only to the extent that smog levels, etc., are lower than they would have been with unhindered car use and to the extent that their tax burden has been reduced by the taxes imposed to limit auto use.

12. Walter Adams and Joel B. Dirlam, "Big Steel, Invention, and Innovation," *Quarterly Journal of Economics* 80 (May 1966).

13. Though the parts suppliers will also be in this fraction, the auto companies' influence should be dominant in any trend.

14. From *Federal Reserve Board Bulletin; Monthly Labor Review;* U.S. Bureau of Labor Statistics, "Indexes of Output per Manhour in the Private Economy." Mimeographed. Washington, D.C., March 1968.

15. It is worth pointing out, however, that the companies have never asked for

special tariff protection against imported cars, a not inconsiderable feat when measured against the protectionist wails of the steel industry, the textile industry, the oil industry, and others.

16. See, for example, Dan Cordtz, "The Face in the Mirror at General Motors," *Fortune* 74 (Aug. 1966).

17. This sort of impression often seems to appear, for example, in Nader's book.

18. Because of the special conditions of the 1946–1948 period, 1949 is a more relevant year for the beginning of comparisons than is any earlier year.

19. Zvi Griliches, "Hedonic Price Indexes for Automobiles: An Econometric Analysis of Quality Change," *The Price Statistics of the Federal Government* (New York, 1963).

20. On the other hand, there have been frequent complaints that modern cars are designed to be much more expensive to repair than were cars of an earlier vintage.

21. Franklin M. Fisher, Zvi Griliches, and Carl Kaysen, "The Costs of Automobile Model Changes since 1949," *Journal of Political Economy* 70 (Oct. 1962).

22. The authors listed it as $700 per new car plus $40 per year in extra gasoline costs.

23. Their estimate of the tooling costs is somewhat exaggerated, since they applied companywide amortization figures just to passenger cars, and they ignored the effects of increasing volume on tooling costs. But they neglect the engineering and development costs of models, which offset their exaggeration to an unknown degree.

24. Where does technological change leave off and styling change begin? Is more glass area in a windshield a styling change or a technological improvement?

25. Part of the increase has come through a faster pace of model change and part has come through greater emphasis on styling (e.g., more wrinkles in the sheet metal requiring more dies).

26. This should not be very large because suppliers mostly provide items for which specifications will not change very rapidly.

27. Since $30–$50 of the price cut was really just a reduction in the dealer's nominal margin, our $130 estimate seems to be of the right order of magnitude.

28. See *A Study of the Antitrust Laws*, part 7, pp. 3544–3545; part 8, p. 4044.

29. General Motors' superior management techniques are generally attributed to its system of decentralized management. For discussion of this system, see Alfred P. Sloan, Jr., *My Years with General Motors* (Garden City, N.Y., 1964); Peter F. Drucker, *The Concept of the Corporation* (New York, 1946); and Alfred D. Chandler, Jr., *Strategy and Structure* (Cambridge, Mass., 1962), chap. iii.

30. Also, perhaps, General Motors' decision to investigate Ralph Nader might qualify, though the damage may have been far more serious in terms of public relations than in terms of profits; though Corvair sales declined, it is likely that many potential Corvair buyers bought Chevy II's or Chevelles instead.

31. Assuming, of course, that auto production revenues and costs mirror those of the overall corporation.

32. The presence of imports would be an important constraint here. Though a domestic firm, once driven out of business, would be very unlikely to start up again, it would be a great deal easier for foreign producers to withdraw temporarily from the United States market and enter again when times were more favorable.

33. Martin Shubik, *Strategy and Market Structure* (New York, 1959), pp. 306–307.

34. Shubik was writing during the 1950's. With the presence of imports the future profitability of the project would be even smaller than when imports had not been an important factor in the market.

35. U.S. Senate, Committee on Banking and Currency, *Stock Market Study*, 84th Congress, 1st session, 1955, pp. 830–831.

36. For another discussion of this general area, see Harold G. Vatter, "The Closure of Entry in the American Automobile Industry," *Oxford Economic Papers* 4 (Oct. 1952).

37. U.S. Federal Trade Commission, *Report on the Motor Vehicle Industry*, p. 29. All of the FTC figures appear to include export sales.

38. The Maxwell Corporation was able to make healthy profits in 1922–1924, while selling 50–60 thousand cars a year. See Ibid., p. 549.

39. See the testimony of Robert S. Morrison of the Molded Fiber Glass Co., in *Economic Concentration*, part 6, p. 2848.

40. They were Studebaker, Hudson, Nash, Packard, and Willys. Graham-Page selling 544 units, Bantam selling 138, and Hupmobile selling 103 were still technically in the industry, but none of the three bothered to tool up for the short-lived 1942 model year.

41. Total advertising by the five Independents during the Korean War was only one-third of that spent by General Motors alone.

42. See MacDonald, chap. vii. Studebaker had an especially bad reputation for high labor costs. It is claimed that many Notre Dame students worked their way through college, studying on the night shift at Studebaker. See Richard Hammer, "Welcome, Sherwood Egbert," *Fortune* 64 (Dec. 1961).

16. Recommendations for Public Policy

1. Why had each company not simply concentrated on one or two volume models to achieve the economies of scale? One suspects that the dynamics of the oligopolistic quality rivalry discouraged any such tendencies.

2. As of the 1969 model year, though, Canadian prices still had not fallen to United States levels. Since individual consumers must still pay a tariff on bringing a car across the border, the Canadian market can remain buffered in this way. But the question still remains, why do the auto companies see the optimum auto price as higher in Canada? Perhaps Canadians have a more inelastic demand for cars. Perhaps Canadian cost levels are still higher even after rationalization. Or perhaps old habits die slowly.

3. For a more complete discussion of this area, see Whitney, chap. viii.

4. *U.S. v. Ford Motor Co.*, 286 F. Supp. 407 (1968).

5. *U.S. v. General Motors Corp.*, 1968 Trade Cases, no. 72356.

6. *U.S. v. General Motors Corp.*, 121 F. 2d 376 (1941).

7. The government was able to obtain consent decrees from Ford and Chrysler in 1939, in which they agreed not to pressure dealers to use specific finance companies. Prior to that, Chrysler had been urging its dealers to use the Commercial Credit Corp., and Ford had been pushing Universal-CIT.

8. *U.S. v. General Motors Corp.*, 1952–1953 Trade Cases, no. 67323.

9. See U.S. Senate, Committee on the Judiciary, Subcommittee on Antitrust and

Monopoly, *Auto Financing Legislation*, Hearings, 86th Congress, 1st session, 1957; U.S. House Committee on the Judiciary, Antitrust Subcommittee *Auto Financing Legislation*, 87th Congress, 1st session, 1961.

10. *U.S. v. E. I. du Pont de Nemours & Co.*, 353 U.S. 586 (1957).

11. *U.S. v. General Motors Corp., 1965 Trade Cases*, no. 71624.

12. R. G. Lipsey and K. Lancaster, "The General Theory of the Second Best," *Review of Economic Studies* 24 (1956–1957).

13. One would feel better about the taxes being levied by government than by the auto companies, as is currently done in effect through their reaping the excess profits on sales.

14. Meyer, Kain, Wohl, p. 62.

15. Insofar as the liability principle is a drag on insurance company response in this area, the self-insurance plans, such as the Keeton-O'Connell plan, that have been proposed as a substitute for liability insurance, should prove beneficial.

16. There has been one postwar example of a department store entering automobile retailing. In 1951, Sears began to market the Allstate, a slightly modified Henry J. made by Kaiser. The car sold poorly (only 2,600 units in twenty months) and was dropped. In the process, Kaiser managed to demoralize its entire dealer body. A paradox exists here: the manufacturer of a successful make would probably not be interested in experimenting with department store retailing; an unsuccessful manufacturer's make would probably sell poorly anyway.

17. This may provide an additional reason for the detailed supervision that the auto companies maintain over the franchised dealers. Lax supervision could lead to catalogue stores and eventually lead to company entrance into retailing, which they presumably wish to avoid.

18. Crandall has argued, supporting his argument with prewar evidence, that the companies are very likely earning excess profits in the repair parts market because of the advantages to be had from producing the same parts for both original production and the repair market. If this is true, then divestiture of the parts operations would be justified to improve performance in the repair parts market, though it would not improve performance in the automobile market. See Crandall, "Vertical Integration and the Market for Repair Parts in the United States Automobile Industry," *Journal of Industrial Economics* 16 (July 1968).

19. One can theorize about other possible ways of creating more centers of initiative. The government might, for example, subsidize and encourage foreign car producers to begin manufacturing on American soil, but the political possibilities of this occurring appear to be even more remote than the possibilities of antitrust action.

20. The market for domestic manufacturers will surely grow to 10 million units in the early 1970's, but the economies of scale may also change. Consequently, it is safer to deal in terms of current volumes and technologies.

21. Both cases are legacies of World War II. Government ownership of Renault came as a punitive action after the war for wartime collaboration with the Germans. The British occupying forces relinquished control of Volkswagen to the West German Government after the latter was formed.

Index

Adams, Walter, 2, 257, 313, 339
Advertising, 49, 222–227, 253, 264–265, 272, 274, 334
Air pollution, 17–18, 228–237, 259, 274, 280–281, 335
Allison Engineering Co., 89
Altorfer Brothers Co., 91
American Bosch Corp., 213
American Metal Products Co., 213
American Motors Corp.: advertising, 223; air pollution, 232; assets, as a guide to entry costs, 58–60; compact cars, 16, 182–183; diversification, 7, 64, 91, 314; formation by merger, 15, 317, 319; integration, 50, 82–83, 86, 323; pricing, 116, 123, 129, 130, 132–133, 264; problems of survival, 16, 44, 55, 75, 268, 271–272; product strategies, 47, 208, 219, 260; production economies, 50, 53; profits, 252, 267; retail distribution, 167; subcompacts, 17, 188; tooling, 317
American Motors Sales Corporation v. L. G. Semke, 150, 166
American Tobacco Company v. United States, 125, 326
Antitrust policy: past, 75, 89–90, 278–279, 324, 335, 341; proposed, 285–288
Assembly plants and technology, 24–29, 38, 41, 43–44, 50, 59, 77, 315–316
Atkinson, L. Jay, 326
Automobile Dealers' Day in Court Act, 162, 165–166
Automobile insurance, 237–238, 245–246, 281, 336, 342
Automobile Manufacturers Association (AMA), 1, 215, 219, 231, 313, 324, 332

Automotive components and parts, 2, 79, 83–87, 211–216, 285, 313, 323–324, 332. *See also* Technology; individual components manufacturers
Automotive Information Disclosure Act of 1958, 109, 120, 325

Bain, Joe S., 38, 51, 52–55, 57, 59, 61, 314, 317, 319, 320, 325
Banner, Paul H., 2, 66, 313, 321
Bello, Francis, 334
Bendix Aviation Corp., *see* Bendix Corp.
Bendix Corp., 12, 85, 89, 212–213
Big Three: compact cars, 16, 178, 183-187, 203-204, 210, 217, 259; diversification, 7, 87–91; general, 5, 10, 14, 42, 262, 269, 271–272, 286–287; integration, 82–87; pricing, 115, 121, 126, 129–130, 132–133; product strategies, 75, 193, 205–207, 209, 213, 215, 218–219, 273–274; profits, 252; retail distribution, 148, 150, 152, 158; safety, 260; tooling, 39, 204. *See also* Mutual interdependence recognized; individual companies
Bogart, Harold N., 315
Borg-Warner Corp., 14, 36, 83, 85, 216
Bootlegging, 41, 159–160, 164
Bradley, Albert, 112–113
Breech, Ernest R., 12, 83, 314
Bridenstine, L. H., 328
Briggs Manufacturing Co., 75, 82
Brooks, John, 72, 74, 323
Brown, Donaldson, 112–113
Brownell, Herbert, 329
Budd Co., 84, 212
Bureau of Labor Statistics, 118, 121, 125,

343

128–130, 132, 194, 196, 254, 257, 261, 325, 329, 331, 339
Bureau of the Census, 313
Burns, Joseph W., 112–113

California, efforts at pollution control, 231–233, 260
Casting technology, 22–23, 38, 50, 60
Caves, Richard E., 314
Celler, Emanuel, 164
Chamberlin, Edward H., 110, 138–139, 325
Champion Spark Plug Co., 81
Chandler, Alfred D., Jr., 340
Chapman, Bernard A., 319
Checker Motors, 5, 64
Chow, Gregory, 192, 331
Chrysler, Walter P., 269–271
Citroen, 258
Clague, Charles A., 337
Clayton Act, 89, 278
Colbert, L. L., 114, 116, 184–185, 325, 328
Cole, Edward N., 183–184
Commerce Department, 334
Commercial Credit Corp., 341
Compact cars, 16–17, 71–72, 106, 129–130, 170, 177–188, 259–260
Congressional pressures: air pollution, 17–18, 232–233, 336; horsepower, 219; retail distribution, 157, 160–165; retail prices, 109, 127, 326–327; safety, 18, 241–242
Conrad, Gordon R., 250, 252, 338
Consumers Union, 69, 200, 245, 322, 337
Continental Motors Corp., 68, 79
Cordtz, Dan, 240, 337
Cornell Aeronautical Laboratory, 239, 337
Crandall, Robert W., 79, 313, 323–324, 332, 342
Crawford, Howard E., 150, 166
Crosley Motors, Inc., 10, 13, 70–71, 181, 236, 318
Curtice, Harlow H., 160, 184

Dana Corp., 84, 212, 323
Datsun, 63, 75
Davis, Gary, 321
Davisson, Charles N., 313
Dealers, see Retail distribution
Defense sales, 13, 88–90
Demand for automobiles: by consumers, 92–104, 120–121; by fleets, 92–93, 100
Denison, Merrill, 2, 313
Design, 29–37. See also Styling
Diesel engines, 199, 258
Dirlam, Joel B., 257, 339
Diversification, 7, 33–35, 87–91, 252–253

Dixon, Robert L., 316
Dodge, L. L., 323
Donner, Frederick G., 44, 318
Donovan, Frank, 2, 313
Drucker, Peter F., 340
Duesenberry, James S., 333
Du Pont Company, 213, 279
Durability, 190–198, 209, 331, 333
Durant, William C., 89, 268
Dyckman, Thomas R., 326

Economies of scale, 21–22, 24, 28–29, 38–53, 269, 272
Edsel, 3, 15, 44, 72–76, 172, 174, 176, 205, 250, 265, 270, 322, 333
Edwards, Charles E., 2, 313, 314, 317, 318
Electric Auto-Lite Co., 83, 86, 90, 213, 278, 324
Electric vehicles, 64, 235–236, 258
Enternalities: air pollution, 228–231, 255; car use, 255–256; model changes, 333; safety, 237–239, 246–247, 255
Entry: barriers to, 54–63, 273, 284; past, 65–76; potential entrants, 62–65
Ethyl Corp., 89
Euclid Road Machine Co., 89, 278

Faltermayer, Edmund K., 324
Federal Trade Commission, 2, 151, 157, 168, 313, 323, 341
Fellner, William, 110, 325
Fiat, 75
Fisher, Franklin M., 243, 340
Fisher, I. N., 338
Fleets, 92–93, 100, 133–135, 324
Forbes, Howard, 317
Ford, Henry, 12, 80, 83, 216, 270
Ford, Henry, II, 12, 83
Ford Motor Co.: advertising, 223–224; air pollution, 231–232; antitrust, past, 278, 324; compact cars, 178, 183–186, 188; diversification, 7, 88–90, 279; general, 3, 5, 7, 10–13, 15, 269, 273, 315, 323, 331, 334; integration, 81, 83–86; manufacturing technology, 29, 33, 37, 60, 222, 315–316; possible antitrust restructuring, 286–287; pricing, 111–112, 121, 124, 126, 132–135, 325; product strategies, 174, 202, 205–207, 216, 219–220; profits, 55, 250, 253, 267; retail distribution, 147–148, 163, 167, 329, 341; safety, 239, 240, 243–244; sub-compacts, 17, 188; warranties, 220
Ford Motor Co. v. Kirkmeyer Motor Co., 328
Frazer, Joseph W., 67

Freight costs, 41–44, 115, 127, 159, 318
Friedman, Milton, 314

Galbraith, John Kenneth, 314
Gemmer Manufacturing Co., 85, 212
General Electric Co., 64
General Motors Corp.: advertising, 223, 341; air pollution, 232; antitrust, past, 278–279; compact cars, 178, 183–186, 330; diversification, 7, 88–89, 321; general, 5, 10, 44, 63, 75, 189, 268–271, 273, 325, 330, 337; integration, 81, 83–86; manufacturing technology, 27–29, 314–318, 323, 339; possible antitrust restructuring, 286, 288; price leadership, 105, 111–115, 127, 131–133; pricing, 121, 125–126, 128–129, 132–133, 135, 326; product strategies, 198, 201, 205–206, 216, 219; profits, 55, 248, 250, 253, 255, 265, 267, 324; retail distribution, 150–151, 156, 158, 160, 163, 166, 329; safety, 240–241, 243–244, 338, 340; sub-compacts, 17, 188; superior management, 253, 265, 324
General Services Administration, 18, 242–243
General Tire and Rubber Co., 13, 71
Gordon, John F., 185
Gossett, William T., 147, 150, 334
Graham-Paige Motors Corp., 67, 341
Greyhound Corp., 89
Griliches, Zvi, 261, 263, 326, 340
Guardian Frigerator Co., 89
Guest, Robert H., 315

Hahn, Kenneth, 231–232
Hall, G. R., 338
Hammer, Richard, 341
Harberger, Arnold, 331
Harris, William B., 330
Hart, Philip, 326
Health, Education, and Welfare Department, 334
Henderson, James M., 139, 327
Hertz Drivurself Corp., 89
Hewitt, Charles M., Jr., 327
Higdon, Hal, 331
Hill, Frank E., 314, 323
Hillman Minx, 31–32
Hoffmann, Paul, 51–52, 66, 269
Holden, 88–89, 179
Horsepower, 218–220, 259, 274, 334
House of Representatives: Committee on Interstate and Foreign Commerce, 329, 337; Committee on the Judiciary, Antitrust Subcommittee, 147, 150, 342

Huang, David S., 96, 324
Hudson Motor Car Co.: compact cars, 180–181, 207–208; general, 14, 270–272; merger, 15, 279, 317, 319; orphan phenomenon, 318; pricing, 71, 126, 181; product strategies, 208, 216, 219, 270. See also American Motors Corp.
Hufstader, William F., 156

Imports, 15–16, 62–63, 75, 182–185, 187, 273, 337, 340
Independents: advertising, 272, 341; compact cars, 176, 178, 180–181; decline, 270–272; general, 5, 13–14, 262, 268, 279, 339; integration, 82–84; pricing, 115–116, 121, 125–126, 130; product strategies, 199, 207–209, 213, 216, 218, 274, 334; profits, 250, 253; retail distribution, 148, 150, 152, 154, 163. See also Mergers; individual companies
Intermediate size cars, 16, 106, 129–130, 170
International Business Machines Corp., 332
International Harvester Co., 5, 63–64
International Nickel Co., 212

Jones, James, 339
Jones, Keith A., 327
Jung, Allen F., 107, 128, 325
Justice Department, 55, 89–91, 162–163, 278–279

Kain, John F., 339, 342
Kaiser, Henry J., 67
Kaiser-Frazer Corp.: cessation of production, 15, 47, 70, 72; compact cars, 70, 181; jeep, 63–64; merger with Willys, 14–15, 70, 271, 279; problems of entry, 10, 12, 66–71, 75–76, 79, 268, 318, 321, 323; product strategies, 216, 219, 333; retail distribution, 56, 152, 342; share of American Motors, 321
Kaysen, Carl, 263, 340
Kefauver, Estes, 51, 127, 184
Kelsey-Hayes Co., 212
Kelvinator, 7, 59, 61, 91, 314
Kettering, Charles F., 218, 334
Killbridge, Maurice D., 253, 339
Kinetic Chemicals, Inc., 89
Kneese, Allan V., 229, 335
Kotula v. Ford Motor Company, 150

Labor Department, 159
Labor relations, 2, 7, 10–11, 68, 79, 81, 125, 253–255, 314, 326, 339, 341

Lancaster, Kelvin, 342
Lanzilotti, Robert F., 313
Lear, William, 65, 237
Libbey-Owens-Ford Co., 84, 323
Liberty Mutual Insurance Co., 246
Lincoln, Freeman, 323
Lipsey, Richard G., 342
Lorenz, Paul F., 147
Loewy, Raymond, 82

Macaulay, Stewart, 165, 327, 329
MacDonald, Robert M., 83, 253, 314, 323, 339, 341
Machining technology, 23–24, 38, 50, 52, 59–60
Mack Truck Corp., 91, 278
Madsden v. Chrysler Corporation, 166
Mass transit systems, 236–237
Maxcy, George, 51–52, 319
Maxwell Corp., 341
Menge, John A., 317, 333
Mercedes, 199, 258
Mergers, 14–15, 70, 181, 268–271, 279, 319
Meyer, John R., 339, 342
Mitsubishi Heavy Industries, 188
Model A (Ford), 269–270
Model changes, 39, 87, 201–202, 263–264
Model proliferation, 202–205, 253, 262–263, 333
Model T (Ford), 28, 178, 269–270
Modigliani, Franco, 319
Molded Fiber Glass Co., 341
Moore, Donald A., 313
Morrison, Robert S., 341
Motor Vehicle Air Pollution Act of 1965, 18, 233
Motorola, Inc., 213
Multiple makes, 45–49, 318
Mustang, 3, 17, 37, 44, 123, 172, 206, 265, 314, 316
Mutual interdependence recognized: advertising, 222–223, 226–227; compact cars, 177–178, 184; general, 173, 260; prices, 109–116; product behavior, 173, 175, 284; warranties, 221
Myers, Arthur, 336

Nader, Ralph, 45, 243, 318, 326, 337
Nash-Kelvinator Corp.: compact cars, 180, 207–208; general, 10, 14, 101, 270–272; merger, 15, 279, 317, 319; orphan phenomenon, 318; pricing, 126; product strategies, 216, 219; tooling, 317. *See also* American Motors Corp.
National Automobile Dealers Assoc. (NADA), 160, 165–168, 196, 328, 334

National Highway Safety Bureau, 244–245
National Lead Co., 212
National Safety Council, 238, 336
National Traffic and Motor Vehicle Safety Act of 1966, 18, 243–244
Nelson, Walter Henry, 321
Nevins, Allan, 136, 314, 323, 327
North American Aviation, Inc., 89
NSU, 258

O'Connell, Jeffrey, 336
Office of Price Administration (OPA), 11, 125
Oligopoly, *see* Mutual interdependence recognized
O'Mahoney, Joseph C., 114, 184
Opel, 63, 88, 184
Organization for European Economic Cooperation, 52
Owens-Corning Fiberglas Corp., 36, 317

Packard Motor Car Co.: general, 10, 14, 70, 75, 82–83, 208, 270; merger, 15, 271, 279, 319; pricing, 126; product strategies, 207, 219, 270; retail distribution, 136. *See also* Studebaker Corp.
Pashigian, Bedros Peter, 49, 138–139, 145–146, 148, 151–152, 319, 327–328
Patents, 56, 213, 215
Paton, William A., 316
Patterson, Charles H., 316
Pearson, Charles T., 321
Perfect Circle Co., 213
Phantom freight, 41, 159, 164
Philco Corp., 7, 90
Pittsburgh Plate Glass Co., 83–84, 323
Planning of new models, 29–37, 186
Playboy Motor Corp., 66–67
Plotkin, Irving H., 250, 252, 338
Pollution, *see* Air pollution
Predatory behavior, absence of, 75–76, 266–268, 284–285
Price leadership, 111–115, 127–128, 131–133, 273, 276
Prices, *see* Retail prices
Proctor and Gamble Co., 223
Profits: manufacturing, 14, 248–256, 265–266, 274; retail distribution, 152–155, 328

Quandt, Richard E., 139, 327

R. L. Polk and Co., 193, 196, 331
Radio Corporation of America, 64
Rae, John B., 2, 313
Rambler, 16, 47, 76, 99–110, 116, 130, 133,

181–183, 217, 236, 243, 268, 317. *See also*
American Motors Corp.
Ranco, Inc., 91
Rates of return, *see* Profits
Redisco, Inc., 91
Renault, 75, 185, 235, 288, 342
Repair costs, 168, 194, 331
Retail distribution: advertising, 224; and
retail prices, 106–107, 109; as a barrier
to entry in auto manufacturing, 56,
283–284; congressional pressures, 160–
164, 259; economies of scale, 49, 155–
156; entry into, 147–150; exclusive dealing, 137, 151–152, 283–284; forcing
model, 137–156, 158, 320, 327–330;
history, 136–137, 155–164, 269; manufacturer-dealer relations, 136–137, 155–
170; possible changes in structure, 282–
284, 342
Retail prices: definition of, 105–106; determination of, 109–116; discrimination,
106–107; elasticity of demand, 93–95,
120–131; flexibility, 116–120; nature of
BLS price index, 121, 123; postwar
history, 121–133, 260–262; quality adjusted, 123, 129, 131–133, 261–262; to
fleets, 133–135; Washington influence,
132
Retail sales, 5–7, 11, 14–18, 72–73, 290–306
Ribicoff, Abraham, 243
Ridker, Ronald G., 229, 335
Risk: and economies of scale, 44–49, 53;
and entry, 61; and integration, 79–80;
and product strategies, 172–173, 199–
200, 209, 330; and profitability, 250–252,
338–339; and retail distribution, 141,
154–155; general, 3, 7–9, 265–266
Robinson-Patman Act, 134, 168
Romney, George, 51–53, 57, 59, 61, 317,
320
Roos, C. F., 326
Rootes, 90–91

Safety, 17–18, 237–247, 259, 274, 281,
336–338
Savage, L. J., 314
Schelling, Thomas C., 110, 325
Scitovsky, Tibor, 328
Scrapping, 195–198
Senate: action on safety legislation, 243;
Committee on Banking and Currency,
341; Committee on Commerce, 327, 337;
Committee on Interstate and Foreign
Commerce, 44, 318, 329, 336–337; Com-
mittee on Government Operations, Sub-
committee on Executive Reorganization,

254, 326, 336; Committee on Public
Works, 336; Committee on the Judiciary,
Subcommittee on Antitrust and Mo-
nopoly, 2, 51, 57, 88, 112, 116, 127, 147–
148, 150, 160–161, 166, 313, 317, 324,
327, 341–342
Sheehan, Robert, 330
Sherman Act, 164
Shubik, Martin, 267, 340
Siekman, Philip, 324
Silbertson, Aubrey, 51–52, 319
Simca, 36, 90–91
Size, as area of rivalry, 182, 187, 216–218,
259
Slack, Lyman, 328
Sloan, Alfred P., Jr., 270, 340
Smith, David K., 68, 321
Smith, Philip Hillyer, 2, 313
Speno, Edward J., 241
Stamping technology, 20–22, 38, 50, 52, 60
*Standard Oil of California and Standard
Stations, Inc. v. U.S.*, 151, 328
Steam vehicles, 64–65, 237, 258
Steiglitz, William V., 337
Stotz, Margaret S., 326
Studebaker Corp.: compact cars, 183; di-
versification, 91; exit from industry, 17,
91; general history, 10, 12, 14, 16–17,
268, 270–272; merger, 15, 271, 279, 319;
product strategies, 208, 212, 216, 219,
270; pricing, 116, 126; safety, 241, 260
Studebaker-Packard Corp., *see* Studebaker
Corp.
Styling, 15–17, 82, 198–201, 205–210, 253,
273–274, 316–317. *See also* Tooling and
tooling costs; Model changes
Sub-compact cars, 17, 106, 170, 188
Supreme Court, 164, 279

Tariffs, 277, 280
Taunus, 90, 186
Taxes: excise, 106, 129, 131, 256, 278, 280;
gasoline, 280–281, 339
Technology: manufacturing, 20–29, 221–
222, 256–258, 340; product, 211–216,
258–259, 274
Temporary National Economic Committee,
50–51, 319
Tennessee Valley Authority, 288
Thompson Products, Inc., 213
Tooling and tooling costs, 33–37, 39–41,
52, 64, 204–205, 263–264, 277, 314–317,
334, 340. *See also* Styling; Model
changes
Townsend, Lynn A., 339
Toyota, 63, 75

Transportation Department, 244
Truck manufacturing, 2, 60, 63–64, 199, 313
Truman, Harry S, 66
Tucker (car), 67, 321
Tucker, Preston, 66, 321
Turbine engines, 199, 258
Turner, Graham, 316

Unions, *see* Labor relations; United Automobile Workers
United Automobile Workers, 7, 68, 125, 253–255, 326. *See also* Labor relations
United States-Canadian Automotive Agreement of 1965, 277–278, 317, 319, 341
U.S. government agencies, *see* individual agency names
U.S. Rubber Co., 213
U.S. Steel Corp., 325
U.S. v. Aluminum Company of America, 326
U.S. v. Arnold Schwinn and Company, 164
U.S. v. E. I. du Pont de Nemours and Co., 342
U.S. v. Ford Motor Co., 324, 341
U.S. v. General Motors Corp. (1941), 341
U.S. v. General Motors Corp. (1952–1953), 341
U.S. v. General Motors Corp. (1965), 342
U.S. v. General Motors Corp. (1968), 341
Universal C.I.T. Credit Corp., 90, 341

Vatter, Harold G., 341
Vauxhall (General Motors of England), 88, 184

Vertical integration, 7, 77–87
Volkswagen: advertising, 334; dealer service, 209; demand for, 100, 101, 185–186; entry into U.S. market, 62–63, 65, 75; government ownership of, 288, 342; prices, 121, 123, 187; sales and selling strategies, 7, 49, 235, 273, 320, 323; size, 71; technological improvements, 258
Volvo, 63, 75, 321
Von Szelski, 326

Wages, 254–255. *See also* Labor relations
Walker, Charles R., 315
Ware, Peter, 316
Warranties, 168, 174, 176, 220–221, 331
Weiss, Leonard W., 2, 313, 317
Westinghouse Electric Co., 64
White Consolidated Industries, Inc., 91, 314
White Motor Corp., 63
Whitney, Simon N., 2, 313, 341
Whittaker, Charles, 329
Willow Run, 66–67
Willys-Overland Motors, Inc.: compact cars, 180–181; cessation of production, 15, 72, 318; merger with Kaiser, 14–15, 70, 271, 279; reentry into U.S. market, 71–72, 76, 271, 322, 341
Wohl, M., 339, 342
Wolf, Robert, 336

Yntema, Theodore O., 113–114, 127, 316